For Better
for Worse

Also by Christine Hamilton

The Book of British Battleaxes

For Better
for Worse

Christine Hamilton

Her Own Story

ROBSON BOOKS

First published in Great Britain in 2005 by Robson Books, The Chrysalis Building, Bramley Road, London, W10 6SP

An imprint of **Chrysalis** Books Group plc

British Library Cataloguing in Publication Data

A catalogue record for this title is available from the British Library.

ISBN 1 86105 670 2

Typeset by SX Composing DTP, Rayleigh, Essex
Printed by Clays Ltd, Bungay, Suffolk NR35 1ED

To my parents, Ted and Megan Holman, who gave me strong roots and also wings to fly; my brother, James, for the constant support he has given to his sometimes wayward sister; and, of course, Neil, without whom I might have had a more tranquil, but far less exciting life.

Contents

Acknowledgements

Jeremy and Carole Robson, for their unstinting friendship and support which set me on my literary path. Jeremy's determination that this book would see the light of day was crucial – without his pesterings I would never have put pen to paper.

The gang at Robson Books – Jeremy's long suffering secretary Melanie Letts; Barbara Phelan, who painstakingly coordinated the editing of the book, ably assisted by Sarah Barlow and Ian Allen – without their eagle eyes and superior grammatical knowledge, I would have committed some awful howlers; and Sharon Benjamin for her boundless energy in helping to promote the book.

Douglas Thompson, for his invaluable help at an early stage in sorting out and making sense of my ramblings.

The legions of lawyers who have acted for us through thick and thin and to whom we owe so much and in so many ways: Anthony Boswood QC; Desmond Browne QC; Godwin Busuttil; the late Peter Carter-Ruck; Michael Coleman; David Eady QC; Richard Hartley QC; Adrienne Page QC; Sarah Palin; Alasdair Pepper; Howard Pinkerfield; Richard Rampton QC; Victoria Sharpe QC; Andrew Stephenson; Tom Lowe; the late Lord Williams of Mostyn QC and, of course, Rupert Grey, who not only held our hands through all the Fayed dramas but supported us when many did not and worked long hours in the hope of securing justice. He also ensured that some of my more exuberant (but wholly justified) excesses were curbed.

The Rt Hon Lord Harris of High Cross (Ralph) and the late Norris McWhirter, who founded the Fighting Fund, and all the contributors, the great majority unknown to us, who enabled us to battle on to the end.

All our friends, neighbours and supporters who kept faith, in particular those in the Tatton constituency who maintained steadfast loyalty in the face of impossible odds.

Jonathan Hunt, whose meticulously detailed research uncovered the truth about the 'cash for questions' saga. For the full story visit his website www.neil-hamilton-is-innocent.com, or read his book *Trial by Conspiracy*.

Ida Eyres, Audrey Hedley and Chris Pendrigh, who looked after us so well at Laburnum Cottage and the Old Rectory – their dedication and infinite capacity for hard work ensured we maintained high levels of cleanliness and tidiness but, even more importantly, their arrival was always a cheery, rejuvenating tonic when times were hard.

And finally, to all the manifold villains who, by their actions, have so enriched my life and without whom this book could never have been written; they know who they are – read on, and so will you!

CHAPTER ONE

Birth, Survival and the Lure of the Sea

The first attempt on my life occurred at 2.35 p.m. on 11 November 1949. I had arrived in the world noisily, just in time for tea, the previous day. Like many older siblings, my brother, James, aged two and a half, did not much like the attention being lavished on the little bundle adjacent to his beloved mother's bed. He put a pillow over my face and sat on it. Luckily, although some may not agree, that assassination attempt was foiled.

Born in a nursing home near Bournemouth, in a seafront room with bay windows overlooking the water, I was a pathetic sight – underweight with spindly legs and a yellow skin from infantile jaundice. My mother described me as 'a poor little scrap'. Happily, the jaundice quickly faded but the legs became the rather more robust ones I possess today, my modelling career stymied at conception.

Fathers, even if doctors, were not present at birth in those days, so Daddy was taking his afternoon surgery as normal, waiting anxiously for the news that his daughter, always known to him as 'Blossom' (yes, hugely embarrassing), upon whom he was to dote until his dying day, had safely arrived. I was fortunate to survive at all because my parents went skiing in Davos while my mother was in the early, volatile stages of pregnancy. She fell on the slopes and, for a while, my future lay in doubt – the first of my many mishaps.

My father was an indulgent progenitor and my mother sometimes had to urge him to impose the necessary discipline upon his daughter. Freud certainly had no place in our upbringing. Looking back after more than half a century, I see that my childhood was idyllic, and no deep complexes haunt me later in life. I was uncomplicated then and remain so to this day. I wore and wear my heart on my sleeve.

My mother, Mary Megan Morris (like me, always known by her second name), was born in Ormskirk, Lancashire, in April 1914. Her father, James Albert, was a railway official based in Liverpool. His first wife died tragically young of pneumonia and his second wife, my grandmother, was a friend of hers. Born in 1890, Margaret Lucas Flitcroft was an active suffragette and became one of the earliest women journalists, writing for the *Bolton Evening News* under the pseudonym 'Penelope', to avoid outraging readers who took a less emancipated view of women in this role. My mother was the first of three more daughters for my grandfather to join their half-sister, who was only three when her mother died. Their names reflect my grandfather's Welsh roots — Gwyneth, Megan, Olwen and Dilys. I also have a cousin, Myfanwy — it's amazing I wasn't christened Blodwen!

My father, Edward Theodore Holman, was born in December 1910 in Bury, Lancashire, where his father was headmaster of the high school. My grandfather, Edward Walter, was rather frightening to me as a child and I disliked his bristly moustache. My mother argued with him about everything, in particular religion and politics, and she generally found her in-laws difficult to cope with, her nonconformist upbringing clashing with their more conventional views.

My grandfather retired before the outbreak of World War II and moved to Essex where my grandmother, Harriet Holman, died towards the end of the war. To free a younger person for the Services, my grandfather had returned to a school in Braintree, where a young biology teacher called Pauline caught his eye. In due course they married; he was 72 and she only 27, the palindrome capturing press attention. I do not remember ever wondering about the age difference — they were just Grandpa and Pauline.

My parents met at Manchester University in 1932, where my mother read Honours General Science in physics, chemistry and maths. She became president of the Women's Union, a platform for her considerable administrative, oratorical and leadership skills. My father read anatomy and physiology, aiming for a medical career. He had difficulty with the mandatory Latin, a deficiency I inherited.

Uninterested in politics of any kind, he was content merely to be on a subcommittee of the Men's Union. According to my mother he was 'a very humble member of the committee and did absolutely nothing for the Union'. My father was instantly smitten by the vivacious Megan Morris but she was not so easily won, declaring, 'I don't care who takes me to the Union Ball but I'm not going with that Ted Holman.' He persevered and they were married on 26 November 1938 at the Methodist Chapel in Sale. They would have married a week earlier but my mother's father died after a long illness, now thought to be cancer but then undiagnosed. He was buried in the little churchyard at Eglwysbach in the Conway Valley on what should have been their wedding day, further marred by the appalling threat of war menacing Europe, with unknown consequences especially for young people.

Their brief honeymoon – one night at the Long Mynd Hotel in Shropshire – presaged my own nonexistent honeymoon 45 years later. It will come as no surprise that neither I nor my mother promised to 'obey', as we had no intention of doing any such thing. She told the minister, 'Just cut it out.' Her father would have approved. With four daughters he was very much in favour of women's rights and brought up his girls to question everything, 'If you've got anything to say, say it loud and clear and let it be heard.' Like her mother before her, my mother is highly intelligent, a clear thinker and a motivational force. Even at the age of ninety she knows her own mind and speaks it with great clarity, never fearing to express her opinion. All who know her love her for her outspokenness.

My father's first proper job was as an assistant GP in Blackpool. Medicine was a reserved occupation, so he could have avoided call-up, but volunteered immediately. It was 'Navy or nothing', and he joined the Royal Naval Volunteer Reserve. My mother was soon attracted by an advertisement for a job with the Admiralty, following its evacuation to Bath, and became Outports Welfare Officer, responsible for civilian welfare at bases all over the country. Megan Holman's arrival put the fear of God into the poor admirals – there was hell to pay if anything was wrong when she came to inspect! Based at the old Empire Hotel in Bath, she sallied forth to Plymouth, Portsmouth, Chatham, Greenock and Rosyth, checking on facilities for women who, employed by the Admiralty for the very first time, could not rely on even such basic necessities as a lavatory.

My father had reported to the destroyer HMS *Atherstone* in Chatham as a fledgling surgeon lieutenant, later promoted lieutenant commander. Officers had to buy their own uniform and wore trilby hats until their naval caps arrived so they had 'something to raise when the ratings saluted' – pure 'Dad's Navy'! *Atherstone* was initially engaged on Channel and Atlantic convoys and then Daddy was sent to the Mediterranean. Careless talk costs lives so, as a smoke screen, crew were issued with Arctic kit to obscure their actual destination, the 1943 Sicily landings.

My father was then appointed director of the British military hospital on the island of Ischia, in the Bay of Naples. He was a remarkable but private man; only much later did I discover and fully appreciate just what an impact he had made on the people of Ischia. He arrived on the island on 20 August 1944, and found them half-starved by German troops and plagued by smallpox. Dashingly handsome, he cut a fine figure in his white naval shorts, limbs bronzed by the Italian sunshine. Little wonder the local girls fell for '*il dottore inglese*'. Modest to a fault, he never sought publicity or glory but was eventually rumbled by a British journalist, Rex North, holidaying on the island in 1953. Joseph Iacono, my father's interpreter, was astonished North had not heard of the legendary Dr Holman. 'See that white villa? Churchill stayed there. He is a very nice man. But Dr Holman is the greatest man who ever set foot on this island. The doctor worked 24 hours a day to save hundreds of lives. I will take you to scores of people who owe everything to him.'

Iacono introduced the journalist to people my father had treated beyond the call of duty. Prompted by the overwhelming gratitude he found among the islanders, North wrote an article in the *Sunday Pictorial*: 'The Uncrowned King of Ischia – If Only He Knew It'. Unused to publicity of any kind, my father was horrified. When he left the island in 1945, he was made an honorary citizen, given a gold medal and presented with a large oil painting of its magnificent Aragonese Castle which, fully framed and carefully packaged, came home intact at the end of the war. Fortunately, so did he, taking rather longer than he might because he refused to fly back. 'I volunteered for the Navy and I am coming home by sea.'

My mother was first aware of his arrival when she received a telephone call, 'Darling, I'm back. Can you fix some transport?'

I think she can be forgiven for pulling strings.

'Car needed immediately at Bath Station.'

So Daddy came home, bearing not only his gifts from Ischia, but also a single banana, an unheard-of luxury in wartime Britain, picked up in Gibraltar and carefully guarded as a present for my mother.

Civilian life resumed. The National Health Service was looming and my father was anxious to have his own practice. They arrived on April Fool's Day 1948 at Cornerways in the market town of Ringwood, Hampshire, with my brother James, a seven-month 'little bundle of nothing'. Two hours later Daddy was taking his first surgery despite the fact they had been left just one light bulb in this large Edwardian house.

With no receptionist or appointments Daddy would sit behind his large brown leather-topped desk, cigarette constantly in hand, overflowing ashtray to his right, waiting to see who came through from the waiting room. It is astonishing now to think of a doctor smoking at all, let alone receiving patients with nicotine-stained fingers, but then everyone did it. I clearly remember the day when he, along with other doctors, suddenly got the message and stopped overnight – forty one day, the next day none. He became a sometimes embarrassingly intolerant convert, anxious that neither of his children should adopt the habit. Generally speaking he succeeded, although I do succumb from time to time on a social basis.

There was no cut-off point and surgery continued until the last person had been seen. An early patient was Lady Caroline Agar, sister of the Earl of Normanton, whose stately home, Somerley, was nearby. She was one of seven sisters, her poor mother having been obliged to keep producing until a son and heir was born. 'Boy' finally arrived, the church bells rang and she could relax. Auntie Lina became my godmother and a constant source of amusement and delight, devoting much time and energy every week to James and me. After walks, me in my shower-proof, pink bunny-rabbit suit, complete with ears and gloves attached, she always gave us our firm favourite: Birds Eye frozen Victoria sponge cake, with a layer of real cream and strawberry jam inside.

Lina had been dandled on Queen Victoria's knee as a child, her Danish mother being lady-in-waiting to Queen Alexandra with whom she had arrived from their mother country. She was full of entertaining stories and wild tales of her youth: early days of motoring; sailing exploits at Cowes when the Prince of Wales, later Edward VIII, put an ice-cube down the front of her dress and then tried to retrieve it – a trick he apparently tried with numerous young ladies. Lina always had a twinkle in her eye and was the instigator of many jolly japes as she drove us out and about in her little black Ford.

Another devoted spinster who spoiled us was Eileen Amery-Parkes, who lived alone on the fringes of the New Forest. Her short, wavy, mid-brown hair, in texture akin to a wire pan scrub, was invariably topped by a jaunty hat. Born an Edwardian in 1906, she retained to her death the characteristics of that glittering era. Always known as Parkii, she was an exciting, dashing figure to us children. Immaculate and stylish, with red fingernails, she was adorably dotty and eccentric, effervescing like a permanent party popper. She would invariably answer her telephone with a loud shout of 'cock-a-doodle-doo', having not the slightest idea who was calling. She kept a sturdy wooden truncheon, with an exceedingly heavy metal end, close by her front door in case of emergency. This had been brought from Hong Kong by her brother and we were convinced by her story that the stains were blood from the head of a sorry victim of police brutality. Appropriately, in view of my 'Battleaxe' image, this offensive but rather attractive weapon now belongs to me!

Parkii ingeniously circumvented the worst rigours of petrol rationing during the Suez crisis. Coupon rations were linked to the cc of your car and Parkii possessed both a large impressive Rover and a very small pale blue Gogomobile. Claiming coupons against the cc of the Rover and bombing around in the Gogo ensured she had no difficulty at all. It was a 'Noddy' car, utterly ridiculous, but very economical. I was then only six, and my brother was already developing long legs, so I was always the one doubled up in the back of the Gogo as we trundled off on forays into the New Forest and to Poole Harbour. Parkii's beloved motorboat, *Kingfisher*, was as odd and quirky as her owner, and we had hours of fun in Studland Bay and off the Old Harry rocks swimming, fishing and larking around.

These and other friends took us off my mother's hands so she could employ them more usefully. The family would never have run smoothly without the daily devotion of Mrs Phyllis Bennett, who cleaned, cooked, ironed, laundered and generally coped with all the detritus of Holman life. I learned a great deal from Mrs B, but dearly wish I had spent longer at her elbow. She was a pastry cook par excellence and although I hovered, waiting always to dip my finger into the delicious raw butter, flour and sugar mix, I never applied myself to serious apprenticeship. It was my mistake. Her deft hands created masterpieces, from tarts and pies to biscuits, Christmas cakes, airy Victoria sponges and light-as-a-feather pastry. My mother and all of us would have been lost without her.

My childhood memories are a haze of happiness. The sun seemed always to shine, days were long and carefree, spent splashing happily in the swimming pool, breaking the larder window with a careless tennis ball, pretending to be a lady in my grandmother's pink and lacy wedding gown. I was bribed by my father at three old pennies a colander to clamber among the branches and pick the cherries before the birds devoured them all. I remember striking the bargain, easily beating him up from 2d to 3d, and my heart sinking at the size of the colander he handed me when each cherry seemed so small and some so unreachable.

As I grew older I became aware that not everyone had large gardens, let alone a tennis court and swimming pool. The latter was modest, most unhealthy by today's standards, being just a hole in the ground lined with concrete. Every couple of days we would tip in chlorine to keep the germs at bay. Twice a summer the pool was emptied, the algae scrubbed out – a back-breaking task we all sought to avoid – the walls repainted with Snowcem and it was filled up again over two days from a large hose. I could swim before I could walk, the former being more important with such a potentially lethal weapon lurking at the top of the garden and I learned to share. The pool was a magnet and it was fun to have extra company, though I resented being told by grown-ups that I was not to jump in and splash in 'my' pool in case I capsized little Johnnie. Water brings squeals and shouts of fear and delight from the young. It must have been an intrusion for my parents when so many friends turned up with their offspring to cool in the pool, but they seemed more than happy to share their good fortune.

We lived in a town but, with space, hens, rabbits, hamsters, mice, guinea pigs, cats and dogs, it felt like the country. Yet even a happy childhood contains minor irritations and setbacks. I was denied a Pekinese dog which, for some unaccountable reason, I had set my heart on. I wouldn't eat meat, so there were battles about that. Within certain bounds, my parents were pretty liberal in their attitude to discipline and relaxed about food fads. Salt came in blocks, highly concentrated orange juice came from the State, and Wagon Wheels, Arctic Roll, tinned fruit salad and evaporated milk were weekly treats. For a while, my brother would eat nothing without custard: sausage and custard, bacon and custard . . . everything had to have custard. My mother went along with it; if that was what he wanted then give it to him.

Though my parents were strict about standards of behaviour, politeness, right and wrong, it was a very easy-going household. My night-time treat was to be bounced up and down in bed, preferably by Daddy who had less care for the bed springs, and we always had 'nights and mornings' by the bedside – two little pieces of chocolate – it is amazing my teeth have survived.

The New Forest was unfenced and ponies trotted around Ringwood at will, which was charming until their hooves created havoc on the lawn, so we were always on 'pony alert', rushing to shut the gates. I was horse mad, trekked all over the New Forest with the local riding school and came to grief several times, the worst when my pony bolted, lurched round a corner, when I lost my tenuous grip on her mane, landing headfirst in a muddy ditch. No chance of clambering back on board – the culprit was already munching hay back home.

Later, I rode the horses belonging to a family friend, Robin Thompson, and had all the fun without my parents having to foot the bills. I would bicycle over every available day, blissfully happy whether riding, mucking out, cleaning tack or just sweeping the yard. It didn't matter as long as it and I were connected with the equine world. Robin was delighted to have her horses exercised and I rode all over the forest for hours on Storm, a vivacious and lively skewbald gelding, or led her children round the fields on Moppet, a prototype for Thelwell. I entered gymkhanas and learned the delights of the blacksmith, where I became addicted to the smell of burning hoof. Despite all, I felt deprived because I did not have a pony of my own. How ungrateful can children be?

My mother had given up her career and become unpaid secretary and receptionist for my father, working long hours for the NHS. He was on duty 24 hours a day. There were no partners, no mobiles or bleepers, so he was effectively 'tagged' by the local telephone exchange, which always had a forwarding number. Daddy provided a 365-day service, paying a locum during precious holidays.

Despite running the practice and two small children, my mother devoted considerable energy to community work. In particular the Ringwood Carnival, which became an increasingly ambitious annual extravaganza, raising money first to build a swimming pool for the town and, eventually, to buy a beautiful Georgian house, Greyfriars, still the thriving local community centre. Flicking through the quarterly magazine of Greyfriars a couple of years ago, one entry caught my eye. A local village Women's Institute reported great success in weaving baskets from recycled materials. Unable to imagine exactly what that meant, but with a mental vision of old bottle tops and used newspapers, I started to giggle.

'Stop it, child!' said my mother, 'That is the warp and weft of life – you are just the froth.' Whether ticking off celebrities or chiding me, she has always spoken her mind and is usually right!

The carnival, on Carvers Field every September, with many ancillary events in the preceding week, provided me with hours of purposeful diversion. With boundless energy and enthusiasm, I would race up to Carvers every day, becoming more useful as the years went by. I painted endless red and white stripes on what seemed like miles of roofing felt, used to decorate the front of the stalls and sideshows. Thousands came from miles around to enjoy the fun.

A major attraction was Adlam's Fun Fair. Florrie Adlam struck the deals and riveted us children. She came from the other side of the track, with peroxide blonde, beehive hair, usually topped by a cheap chiffon scarf, a cigarette permanently between her teeth. Florrie was born and had lived in a caravan all her life, travelling around with the family business. Every year she would come to our house and pay her dues to the carnival, always in dirty pound notes. Florrie enthralled us with romantic tales of bohemian life on the road. She and my mother, although about the same age, could not have been more different, but she recognised Florrie's many sterling qualities and developed a very soft spot for her. So did I but perhaps for slightly different reasons. Florrie was always to be found in the box by the side of the dodgems, fag in mouth, receiving the money from the tattooed toughies who leaped from car to car. Together with James, or separately with friends, our rides were always free and for as long as we liked. It was pure heaven; I can hear and smell it now.

For a couple of years at carnival time I spent many hours lying in a bed wearing a baby-doll nightie. 'Tip the Lady out of Bed' was always a popular sideshow and a good money-spinner – there were no prizes beyond the satisfaction of seeing me fall if you hit the target with a ball. I changed ends frequently, to fall on a different side, but still ended up with enormous bruises on my thighs.

My mother's inspiration for all this had been the Queen's Coronation in 1953, which lifted the gloom of post-war austerity on the day we also heard man had conquered Everest. My parents hung their climbing boots on one of our front gates as a patriotic gesture and the whole town repaired to Carvers to enjoy a double celebration. James and I came back with gifts of Coronation mugs and I innocently enquired, 'Is the Queen always at Carvers?' My mother was determined to harness this tremendous spirit for the continuing good of the community and so began a succession of fundraising activities.

I gradually became conscious that my parents were significant and respected figures locally. I had a privileged life and was aware of the reflected glory we received as their children. We unashamedly traded on that, hanging around the local sweet shop hoping a patient of Daddy's would come along and treat us. My mother always knew where to find us. The local chemist was my godfather, a soft touch whenever I went into his shop – barley sugar twists being my favourites.

Today, if you call your doctor in the middle of the night, you will be referred to a deputising service but in the Sixties your doctor himself would be disturbed from sleep. Daddy was sometimes out two or three times a night. Early one morning in 1963 he was woken by a patient who had a guest with severe abdominal pains. Could he come immediately? He got out of bed, rushed to treat the girl, suppressed the pain and reassured her it was nothing serious. Back home, he slid into bed and resumed his sleep. The next morning my mother asked what it had been about. 'Oh, it was a girl called Mandy Rice-something.' My mother was astonished. 'Good heavens, don't you know who she is?' Daddy had been blissfully unaware of examining one of the most notorious and beautiful bodies of the time – Mandy Rice-Davies, hiding from the press at the height of the Profumo affair.

My father loved the sea and hankered after his own boat. But, before he could afford one, we spent several years caravanning on the Gower peninsula in south Wales. With friends and relations, we parked our vans and pitched a small marquee on a farm by the coast. It must have been hell at times for the grown-ups but it was glorious for the children. A photograph records my presence, firmly sitting on potty, baggy white knickers around my ankles. All the fun of the farm was at our disposal and the sea and rock pools just down the cliff. I soon displayed a disdain for physical danger, jumping ahead on the rocks while my brother held back. Seeking to encourage, and probably wanting some peace, my mother urged him, 'Why don't you go ahead on the rocks with Christine?'

'No,' James replied solemnly. 'It's different for Christine. She doesn't understand about dying.'

As soon as they could afford it, and we were old enough, sailing took over. My earliest memories are of *Wanda*, a little, pale blue, clinker-built boat. She had no standing headroom for my parents but I never thought of their discomfort, bent double for a fortnight's holiday. My mother coped brilliantly; meals would appear from a tiny one-ring Primus stove, Smash and fried Spam being firm favourites. Much food was stored in the bilges and there was a tendency for labels to float off, but occasional surprises only added to the fun when a tin of sausages turned out to be fruit salad. Family life on the ocean wave was joyous and, despite the vagaries of British weather, I recall little mutiny. In the early days our boats were based at Poole or Keyhaven, and we would potter over to Yarmouth, anchor in Alum Bay, running up and down the cliffs of coloured sand, or sail to Cowes and Bembridge, marvelling at the *Queen Mary* and other great liners steaming past. It was paradise.

Our next boat, *Elka*, built in 1936, was a white 28-foot cutter with bowsprit, canoe stern and tan sails – Daddy's pride and joy. James and I were beginning to shape up as useful members of the crew. In 1960, when I was ten, we made our first Channel crossing, crashing through the waves with me vomiting over the side. But I never stayed ill for long, and would buck up on arrival in Cherbourg as I hopped ashore, always barefoot, for a paper twist of '*pommes frites*' from the little stand on the quay. In Cherbourg my parents met Joachim Lepelletier, an elderly French widower who frequently sailed alone and tied up next to them one day in his beautiful old black sailing boat *La Mascotte*. Jo's house at Carentan, Normandy, was an elegant time capsule, the salon still displaying wartime bullet holes. After D-Day, slates and brickwork were damaged almost nightly but Jo always insisted his workmen repair the exterior damage the next day to show his defiance of the Nazis. The house and Jo himself were part of a rapidly fading era. In its heyday it had bristled with staff, and Jo still cured his own hams and made his own Calvados, giving me my first introduction to the Normandy nectar. A genuine *bon vivant* and gourmet, he once embarrassed me hideously. Flying from Heathrow, he took us to lunch at the Post House Hotel. Service was slow, but all was vaguely under control until the red wine arrived – in a basket. This was common practice, if pretentious, as a basket is superfluous where wine has no sediment. Not impressed by this harmless flourish, Jo, whose patience had been tried by bad service, stood up, glared at the wine waiter, grabbed the bottle by the neck, declaiming loudly, 'Zer is no wine in zis restaurant, zat is fit for a basket!' and flung the basket across the room where, fortunately, it landed in the sweet trolley, splat in the middle of some creamy concoction. I would have been delighted by the scene today but, aged fourteen, I was mortified as the whole restaurant turned to stare in astonishment. Back on board, my mother did the navigating. It was only sixty miles across the Channel but, in a small yacht, making only an average of five knots, it took about twelve hours. We had plenty of adventures which I mostly relished but I was very frightened several times.

In 1962, approaching Cherbourg after a difficult sixteen-hour crossing, a sudden gale blew up. I was tired, sick and wanted to be anywhere but in a small boat, at the mercy of the elements. The wind direction was totally wrong, we were being blown on to the rocks at the harbour entrance and *Elka*'s small engine wasn't strong enough to fight wind and waves. I was terrified. Daddy tried to keep our spirits up, assuring us there was no danger. We could always turn and run back to England. Having just endured sixteen hours at sea, that was a worse prospect than hitting the rocks. Suddenly, a French minesweeper appeared, my mother waved a red towel, and the sailors waved back. It was a salutary lesson: if you need help, make it obvious. Daddy fired a red flare, the recognised signal for distress, and the minesweeper reacted swiftly, towing us safely into Cherbourg. The incident reinforced my healthy respect for the sea.

In 1963 we sailed over to Le Havre, stored the mast, and off we went up the Seine to Paris. It was a fascinating trip, chugging along in the sunshine, shopping for fresh food in little villages, visiting the ancient city of Rouen, passing through the vineyards (of Champagne), sharing the river and the locks, sometimes perilously, with working barges of all descriptions. In Paris we tied up at the Touring Club de France pontoon, adjacent to the Pont Alexandre III, for two shillings and sixpence (less than 15p) a night – for a family of four! We sallied forth, an incongruous sight in yellow oilskins and sailing shoes as we sauntered up the Champs Élysées. The shops and cafés beckoned and I always wanted to collapse into their arms but my mother struggled to ensure we succumbed only once a day. A round of coffee or lemonade for four was about a pound and, therefore, a treat.

In Paris we found another English boat, *Mistura,* belonging to a splendid Gloucester doctor and his wife. Their son, John Green, was two years older than me and we had romantic illusions for a couple of years, largely carried on through copious correspondence while he was at King's School, Bruton. We had good times but drifted nowhere. Our paths were destined to cross again some forty years later when, in May 2003, we went to the Theatre Royal in Bath to do a one-night stand *An Evening with the Hamiltons*. John revealed himself during questions as an early boyfriend of mine. He had been re-reading his holiday diaries and told the audience that we had clambered up the Eiffel Tower together. At the *2ème étage* he had decided that was enough but, his diary records, 'Christine insisted on going all the way.' We had supper together after the theatre when he disclosed, to my horror, that he had kept all my letters and reminded me it was my thighs to which he had first been attracted some forty years earlier. Fortunately, I was wearing trousers, so his fond memories were not shattered by the visible and adverse effects of time.

Sailing continued to be a passion and, in our teens, James and I raced in yachts in Poole and Cowes Weeks, with ocean races further afield. Becalmed or battered by storms, I loved it all – the salt, the wind, the waves, the hardship, the exultation. Sadly, I never achieved one of my early ambitions, to sail round the world. I could never do it now – I would positively hate it – but I still harbour dreams of rounding Cape Horn. My philosophy in life is that you regret what you fail to do rather than what you actually do. It's the boys I *didn't* kiss I regret, not the odd mistake I made!

Chapter Two

Schooling and Skating on Thin Ice

At school, I coasted rather than strived. Aged three, I arrived at St Katherine's kindergarten, hardly more than a large wooden hut with several rooms. My school reports were encouraging but, looking back, the warning signs were there: 'Christine is full of confidence . . . her one weakness is her inability to slow down her brain, which races ahead of her tongue and her pencil.' But I was an attentive child, eager to do well. 'Christine is so anxious to please and to be appreciated – it has been a sheer joy to teach her.' My gymnastics reports attest to little regard for physical danger: 'A daring little performer – Christine is fearless.'

I progressed to Blynkbonnie, a small private school in Ringwood, where I had the usual medley of teachers. Mrs Goldmanis (who my father, in an early, uncharacteristic bout of political correctness, referred to as Mrs Silverwomanis) taught history and geography and was rumoured to have been in a concentration camp during the war. With her very twisted fingers and no bosom, our theory was that the hands were the result of torture and the bosom had been cut off by the Nazis. She was probably just flat-chested and arthritic but childish imaginations ran riot. Maurice Tilley taught maths and ran the school National Savings scheme. Every week I bought a Charles and an Anne, thinking it unfair the Princess's stamp was cheaper than the Prince's. I stayed at Blynkbonnie until the age of ten, my greatest achievement being to become hula hoop champion. I began to learn the facts of life, but nothing too serious.

Early reports were fine: 'Christine brings a gay and happy spirit into class . . . She approaches work with a zest and ability . . . Her enthusiasm carries others along – she is already developing qualities of leadership.'

But later reports began to hint I was not quite so content to be the good little girl. 'Christine must achieve more self-discipline . . . Her general development is good but there have been too many occasions when she has had to be admonished . . . There are moments when her over-exuberance creates a disturbance.' My 'over-exuberance' had already caused problems for my maternal grandmother, who refused to sit next to me at mealtimes because of my hyperactivity. Even now, Neil despairs at my inability to relax.

When widowed for the second time, my grandmother frequently stayed with us for several weeks at a stretch. Handsome, gentle, loving and gracious, she had firm views and a determination which has inspired me over the years. She was 79 when she died in her sleep while at Cornerways. I was ten and stole into her bedroom, uncertain about but intrigued by death, unsure what I would find. I stood by her bedside, afraid to turn back the sheet that had been lovingly placed over her, and merely looked at the outline of her face, wondering, trying to comprehend the awesome finality of death.

Another regular visitor was Great-Uncle Charlie, large, beaming, almost bald and very, very deaf. We took it in turns to shout at him and he smiled benignly back, having switched off his cumbersome hearing aid. Charlie was good with words, enjoyed a game of Scrabble and, infuriatingly, always beat us; there was no nonsense about 'letting the children win'. This was a laudable philosophy but my mother one day took a cursory glance at the board: 'That's not a word – who put that down?' she asked, pointing at 'konez'. Charlie smiled and quickly left the room. He had been caught out!

I was on my own at home during term because James had been sent to a boarding school, Durlston Court, at Barton-on-Sea. Just eight, he trotted off bravely in his little grey shorts, grey shirt and grey blazer with white edging. The school emblem was a magnificent eagle and the motto, *Erectus non elatus* (upright but not proud) ultimately proved very apt for him. I was intrigued by the paraphernalia of his departure. He seemed to be getting too much attention and a brand new tuck box of which I was very envious.

His headmaster, Pat Cox was an enthusiastic patriot and militarist whose morning Bible readings gave way to 'Early Morning Dispatches' during the 1956 Suez crisis as he enthused the boys with news from the front. 'Cockeye', according to James, possessed a 'tin bum' (they had heard it clanking) as a result of injuries in World War I. This was an absorbing fact to a little girl and I would watch his posterior with awe as he lorded it over sports day, shouting orders through his megaphone.

Also at Durlston was David Straton, whose parents, Tom and Rae, both doctors, were great sailing friends. The boys were allowed one day out either side of half-term with their parents and one with someone else. Needless to say, the four parents hit upon an obvious wheeze. Alternately, they would collect both boys, keep their own, and drop the other at his home for an additional day with his own parents. When this was put to my brother, he was pensive for a moment and then gravely responded, 'But Mummy, wouldn't that be rather sly?' My parents, momentarily chastened by this moral reproof from their eight-year-old son, soon overcame their scruples, made the swap and neither boys nor school suffered one iota.

In my early years all I wanted was to be a farmer's wife. I loved animals, spent most of my spare time with them and it seemed the ideal lifestyle. I even had the perfect farmer lined up: Bill Lovelace, a Dorset farmer's son, my brother's greatest friend at Durlston. One memorable summer the three of us went camping in the New Forest, pitching our tent in a field at a rundown smallholding called Tits' Paddock, the name causing much giggling. The gypsy-born owner invited us to her caravan to read our palms. I would have a happy life, go abroad and work in a hot country. For Bill, she could see only death. We laughed; we would all die in the end, and thought nothing more of it. When he got home, one of Bill's geese had died. We hailed the lady as a genius – how did she know? But, aged thirty, Bill had an emergency operation for a brain tumour. At a routine check-up, two years later, he was told he had only a fortnight to live. 'Bugger it, Mum,' he said, 'I'm going hunting.' He spent his last days riding, hunting, living life to the full and, indeed, was dead in two weeks.

My parents felt I needed a more challenging environment so in autumn 1959 I was dispatched to Wentworth, a boarding school on the cliff top in Bournemouth. Although the school was set back from the coast, just over the lacrosse pitch, through the woods and down the ravines was the sea – very bracing and good for the 'gels'! I was delivered to the door, trunk packed with mid-blue uniform, grey knee-length woollen divided shorts for winter games, navy serge knickers for gym, white gloves for church and pale pink Bri-nylon pyjamas.

'Wenties', even by the standards of those days, was pretty strict. It was a gracious building, previously the seaside home of Lord Portman, whose portrait stared down at us in the central hall. I was not particularly rebellious or deliberately naughty, but did feel constrained by pettifogging rules that seemed worthy of flouting. Don't do this, don't do that and for heaven's sake don't do the other. I could see no valid reason why I shouldn't do them all. We had such fun and I admit I was the instigator of much of it. Midnight feasts in the woods, accessed down the rickety fire escape; getting deliberately 'lost' out on walks; placing toy-gun caps strategically under the legs of desks used by the hapless French 'mademoiselles'. Poor darlings, they were probably only twenty and suddenly bang! bang! bang! Friction set the caps off, we rushed for the doors and the lesson collapsed just as I had planned. A key ambition was to 'faint' in Assembly in the gymnasium, where we had to stand most of the time. We crammed blotting paper in our shoes, the theory being it would draw the blood away from our heads. Occasional faints had nothing whatever to do with blotting paper and more to do with growing up, but it gave endless cause for smirking and knowing looks as we marched in.

I had high spirits, found petty restrictions irksome and was sometimes caught out. I spent a ridiculous amount of time outside the headmistress's study waiting to be told what a silly girl I was, but she made the fundamental error of taking me seriously. Instead of just handing out the task deemed necessary, she felt obliged to say, 'Christine, don't you realise, if you suggest something the class will follow?' I stood there, eyes dutifully down in pseudo-contrition, thinking, 'Gosh, I wonder what I can get them to do next.' Lack of basic child psychology gave me unnecessary encouragement. As well as learning large chunks of poetry and the Bible (which, happily, I have largely retained), I was made to spend time cleaning endless pairs of prefects' white sports shoes. I retaliated by peppering them with itching powder, secreted from Matron when I checked in at the beginning of term. I never saw the results but cleaned away with a smile, turning my punishment on its head.

Today, it is apparently against some Euro law to deprive children of instant communication with the outside world. But in the 1960s we had to queue up after supper and ask permission of the headmistress before making a telephone call. The excuse had to be good — a death was great, although Dad or Mum's birthday usually sufficed, but woe betide if you forgot how many birthdays they had already had that year. The one available telephone kiosk was very public, in the corner of the central hall opposite the staffroom door and perilously close to that of the headmistress. Nevertheless, I concocted a suitably believable story many times in desperation for contact with sympathetic beings.

Compulsory letter-writing took place every Sunday afternoon when we had to write one to home and one to somebody else. Fed up with writing to maiden aunts, one Sunday I wrote to Elvis Presley, whom I adored and still do, firmly believing he would read my letter personally. It was vitally important he knew how I felt about him and I invited him to meet up next time he was in England. Needless to say, the envelope did not escape the eagle eye. I was hauled, yet again, before the headmistress and made to feel foolish but I didn't care – I had my thrill telling the great man how much I loved him.

I enjoyed and was good at sport. We played lacrosse rather than hockey (so much better for the posture) and the freedom of lacrosse appealed to my anarchistic instinct. There are no white lines down the side of the pitch, the game is fast and furious and you are not offside the minute you go over a line; you just career after the ball and wait for the whistle when the referee thinks you've gone far enough. I adored the rough and tumble of sports and was in many school teams: lax, tennis, rounders, netball, swimming – I revelled in it all.

These were the days before competition was regarded as detrimental to the less able and I was taken off to sit my 11+. My parents were keen for me to pass so that if anything happened to the family fortunes I could go to a grammar school. It proved a wise precaution a couple of years later. In the meantime, I thrived in the camaraderie of the dormitory, seldom more than six to a room, but the staff were something else and I can remember many of them all too clearly. My maths teacher, Mrs 'Daisy' Weir, was an alarmingly ferocious woman with wild grey hair, who took a sadistic delight in scraping her long scarlet fingernails down the blackboard. To make matters worse, she used a sharp-edged Crawford's shortbread tin to draw lines on the board; the combination was excruciating. Even now I wince at the memory of the screech. She may have been a very kindly lady but to me she was sharp and strict, with eyes in the back of her head. Writing on the blackboard she would snap, 'Christine. Bring that note here.'

How on earth did she know I had even written, let alone passed a note to anyone? She also taught classics and Daddy, remembering his own struggles, was indulgent at my failings in the Latin quarter.

Our music and singing teacher, Miss Bechervaise, was possibly the worst of all. Pretty unappealing to look at, and utterly ridiculous when conducting, her tight dress rode up her stout body as she waved her arms in the air. Totally unable to keep discipline with us juniors sitting on forms in the gym, her patience gave way and she resorted to kicking me on the shins with her pointed shoes, for which she would be dismissed today. It must be her fault I have never been able to sing a note in tune.

Wentworth was an education in the sometimes painful business of growing up, learning to live with others and cope with adversity. Nowadays, pupils seem to come out of school whenever they like, but then days out were few. You had to look to the other girls for support. Everyone needed a 'best friend' for self-esteem. If no-one wanted to be your 'best friend' you were an outcast. The relationship was frequently transitory and we chopped and changed, sometimes with cruel effect. 'Will you be my best friend?' was great but 'I don't want to be your best friend any more' could be devastating. It was also essential to have a 'Pash', a senior girl on whom you had a crush. You had to pluck up courage to approach the object of your affections: 'Will you be my Pash?' If you chose wisely, your Pash could be a source of comfort, advice and help. I knew my mother disapproved strongly, probably thinking it encouraged unhealthy attitudes, but there was nothing remotely sexual about it. Indeed, we little ones were totally unaware of the concept of a lesbian, as sex itself was still waiting to be invented. Unknown to us, it was lurking around the corner.

Our headmistress, Miss Everett, could not be described as inspirational. She must have been in her late forties, blonde with a protruding stomach ensuring her straight skirts never hung properly. She was particularly friendly with Miss Freemantle who taught geography. Their bedrooms were adjacent and they holidayed together. Furthermore, Miss Freemantle was frequently seen disappearing into Miss Everett's bedroom, at the top of the main staircase. Even at our age, we sensed this was perhaps more than an ordinary friendship but there was only one possible explanation. After much excited giggling in the dorm we concluded Miss Freemantle was a man in disguise. Certainly she was very butch and always wore totally flat shoes, but her bosom was so monumental that it is difficult to imagine it was anything other than real.

One day a gaggle of juniors noticed some graffiti on the wall in the music wing – a red heart pierced by an arrow, at either end of which were Miss Everett and Miss Freemantle's initials. Underneath was written 'Miss Everett is a lesbian.' We had never encountered this word and wondered what on earth it meant. Suddenly the penny dropped. I piped up triumphantly, 'I know, it's French! "Les biens" means "the goods". Miss Everett is the goods! Miss Freemantle has just spelt it wrongly!' Subsequently, whatever had or had not taken place between them, they were both sacked by the governors.

After our first year, we were allowed to wear stockings for church and special occasions. I arrived at the beginning of term thrilled with my white suspender belt with little pink rosebuds. My mother thought it ridiculous and, despite my entreaties, would allow me only one pair of thirty denier. I walked to church, hugely proud of my nylon-clad limbs, despite a large ladder up the side of my right leg, inflicted as I put them on for the first time. That afternoon, compulsory letter-writing home was welcome and I poured out my heart, begging for more stockings. My mother's heart melted and three pairs arrived in the post by return.

Despite tears at the beginning of term, I loved being at Wentworth. My greatest difficulty was a vehement dislike of meat, except sausages or, at a pinch, mince or chicken. The rule was you had to eat enough to cover a three-inch circle. We sat at tables of six with a senior girl at the head. Some were tolerant but others were sticklers so a strategy had to be developed. It was not always easy, especially if sitting adjacent to the gorgon, but I became adept at sleight of hand, shovelling all manner of protein into my napkin and flushing it away afterwards. I always declined gravy to avoid the problem of 'oozing'. Staff and seniors knew some pupils would do anything to avoid eating certain foods so, if I sensed surveillance, I would chew enthusiastically until their attention was distracted, storing the masticated food in my cheek much like a hamster and then spitting the remains into my napkin. It sounds disgusting and it was, but desperate situations call for desperate measures. I would not eat meat and that was that.

The worst weekly horror was the plate of ham on a Sunday morning before church, presumably regarded as a treat. That was easy – being dry it went straight into my pocket so the napkin was unnecessary. In rotation we all had to sit on the high table, raised up by eighteen inches, where a senior mistress or the headmistress presided. I can still recall the horror of knowing I was going to be up there but not knowing what food would be put in front of me. It was pretty difficult spitting things out into your napkin when sitting next to the headmistress, on a podium in view of the entire room, but I managed it time after time.

Table manners were strict. You were not allowed to help yourself to anything – salt, pepper, water – even if immediately in front of you on the table. You had to enquire solicitously whether your neighbour would like the item and she would reply, 'No, thank you, but do help yourself.' Without that preamble it was a capital offence to reach for anything. Food was contraband, like drugs in prison so, after outings at home, we would all smuggle back goodies. In addition to biscuits and cakes, favourites were tubs of thick chocolate spread, which we would eat with our fingers, and condensed milk in a tube, which would be sucked directly into the mouth as we lay back on the pillow. There were no carpets, just a small mat by each bed, so the floorboards were easily accessible and the food hidden underneath to be retrieved later when the enemy thought we were safely asleep. We each had a tuck tin, securely locked away, from which, twice a week, under the housemistress's eye, we were allowed to extract items according to size and type, in a mathematical ratio that defied logic – for example, a four-bar KitKat would equate to eight boiled sweets or five chocolates from a selection box.

Washing facilities were primitive. By rota we filled large white plastic jugs with hot water in the bathroom and brought them back to pour into a ceramic bowl in the bedroom. After a rudimentary wash, the slops were poured into a bucket (no wonder we did not have carpets!) and emptied in the bathroom. We had a bath three times a week but hair was rather different and washed only once a fortnight unless your parents, in writing, specified greater frequency.

We were permitted to keep modest, caged pets (no snakes). During one holiday, I found a tiny, wild, baby mouse half-starved in the garden, brought this scrap of bones and fur into the house, fed her up, and called her Lulu. Term was looming, and I desperately wanted to take Lulu back to school. Reluctantly, it was agreed I could. Wild mice are not ideal pets but I was dedicated to Lulu's welfare, visiting every day to feed, clean and handle her, always conscious that, if I opened my hand too far, she would leap out. I was confident I could win her trust and she would return my love and affection. One day, inevitably, Lulu took her chance, jumped out of my hand and made her escape. I was inconsolable but not, of course, allowed to telephone home, despite having queued for half an hour outside the headmistress's room to make the request. Stonily, I was told, 'This, Christine, is something you will have to deal with yourself.' Every day I put out fresh food for Lulu, hoping she would see sense and come back. Again, I poured my heart out in letters home, causing untold anguish to my mother who could not bear to think of me so upset — exactly why they had opposed taking Lulu to school.

My parents gave me a wonderful start in life but one incident still rankles. A major epidemic of mumps sent girls down like ninepins. Having escaped infection, I went home for one of my days out. When it was time to return I complained about aches and pains in my neck. My father, sensing a try-on, dismissed my fears and packed me off to school. The next day I was hugely swollen and very unhappy. Instead of being indulged and cosseted at home, I had to endure mumps in the sick bay, looked after by Matron. She was a kindly soul, but rushed off her feet, with little time for niceties. How could my father do this to me? We laugh about it now but he should have realised I had mumps; had I been anyone else's child he might have given me the benefit of the doubt.

I wanted to please my parents and do well at school. I knew they made a lot of sacrifices to send me to Wentworth. Although we had a comfortable middle-class existence, school fees for two children were a huge burden. I thought I worked quite hard but my school reports were always peppered with remarks like 'Christine has great ability but will not use it . . . Will go far if she realises her full potential but there is little sign of that yet.' Miss Everett's parting shot was 'Christine needs to exercise self-control in her behaviour, particularly with others of her own age.' She was a fine one to talk! Her successor, Miss Hibbert, took up the cudgels: 'Christine must exercise more self-control in her behaviour' and 'Christine is noisy and uncontrolled in class.'

I was always in trouble and the school was fed up with me. This came to a head during summer sports day in 1963. All the parents were there and the last race was the relay in which I ran the final leg for my house. I trailed in last, having run my little heart out. My mother quickly understood why we had done so badly. The race had been run four times round the circuit, so my team, in the outside lane, needed a factor of four start, instead of the one they had been given. It was a mistake and the race could easily have been run again another day. Not one teacher had realised this and, despite my mother's protests, the cup was duly handed to the 'winning' house. My parents could scarcely believe that not even the maths teacher, Mrs Weir of the scarlet fingernails, had been prepared to correct the error, which set such an appalling example to the girls.

My mother telephoned the school the following day, to speak to Miss Hibbert. Her response came back through the impossibly unsympathetic school secretary, Miss Pitman, who returned her call: 'Miss Hibbert feels everyone was having such a happy afternoon. We didn't want to spoil it then and don't think it necessary to raise it now.' My parents were furious and expressed their dissatisfaction, not just because of the incident itself but because of what it indicated about the school. My mother telephoned the chairman of governors, who took Miss Hibbert's side and would not discuss it. The chairman knew nothing about my conduct, except what a biased headmistress had told him. However, in his ignorance, he voiced his doubts about me as a pupil, told my mother I was a disruptive influence and that the school would be better off without me. Total war was declared and I left soon afterwards.

And so I arrived in a brave new world of co-education at Christchurch Grammar School. I joined the third year, the senior form as it was a new school filling up from the bottom. With no older pupils, there were no prefects above us, but there were boys. I would never have wanted to miss the experience of a girls' boarding school but this was something different. Wentworth was just a single-sex interlude, as I had studied with boys at St Katherine's and Blynkbonnie, so I quickly settled in and enjoyed the rough and tumble. I didn't like everything. The boys soon nicknamed me 'Hormones', deriving from my surname, Holman. I was not one hundred per cent certain what hormones were (I don't suppose they were either) but we all knew they were something to do with sex. Teenagers nowadays are saturated with sex from television and magazines but for us there were still some mysteries. I hated being called Hormones but never showed it – that would have been fatal.

I revelled in the boys' company. We were getting older, some were 'dating' and there was endless fascination trying to work out who had done 'IT'. One girl, notorious among the older boys, was looked on with wonder but also some distaste. The same gossip goes on in schools today but the guessing probably begins far earlier. I had male teachers again, one of my favourites being Mr Finlayson, who taught geography. A character, he was not averse to caning a boy on rare occasions but had a light touch and defused situations with great humour.

A dark, handsome boy called Croucher had a thing about me. One day, Mr Finlayson burst into the classroom and noticed someone had drawn a heart on the blackboard with my and Croucher's initials at either end of the piercing arrow. Mr Finlayson grabbed him by the scruff of his neck and the seat of his pants and proceeded to rub his mop of thick, black hair up and down the board to erase the offending heart. I was embarrassed but flattered and the rest of the class roared with laughter. Later, I willingly gave Croucher a compensatory kiss behind the sports pavilion.

My best girl friend was Marilyn Ward, who was brilliant academically and sailed through school always getting A grades in every subject. She was invaluable with homework, particularly in Russian, maths and chemistry, where I needed help. Life is unfair and Marilyn was also stunning with luxuriant long hair and a fabulous figure, destined to be a real beauty. She followed her dreams and joined the glamour world, becoming Miss United Kingdom and runner-up to Miss World.

Chemistry and I were like oil and water. I was fascinated by gurgling test tubes but found all the symbols just too much bother and longed to dump it. I also found the chemistry teacher unsympathetic (his comment in my 1965 report was dismissive but probably correct: 'Christine is too content to take life easy') and I don't think he was unhappy when I suffered two accidents in the lab. I inadvertently burned off my left eyelashes in a Bunsen burner – I was lucky not to lose my sight. Only three weeks later, I was sucking up sulphuric acid in a pipette (something I should never have done), sucked just a bit too hard, and had to rush for the alkali solution to wash my mouth out. I could hardly eat for a week – a great diet!

Getting to school was a bother – the 38 bus from Ringwood, change once and then on to school. I did this for three years in the company of Robert Bradley, with whom I had grown up and whose parents were longstanding friends. Robert and I sat together plotting on the back seat of the top deck, in particular, how to get away – we had had quite enough of school.

My stock rose through the roof when I acquired a handsome boyfriend, three years older than me and the proud owner of a white Sprite sports car. He would wait outside the school gates. Picture the scene –

me in my purple blazer and grey skirt, bending low into a dashing sports car, while my chums trudged off to catch the bus. I had met Richard at the Webbs'. Philip Webb and his wife were lifelong friends of my parents, having arrived in Ringwood at almost the same time. Webb parties were legendary and it was at one of them that I became drunk for the second time in my life.

I introduced myself to alcohol at an early age and have never looked back. My parents threw a party for their friends when I was four. As they were outside saying goodbye, I circumnavigated the drawing room, draining the interesting dregs from as many glasses as I could reach – a heady concoction of wine, gin, whisky, sherry and assorted cocktails. By the time they came back, I had capsized in the middle of the floor hiccuping bubbles. I suffered no adverse effects, but it had given me the taste!

My second memorable brush with alcohol was at the Webbs'. Philip and his wife, both dentists, had their practice at home. The party somehow overflowed into Philip's surgery, which sounds dangerous, alcohol and dental drills not being natural partners. I was about fourteen, imbibing heavily with little idea what I was doing until I was violently sick and collapsed in the dental chair. My mother was mortified – how could I do such a thing in front of all her friends? – but I was too far gone to worry about her reactions.

So it was at a convivial and gregarious household that I met Richard and we 'went out' for about eighteen months. We had enormous fun, although my mother always waited up for us, knowing when the film, or whatever, ended. She calculated the time home and was deeply suspicious when, occasionally, the Sprite broke down. There were no mobiles so there was nothing we could do but wait in a lay-by for help. A low-slung sports car is not the ideal passion wagon but we passed the time. It was a happy relationship and, looking back, I wish I had given in to Richard's persuasive charm as he was a sympathetic, caring and gentle lover, more deserving of my virginity than he who eventually claimed it.

Finally I rebelled. Having achieved O levels, I was tired of school restrictions and had had quite enough of purple blazer and grey pleated skirt. I gave my parents an ultimatum: either I left and did A levels at college or not at all. They bowed to the inevitable and with Robert Bradley I continued to catch the 38 bus every day, but up the Avon Valley instead of down. The destination, Salisbury Technical College, gave me the freedom I yearned for. I suspect part of my inspiration for this move came from the steady advancement of my brother, who went up to Exeter College, Oxford, in 1965 to read philosophy, politics and economics. I could see the liberty he was about to gain and wanted some myself.

I had some carefree relationships at college but nothing serious. My mother was always dismissive of any man in focus but tended to lament when the relationship was concluded as I was again available and on the lookout. Naturally, she feared the predators. I met a few at Salisbury but managed to emerge virgo intacta, despite various near misses. I was locked into a bedroom by Alan, one of the older students, who had stalked me for weeks and could not believe I did not find him irresistible. Looking back, I am not sure why either – he was attractive and charming – but something just told me, 'No. Not this one.' At a seventeenth birthday party one weekend he manoeuvred me into a bedroom and tried sheer brute force to persuade me. It was only by biting his arm and kneeing him in the groin, rendering him helpless, that I was able to escape. He was subsequently imprisoned for rape so perhaps my better judgment was beginning to take hold.

On the academic front, I enjoyed English literature and economics, Shakespeare, T S Eliot, Chaucer and Virginia Woolf fighting it out with the law of diminishing returns and the elasticity of demand. Despite family holidays, French exchanges, French friends and French letters, I found the subject difficult. The lecturer was unbelievably boring and uninspiring. With everything else going on in life, it was easy to skip French, but I did just scrape the A level.

Teenage exuberance, overconfidence and scrumpy, that rough, raw, highly potent cider, nearly cost me my life. Robert's father owned a beautiful 1940s Rover convertible and incautiously relented when Robert begged to borrow it. The Forester's Arms, a tiny unspoilt pub in the New Forest, sold scrumpy for 2d a pint. With a mutual friend Stuart, Robert and I had been enjoying ourselves, and the scrumpy, and left for home. It was a summer's evening, the roof was down, and we were in high spirits. All the warning signs were there but we were young and Barbara Castle's breathalyser was even younger. We gave someone a lift home and he was well away, enjoying the delights of the old car. 'Go on, Robert, give it some stick, give it some stick,' he shouted repeatedly. Thankfully, we dropped him off but Robert hit the gatepost on the way out. Undeterred, we sailed on and shortly joined the main A338 – yes, the route of the 38 bus, so we were on familiar territory. The next thing I knew I was waking from unconsciousness on the wide grass verge, the car upside down beside me, Robert hovering in a daze and Stuart nowhere to be seen. There was a terrible sound of buckling metal and a human scream.

Jolted from our knockout, Robert and I realised Stuart was trapped. Somehow, we managed to hold the car up and pull him out. Miraculously, he and we emerged unscathed, apart from cuts and bruises – I now have a triangular scar on my bum where a piece was gouged out by a sharp metal edge. But it was a lesson and gave us all a huge fright. About two minutes after we pulled Stuart out, the police arrived and, after checking we were OK, one remarked, 'It's lucky for you lot we haven't had our breathalysers issued yet.' My parents were so relieved to see me in one piece I was able to gloss over scrumpy's role. In truth, it may not have been entirely to blame. It was clear from the tyre marks that we hit the nearside kerb, spun out of control, hit the far side, back to the near side, then the far side, mounted the grass verge and turned the car over. Luckily, nothing was coming from the other direction. Robert was clearly a little the worse for wear but, also, the steering was not a hundred per cent aligned. Fortunately, it was before the days of seat belts, and Robert and I were thrown clear; with seat belts we could well have perished as our heads scraped along the road.

I had a splendid time at Salisbury, never regretted the decision to leave school and just assumed I would go to university. I did not apply for Oxbridge, feeling I was not sufficiently academic, but was offered a conditional place at York, my first choice. Having lived all my life in the south I wanted to go north. York had a first-rate reputation, is a beautiful city surrounded by glorious countryside and the university and hinterland offered excellent facilities. One of my friends, asked why he had applied, responded, 'Because it is near five racecourses.'

But, while waiting for A level results, I had a crisis of confidence and toyed with other alternatives. I had no idea what I wanted to do with my life and, for some extraordinary reason, I investigated the possibility of the armed forces. It might have seemed natural, with my love of the sea and my father's devotion to the 'Senior Service' to go for the Navy, but I was put off because women were not then allowed anywhere near a ship and I thought, what's the point? Totally inexplicably, I applied for the RAF selection course for officer cadets.

I needed an outfit and bought a smart little suit with pastel checks. On the train to Biggin Hill, where I sat full of eager anticipation, the attendant spilled coffee all down the front of my pale jacket and skirt. I was horrified. This was my first big interview, the beginning of my triumphant career, surely culminating in my appointment as Air Vice-Marshal, and I looked like a seedy waitress at the end of a bad shift. I sailed, I mean flew, through the weekend and loved it, relishing the physical challenges, problem solving and tactical discussions. At the end we were asked who, in a real situation, we saw as the natural leader. I hesitated, not wishing to appear pushy, but said I thought it would probably be me. I subsequently learned all the other girls had nominated the same person. I was offered a place the following week but wanted time to consider, perhaps realising my destiny lay with Battleaxes not Spitfires.

My results arrived; I put aside aberrant thoughts of the RAF – I would have hated all that regimentation. I was destined for York. But, before I parachuted blindfold into the wicked world of student politics, I spent a glorious summer sailing, earned a useful pittance on the production line and learned rather too much about the allure of an older man.

Chapter Three

Pink Spots to Candy Stripes, the Seeds of My Downfall

I've taken many jobs over the years to raise much-needed finance. My first Saturday job was at Guards, a Ringwood clothing store, where life sauntered on with an old-fashioned courtesy now long-vanished. I earned two shillings and sixpence (12.5p) per hour, ten shillings (50p) for a Saturday morning and £1 if I worked all day. Confined to haberdashery, I started by tidying away after others but soon progressed to measuring out yards of ribbon and buckram. However, my most important task was taking the ladies' bun order and purchasing the items for their mid-morning break. I sallied forth for bagfuls of doughnuts, iced Bath buns and rock cakes. Two beleaguered males, who worked in the gentlemen's outfitters, had a segregated break. I never knew whether they had buns or not.

When I was about fifteen, I stayed for a couple of weeks with my friend Philippa Hare and we decided to try our hand at waitressing. With the optimism of youth, we assumed Bournemouth hoteliers would welcome us with open arms. We started at the top, presenting ourselves at the Royal Bath, a magnificent five-star hotel overlooking the sea, where we were politely turned away. Undeterred, we walked to the Highcliffe, an equally classy establishment, and received the same response. Just a little dispirited, we persevered, descending the hierarchy to mere three-stars.

After being turned away from the second of these, the penny dropped. We urgently needed to address the key question of 'experience' and acquire some without delay. We sat on a bench in the sunshine and agreed we had waitressed at a hotel in Cornwall the previous summer. Cornwall seemed suitably far away to ensure no embarrassing checks would be made. Our next target was the genteel Fullers Tea Room, where the 'Cornish experience' did the trick. We were issued with nylon uniforms – blue short-sleeve dresses, with press studs up the front and white frilly pinnies covered in large pink spots – and let loose on the unsuspecting customers. It was jolly tiring and fraught with danger. We coped with teas, coffees, chocolate buns, eggs, chips, beans and macaroni cheese, but a prawn and smoked salmon open sandwich was nearly our undoing. Philippa and I were on our own when this exotic delicacy was ordered. After hasty confabulations and much brow-furrowing, we did our best and I was about to sail out with a sorry little offering – a piece of buttered white bread, a slice of smoked salmon and a few scattered prawns. We knew it wasn't right but were unsure how to rescue the situation. The supervisor returned just in the nick of time from her coffee and fag, dismissed the offending plate and rapidly created a magnificent, towering construction with exotic twirls and flourishes, rising from a sea of salad.

In our lunch break we stuffed our pockets with wonderful light, creamy chocolate-covered buns, wandered down to the seafront and sat munching on the stone steps, looking like a Donald McGill seaside postcard, in our blue and pink frilly nylon. We soon learned how to inveigle the best tips, especially from young men on their own. A near spill of the coffee, not too much and certainly not over them, was a sure way of entering into conversation. 'Oops, er, sorry!' – big smile, look into their eyes – 'I'm not used to this, I'm only a student.' We began to amass a small fortune in the jar on the fridge at Philippa's house. We earned more in tips than our basic wage, even allowing for Fullers' initial error. We realised at the outset we had been signed on at the full adult rate, rather than the student pittance, and anticipated an attempt to short-change us. They tried it on but any union would have been proud of us as we fought for our rights.

In the great outdoors, I worked three Easters on a farm in Somerset. During a couple of idyllic weeks I was surrounded by sheep, horses and all the joys of a farm. It was lambing time so we had a night rota and I would be up at 3 a.m. to go round the pens, seeing who had lambed and sorting out any difficulty. There is a technique to pushing your lubricated hand up inside a sheep, reaching for the lamb and gently pulling it out, while encouraging the terrified animal to push at the same time. It is not a one-girl job and if I found any stuck I rushed back to the house for help.

One of the worst jobs was sewing them up after a prolapse – when the womb turns inside out and shoots out of the back. My task was to hold the sheep firmly down with its bum in the air while the farmer pushed the womb back and performed the delicate stitching. The blood and gore of the lambing pens was offset by hours of riding, looking after the horses and generally revelling in farm life. It was not always easy to tuck into lamb for supper after watching the farmer cutting open the internal organs to ascertain the cause of death (not, I hasten to add, of the one we were about to eat) when putrid yellow pus spurted everywhere, confirming disease.

In 1968 I needed money before setting off for York. My mother had seen an advert in the local newspaper for students as temporary production-line staff at Max Factor in Poole. Doubting my resolve, she applied for me and I found myself catching a hideously early bus from Ringwood to the factory. The basic pay was dismal but supplemented at the end of the week, if you worked five full days and were punctual every day. It goes without saying, I managed to miss the bus at least once a week and I always wanted Friday afternoon off to go sailing, but what I lacked in financial reward was more than compensated for by the life experience it gave me.

Max Factor employed many student casuals and always ensured a regular employee headed any production line, keeping it rolling at professional speed. I had a variety of jobs. I sat round a table packing pale blue mascara wands into boxes. Five folds, two tucks, pop one end of the wand in, another fold, another tuck and the other end was secure. I am reasonably adept with my fingers so, after a few crumpled offerings, my pile mounted up creditably and did not look noticeably smaller than the others. I was later placed on the Primitif line, responsible for plonking bottles of perfume into the slot as Christmas gift boxes whizzed past, to be filled with talc and a cake of soap further down. It was hardly rocket science but the wretched boxes shot past like bullets. Most days, I managed to drop a bottle early on, and spent the rest of the day with my overalls and the concrete floor reeking of Primitif – not a pretty smell.

It was a different world. The regular girls chattered away about men, sex, clothes, make-up and TV and I was so riveted by their conversation it was difficult to focus on the job in hand. They were so used to their manual tasks, they didn't need to concentrate. I learned a lot about lives far different from my own but had no problem getting on with the girls. We were warned that some might resent students but I enjoyed talking with them and we had many laughs, often at my expense.

Poole Week dawned and I tore myself away from Primitif and factory gossip. James and I were then crewing in a boat called *Aimée*, owned by Godfrey Verner, who sailed out of Poole. Godfrey was a master tactician and helmsman, and *Aimée* was a wonderful boat but, being wooden, she was too old-fashioned and heavy to compete with the sleek new racing machines. So, at the invitation of the owner of *Judy Too*, the entire crew from *Aimée* transferred for the duration of Poole Week. With this black, shiny, mean machine underneath us, we trounced the opposition, easily winning Class I every day. I was bronzed and fit, it was exhilarating, heady and we attracted a lot of attention both at sea and in the club in the evenings. The week was not, however, only about winning. We won the trophy but I lost something else.

It was a classic case. Older man, exuding considerable charm and sophistication on a vastly younger, impressionable girl. Looking back, I now wonder how I could have been so stupid. But I was ripe for picking. Not only was it physically electrifying battling with the elements; there was an additional frisson because he and I were sailing in competition in the same class and I was beating him every day. It was a gloriously hot week and I did not help my cause by wearing rather brief navy shorts and a sleeveless, stretch candy-striped towelling top.

He was attractive and I was flattered by his attentions. If only I could have looked at myself and said: 'Hey girl, what do you think you are doing? Can't you tell what's in his mind? It's you today and her tomorrow.' It is frightening now to see how easily he took advantage of me. I was sensible, well brought up, educated and had plenty of men my own age paying court. Indeed, there was one particular handsome, charming enthusiast during that same Poole Week, but he suffered a comparative lack of maturity.

My Lothario invited me for dinner on the Friday evening at the Dolphin Hotel in Poole. I was tanned, toned and sun-kissed and wore a simple but sexy white dress with low neck and large mesh fishnet sleeves. What was I anticipating, even to have packed such an item in my kit bag? I was light-headed with the euphoria of the week and the prospect of university ahead. Life was good. I was enjoying it to the full and radiated that to everyone I met. I remember the scene as if it were yesterday and could take you to the very table at which we sat. My companion paid me endless compliments while he topped up, and topped up, my glass of champagne. He disappeared for a brief while and I assumed he was answering a call of nature. He was, but not of the kind I had anticipated. While we lingered over coffee, the waiter came and said quietly, 'Yes sir, we do have a room available.' If I hadn't already realised, I did then. But it was too late. Of course, I should have backed out. I cannot remember what was going through my head, apart from the effects of the champagne, but I found myself in said room and the inevitable happened. Clearly, it meant nothing to my friend and it certainly meant nothing to me. He was tender and loving and, possibly sensing my racing thoughts, enquired, 'Hell, that wasn't your first time was it? Were you a virgin?' I looked at him and my silence spoke volumes. He hugged me, smiled, and said, 'Well, you're not now.'

We returned to our respective boats and I crept back on board so I would not wake anyone. The next day, after the racing, when I took an even greater satisfaction in beating him, we were tied up alongside each other. His crew, who clearly knew exactly what had happened, broke into song: 'Who were you with last night? Who were you with last night?' I was deeply embarrassed but could only smile. They must have watched the chat-up process during the week with wry amusement. I am sure they had witnessed it many times before.

I don't regret the incident but nor do I look back on it with any pride. He was married. I knew that and should have steered clear. He must have been about 45 or 50 and I was 18. He didn't offer any of the usual excuses, so I never knew whether his wife did or did not understand him. We didn't talk about anything like that – our conversation was full of sailing and racing. In my defence, I was vulnerable and he took advantage of my youth and naïveté. He may well be dead but I would welcome meeting him now to laugh about it, although I doubt Lothario would remember it at all. The power of an attractive middle-aged man to seduce a young girl is frightening unless, of course, one happens to be that middle-aged man.

I had made for myself the candy-striped stretch towelling top which, with the brief shorts, had contributed to my downfall. When I was sixteen my parents agreed a clothes allowance of £20 a month, never enough of course, but I was thrilled with the independence it gave me. My very first purchase was a white, shiny PVC mac, trench-coat style with black buttons and black edging around the collar and sleeves. I looked like a lollipop lady but it was extremely trendy. From a young age I made many of my own clothes on my mother's ancient treadle Singer sewing machine, which had belonged to her grandmother. I beavered away, running up everything from skirts and dresses to suits and long evening wear. It eked out the clothes allowance so I could buy the fashionable essentials. Some garments were crashing mistakes but I loved everything at the time. I have always been addicted to colour, in particular red, and my motto now is 'Why wear one colour if six will do?' Far less confident in those days, I went through a phase of navy, navy, navy, thinking it would make me look slimmer. The shiny white mac? Yes, it was an aberration, but it did stop the traffic at pedestrian crossings!

A childhood friend of ours, Judith Rossiter, lived on the outskirts of Ringwood. Judith was a couple of years older, very fashion conscious and with a great figure. As soon as she could escape from school, she rushed to the bright lights and worked in London for *Honey* magazine, quickly becoming accessories editor. It was the sixties and Judith had a flat very near the King's Road, the epicentre of 'Swinging London'. She would come home to Ringwood some weekends kitted out in the latest things. She had wonderful legs, wore tiny miniskirts, always with the latest groovy tights, sported a long blonde wig, false eyelashes and had the flair to carry it off. It seemed wondrously glamorous to me and I felt terribly gauche, very much a country cousin.

I went to stay with Judith (by then calling herself the far more trendy 'Lisa') in London, arriving one evening eagerly anticipating actually setting foot the next day on the King's Road, *the* place to see and be seen. Judith went off to work and I was alone to pursue my great adventure. It was a fabulous sunny day, and I was in high spirits, agog with excitement as I walked down the road. I turned left and there it was – the hallowed tarmac. I had expected to see at least a Beatle, a Stone, a Shrimp or a Twiggy walking towards me. But it was just an ordinary road. It could have been Ringwood High Street. What was all the fuss about? Silly me. I was at the wrong end! So I ploughed on, with heart pounding until I reached the bit that mattered – the boutiques, the bars and everything important in life. I immediately fell under its spell and spent all day gawping at people, clothes, hippies and hairstyles, intoxicated by the whiff of decadence. I knew I was out of my depth, too provincial and unsophisticated to interest anyone, but I fell under the spell of its atmosphere. The King's Road is now fashionable all over again and, although many exotic, individual shops have made way for chain stores, some gems remain, like the imaginatively named shoe shop, R Soles. I love walking up and down in the sunshine, watching a new generation captivated by its buzz, fizz and excitement.

Chapter Four

University – Hellenic Passion – Enter Neil

I was growing up fast, mapping out my way in the world at an age when people and places make impressions that remain with you for life. While I was finding myself, a young man who was to prove important in my life was doing the same.

Mostyn Neil Hamilton was born just in time for breakfast on 9 March 1949. His timing was impeccable, as meals have always assumed primal importance for him. Both his grandfathers were coal miners, although his maternal grandfather simultaneously ran a pub, the Masons' Arms at Blackwood, Monmouthshire. His father, Ron, left school at fourteen, continuing his education at technical college and night school. A brilliant mathematician, who had to turn down a place at Cardiff University for lack of means, he rose rapidly to become the National Coal Board's chief engineer for Wales. A talented rugby player, he played for Blackwood RUFC and it was a combination of rugby and pub that brought Neil's parents together. The ground was nearby and the players slaked their thirst at the Masons'. It was there that Ron met Neil's mother, Norma, helping her parents behind the bar. They moved into the pub after marriage, and Neil spent his formative years there, which explains a lot.

The places where Neil grew up were hardly less likely to nurture a Tory politician. He was born in Fleur-de-lys, a romantic name for a pit village where the river ran black with coal dust, the surrounding hills were capped by slag-heaps, and voting Labour was an article of faith. To be a Tory in the post-war Welsh mining valleys was eccentric to say the least. Neil was an unusual little boy, fascinated by politics. He started debating when twelve, at the Amman Valley Grammar School in Carmarthenshire, another mining area where his family had moved. His best friend at school, Roy Davies, was a strong Labour supporter whose father ran the local Co-op and they constantly argued about politics. It was a lonely battle for Neil. The Llanelli constituency had no Conservative branch but did nurture future Tory leader, Michael Howard. In the holidays, Neil escaped this socialist wasteland to join the Young Conservatives in Portsmouth South, then solid Tory territory to which his maternal grandparents had retired. Back at school he fought his first political contest as Conservative candidate in a mock election in 1964. Seventy-five per cent of the locals spoke Welsh and Plaid Cymru won, with the communists as runners-up. Neil lost the election but won admiration for his eloquence, even if wasted on an incomprehensible cause.

As a teenager, politics were of little interest to me. My father was an *Express* reader and had a challenging home life, as my mother read the *Guardian* and *Observer*. She was the intellectual partner and political force. She was later to say I derive all my gentle characteristics from my father and all my aggression from her; she is a little hard on herself but I see her point! My father was instinctively conservative but my mother, with her strict Nonconformist background, was always a staunch Liberal.

The passion of politics was first brought home to me at the 1966 general election. James had Liberal inclinations and was caught up in the excitement while I concentrated on important things like riding and make-up. On election night we gathered for a party at the home of Liberal friends and the New Forest Tory MP cantered home with an enormous majority. When the result flashed on the TV, James tore off his glasses and threw them into the blazing log fire, shouting, 'Those ****ing Tories.' Being a sensible chap, he immediately realised the foolishness of his grand gesture and frantically scrabbled in the fire to retrieve his specs as they melted away along with the Liberal hopes. To see him so angry and emotional, momentarily losing control, was an eye-opener. I was also amazed and embarrassed; he had used *that* word in front of our parents — something then quite shocking. It was an early lesson in the passion of politics, which had yet to touch me.

It was another two years before I first dipped my own toe into those murky waters. I went on my excited way to York in 1968. At the end of the '60s the streets worldwide were an ocean of protest. Paris was filled with barricades and tear gas as students rampaged through the city, full of revolutionary zeal and fervour, the sons and daughters of the privileged shoulder to shoulder with the poor, paralysing the government of General de Gaulle. Bobby Kennedy and Martin Luther King Jr were assassinated and London witnessed violent anti-Vietnam demonstrations. Students everywhere were revolting against authority. If my brother's grand gesture had begun to awaken my political consciousness, the event that had the deepest and most lasting impact on me was the self-immolation of Jan Palach, who set fire to himself in Prague's Wenceslas Square in protest against the Soviet invasion of Czechoslovakia. I admired his courage, but was deeply shocked and moved that he could sacrifice his young life in such a horrific way.

Politics may not have been much in evidence at Max Factor but it certainly was on the York campus. Top of the agenda for political groups was to enlist newcomers to their cause. 'Freshers' were romanced by all the organisations and societies that were pitching for members at the Societies Mart. My innate leanings took charge and I wandered over to the Conservative stall where a tall, slim, third-year introduced himself as the chairman. Harvey Proctor was later elected Tory MP for Billericay in 1979 and subsequently forced to resign when the *People* allegedly set him up with an underage rent boy. But all those horrors were ahead. In 1968, Harvey was full of political zeal and very persuasive. I duly joined and, within 24 hours, found myself social secretary, which entailed organising parties and gatherings and, infinitely more difficult, enticing MPs to come and speak. It was a long way from Westminster and some politely declined, but we were a lively association and many made the trip, including Enoch Powell and Gerald Nabarro.

It was not easy being a student right-winger in the sixties when the world was undergoing a cultural, social and sexual revolution. Tory Central Office contrived to make life even harder by naming their student wing the Federation of University Conservative and Unionist Associations. These were more innocent days, before FCUK. Fortunately, the penny eventually dropped and it became the Federation of Conservative Students, with more user-friendly initials. Amazingly, we were the largest political group, with Labour second and the far left splintered into innumerable sects such as Spartacus, Trotskyites and Ice-pick (anti-Trots – Trotsky was murdered with an ice-pick).

I originally wanted to study economics, having so enjoyed A level, but eventually decided on trendy new Sociology. In the first year we had lectures in all the social sciences and the economics lecturer was a tedious statistician. This reawakened my prejudice against maths and confirmed I was right to choose the softer option. Laurie Taylor, now a regular radio broadcaster, was a junior lecturer in sociology and the only person who could get students out of bed on a Monday morning. Rumours abounded of how many he got into bed as well but I could not possibly comment. He was magnetic, charismatic and his lectures were always full. Sociology was a wonderful way to idle away three years. We had few lectures and as long as you mugged up on basic facts, it seemed largely opinion and interpretation. While chemistry undergraduates sweated in laboratories every day, I breezed in and out of three lectures and two tutorials a week. That was it.

Having a good time and dabbling in politics absorbed most of my energies. York is a noble city, always providing plenty of diversion. In my first two years I lived with a local solicitor and his wife, Peter and Jeannie Gildener, who let out two rooms to students at the top of their house in Burton Stone Lane. We were deliciously close to the chocolate factories and, with the wind in the right direction, the smell of Rowntree's After Eights or Terry's Chocolate Orange wafted tantalisingly over. I was happy with the Gildeners, enjoyed the company of their two young children, and was glad to be able to escape the campus. Peter and Jeannie were very involved with the Arts Theatre and I spent many a happy hour helping behind the scenes, suitably star-struck, meeting young actresses like Judi Dench and Francesca Annis. The race course was a popular haunt, the surrounding countryside glorious and I spent long days out in the Dales, walking, pubbing and just being young.

There were no undergraduates to whom I was particularly attracted. They all seemed too young. Perhaps I was subconsciously looking for another older man. My first romantic attachment came in the form of a Greek Adonis called George. It was a straight pick-up but he was disarmingly charming and, as I was shortly to discover, totally irresistible. I was sitting alone in the window of a coffee bar in Stonegate on a Saturday morning, summoning the strength to walk home. My shopping was heavy but I was on an economy drive and it was cheaper to walk than catch the bus. I was absorbed by the newspapers when suddenly a shadow stole across the page. I looked up to find a tall, dark, lithe man in his mid-thirties with a mane of thick, gently wavy black hair. His eyes were like deep, brown forest pools. He bowed slightly and, with a captivating accent and delightfully muddled grammar, said,

'When you are ready, I take you home — yes? I am going in your way.'
I protested that he didn't know where I was going. 'But, I have. I watch
you for the days.'

George did indeed know exactly where I lodged and he genuinely
lived in the same area. There seemed nothing wrong with accepting a lift
except that he was, quite simply, gorgeous. Sex on rather beautiful legs.
I sensed danger but he was delicious and my carrier bags were many.
With pounding heart, I clambered into his stylish, sporty, white
drophead, wishing I had put on a bit more eye make-up before sallying
forth that morning. We almost fell into bed there and then. With even
one glass of wine I suspect I would have thrown caution to the wind, but
on a mug of coffee I was able, just, to keep my balance. His very touch
was electric and I knew it would not be long. He took me for dinner the
next evening and so began a whirlwind relationship that did not fit at all
with my burgeoning, all-too-conventional involvement with student
politics. I kept George very much on the side and to myself. He would
scarcely have blended at a 'wine and cheese'!

We came from different worlds. About fifteen years older, born in
Athens, George had arrived here with his parents some twenty years
earlier. He was bohemian and nomadic at heart so we were never
destined for a long-term relationship. He was impossibly romantic
and glamorous but, although we berthed happily and passionately
together, we were destined to be ships that passed in the night. We
began to see less and less of each other and cast adrift amicably after
about six months.

Politics was taking hold. In September 1969, I attended my first
Conservative student conference at Swinton Castle, near Ripon;
surrounded by a deer park, it was a magnificent place with huge baronial
rooms, imposing staircases, magnificent paintings and castellated battle-
ments where, naturally, I felt quite at home. Lord Swinton lived in one
wing of the castle and lent the rest to the Party. Once a year, two
representatives from each university attended, at the Party's expense.
These conferences were an important part of student politics. Some
went to be seen and to make their mark, others just to have a good time.
Among the people I first met at Swinton were Ann Widdecombe, David
Mellor, Andrew Neil, David Davis and Richard Ryder.

I arrived at Swinton together with the newly elected chairman of our
association, Michael Young, a mature student. He and I lived at the same

address in York, a fact that appeared in the conference handbook. Naturally, people drew the obvious (but wrong) conclusion, compounded by our sticking together at first, not knowing anyone else. There were plenty of eligible and interesting young men, plus the usual nerds and tossers always present at any political gathering. Casting my eye around I was instantly attracted by a young man with large bushy black sideburns, standing in the middle of a group, clearly trying to win an argument. I distracted his attention, our eyes met and I thought, 'Yes. That'll do me for the weekend.'

Neil Hamilton, standing for election to the FCS Committee, needed the right girl on his arm. I could tell he was attracted. The hours went by but he made no move. I wondered what was wrong with him. We had arrived at noon, had had lunch, an afternoon session, dinner and still nothing. The next day, the same. Time was fast running out. Positive action was required. That evening, relaxing after the sessions, waiting for dinner, Neil was idly tinkling the ivories on the piano. As the others moved into dinner, I lingered, draped myself across the piano and flashed my own pearly whites. He had thought I was shacked up with Michael Young. I quickly disabused him, we went into dinner and our lives have been entwined ever since.

My romance with Neil was a long-distance student affair. I had nearly two years left at York and Neil did a further degree at Aberystwyth, unwilling to face the harsh realities of the real world. Little did I know then he was to take yet a third, this time in law at Cambridge. We met regularly at political junkets and, in between, wrote copious love letters, Neil addressing his envelopes in an elaborate gothic script with twirls and flourishes, which intrigued those who saw them, particularly my parents.

The telephone bills of innocent third parties mounted. Our respective parents subsidised lengthy calls, as did my landlord, Peter Gildener. Fortunately, itemised bills were unknown and he could only rail at his student lodgers with his totally justified suspicions which, of course, we all strenuously denied. Peter watched the pennies and would not allow us to have an electric fire in our rooms but I circumvented that petty nonsense by keeping two hair dryers blowing for hours and hours, which did the trick instead.

From time to time Neil would send me parcels through the post. I particularly remember one birthday receiving a small package which I opened in eager anticipation. My hopes were soon dashed as I discovered a slim volume, with a garish purple and red cover, entitled *Right Turn*. Neil, realising I was dangerously left-wing, thought it his duty to educate and improve. This was the first of a series produced by the Constitutional Book Club to which he had subscribed on my behalf. Other volumes followed at monthly intervals – *Down with the Poor, Goodbye to Nationalisation*, and so forth. I never did read any of them but they still grace our shelves as an amusing, if unromantic, reminder of times past. All the policies espoused therein are now firmly part of Labour thinking and most already set in legislative concrete. As always, Neil and his fellow travellers were ahead of the pack.

Organising 'cheese and wines' was a doddle, but formal dinners were more taxing. One year we were thrilled to receive the legendary but highly controversial Enoch Powell. Enoch was *the* hate figure. The Left, seeing him as their ultimate challenge, were desperate to picket, heckle and generally destroy the event. Determined to outwit them, we leaked false information. A bogus menu, complete with the wrong location and time, fell into the hands of the enemy. They thought they had rumbled us at the magnificent Merchant Taylors' Hall. The police co-operated fully, posting a few boys in blue outside the hall, duly hoodwinking the lefties until too late. With placards and megaphones, hundreds massed outside in a baying mob, while several hundred Tories were safely and happily ensconced five miles away at the Chase Hotel. I sat down at the top table with a huge sigh of relief, exhausted and starving; food had seemed an irrelevance all day. But we had done it.

I have ridiculously large handwriting and had penned many letters to Enoch to arrange his appearance. When introduced before dinner, he bowed low, 'Ah! The lady with the large hand!' I was seated between him and Brian, an FCS officer. I was glad to have his undemanding, easy company to counterbalance the more intimidating presence of Enoch, one of the great brains of the century, a professor of Greek by the age of 25. The menu was chosen with an eye to economy and dessert was a choice between trifle and fruit salad. Brian and Enoch opted for the latter. I was hungry, plumped for the trifle, and an enormous helping was plonked in front of me. Secretly thinking, how splendid, I held up my hands in mock ladylike horror, 'Good heavens, I can't possibly eat all that.' Enoch turned to me, took both my hands between his, looked straight into my eyes with his steely blue stare and said, slowly and deliberately, in his unmistakable voice, 'Christine, there is nothing more attractive in a woman than a healthy appetite.'

'Oh really, Mr Powell. How wonderful!' I eagerly wolfed the lot! Enoch then told me how disappointing it was to take a lady for dinner if she merely toyed with her plate, declaring he loved seeing women enjoying their food. I think of him now, looking down on me reprovingly every time I decline the chips or a pudding!

Food and seduction apart, he was a difficult neighbour. I was outclassed and it did not help that I was tired, my mind having been full of administrative minutiae all day. I ventured to use the word 'moderate' during a conversation about student politics. Again the gimlet stare. 'Ah, Christine, what do you mean by "moderate"?' he enquired. 'Well, you know, everyone knows what we mean by "moderate".' It was no good. I had to define my terms before he would continue with the conversation. 'Moderate' was an important word in politics. We were constantly battling to distance ourselves from the right-wing Monday Club. I suppose all the student infighting prepared me for the endless back-stabbing of grown-up politics. I hated it then as now, but it was a world I was destined to inhabit for nearly three decades and I was about to meet someone who would play a large part in that life.

I graduated from York in 1971 with a 2:1, which was OK for not trying. Just after finals, the guest of honour at our annual dinner was Sir Gerald Nabarro, MP for South Worcestershire. Universally known as 'Nab' and a great rabble-rouser for the Party, with huge bloodhound eyes and handlebar moustache, he was a gift to political cartoonists. Seated next to him at dinner, I was enchanted by his humour, his twinkling eyes, his sense of fun and naughtiness as he quizzed me about my future career. On hearing I wanted to be an MP, and planned to get a job to see how Westminster operated at first hand, he stroked his impressive moustache and boomed, 'My dear, I don't have a vacancy now, but let me know when you arrive and I will look after you.' True to his word, he did.

CHAPTER FIVE

The Palace of Westminster

Looking back, I wish I had taken a gap year before plunging into the world of work. The options seemed to be either VSO or a kibbutz in Israel and neither seemed appealing. I was desperate to forge ahead, get on with life and my ambitions. Good works could wait. So, two months after graduating, I found myself working as research assistant to Wilfred Proudfoot, MP for Brighouse and Spenborough.

I was ecstatic. I had a paid job in the Gothic splendour of the Palace of Westminster. My glass bubbled over, my political career had begun and even prosaic reality could not dampen my enthusiasm. Proudfoot was a lively, engaging fellow, a dedicated Yorkshireman who owned a little chain of supermarkets. He was never going to change the world, although he tried, but he was kind enough to take me on, and I was hugely grateful for a foot on the ladder. I earned £800 a year – good money considering I had zero experience, could neither type nor do shorthand and was totally ignorant of parliamentary and office life. I joined in September, living in a caravan in his Scarborough garden while I began to accustom myself to the man, the constituency and political life. My mother was horrified at the caravan but, frankly, I was delighted to have the privacy, obviating the need to spend evenings *chez* Proudfoot. Parliament returned in October and I arrived at Westminster with eager anticipation and boundless optimism.

Life with Wilf was not exactly the epicentre of political intrigue and power, but I was in my element and agog with excitement when the practicalities of life bore down. I needed somewhere to live in London. My aunt and uncle in Dulwich were very hospitable but after the freedom of York, the last thing I wanted was to be in the clutches of the family.

Equally, I didn't want to share, I needed my own retreat, somewhere I could be alone. I didn't want anyone else's things hanging around, neither their tights over the bath nor their boyfriends slouched in front of the telly. However small, I was determined to find a place of my own and so I settled in now fashionable Battersea, which had not then 'arrived'.

The block was built in 1968 by a Co-ownership Housing Association, funded by a Housing Corporation mortgage. About half of what you paid monthly was rent, while the rest paid off the common mortgage. If you moved on, you received a percentage refund that increased over time. It was a toehold in the property market. By 1980, I had moved twice within the block, to larger and higher flats, when suddenly there was an unforeseen change. Margaret Thatcher gave council and co-ownership tenants the 'right to buy' and I became an owner overnight, paying a mere £4,500 for a two-bedroom flat with underground parking, overlooking Battersea Park. The block remains a classic example of everything wrong with late 1960s architecture. In a road of handsome Victorian buildings, it sticks out like a sore thumb but enjoys superb views over the park and proximity to the river and the Albert Bridge, London's most beautiful.

My first flat was just a glorified bedsit with bathroom and kitchenette, but it was mine. I did not have to answer or explain myself to anyone. Living in my own little castle, with my own little job in the palace of my dreams, the world was at my feet. But I was already restless, frustrated by the limitations of working for Wilf and actively keeping my ear to the ground for something more stimulating, when I received a telephone call.

Gerald Nabarro had a difficult start in life. When he was seven his mother died in childbirth, the same year his tobacconist father went bankrupt. Aged fourteen he spent a year working in a ship's galley, ending up scavenging for food in Seattle docks. Back in England, he added three years to his age and, at fifteen, joined the King's Royal Rifle Corps, a regiment he deliberately chose because they traditionally recruited short men. He was five foot six. Through intelligence and aptitude, he used the next six years to fill the gaps in his education but, with no private income, was unable to accept a post at Sandhurst. He joined the Territorial Army, spent the war on industrial duties and training the Home Guard, developed an interest in politics and joined the Conservative Party in 1945. Five years later, by then a successful businessman, he was part of the 'Great Tory Vintage' of 1950, his new colleagues including Ted Heath, Enoch Powell, Bill Deedes, Iain Macleod and Reggie Maudling. Nab stood out immediately, not just because of his physical appearance and booming voice but for his decided opinions and apparent love of controversy. He suffered two serious flaws for a politician: he was a nice man and had a sense of humour. The TA had brought him together with the beautiful Joan im Thurn, the colonel's daughter, whom he picked up at a bus stop in the pouring rain and married at the end of the war.

By the time we met, Nab had found himself cornered by two other women. Margaret House had been his secretary for thirteen years and he was very close to her. The complication was Margaret Mason, who ran his fledgling publishing business in Birmingham and drove him to many engagements all over the country. One Margaret was enough – two were jealous. Something or someone had to give. Margaret House gave up the unequal struggle for dominance and quit suddenly, leaving him with no secretary.

And so the telephone rang and Nab asked if I would join him for a drink that evening. I duly presented myself in the Central Lobby and we repaired to the Pugin Room, overlooking the Terrace and the Thames. Wilf had never even taken me to the canteen, so I was delighted and thrilled. I was 21, enjoying the attention of one of the best-known, most active and energetic political figures of the day, a regular radio and television performer, entertaining, universally recognised, a controversial figure whose abilities were acknowledged more often by his adversaries than by his colleagues. He came quickly to the point. His secretary of thirteen years was leaving and he wanted me to take over. I had thought the meeting was purely social, a kind enquiry about how I was faring in my new world. I was flustered, and blustered that I wasn't equipped to be a secretary, I couldn't do shorthand, could barely type, was only fit to be a research assistant and pretty new at that. He waved my protestations aside, saying he would engage someone else to do all that. What he wanted was someone to organise and look after his life. I suspect he wanted the status of a graduate secretary. He made it difficult to refuse. I was earning £800 a year and he offered me £2,500 plus an all-expenses-paid car. In 1971, MPs themselves were paid only £3,250 so it was a monumental offer, even without the car. I enjoyed his company, felt we would get on well and so, after extracting firm promises of someone to help me, I took the job and the wheel of NAB

4, a racy Mini Cooper. Nab was ludicrously indulgent, insisting I put all my petrol on a credit card, which he paid, telling me I had 'more important things to spend my money on'.

He was a dedicated motorist and early fan of personalised number plates. AB is a Worcestershire suffix and in those days you could earmark particular plates with relative ease. As well as NAB 1 to NAB 10 he had others – NAB 999 and NAB 333. His two gardeners even drove mopeds with NAB plates. With little regard to economy, he changed his cars every year. The family lived in The Orchard House, a large and beautiful Cotswold stone house in Broadway with generous gardens and, as I was soon to find out, ever-abundant hospitality.

Age-wise I came in the middle of his four children and was regarded as an extension of his family. I loved working for Nab, though he was a demanding taskmaster, sometimes forgetting everyone needs time off occasionally. He was criticised, not always unfairly, for being bombastic and pompous but he had a big heart, a great sense of fun and we got along famously. As good as his word, he employed Lilian, who had brilliant secretarial skills, and together we coped with his prodigious workload – and him! Needless to say, my arrival did not go unnoticed by the press, and Nigel Dempster wrote in the *Daily Mail* that Nab had bribed and 'stolen' me by offering more money. There was the usual 'blonde 21, nudge, wink', but he was careful not to libel us. After having a middle-aged secretary for so long, Nab was amused to have a youngster working for him. I think he was probably amused by the innuendo – but his wife Joan was not.

When I began working for him in January 1972 he was already embroiled in a court case, having been prosecuted for dangerous driving, and its ramifications caused an almighty upheaval in his life and career. In May 1971 he had addressed a meeting in the New Forest and set off for London with Mrs Mason at the wheel. He was subsequently charged with dangerous driving, NAB 1 having apparently driven the wrong way around a roundabout. You might think that was impossible but this one was lozenge-shaped. Others had made the mistake before and the road system was changed shortly thereafter. Two witnesses said Nab was the driver. He and Mrs Mason said she was. I knew nothing of this at the time but the case came to court when I had been with him for one month. He was found guilty, fined £250 and given a two-year ban. There had been almost no publicity in advance but then my telephone at the House of Commons went mad. I was fielding endless media enquiries when more important callers came through. Three independent people said they could not believe the verdict. They had seen the car, just before and just after the roundabout. Gerald Nabarro had not been driving. NAB I was a car you would remember if you saw it. Letters then arrived from others, confirming the same thing – he had not been at the wheel. On the basis of this new evidence from independent witnesses, a retrial took place that October, when Nab was acquitted by a unanimous jury verdict and awarded costs of £10,000.

It was a mammoth victory for him but the strain had taken its toll and dominated what were to be the last years of his life. Did it matter who was driving? It would have been much easier for him to plead guilty and get on with living. A bit of 'dangerous driving', with no accident and no-one hurt, could have been shrugged off with his usual aplomb. But he was determined to prove his innocence. I thought I understood this fully at the time and I certainly do now. To be accused, never mind convicted, of something you have not done is not easy to live with. All your natural instincts are to fight and fight on. No-one can ever know whether they would have occurred anyway but Nab suffered two strokes. Having seen the months of worry and mental torment he endured and now knowing myself the agonies and stress of a high-profile court action, I will always suspect they were brought on by the prosecution.

But that tragedy was still ahead. Sir Gerald celebrated victory in the obvious way by replacing his fleet of cars, including my NAB 4, and I took delivery of a brand-new bright purple Mini 1275 (successor to the Mini Cooper), with red leather seats. It was heaven. Nigel Dempster telephoned – was it true? It was hardly news. I had driven in and out of the Commons, often with Sir Gerald in the passenger seat. It was my first lesson that journalists can distort the facts to their own ends. I didn't say anything wrong, I just told Dempster the whole truth. Yes, I had a new car, but merely as part of general car-replacement therapy for Sir Gerald. I was so innocent, so trusting, so naïve. He asked me what my car was like and, probably overenthusiastically (well, I was thrilled with it), I told him all the details.

Joan Nabarro was far from happy when she opened her *Daily Mail* the next morning and saw the screaming headline: 'From Sir Gerald to Christine with love, a brand new Mini . . . as a reward for standing by him loyally in court, Christine, blonde, 22 . . .' All the innuendoes were there. Dempster didn't say anything untrue but conspicuously failed to point out I was not the only one having a new car at the time. Joan had every right to be upset and, for the first time, I was reduced to floods of tears by an inaccurate and distorted press report. I felt I had let the family down but also betrayed by Dempster. It was a lesson I was to learn many times more.

I arrived at the House of Commons wanting to be an MP but was clearly too young and inexperienced to seek any nomination. I threw myself into local Battersea politics, canvassing, jumble sales, the general melee of grass-roots activism. I had boundless energy and enthusiasm for the cause. Battersea was a hopeless case for the Tories but we leafleted manically, canvassed the tower blocks in pairs, and ended up in the pub. I had lost none of my passion for politics itself but began to realise I did not, personally, want to be in the firing line. Some people may find this hard to believe but I do not like confrontation and am always happier when at ease with those around me. I tend to back away from arguments and look for consensus. The prospect of antagonistic debate did not and does not appeal. I started to recognise I did not have the necessary political ambition to carry me through the battles and personal hostility inherent in being an MP.

Besides, I was having a ball and life was good, very good. Living on the top floor was a delightful man called Jimmy Sanders, who had a grown-up family and a girlfriend in Surrey, but who spent his weeks in London attending to his large empire of jewellery shops. In the nicest and most wholesome way, Jimmy was my Sugar Daddy, loved and adored by my circle of young friends and always an essential ingredient at my dinner parties. He would frequently escort me to restaurants, my favourite always being Pomegranates, still presided over by the exuberant and effervescent Patrick Gwynn-Jones. I gawped at Michael Caine and Peter Sellers, while Robert Morley's chins quivered like jelly as he tucked in with relish. I still love Pomegranates today and am happy to say that neither the menu nor Patrick has changed in thirty years.

All London could offer was opening up and I was blossoming in my chosen environment. Earning far more than I had ever dreamed possible, I had a racy little car, a charismatic, vivacious employer, my own flat and plenty of men paying court. I was at the centre of a fast-moving scene. History was being made around me as I flitted through the corridors, canteens and bars, making friends with all and sundry, MPs, ministers, secretaries, police, journalists and staff of all descriptions. I could hardly believe everything had fallen into place so easily. The Palace of Westminster was alive with opportunities of every kind and I flirted with them all. Aberystwyth seemed a very long way away.

Chapter Six

Exit Neil – Unholy Alliances – Farewell to Sir Gerald

Meanwhile, Neil was doing his second degree, stuck out in mid-Wales, with no financial support either from the state or from his father, who had decided it was time he fended for himself. He was spending much time on Party matters, entitling him to travel and accommodation allowances for conferences and meetings, and we frequently met in London. He was vice-chairman of FCS and a member of the Conservative National Executive, entitling him to a room at the Metropole Hotel, Party HQ at the Brighton Conference. He rang in great excitement to tell me he had been allocated a double room. It was brilliant staying at the heart of the conference with all the Ministers and hierarchy, instead of a cheap B&B miles away. However, it is not easy to cover your tracks and the hotel duly charged the Party for two occupants. They passed the excess on to Neil, making a huge dent in his paltry finances, but he was too gentlemanly to mention it at the time.

The shores of Cardigan Bay were a day's journey from London, Neil was a penniless, seemingly perpetual student and romance at that distance was difficult. If he had come to London things might have been different but, through circumstances, we were drifting apart. Life was thrilling for me and Neil's world seemed light years from mine. I felt I had outgrown him. Did I need a boyfriend like that? For a time, geography ensured I did not have to confront reality; however, something had to be done. We attended a Northern Region FCS dinner at the improbably named Dixieland Palace at Morecambe, Lancashire. Prime Minister Edward Heath was guest speaker and Neil drove across from Aberystwyth while I travelled from London. I have no memory of the dinner because my mind was fixed on the task ahead. Afterwards, among the potted plants of the Palm Court, I plunged the knife. Neil said nothing. The blow was totally unexpected and he was crestfallen and bewildered. Me? I felt as though I had kicked a dog, guilty and horrified. We parted, with no reason to think we would meet again, and Neil drove himself into the sea.

He was staying overnight on the other side of Morecambe Bay and had reached the Dixieland Palace across a causeway, although he didn't realise it at the time, passable only at low tide. On the return journey, the tide had turned, the rain was beating down and the estuary high. Together with a couple of friends, he was packed into the sardine can he cheerfully called a car – a rusty NSU Prinz. They were deep in earnest conversation, trying to analyse the weird and wonderful ways of women, when an oncoming car flashed its lights. Neil charged on obliviously and suddenly hit a wall of water, which gushed in through the pedals and under the doors, quickly rising to their knees. The car was flooded and stalled; they were about to drown. Urgent action was required. For all its faults, the sardine can rose to the occasion. It managed to chug backwards to firmer ground, where they were shortly rescued by the very police who had frantically signalled them to stop. Neil retells the story as though, blinded by grief, he was trying to kill himself, but he's not that daft!

Blissfully unaware of this drama, I did not realise what a blow I had delivered. Quite apart from wounded pride, I had damaged his chances at the impending FCS elections. It was undoubtedly helpful to have the right girl and I had left him little time to acquire another. But that wasn't my problem. I was beyond student politics, the future was beckoning and Neil represented the past. At first we still exchanged birthday cards, but those petered out and Christmas greetings became the only contact.

Back at Westminster, though Nab was demanding, I had time for a private life and loved entertaining. My flat was small, the cooking facilities limited, but it was the company that mattered. As my visitors' book testifies, I had endless uproarious evenings around the circular pine table, which later witnessed so many extraordinary events in my life. One visitor was Andrew Neil, an FCS contemporary from Glasgow University. Andrew is now a wealthy, established and respected media figure, formerly editor of the *Sunday Times*. In his 1996 autobiography

Full Disclosure he makes no mention of me, so his title was not entirely accurate. He did refer to Neil, rightly boasting he had beaten him to become national chairman of FCS. Earlier, I had voted for Andrew in a similar election, despite being on Neil's arm at the time, thinking my Neil was too right-wing!

After a particularly jolly evening in the flat, Andrew and I found ourselves alone. I am not sure how it happened. I don't think it was his intention to help with the washing-up (he didn't) and I doubt whether anything was planned, but the other guests had gone and he remained. There was only one room and the bed was the obvious place to relax and enjoy yet another glass of wine. It was comfortable, set against the wall and piled high with a large bolster and plump cushions. Why do these things occur? It was as much a surprise to him as me and we laughed about it afterwards. I have no regrets about it and I hope he doesn't. We were young, single and fancy-free.

While I was sowing my wild oats and Neil was munching his Weetabix, I indulged in some liaisons which were inappropriate, largely because the men concerned were married. I do not seek to excuse my behaviour, and my protestations that I was young are explanations not exculpations. I knew better and my actions were wrong. I am sorry to disappoint the scandalmongers (and my bank manager) but I do not intend to name anyone, although one was at the time and another became a Minister. They are both still alive, as are their wives. I wish now I had never become involved.

There is one man I will name with whom I had a liaison. He was a well-known Lothario, I was but one of many, he is dead and his attractive and vivacious wife knew all about his philandering. He happened to be a Labour MP, which made it interesting. After John Profumo resigned, there was a by-election in Stratford-upon-Avon. The Labour candidate, Andrew Faulds, received rapturous reviews from the intellectual, future Cabinet Minister, Richard Crossman, who said he had made quite simply the best speech he had ever heard from a by-election candidate. Three years later Andrew, tall, bearded, aggressively handsome, became MP for Smethwick. As a distinguished Shakespearean actor, he was already typecast as a romantic hero, with a magnificent, wonderfully modulated voice that lent itself to stage, screen, radio — and Parliament. Andrew's stage whispers could be heard all over the Chamber. When opposing David Steel's Abortion Bill, Norman St John Stevas, MP, was accused by

Andrew, sotto voce but heard by everyone, of being 'unlikely to put a bun in anyone's oven'.

Described in a Parliamentary profile as a 'sextrovert', Andrew's amorous adventures were well known and he had a massive reputation in the Commons and elsewhere. I was unaware of this and was an easy target when he unleashed his very considerable charm offensive. I was quietly waiting for Sir Gerald in the Central Lobby, a wonderful place to sit and watch the world go by. You never know who will arrive next. From presidents to pop stars, all are seduced by the romance and excitement of Westminster. Suddenly this man, whom I recognised as Andrew Faulds but of whom I knew little, made a beeline for me and introduced himself. I suspect he knew exactly who I was and what I was doing there but, nevertheless, asked me the two questions. I told him my name and explained I had recently started working for Gerald Nabarro. He smiled, twinkled his eyes, bowed his head, and said, 'Welcome. You are an adornment to the already beautiful Palace of Westminster.' With that, he went on his way and I thought nothing more of it but, clearly, the seeds of lust had been planted in his mind. Within hours he telephoned and began gently to plague me with calls. To my credit (please!) I was very cool and rebuffed his advances, repeatedly declining to meet him for a drink. I was intrigued but must have sensed he was dangerous to know. Quite apart from anything else, he was some 27 years older than me. However, he persevered and, of course, I was flattered. Whether by accident or design on his part, we seemed to keep meeting in the corridors and I could feel his eyes on me. Whenever I dared look at him, he was smiling, one hand caressing his luxuriant beard, obviously delighted to play with the young salmon so clearly, nearly, taking his bait.

Eventually (let us be honest, it was after only a week) I agreed to meet him for a drink and we then went for dinner in the Strangers' Dining Room. The ever discreet and inscrutable Mr Graham, who ran the SDR for all my Commons years, was accustomed to seeing Andrew come in with yet another woman but even he must have paused in his tracks. I was a regular in the SDR with Sir Gerald, and Mr Graham knew me. Always the perfect gentleman, he showed us to our table, his face betraying nothing.

As night follows day, the experienced and professional lady-killer had his way. Andrew taught me a great deal and we had many splendid, if clandestine, times together. He had the consummate ability to make me feel like the only woman in the world, gloriously swathed in mink yet undressed at the same time. He had that warm, embracing glance in public, heady at any time but particularly when you are young and impressionable. Although I knew he had a large directory of women, at that tender age you cherish illusions you are special. He was mature, magnetic, sexy and, frankly, irresistible! He had a flat in Albemarle Street, Mayfair, where, usually after an intimate dinner at Brown's Hotel across the road, we went frequently over several years. Andrew occasionally suggested there should be additions to our situation, but I resisted, having no interest in extending the relationship beyond the pair of us. He, we, would never have got away with it now. The staff at Brown's knew him of old and would not have dreamt of betraying a customer for thirty pieces of silver but, of course, the tabloid press was not then what it is today.

I harboured no romantic illusions about Andrew but it was more than pure sexual attraction. We had a lot to talk about, which, I guess, was not the case with some of his girlfriends, and we both found the cross-Party element of our liaison added a special frisson. When I first found myself in his bed in Albemarle Street, I thought, 'What the hell am I doing here?' Unable to answer the question rationally, I just floated along with the tide. Andrew was tremendous fun, a great companion, a wonderful lover and we had a good time but that was that, no future. I was swept off my feet by an older, experienced, charming, educated and cultured man.

The most extraordinary thing was Gerald Nabarro's attitude to the affair. The Whips' Office was administered at the time by John Marling. 'Darling' sidled up to Nab one evening in the Members' Lobby. 'By the way, do you know Christine is having a dalliance with Andrew Faulds?' Sir Gerald, who did not know, instantly responded, 'What Christine does in her spare time is entirely her own affair.' He must have been startled but, to his eternal credit, he appeared unconcerned and, if he was taken aback, he was certainly not going to display such emotions to Marling. Over dinner in the Strangers' Dining Room ('My dear, you have better things to spend your money on than food') he told me what Marling had said and his response. It was his way of telling me to be careful. He was not warning me off, just letting me know the gossip was there. He would have been entitled to object. He was a high-profile Tory and could have been horrified by my consorting with a Labour MP. But they had a mutual respect and Nab recognised in Andrew a kindred spirit, another 'Jack-the-lad'. In truth, I think he was tickled by the idea that his young secretary was being romanced by him.

When Andrew died in 2000 at the age of 77, his obituaries made mention of his lady-killer reputation, and 'turbulent marriage'. He was a remarkable and talented man. I was privileged to know him better than many and I remember him with enormous affection. He never accorded me anything but the greatest respect and courtesy and I would not have been without that chapter in my life. It is a disgrace he never went to the House of Lords when he retired, but his strongly pro-Palestinian views probably put paid to that.

Andrew didn't need it, but power, even the illusion of power, is an amazing aphrodisiac and this undoubtedly enables male MPs to attract women who would not give them the time of day on their physical appearance or personality alone. I never ceased to be staggered by the gorgeous young women on the arms of dismal men who just happened to be MPs.

I was having a splendid time. Many weekends saw me at the Orchard House, where I would join the family fun but was also expected to put in a few hours with Nab. He liked having me around because if there was any lapse in the proceedings, I was a perfect excuse to repair to his library and get on with things. Life, although incredibly busy, was relatively uncomplicated emotionally until I embarked on a love affair. It began, unknown to me, on the telephone. He and I had spoken many times over several months arranging the detail of a conference Sir Gerald was due to address. When we met at the conference the attraction, already simmering down the telephone lines, was powerful and instant. He subsequently told me he had already fallen head over heels in love with me and, when I walked into the room with Sir Gerald, he could not believe it – apparently, I exceeded his wildest hopes. Mr S was thirteen years older than me and was then 36. The conference passed in a haze, our eyes meeting rather too often, and we parted, both knowing we would meet again. I was unattached at the time and excited about the prospect of a new relationship. I knew he would ring. Indeed, he was on the telephone next day, ostensibly to thank me for my part in the success of the conference but also casually to enquire whether I would like to watch Trooping the Colour the following weekend. He had a couple of tickets and we could make a day of it, taking a picnic to St James's Park afterwards. It sounded terribly romantic. I put the telephone down and went singing along the corridor to the photocopier.

It was a memorable day, the sun shone but not too brightly and the pageantry of the occasion touched us both. S took my hand to guide me through the crowds and make sure we were not parted and we wended our way through St James's Park to settle on the grass for a simple picnic he had prepared. I could not believe I had met Mr Wonderful and my mind was already racing ahead. We ate, drank, walked and talked, finding out about each other, yet feeling we had been friends for ages. Everything was so right, so perfect. We were lying on the grass, each propped up on an elbow, and, if I was thinking at all, I assumed we would spend the evening together. Then came the bombshell. 'Christine. I've had the most delightful day with you. But I have to tell you something.' My heart stopped. I must have known what was coming. He was considerably older than me. He was far too attractive to have remained unattached. 'Christine.' He took my hand and looked me straight in the eye. 'I am married.'

Those three simple words shattered my idyll. Of course, that is the moment I should have walked away. But I look back now with the wisdom of a woman in her mid-fifties. This was more than a mere physical attraction. I had to see him again, I did not have the will to leave. I was already in too deep and sinking fast. Others caught in a similar situation will know what I mean. By the time you realise you should be getting out, it is already too late. S told me he had no children, which made me feel marginally less guilty even though I had not yet committed any offence. I didn't even ask for time to think. Trying to hide how desperate I felt, I said I did want to meet him again, despite the devastating information he had just imparted. We went our separate ways at the end of the afternoon, which was destined to become a pattern. We had been seeing each other for about four weeks before we made the ultimate physical leap. It was he who decided we should wait. Had it been left to me I would probably have ravished him in St James's Park that first afternoon but he wanted to delay. He did not need to be sure but wanted to show me he was serious. It was difficult but he was determined.

Oh, the agony and the ecstasy of a serious affair. Ask anyone who has been there. The highs are exquisite but the lows, both major and minor, are terrible. The secret nature of meetings is exciting at first, but if you are never able to spend the night together you can never experience the joy of waking up in the morning alongside the person you love. As time went by, it became more and more frustrating not being able to do normal things, especially in public, in case we were spotted.

Although I went to his house during the day only once did I stay overnight, when his wife was away on business. We both knew we should not have done it but the temptation proved irresistible. We could have spent the night at my flat but he needed to be at home to answer the telephone when his wife called and, in any event, he wanted to entertain me rather than the other way around. We slept in a spare bedroom but that was no excuse. I should not have been there. It was our undoing. Despite checking, rechecking and checking again, I left something behind. His wife spotted the evidence almost immediately. She already knew he was seeing someone but this was hard proof. It must have been a devastating blow for her. I will never know what passed between them but he explained to her this was not just a fling. We continued to see each other, agonising for hours over what we should do, me frequently in tears of frustration and heartache. It was terrible not being able to ring, to talk when I wanted to. We couldn't share things properly. When you are in love, you yearn to give, to share. Looking back, it all seems so petty and self-centred compared with what his wife was suffering, but then these little things mattered hugely.

If there had been children it would never have happened. I am sure he would not have embarked on the affair and I would certainly not have pursued it. He is a kind, gentle, thoughtful man who would never willingly hurt anyone. A man of decided views, he has a sense of humour that I loved and enjoyed, although I never fully understood it. I was not the first woman he had strayed with. There have possibly been others since, but he still maintains, and I believe him, that I was the love of his life.

Our affair had been raging for about a year when Sir Gerald had a mild stroke. I kept the show on the road as best I could, but he soon suffered another, this time more severe, leaving him paralysed down his right side and with seriously impaired speech. He announced he would leave Parliament at the election and began to make a slow recovery, regaining movement and some speech. He left hospital to convalesce at home and we all thought he would recover enough to lead a fairly normal life. I was with my family in Ringwood when, on a Sunday morning in

November 1973, the news came through that he had died peacefully at home. The weeks running up to Christmas that year were sad. There was Nab's funeral and memorial service to be arranged and all the parliamentary, constituency and personal ends to be tied up. There were hundreds and hundreds of letters, not only from friends but also from members of the public who had appreciated Sir Gerald's many contributions over the years. But, by early January, there was little more I could do to help Joan so, although I continued to do odds and ends for a few weeks, I was free to take alternative employment. My happy days as part of the Nabarro family were over.

CHAPTER SEVEN

New Job – a Lucky Escape – Welcome Back Neil

After Sir Gerald died, several MPs approached me, all probably assuming I was a top-flight secretary because Nab would tolerate no other. Little did they know, my secretarial skills were still rather basic. I could compose good letters myself and anything that needed dictating could be done on a dictaphone. Looking back, I wish I had learned shorthand at the appropriate moment but then it seemed too much like hard work.

I decided to accept an offer from Michael Grylls, MP for Chertsey but shortly, under boundary changes in February 1974, to become MP for North-West Surrey. I could not have predicted how much that choice would alter the course of my life some twenty years later, its effects still reverberating today. Michael was a wine importer; his company represented many well-known brands and owned a delightful basement wine bar in the City. It was a happy combination, politics and wine, with obvious perks from the latter. I had little time to lament the passing of the Nabarro chapter in my life. I had a new boss, a new constituency and, although we did not know it at the time, two general elections that year.

In what I regarded as a huge backward step, I had to move out of my office in the Palace of Westminster itself to an outbuilding, Michael being too junior to qualify for an office within the precincts. Worse still, I would have to share. Sheila Childs was running a recruitment consultancy when a job came in, working for Sally Oppenheim, MP for Gloucester. With an election looming, Sheila decided she would take a break from recruitment and dabble in politics. She arrived in 3 Dean's Yard a few months before me, enjoying a large room to herself. Like a bombshell I descended, destined to occupy the desk immediately opposite her. I was doubly disgruntled, being relegated to an outbuilding and having to share, and Sheila certainly did not want an intruder in 'her' office. We glared at one another for 24 hours, and have had the firmest, closest, unbroken friendship ever since.

Dean's Yard is a delightful courtyard in the shadow of Westminster Abbey. On a practical level it meant walking to and from the House, enjoyable in the sunshine but not much fun in winter. In June 1974 I first encountered personally the dangerous side of politics. I was used to getting to work early, a habit instilled in me by Sir Gerald but now there was an additional reason. I no longer had my little NAB 4. It was a very grim moment when I lost my wheels. Battersea is not well served by the tube, so I had to juggle various options, beginning with either a bus or a twenty-minute walk to Sloane Square underground. Either way, it made a huge difference to be ahead of the rush. Arriving at Westminster, I collected the post, cut down through Westminster Hall and out across Parliament Square to Dean's Yard. It was uplifting to walk through Westminster Hall, especially when deserted in the early morning. The oldest part of the Palace, it is a stupendous achievement of medieval engineering with a soaring angel-laden, hammer-beam oak roof. It was the cradle of justice, the meeting place of Parliament, the home of kings, bearing silent witness for nearly 1,000 years to historic tragedies and pageants.

One cannot fail to be under the spell of the past in Westminster Hall, despite the best endeavours of the current lot to destroy the atmosphere with a souvenir kiosk in the corner. The window over the main entrance was magnificent and I never forgot to look up and admire, however fleetingly, the sheer beauty of the stone tracery and the delicate glass. That lovely June morning I walked out from Westminster Hall, skirted New Palace Yard to the main entrance off Parliament Square, a distance of about 100 yards; where I exchanged a cheery 'Good morning' with the policemen. I had scarcely moved on when there was an ear-shattering noise and I felt the thrust of the blast. A couple of minutes earlier, I had casually walked past the bomb as it ticked towards its predestined time for explosion. I could so easily have been caught in the full horror. The IRA had planted it, timed to avoid casualties as far as possible, but the old glass was shattered, destroyed for ever. It was a narrow escape.

My affair continued, though I was beginning to have doubts. S was talking about getting a divorce. My heart had ached for him not to be married but when faced with the reality I realised I could not go through with it. I had already done far too much to destabilise and wreck his marriage. I could not allow a terminal separation because of me. We just did not have a future together. We parted slowly and tearfully over the coming weeks. It was desperately difficult but we both knew it was the right thing to do, not for pious reasons – it was too late for that – but because our relationship would not hold. We remain good friends although we seldom meet now. He and his wife are still together today and I dare to hope that the hurt has been sufficiently cauterised by the passage of time and she has forgiven me. It is easy to condemn but anyone can find themselves at a point where a power takes over and all their moral instincts become swamped. I had not personally taken any marriage vows but that is poor defence. Because of the obvious strength of our marriage, Neil and I are often asked to comment on high-profile marriage break-ups or sexual shenanigans. Despite my youthful failings, I do disapprove of adultery, although I know I lay myself open to charges of hypocrisy.

Neil had appeared like a ghost in the middle of the affair. While I was finding my feet with Michael Grylls, with no thoughts of my erstwhile boyfriend, Neil fought the February 1974 election in Abertillery, in the mining valleys of south Wales, then the safest Labour seat in the country. Striking miners were holding Britain to ransom and Edward Heath called a snap election asking: 'Who governs Britain?' He got his answer. He was booted out and Harold Wilson was in. As for Neil? He lost his deposit and reduced the Tory vote from 10 per cent to 6 per cent! But he had cut his electoral teeth. From the bottom the only way was up. Had Neil been elected in 1974 we would suddenly have been thrown together again physically and, perhaps, might have taken up where we left off rather sooner than we did. But it is idle to speculate.

We had remained in desultory contact and he wrote saying he was coming to London and proposed taking me out for lunch. My affair was in full spate but I was happy to see Neil for old times' sake. We met at the Gay Hussar in Soho, a legendary Hungarian restaurant, favourite of politicians, especially Old Labour, for more than fifty years. At an intimate table for two, Neil eagerly lapped up their famous cherry soup, together with my Westminster experiences, while I listened to his news and intrigues. After lunch, we wandered through Soho, parting company on the corner of Whitehall and Parliament Square. I gave him an affectionate peck on the cheek and waltzed back into the Palace, the building symbolising his hopes, dreams and frustrated ambitions. I now know he harboured hopes for our getting back together. Not only that, but I encapsulated for him the life he yearned for, that might be, someday, if things worked out . . . For me it was just a carefree interlude but for Neil, not only was my indifference a massive disappointment but he had a more immediate problem. The Gay Hussar is not cheap and he had invested about three months' living expenses on lunch with nothing in return. I would have been horrified had I known but naïvely assumed he had taken me somewhere he could afford. I can see him now, as we parted, standing on the corner with the impressive façade of the Treasury behind. Perhaps I noticed he looked somewhat wistful but any compassion was momentary. I certainly still found him attractive and, if I had not been otherwise involved, I might have been tempted, but I was not free to revisit old territory.

A few months after my lunch with Neil, I ended the affair with S. Had the meeting with my former love destabilised things? I don't know. I could not easily separate the whirling emotions I was experiencing, but I wanted to move on. I saw various people in various ways but nothing meaningful developed. Footloose and fancy-free, I was positively not seeking another intense relationship. I had dramatised to my parents the cold at the Battersea Bridge bus stop, and highlighted my brother's four years at university plus time as an impoverished pupil barrister when they had supported him financially. I reminded them that I had spent merely the statutory three years at university and immediately started earning, thereby taking myself off their hands. The penny dropped and I became the proud owner of a brand new Ford Fiesta.

In December 1977 a viral infection hit me almost overnight. I couldn't do anything, had no energy at all and could barely even open a book or a newspaper. I just lay in bed doing nothing. I went right up the hierarchy of medics to the professor of virology at St Thomas's Hospital and the answer was always the same. It was a virus. It was not glandular fever, but one of the many hundreds of others lying in wait for unsuspecting bodies. I was told there was no cure except rest; it would gradually work its way out of my body. So there I was, stuck in bed in

Battersea, feeling sorry for myself, when a Christmas card arrived from Neil which I treasure to this day. He wrote that he would be in London shortly, studying for the Bar and staying with an aunt near the Oval. He gave the telephone number and asked, in the absence of any etchings, if he could come and see my Bratby. John Bratby was a Royal Academician, who had painted a striking portrait of Gerald Nabarro. His technique and execution are impressive anyway but he also superbly captured the very essence of the man – the shape of the head, great big eyes, large stubby fingers, and the soulful gaze. Bratby saw through Nab's façade and painted a brilliant portrait.

It was a modern work and Sir Gerald was predictably horrified. He disliked the large blobs of oil paint distributed around the canvas, in particular on his face, and refused to buy it. In 1974, my father was in Salisbury Hospital for an artificial hip operation. My mother came across a nearby art gallery holding an exhibition of Bratby's paintings and asked if they knew the whereabouts of Nab's portrait. The gallery was enterprising and, within a fortnight, they had the painting for me to look at. I knew I had to have it. The gallery contacted Bratby who asked for £390. I did not have that sort of money, so I wrote to him to ask if he would consider selling it to me for a lower figure, on the promise of a good and loving home for his work. After an interval, Bratby agreed to let me have it for £300. Very generously, as we were in the process of splitting up, S contributed £100 and I did the rest in £50 post-dated cheques. Bratby wrote me a charming letter expressing his delight that I now owned the painting, recalling he had found Sir Gerald 'quiet and restrained and far from loud and extrovert'. 'We conversed,' he wrote, 'about discerning Individuals as opposed to run-of-the-mill people and he told me he could always tell an Individual because they "fizzed".' Neil knew about the painting, hence his Christmas card reference. It was a none-too-subtle hint he would like to come for dinner.

He duly arrived at my flat at 7.35 p.m. on 17 February 1978. We both remember my first words as I opened the door: 'Gosh, you are looking prosperous!' Nothing could have been further from the truth as he had still not settled into a proper job or career. He had dabbled in teaching, taking a post at St John's College, Southsea, which his mother had lined up for him in desperation to get him out of the house. He then spent a year doing a post-graduate law degree at Cambridge and now, at the ripe old age of 28, was embarking on his Bar finals with eyes still firmly on the House of Commons. The re-attraction was instant. I had prepared a simple dinner. The chocolate mousse sealed our fate and we've been together since that night.

Neil was underfunded and overqualified. His lack of money didn't matter. I had been working for six years, I had the flat, and there has never been any dispute between us over money or possessions. Besides, he soon remedied the financial imbalance by signing up with 'Take-a-Guide'. TAG still arranges personalised tours, principally for prosperous Americans. After passing a London Tourist Board exam to brush up his local knowledge, Neil was let loose on unsuspecting clients. The only problem, a big one, was his car. He had moved on from the 'sardine can' and was now the proud possessor of an old Austin 1800 which was capacious and, on a cursory assessment, passable as a conveyance for rich tourists. However, close examination revealed rust breaking out like a rash of metallic eczema all over the white paintwork.

Clients were often a little surprised when they first saw the car outside their hotel. It hardly matched the photograph on the TAG brochure of an attractive smiling young lady beside a gleaming Jaguar on Westminster Bridge with the House of Commons rising majestically behind. In stark contrast, before their eyes was Neil and his (t)rusty old Austin 1800. He quickly assured them life was an adventure, bundled them into the car and charmed them with his bonhomie, immense general knowledge and ability to supply everything they wanted.

We managed to keep the car looking presentable, but only just. The interior passed muster with the addition of some strategically placed cushions, and some mornings Neil would dab the rust with paint as he set off, hoping it would last all day. The crunch came when the doorman at the Ritz (London, not Paris) complained to TAG. The doormen were on a commission for every client recommended and this one could see his reputation being as tarnished as the car. Neil bluffed his way through and continued unabashed.

Some clients wanted to travel beyond London, and Neil had some memorable adventures. His first victims were a gay couple from Chicago, Eldon and Keith, whose grasp of geography outside the US was sketchy. 'England' (which included Scotland and Wales) is only a small place, and they wanted to see 'everything'! They had booked a circular tour starting at Heathrow, up the west coast to Inverness, returning down the eastern side of the country to spend the last two days in London. It was a delightful itinerary, marred only by having to do it all in seven days! Back in London, the pace was less frenetic and they wanted to go antique-hunting on their last day. Their tastes were eclectic and appetites for retail therapy unlimited – unlike their baggage allowance, which was inadequate for their cornucopia of unwieldy acquisitions. Neil inventively solved the problem and Keith solemnly boarded the aircraft resplendent in full-dress admiral's uniform, including cocked hat and sword, carrying under his arm as cabin baggage a small brass cannon.

Mr and Mrs Woodbury Ransome of Kalamazoo, Michigan, were another delightful pair, elderly and old-fashioned. 'Woody' was a gravel-voiced businessman with a bark worse than his bite, tall, portly, avuncular, bald and bespectacled. Unfortunately, husband and wife had differing notions of holiday activity. He wanted to be driven around the countryside, enjoy a pub lunch – 'I just love your beef hash' (cottage pie) – returning at funereal pace along country lanes to their hotel. Mrs Ransome cried out for culture – especially stately homes, all of which she called 'castles' and fondly imagined were inhabited by a 'dook'. Staying a week at the Lygon Arms Hotel at Broadway, Worcestershire, Mrs Ransome wanted to see the Royal Pavilion in Brighton. For days, Woody grunted and grumbled in the back of the car but eventually conceded. After a three-hour journey they arrived at George IV's oriental fantasy, only for Woody to refuse to get out of the car: 'Well, you seen it now. Let's go home.' So Neil had to retrace their steps with Mrs Ransome's face pressed disconsolately against the window, the Pavilion disappearing from view. On another trip she wanted to see Chatsworth, evoking a similarly negative response from the lovable curmudgeon in the back seat. After several days of grumpy exchanges the matter was concluded when he growled, 'Whad'ya wanna see this Chatsfield place for? We seen it all before. We went to Wilton House last year!' 'Chatsfield' remained unvisited.

However, tourists wane and further action was needed to fund the exchequer. In September 1978 Neil took a job teaching law at Hatfield Polytechnic and was paid a ridiculous sum for working only eleven hours a week. In the days before computer programs, drafting the timetable was time-consuming and fiddly but the timetabler could schedule himself exactly as he wished. Neil instantly saw the advantages of this and volunteered. He fitted all his tuition (with two hours remission for timetabling, only nine hours) on a Monday. He worked hard on those

Mondays — lecturing from 9 till 6, with no coffee or tea breaks, munching his sandwiches running between classes. He received a full-time salary (£10,000) for roughly 24 teaching days a year. The rest of the week he was free to pursue his legal and political ambitions.

On the home front, my parents were not wild about Neil's return into my life. My mother, in particular, was suspicious. It was just too easy for him, using me, my political connections and my convenient flat. But she softened and gradually realised he was a fixture. In 1974 my parents had moved to Cornwall's Lizard peninsula for a Shangri-la existence in the delightful hamlet of Carne, at the head of Gillan Creek just south of the Helford River. They seldom came to London and were usually hundreds of miles away, blissfully unaware what I was getting up to in the big bad city. But I have always been close to them and wanted their blessing on everything, particularly Neil. I knew before he did that he was here to stay and in due course I informed him of his fate.

CHAPTER EIGHT

Tory Victory – Hamilton Defeat – Girl Problems

Most people go into politics aiming for the top even if they admit it only to themselves. We had high hopes for Neil. He is intelligent, articulate, clear-thinking, driven by firm libertarian beliefs and not easily diverted from them. Personally, I am inclined to see more than one side to any question and tend towards the left-wing of the Right. It surprises some people to know we never talk about politics between ourselves; not even in the thick of the political melee. What's the point? I know what he thinks. He *thinks* he knows what I think. Where we differ, things are best left unsaid!

But, at the end of the 1970s, we didn't really know *what* to think. Career decisions had to be made. Neil would soon be thirty and needed to sort his life out. Many opportunities and routes were possible. He enjoyed law and could have earned a fortune at the Bar in his lucrative field of corporate and tax law. I might have been a lady of leisure! Fledgling barristers have to do a year of 'pupillage', an apprenticeship with established practitioners. Neil had just begun his first six months when, in February 1979, he went for an interview at Bradford North, a Labour stronghold with a high percentage of Asian voters where only a major political earthquake could have dislodged the sitting Labour MP, Ben Ford. Looking after the aspirant candidates waiting to be grilled by the selection committee was Annie Bell, a grand Yorkshire woman and Conservative stalwart. Girlfriends did not count, so I could not go in with Neil for his speech and interview, but we knew it was important I should be there in the background. My only opportunity to try to influence things was to make a favourable impact on those I met behind the scenes, foremost among them Annie. It was easy. She was a blunt, salt-of-the-earth character and we hit it off straight away. Neil got through to the final round and, over tea and buns, Annie vouchsafed in her broad Yorkshire accent, 'I want your 'usband to 'ave it.'

She whipped her disciplined troop of helpers and pushed Neil's cause to those who mattered. He topped it off with a barnstorming speech. The burghers of Bradford were impressed he had fought Abertillery in the 1974 miners' strike and wanted a tough combative candidate to fight for them. Neil never had to nurse a seat for very long. The very fact of his selection seemed to precipitate an election. It had happened in Abertillery, was about to happen in Bradford and would again in Tatton.

In March 1979 Callaghan's Labour government faced a combined Tory/Liberal 'no confidence motion'. The tension and frenzy at Westminster was electric. No-one, absolutely no-one, knew who would win. Frantic wheelings and dealings went on behind the scenes. Labour pulled out all the stops, even sending an MP to Northern Ireland to escort Frank McGuire, maverick Irish Nationalist MP for Fermanagh and South Tyrone, personally on to the plane for London. This was truly a measure of desperation. McGuire seldom appeared at Westminster, preferring to stay and run his pub. He had never spoken in the Chamber but occasionally could be persuaded to come across and support Labour. Upon his arrival, relays of Labour MPs were detailed to keep him happy in the bar, another taking over when the alcoholic capacity of his predecessor was exhausted. At last the division bell clanged, bringing MPs scurrying from every nook and cranny, but Frank refused to move. He had come 'to abstain in person' and would not budge from his bar stool to save Callaghan's skin.

Even Michael Foot's brilliant winding-up speech could not save Labour. I had been lucky enough to obtain a good seat near the front of the Gallery and watched the proceedings below. It was like sitting on the rim of an erupting volcano, smoke, heat and sparks flying up in all directions. Political lives, careers and the future of the country were at stake. The government lost by one vote. Frank McGuire ordered another pint, Labour MPs vented their fury by singing 'The Red Flag' and a gaggle of Tories 'conga-ed' through the Central Lobby, in and out of the statues.

Labour was out and we headed north to Bradford, where the weather was as bleak as the political outlook. It had been snowing when we arrived at the end of January for the first interview and it snowed when we left after the election on 3 May. I had my commitments to Michael Grylls and, although he was very generous and often let me slip away early, I had to spend most of the week in his North-West Surrey constituency, racing to Bradford by train on Friday to be with Neil over the weekend.

We enjoyed great camaraderie but electioneering was tough. To maximise support, Neil had his election address translated into Urdu and Punjabi. The politics of the Indian subcontinent loomed large locally in Britain's 'winter of discontent'. For reasons we never fully comprehended, Neil enjoyed the enthusiastic support of the Pakistan People's Party, who supplied a loudspeaker van and a vigorous propagandist to broadcast for us in his native tongue. It was very odd driving around not understanding a word coming out in stereo over my head except for the occasional 'Neil Hamilton' and 'Conservative'. We could only hope he was saying the right things in between.

I also had personal problems to contend with. Before coming back into my life, Neil had enjoyed a friendship with a woman called Sarah. He had other girlfriends but she was the only one who seemed in any way important and I think she thought they would probably get married. There was no reason why Neil should have told me about her initially. He was obviously unsure if our new relationship would last. I had dumped him once before and he did not wish to burn his boats with Sarah in case I did it again. But I soon sensed someone else in the background and the situation became untenable as Neil found it impossible to disengage completely from Sarah, although she must have known he had found a berth elsewhere. The situation caused a certain amount of friction (understatement of the book) between us. Things came to a head one weekend.

It was all hands to the pump and many of Neil's chums came to Bradford to help canvass, including a French friend from Cambridge days called Guillaume, who also knew Sarah. I had heard about Guillaume but had never met him and was delighted to find him at the station when I arrived in Bradford. Guillaume speaks impeccable English and, while Neil went to get the car, he enquired, 'Excuse me, but who are you?' I explained I was Neil's girlfriend, whereupon he looked somewhat bemused, both his expression and his question giving the game away. I sensed problems ahead. Thinking maybe Guillaume had merely not kept abreast of developments in his friend's love life, I did not mention it to Neil but it made me edgy and defensive for the weekend. I was still unprepared for the bombshell which was to drop just before I departed. We were staying in nearby Ilkley with John and Mary Rae, parents of another Cambridge friend. The Raes, an exuberant, extrovert family, kindly offered Neil their house as a base during the campaign. As I was leaving early on Monday morning to catch the train back to Surrey, Mary took me to one side. 'I don't know exactly what is going on, or whether I should even be telling you this,' she confided, 'but I feel you ought to know that Sarah has been up here, staying with us.'

I was horrified. In my wildest imaginings I had never thought that Neil would bring her to Bradford where I was already so clearly known as his long-term girlfriend and where, as such, I had done my bit to secure him the nomination. Quite apart from the emotional trauma, I felt it seriously undermined my position. Neil seemed genuinely unable to see why I was so upset. As far as he was concerned, Sarah had wanted to help out in Bradford and that was all there was to it. Men see things so differently. I was not concerned for the long term as I was confident about our future together, but I was absolutely fed up with things as they stood, knowing Neil was not being straight with me about Sarah or with her about me. Why couldn't he just tell her the truth and then we could get on with our life together? The problem was his gentleness and unwillingness to hurt anyone — he just hadn't the heart to tell Sarah it was over. He was still fond of her and, possibly, harboured lingering doubts that I might change my mind and waltz off again.

We continued to have 'Sarah problems' for some time. By then Sheila Childs and I were bosom buddies and destined to remain so. She had lived through the problems of my affair, was one of the very few people who had met S and was by now a good friend of Neil's as well, understood him and knew all about the situation with Sarah. We end-lessly discussed the situation, like the girls on the Max Factor production line, totally disregarding the constituency or business matters to which we should have been attending. Our love lives were far more important and had to be sorted out. Sheila agreed that although there was no long-term problem Neil had to be bounced into taking action. The situation could not endure, as it was causing untold resentment and stress between us. He had to bite the bullet. Today, Neil knows exactly what to expect when Sheila and I gang up on him, but then he was blissfully ignorant.

There was one ridiculous incident in the summer of 1979. Neil habitually joined a party to Glyndebourne that was organised by his oldest friend, Michael Pearl, and had taken Sarah for several years. That year he was between the devil and the deep blue sea. He did not have the courage to tell Sarah, who had been looking forward to the event, that things were over and neither, understandably, did he have the courage to tell me he was taking her to Glyndebourne. I would have been furious. No wonder he could not face that hurricane! So he invented a pre-posterous story about a wedding, to justify his absence. I knew perfectly well he was off to Glyndebourne and gave him every opportunity to be open about it. Had he done so, I would have gone ballistic, so he was probably wise to try subterfuge.

The charade continued. Sheila and I had decided to let Neil hang himself and not challenge him outright. By then I had moved yet again and we were living on the fifth floor in a two-bedroom apartment. He got up that morning and I lay in a grump. As soon as the door closed I leapt out of bed, went straight to the wardrobe and found the evidence. Instead of his morning suit for a wedding, he had taken his dinner jacket – he had not even had the wit to take them both to try to cover his tracks. I called Sheila, confirmed what we both suspected and we hit upon the brilliant idea of driving down to Glyndebourne, hiding in the gardens and casually strolling past the group while they were enjoying their picnic. We had a lot of fun giggling about it but decided it would be too much hassle. I would have it out with Neil when he got back on Sunday. I laid his morning suit out on the bed and greeted him with the words, 'How did you manage at the wedding without this?'

His return was the catalyst for a major heart-to-heart. Neil was in a turmoil, hoping Sarah would gradually realise and be let down gently. I understood this but had had enough of deception and half-truths. I was not prepared to share my man. We cleared the air but Neil never made a clean break and just allowed the relationship to wither away. Even four years later, when we were getting married, he would not countenance an announcement in the press, which bothered me at the time. I knew it was because he did not want Sarah to see it there in black and white. His big heart created big problems for us both in those early days.

But back to the political fray in Bradford where, despite Margaret Thatcher's triumphant arrival in Downing Street, the Labour majority had scarcely moved. The Labour machine had assiduously courted the constituency's eclectic mix of voters and adopted sure-fire tactics. We frequently encountered Asians who spoke no English but knew they were to vote for 'Mr Ford, Mr Ford' and had been told they would be sent home if the Tories won. Neil even encountered one man who had stopped in the middle of redecorating his house because he thought he would be on the first boat out. The local press were not even impartial, let alone helpful. We had not expected to win but it was frustrating when so many Conservatives, fighting bigger Labour majorities, swept into Parliament on the crest of the Thatcher wave. We could be forgiven for casting an envious eye at some of the others and thinking how different things would have been if only Neil had been elected as well. They were hugely stirring times. Margaret Thatcher had stormed into power as our first woman prime minister, there were dragons to be slain and challenging days lay ahead. The excitement of her victory highlighted our disappointment, knowing we would not be involved in the front line. We said our goodbyes and, as we drove back to London, felt that we alone had not been caught up in the great tide. It was tough for Neil, able only to watch as the revolution began that would change the face of the country for ever. But we had to get over that maudlin nonsense and pull ourselves together. It was back to the drawing board.

By fighting Bradford, Neil had signalled to the Bar, in particular the small corporate and tax section, that he was more interested in politics than law. We did not fully appreciate what a black mark that was. Politics and law tend to attract the same abilities and there has always been considerable interchange. We thought Neil's political achievements would be regarded as a plus when seeking permanent chambers, but times were changing and it was now viewed as lack of commitment. For example, after Bradford, Neil applied for a tenancy in the chambers of Peter Rees, QC, a Tory MP and Treasury Minister. We assumed, because they had him, they would be comfortable with another politician-lawyer, but quite the reverse. Peter's politics reduced his Bar practice. He was occupying space but not paying a pro rata contribution to chambers' expenses. Barristers are organised by clerks who receive a percentage of their earnings. A high-earning QC could make you a fortune while your school-chums were cleaning windows. The last thing a clerk wants is to build up someone's practice only to see him disappear to Westminster.

Only a handful of chambers specialise in tax law and everybody knew Neil was a politician first and a lawyer second. We could see he was not going to get anywhere at the Bar unless he gave up politics, which neither of us wanted him to do. He was well received by various sets of chambers, two in particular wanting to take him on but only if he renounced his political ambitions. It was clear he was in danger of falling between the two stools. The Bar did not want politicians and it was becoming apparent that many constituencies were tiring of lawyers.

As well as earning his keep, Neil needed a job to occupy his intellect. He continued tourist guiding in the summer of 1979, earning a lot of money from his rich American clients. Whether at the end of a day or a week, by the time they got back to base Neil had enchanted them. Some weeks, if you added in the generous tips, he earned more than I did but it was hardly a career. Suddenly two jobs came along at once. In the same week he was offered a tax consultancy by Peat Marwick, a major firm of accountants, promising a good salary and fabulous prospects, and also offered the job of heading up the new European and Parliamentary Affairs Department at the Institute of Directors. Although the IoD was not offering anything like the accountancy salary, it was a job very much in the political swing and we both knew which he should accept.

By 1982 our own problems, hopes and ambitions faded into the background against the developing crisis. Margaret Thatcher was preparing to go to war over the Argentine invasion of the Falkland Islands. The House of Commons was summoned to meet on a Saturday for the first time since the Suez crisis of 1956. This was an historic occasion and I rushed down early to secure tickets. The Gallery and Chamber were packed, MPs crammed the aisles, expectation pervaded the air. Defence Secretary John Nott was mauled by an angry Commons after making a party political speech that disastrously misjudged the House's mood. Also in the Gallery was his secretary Debbie Emerson with whom I shared an office. A couple of weeks later we were quietly gossiping one morning as we opened the post. Debbie suddenly shrieked as she slit open a medium-sized padded bag, 'Oh God, I've got a bomb!' Fortunately she had spotted the wires sticking out. We immediately rushed out of the room and called security. Feeling rather foolish but soon changing our tune when we learned it was indeed a bomb, an 'amateur' device, intended to maim not kill. If Debbie had pulled it out any further, acid would have exploded into her face. It was a frightening and sobering experience.

Security procedures have altered out of all recognition over the decades. It seems impossible to believe now but when I first started working at the Commons in 1971, you just marched in, smiled at the policeman and went on your way into the inner recesses of the labyrinthine building. There were no checks, no passes, no metal or smoke detectors — just nothing. They were innocent days for all of us.

It was an intense and patriotic time. The mood was heady and we were glued to the airwaves wanting to catch every image of the fleet as it steamed south. But the fervour merely underlined Neil's frustrations. Momentous events were taking place, and he wanted to be involved in the political fray, making his contribution to the debate. Instead, he had to kick his heels on the sidelines, hoping to get a safe seat for the next election, possibly as much as two years away.

CHAPTER NINE

Tying the Knot and Tatton

Despite Neil's uncertain future I thought it high time we got married. Never mind romance, there were sound political reasons for this step to be taken now. It made sense for someone seeking a safe constituency to have a fiancée or wife, rather than just a girlfriend. Girlfriends come and go – well, so do wives, but you know what I mean. We needed the magic word 'fiancée' on his CV and also the wedding date. And so, as we were driving up the M1 one day, I informed him we were getting married and that was that. I wasn't expecting a proposal, which is just as well as I never had one.

Having come to terms with each other's foibles, and me having decided we would take the plunge, we needed to tell my parents. Neil had been called for interview in the St Ives constituency where John Nott was retiring. We had mixed feelings about it. It was a glorious area with magnificent scenery, a stunning coastline and the Isles of Scilly, but it was a very long way from London, would have entailed endless journeys on the sleeper to and from Penzance and, even more importantly, could not be guaranteed to stay Conservative for ever as the Liberals were a strongly rising force in the West Country.

We decided to use the opportunity to break the news to my parents. After Neil's interview Daddy took us out to the Admiral Benbow, a jolly dining pub in Penzance. Neil went off and organised a bottle of champagne and when it arrived my mother protested that we were a bit premature in seeking to celebrate Neil's selection for the seat. They could not have been more surprised when we told them our news. They were so used to us living together they had stopped wondering whether we would ever get married. Twenty years later my mother was asked on camera what she thought of Neil when I first brought him home. Her response, after a brief pause was 'Not much!' She has come round since then, recognising his qualities and rejoicing in the close and happy relationship we share, but, being her, she does not seek to disguise her initial reaction.

At the Admiral Benbow we fell to discussing the wedding details and I explained we could either get married at St Margaret's, the parish church of the House of Commons, or in Cornwall. Ever the pragmatist, my mother announced immediately, 'Well, we can do the entire wedding down here for half the cost of the flowers up there.' So it was settled. Neil's mother-in-law-to-be had spoken. I wanted to set a date for early May but Neil thought it would be safer to leave it until June because the weather would be better and it would be easier for people to make a Cornish weekend of it. As always, he brushed aside my worries that we might be running into a general election; although he did not have a seat, we harboured hopes he might by then. My concerns were dismissed and the wedding was fixed for Saturday 4 June 1983.

In the meantime, the constituency hunt continued. One of the first had been Bournemouth West, where Sir John Eden was retiring. It was my home area; we had all the local credentials and felt we might do quite well. There were three finalists and fiancées and wives were invited too. The inevitable question came from the floor: 'What will Christine do to support you?'

'Well', said Neil, 'I think she had better answer for herself.'

I stood up, said my piece and sat down to loud and enthusiastic applause. Neil did not get the seat – we later learned I was thought 'a bit much' by some of them!

A major boundary review was due but had been held up by legal challenges from the Labour Party. None of the changed constituencies could begin selecting candidates until that was disposed of. Then, as though a dam had burst, they all started selecting at the same time in case there was a snap election. Our most action-packed weekend was Lincolnshire on Friday, Cornwall on Saturday, Suffolk on Sunday and Sussex on Monday. We spent hours on the road and in the train mugging up on the totally different constituencies, discussing tactics, weighing up the opposition. Neil was runner-up in safe seats six times and we were beginning to think he would always be the bridesmaid and never the bride.

Shortly afterwards we became aware of the new constituency of Tatton, brought about by major boundary changes in Cheshire. We had no idea where Tatton was when the Central Office form arrived but soon learned there were two sitting MPs vying for it, as Jock Bruce-Gardyne, MP for Knutsford, and Mark Carlisle, MP for Runcorn, both found their seats disappearing beneath them. They were clearly the main opposition and, on paper, there was no way Neil could win. He was a rank outsider. Jock and Mark were given a bye into the final and a couple of hopefuls had to be chosen to put up against them.

There was only one early round (which eliminated Michael Portillo among others) and Neil was suddenly through to the final in three weeks' time. Jock was a Treasury Minister and it looked like a walkover. We assumed he would take the seat and this would be yet more experience in losing. Suddenly we received encouragement from Fergus Montgomery, MP, whose Altrincham and Sale constituency was adjacent to Tatton. I had known Fergus for years. Hugely entertaining, warm and gregarious, with a wonderful ear for gossip, he had been Margaret Thatcher's Parliamentary Private Secretary as Education Secretary and Leader of the Opposition. Fergus was delighted when Neil reached the final and rang me excitedly one Monday morning to report his weekend findings. The 'anti-Jock' movement, about which we were vaguely aware, had gathered pace and it was far from certain that he would get the seat. Jock had not helped himself during the Falklands War when he wrote to financial journalist Sam Brittan saying the war was madness and he was against it. This private letter was taken from Brittan's desk at the *Financial Times* and leaked. Needless to say his views caused outrage among the Tory faithful. Feeling ran so high that the Knutsford British Legion banned Jock from their Remembrance Day parade, which was seriously bad news for a Tory MP whose seat was being abolished. All was not cut and dried. Neil was clearly in with a chance.

The final was on Saturday lunchtime. The constituencies were coming thick and fast and Neil was also in the running for a Welsh seat. He was hot favourite and I feared he would get it, not least because of his many Welsh connections. I was determined nothing would come between Neil and Tatton, which would be a safe seat for ever whereas the Welsh seat, although won by the Tories in the 1983 landslide, was not a good bet in an average year. After endless heart-searching, we agreed he must get out of going to Wales on the Wednesday because he was bound to be selected and would not then be available for the final in Tatton on the Saturday. I just knew, in my head and heart, that he could win Tatton. Neil was more cautious. The Welsh seat was a bird in hand, Tatton an unknown quantity. He hesitated. I decided and went into our bedroom to be private and telephone the area agent who was organising the selection. I said Neil was ill with a knockout bug. It was a monumental fib. I put the telephone down and went back into the sitting room. We looked at each other and wondered what I had done.

We stayed with Fergus that weekend without realising how long we would be squatting with him thereafter! He and his wife Joyce were incredibly kind and we lived with them, their elderly fathers, even more elderly uncle and three large Labradors, for nearly a year. It was a perfect arrangement – well, it was for us . . . We had a spacious room, and came and went as we needed with no ceremony or fuss, Fergus and Joyce understanding only too well the demands of parliamentary and constituency life.

In those days Neil had a scruffy, hideous brown Austin Princess, but it got us around in reasonable comfort. A few weeks earlier, as I manoeuvred in reverse gear, the British Rail North-West Regional HQ suddenly moved, hit us and dented the back of the car. The only paint to hand was white and, in a fit of nonsense, I dabbed this on to stop the dent rusting, thus creating a rabbit's-tail effect and the car became known ever after as 'Bunny Bobs'. We turned up for the final at Tatton in this old banger, which I certainly did not want to be seen by the selection committee. It was not false pride, but would just present the wrong image. It was lunchtime and we were parking by the hotel in broad daylight when some of the committee hove into view, walking directly towards us across the car park. In a panic we slid down in our seats, crouching below the windows until the danger passed. When all was clear we hopped out of the car, quickly disowning it before anyone else appeared.

In the upstairs room the other three candidates and their wives were mustered. John de Courcy Ling, then chief whip in the European Parliament, was the other outsider. Jock Bruce-Gardyne had his Treasury Minister's red box with him and was ostentatiously working on papers while waiting. Former Education Secretary Mark Carlisle and his wife gave us looks bordering on disdain. They were all much older than Neil, with experience and achievements under their belts. Come back Wales, all is forgiven!

After a stand-up buffet lunch, where our juggling skills with plate, food and glass were closely scrutinised, the candidates went in one by one. Neil was in excellent form and gave a corking speech. He took the bull by the horns and said he felt like David against three Goliaths 'but the Biblical precedent was encouraging'. He told them they would get two for the price of one. I would be secretary, wife and all-round constituency partner. We would both give it our all. He entertained and amused but then, to prove he could also inspire, he went into Churchillian mode. It worked. Neil won an overall majority on the first ballot and so became the prospective Conservative candidate for Tatton. It had been an uphill struggle but we had made it and an election was looming. Afterwards, Fergus reported to us that, back at the Commons, Mark Carlisle had remarked, 'He just swept in with his fiancée on his arm, made them laugh and that was that.' He seemed to think Neil had somehow won unfairly. It was obviously a major blow for both him and Jock and we later learned how devastating it is to be rejected by your own constituents. But then we were on the crest of the wave – with a seat for life?

If we had been in any doubt as to what to expect of our new constituency, it was dispelled by Sir Richard Miller, president of the Conservative Association. A splendid old gentleman and lifelong Conservative, bachelor Dick was nearing eighty and, like his identical twin Tony, was impressively tall, thin and elegant. He came over to Neil after his adoption meeting, drew him to one side and whispered, 'You'd better keep an eye on young Christine up here. It's all sex and saddle soap you know!'

Like any youngster brimming with enthusiasm and ideas, Neil was a breath of fresh air, and we worked our socks off. We did everything, never turning down an invitation unless we were already committed elsewhere. It was hard work, we seldom had a weekend off, but we wanted to meet as many people as possible, to become a real part of the local community. In this we had an immediate ally in the form of Neil's new constituency agent, Peter McDowell. Peter was only 27, not a well man and when we first met him, we were not overimpressed. The greatest love of his life was the sea and he had just been invalided out of the Merchant Navy with crippling arthritis. But the frailty of his body belied the lion strength of his spirit. There are few jobs more difficult than being paid organiser in a voluntary organisation, having to deal daily with prima donnas, egomaniacs, bores and time wasters. Peter possessed in abundance both the diplomatic skills of the Vicar of Bray and the patience of Job, and worked long hours in what must have seemed, for his wife Alison, something of a *ménage à trois*. Peter and Neil were political soul mates and never had a cross word, never a disagreement.

We had precious little time before the election was called and also had a wedding to organise. Needless to say, politics took priority! The election was announced for 9 June, just five days after our wedding hundreds of miles away in Cornwall. I was still working for Michael Grylls, interviewing my potential successors, helping Neil in Cheshire and trying to get ready for our nuptials at the same time. We needed a wedding ring and I brought home six on approval. I had already decided which one I was going to have, but thought I had better go through the motions of giving Neil a chance to express an opinion – after all, he would be 'giving' it to me! There was no engagement ring – we just drifted from cohabitation to marriage.

We had been madly campaigning for nearly three weeks, when we had to drive to Cornwall on Friday 3 June for our wedding the following day. Neil had a dreadful cold. I was married in blue, the traditional colour for a bride centuries before white became *de rigueur*. The dress was made by a little firm in Oxford called AnnaBelinda, tucked away, although I did not realise at the time, just around the corner from the stage door of the theatre where, nearly twenty years later, I would appear in the *Rocky Horror Show*. For a brief spell AnnaBelinda was a front for the infamous drug-dealer, once Britain's most wanted man, Howard Marks. Marks tells in his auto-biography *Mr Nice* how Belinda and Anna, two undergraduate friends of his, ran a small dressmaking concern and were short of funds. Telling them he had inherited some money, Marks bought the sewing machines, and set them up in business. They made the dresses and he did the laundering but, unknown to the girls, the money came from international drug trafficking. I am still a contented client of AnnaBelinda – their clothes are beautifully made and totally irresistible. My wedding dress was long and flowing aquamarine silk with a subtle stripe, and delicately quilted front and back panel. I had just one fitting, with the dress only tacked together, before it was posted to Cornwall to await my arrival the night before the wedding. I had expended so much energy on the campaign that I had lost weight, the dress was too long and I tripped as I walked up the aisle.

My parents lived half a mile from the delightful hamlet of St Anthony-in-Meneage. St Anthony church, romantically situated in the lee of the Dennis Head, is only a few yards from the beach and lit entirely by candles. Tradition tells that it was built by a band of shipwrecked Normans caught in a storm crossing from France to England. They vowed to St Anthony that if saved from drowning, they would erect a church in his honour wherever they came ashore. Some credibility is given to this by the tower's fine-grained granite of a kind wholly unknown in Cornwall but found in Normandy.

Many people are nervous at their wedding but I wasn't. I knew we were doing the right thing and never gave it a second thought. Having stayed the night before with Douglas and Valerie Harris, great friends and my parents' next-door neighbours, Neil walked to the church alone. I watched him go past my parents' house, carefully averting his eyes in case he accidentally caught sight of the bride. He was an eccentric and curious sight for a Cornish creek, resplendent in tail coat, Victorian waistcoat and silver-topped cane, wandering down the lane in the sunshine. Our wedding was timed for 2.30 p.m.

We were married by our dear friend, Canon James Owen, vicar of Little St Mary's in Cambridge, who sadly died of cancer a few years later after a brave struggle. James was not alone robed and in the sanctuary. The local vicar, Trevor McCabe, presided over his church and another old friend, Father David Johnson, also a Cambridge friend of Neil's, read the lesson. We had agreed, my mother in particular, that we wanted two hymns before the actual marriage to give people longer to settle down and concentrate on the task in hand. James Owen, keen to get on with the marriage, completely overlooked the second hymn and went straight into the vows. I realised he had forgotten but even I did not have the courage to stop him in full flight, 'Pssst, James, what about "Lead us, heavenly Father, lead us; O'er the world's tempestuous sea"?'

We got to it later, as indeed to the tempestuous seas!

I was deeply moved by James's address. He told the congregation he married many couples and often had a sense of foreboding, feeling the partnership would not endure. He had never married anyone before where he was quite so certain it really was for life. He knew us so well he could say that with total confidence, and how right he was. Neil's best man should have been Nigel Thomas, an old friend from both Aberystwyth and Cambridge. But Nigel was also fighting a seat,

Carmarthen, and felt he could not desert his campaign. Neil told him not to be so silly – the less voters saw of him the better he was likely to do. Nigel was unmoved. He had a fight on his hands and thought he would be criticised by the Welsh farmers if he absented himself for something as frivolous as a wedding. My brother, James gladly stepped into the breach. Apart from a few relations, Neil and I both knew virtually everybody in church, and many were unsure which side to sit on as they had known us as a couple for so long.

We left the church to Purcell's *Trumpet Voluntary* played by a young musician from the local St Keverne Town Band, and departed the fray from the beach by black London cab, festooned with bright blue election posters with 'Mr & Mrs' inserted before the 'Neil Hamilton'. The sun shone, the water lapped the beach, where gaily coloured fishing and sailing boats were drawn up. Our reception was held at Trelowarren, an enchanting manor house nearby where the St Keverne Band (tremendous value at £40 including the trumpeter!) played on the lawn and everyone made merry, banishing all thought of politics. The starring role (apart from the cake made by dear Mrs Bennett who had looked after our family for years in Ringwood) went to my father's home-caught mackerel and crab, used in many and various ways. Daddy had been fishing and crab-potting for weeks and weeks, hoarding the precious meat in the freezer for Blossom's big day.

There were four speeches. James and Neil, of course, rose to the occasion, as did my erstwhile employer, Michael Grylls, who said all the right things about the bride. As you may have guessed, I was not going to let my own wedding pass without having my say, and I leave others to judge whether my contribution was as good as that of the professionals. It was an emotional occasion but I remember saying I knew I was *not* the greatest love in Neil's life, and that it wasn't politics either but books, old books. I felt comfortable about that because, the older, more wrinkled and battered I became, the more interesting I would be to him. I would enjoy languishing on the shelves in his library under 'General but enduring interest' so he could take me down lovingly from time to time and buff and caress my wrinkled leather. Neil interrupted, 'You won't be in the lending section.'

At around 7 p.m. we tore ourselves away from the reception. I had given no thought to a going-away outfit and the result was horrendous. The dress itself was unspeakable and the hat a mismatch, but I didn't

care as we were carted away down the sweeping drive in the back of a
Mini Moke, having taken good care to park our car away from meddling
jokers. I always intended to have my honeymoon in Venice but I have
still never been to the magical city. It was not to Italy that we headed but
back to Cheshire and political reality. Neil had earlier assured me,
'Darling, you don't need one. Life with me will be one long honeymoon.'

We had to be back in Tatton by lunchtime the next day so we set off
to see how far we could get. Instead of the Cipriani in Venice, we spent
our wedding night in the Exeter Crest Motor Lodge Hotel in single
beds. What more could a new bride want? The following morning we
drove on to Cheshire for Sunday lunch with Lieutenant Colonel Sir
Walter Bromley-Davenport, MP for Knutsford 1945–70. He and his
American wife, Lynette, lived in a colossal 'Jacobethan' pile, Capesthorne
Hall, and had always gathered local Tory candidates and wives on the
Sunday before polling day. After he left Parliament they carried on this
great tradition and so the brand-new Mr and Mrs Neil Hamilton
presented themselves for luncheon.

Walter was a great parliamentary character. When Neil was first
selected, we had been summoned to see him immediately. We had
bounced up the immense drive through his parkland, hoping to keep
Bunny Bobs' white tail hidden, anxious not to reveal the poverty of our
conveyance. We need not have worried; Walter had no pretensions of
any kind. We were ushered down a maze of passages into his library,
where we walked into a thick fog of black smoke belching from the open
fire. Walter didn't seem to notice as his large, stocky figure crashed
towards us through the smog. Arms outstretched, he thrust a couple of
glasses of champagne into our hands with the command, 'Get this giggle
water down you.' He was clearly more concerned with thirst
extinguishers than fire extinguishers. With plastered-down hair, dead-
centre parting, wonderful jowls and stentorian voice, he rather enjoyed
conveying the impression of a buffoon. A former Army welterweight
boxing champ, he was robustly unintellectual but far from unintelligent.
During World War II he put his booming voice to good effect when he
joined a crowded train at Crewe and could find nowhere to sit. He
marched up the train bellowing, 'All change at Platform Four.' This had
the desired effect and he took his pick of the vacated seats.

Glass in hand, Walter launched straight into some hopelessly
outmoded advice about the campaign: 'You don't want to bother with

all that canvassing lark. Plenty of people to do that for you. Take my advice – just put your feet up with a large cigar and turn out for an eve-of-poll meeting. That'll do. That'll do.' He did not seem to realise how times had changed.

We had a delightful kitchen lunch and went on our way uplifted by our encounter with a rapidly vanishing breed. Walter's ancestor had been Lord Chancellor under Elizabeth I, another was a Speaker in the reign of Queen Anne, and members of his family had represented Cheshire constituencies since 1806. A few years later Michael Portillo came to speak for Neil and Walter turned out to meet this new rising star. He was getting old and had to sit on the sidelines but Michael went over to chat with him. Making conversation he innocently asked, 'Do you still live locally now you've retired?'

'My boy', Walter boomed, 'my family have lived here since the Norman conquest!'

Poor Michael – it was my fault, I should have briefed him properly.

The culmination of the pre-election luncheon was the traditional forecast of the outcome. I timidly scribbled my prediction of a Tory majority of 69 (it had been only 44 in 1979) and pushed my scrap of paper, plus the requisite pound, into the large silver-gilt tureen in the middle of the table. Some weeks later we learned that Walter had scooped the jackpot of £18, by accurately predicting the massive majority of 144. His method? It was his highest ever score in cricket!

The great old warhorse was thrilled when Neil asked him to speak at his 1987 eve-of-poll meeting. Walter made a tub-thumping speech, concentrating on universal themes like the 'Evils of Socialism'. Neil enquired about the dog-eared pile of yellowing papers he used as notes, and Walter responded, 'I made this speech in June 1945. When I came back from the war'. He had delivered exactly the same speech as at his own eve-of-poll meeting in Knutsford forty-two years earlier – and no-one had noticed!

Neil was duly elected in 1983 with a majority of 13,960. We had arrived at our destination and, as we drove back from the count in the early hours of the morning, we were deliriously happy with each other, our marriage, and our new jobs. We had everything to smile about. We could not have dreamt that our idyll was to be shattered in a little over six months' time.

CHAPTER TEN

The Battle of the Beeb

Although just married with my husband newly elected to Parliament, this made no great difference to my daily life. I was a veteran of the Commons, having worked there for thirteen years and it was Neil who was joining me. I would be showing him the ropes, not the other way around. As a political secretary you cope with various dramas but neither you nor your husband is directly involved. Now, however, I was just one step behind the firing line and it was *my* private life being messed around by votes and *my* weekends that were full of constituency engagements. Although I knew exactly what was coming, at times even I resented the intrusion of politics into our lives.

The divorce rate at Westminster is high and marriage failure rate even higher, but MPs' problems are no different from those encountered by countless others. Service wives, or the wives of high-flying businessmen whose careers come first, experience the same pressures. Many people express incredulity that Neil and I could work so closely together, seven days a week, but we never had any problems and it never crossed our minds to do otherwise. Apart from anything else, I would not have trusted anyone else to do the work as I thought it should be done and it would have been sheer hell for any secretary of Neil's to have to put up with me! I knew I could do a better job as his wife if also his secretary, and vice versa. The dual aspect gave me a complete view of what was going on and the two roles bowled merrily along together.

We threw ourselves into Tatton life with vigour, deriving huge enjoyment and satisfaction from the constituency, both socially and professionally. An MP is blessed with daily opportunities to help his constitutents with a whole range of personal and community issues, sometimes seemingly small, but important to the individual. Occasionally the workload seemed overwhelming and there was no time for anything else, but it was very fulfilling for both of us and we began to forge many lasting friendships.

Neil was either thoroughly pampered or led the gruesome existence of a battery hen, according to your view. He does not like and is not interested in administration. I enjoy it and am naturally ordered and efficient, so I controlled his life, opened his letters, answered his telephone calls, arranged his diary and gave him a daily action card telling him where to be and when. If he had had a mistress, he would never have remembered their assignations and the admin would have been left to me. He was one of the few MPs who would have been in deep trouble if he had not had an affair with his secretary!

Neil quickly established himself as a lively, combative, intelligent backbencher on the Thatcherite right of the Party. His maiden speech, in the debate on the 1983 Trade Union Bill, was well received and he soon acquired a reputation as a provocative and witty speaker, concentrating on economic and industrial topics. He was elected secretary of two influential backbench committees, Trade & Industry, and Finance, and was laying the foundations of a future career. He was on his way.

But an explosion was about to open the ground beneath us. On 30 January 1984, we experienced for the first time the harsh reality of public life, when Neil was targeted by the BBC's flagship programme, *Panorama*. In a piece entitled 'Maggie's Militant Tendency' they alleged far-right extremists had infiltrated the Tory Party, just like the Trotskyite 'Militant Tendency' in the Labour Party. We had known they were making a programme but had not been worried. It was nothing to do with us. However we had reckoned without *Panorama*'s mendacity and irresponsibility.

That evening we were so unconcerned that Neil toddled off without a care in the world to St John's College, Southsea (where he had taught briefly), to talk about the delights of being a newly elected MP. Along with millions of others, I watched the *Panorama* programme out of curiosity, but not because I thought Neil would be mentioned. In those days, facilities for MPs in the House of Commons were basic, few had their own room and there was little provision for their families. In the Families' Room, relatives could wait, read the papers or watch one communal television. On this unforgettable evening about 25 people gathered around it. If I had known how dreadful the programme was going to be, I would have watched in private, with a few close friends for moral support, but I blithely wandered in, happy to sit among strangers. Within minutes I was mesmerised, in profound shock at the horror unfolding on the screen.

The programme-makers produced a disgraceful hatchet job. The *Panorama* team, knowing it to be wholly untrue, claimed the Conservative Party had been infiltrated by a conspiracy of virulent racists, anti-Semites and fascists. Neil was allegedly one of this odious bunch. It was the stuff of nightmares. When the programme ended I could hardly move. I sat in a daze, transfixed by the now-blank screen. I managed slowly to pull myself together, my eyes stinging with tears as I left the room, head down, feeling all eyes were on me. No-one spoke to me as I stumbled through the corridors and down the stairs to the car park. Despite needing windscreen wipers for my eyes, I managed to drive home.

The telephone was ringing as I entered the flat. It was Neil, in a phone box at Portsmouth railway station, cheerful, loving and buoyant as always. Sobbing hysterically, I kept repeating, 'It was awful, awful. Your career is finished. They've destroyed you. They've destroyed you.' He tried to get me to describe what had happened but all I could do was repeat myself.

He simply did not grasp the shocking nature of the programme. 'Darling, please calm down. What are you talking about? It can't be as bad as all that.'

I wasn't thinking straight and Neil hadn't seen the programme, so neither of us fully appreciated the effect it would have on our lives, or that we would spend the next three years dealing with the fallout. It was difficult for me to convey to Neil its dramatic impact, which relied so heavily on visual images. After only one viewing, I was so shell-shocked I could not properly remember what had been said and shown. But I knew that in fifty minutes *Panorama* had wrecked his career and finished him for ever as a serious political figure. Neil had been an MP for scarcely six months. Now, after all we had worked for, it seemed the curtain had fallen just at the end of the overture.

In 1984 *Panorama* was the pinnacle of current affairs broadcasting and the BBC's integrity unimpeachable. Today, after countless media scandals, people are more sceptical, but twenty years ago, if it was on *Panorama* 'it must be true'. I had been the victim of misrepresentation before, but that was mere tittle-tattle. Suddenly I discovered how truth, events and people can be deliberately twisted and spun to produce a pack of lies. I now look back on this chapter of our lives with resigned acceptance that we are all dealt bad cards at times. What matters is how you play them. But then I was shattered and felt a terrible fear and foreboding. What dark and powerful forces were pitted against us? By the time Neil arrived home at midnight, my eyes were red and swollen with tears and I had collapsed in a heap, having drowned my sorrows in the usual way. After a fitful night we went to the Commons and watched a video of the programme. Although scandalised by what it said about him, Neil was unable to take the thrust of the programme seriously. It was patently absurd. The Conservative Party had a Commons majority of 144 and hundreds of thousands of members in the constituencies. How could a loose conspiracy of a few nutters and oddballs take it over? To anybody with the slightest knowledge, the programme was transparently idiotic. *Panorama* had lined up a 'rogues gallery' of cranks and misfits, misrepresented them as serious figures and dumped Neil and others in their midst, smeared through guilt by an association that was tenuous to nonexistent.

The programme opened with a nutcase standing under a portrait of Hitler, screwing in his monocle, putting on a record of German military music and solemnly announcing that Hitler was the saviour of the human race. There followed film of Oswald Mosley at a 1930s rally, National Front marches, a foreign fascist gathering with flags, Hitler salutes and so on, all overlaid by Leni Riefenstahl-style dramatic lighting, commentary and musical accompaniment.

Later, in court, Neil's QC, Richard Hartley, said Neil was 'plunged into this stinking cesspit of unbelievable evil'. With one exception, the *Panorama* team did not link him directly with any of these bizarre individuals or organisations and relied on innuendo – mere juxtaposition created the intended association in the viewer's mind. The reporter, the repellent Michael Cockerell, intoned portentously that at university Neil had dressed up in military uniform and called for the abolition of Parliament and the suppression of the lower classes. A picture of Neil in this supposed uniform flashed on the screen. In fact, the 'uniform' was a crumpled ice-cream vendor's jacket festooned with a home-made sash and chain of office of the president of the student union. The occasion was the 1970 Aberystwyth student union election hustings, the 'sinister armed guards' were students brandishing water pistols and the speech merely a spoof to entertain the audience, mocking the bores of the far left then dominating student politics. The speech also called for the presidency to be hereditary; compulsory full afternoon tea for all students and a steam yacht to be moored off the sea wall for the president's personal use! It was wicked to misrepresent an innocent student prank as evidence of a serious anti-democratic conspiracy.

Neil and Gerald Howarth (newly elected MP for Cannock & Burntwood and one of Neil's closest friends) were also accused of goose-stepping in front of their hotel on an official Conservative visit to Berlin. This, again, was a travesty of the truth. The occasion was a conference on East–West relations at the Konrad Adenauer Foundation, the Christian Democrat Party's think-tank. The group included twelve MPs, half a dozen candidates and two members from the Conservative Research Department. After a convivial dinner, one delegate did perform exaggerated goose-steps outside the hotel. This was Dr Julian Lewis, now MP for New Forest East. As he is Jewish, it is unlikely this indicated Nazi tendencies. Furthermore, far from emulating the Nazis, he was mocking the goose-steps of Communist East German border guards seen earlier that day!

This is but a tiny sample of *Panorama*'s deliberate perversions of the truth. In the cold light of day two decades on, it is difficult to imagine anyone taking seriously such a catalogue of patent absurdities. But they did. Saturation coverage in the press and a widespread public tendency to believe 'no smoke without fire' combined to cause us maximum damage and distress. I was knocked sideways and it was all too much for Neil's family, not only his parents and sister, but also his 95-year-old grandmother and her sister of 88. They watched the programme and were completely bewildered by its savaging of Neil. We received a heart-rending letter from our old friend, Annie Bell, our greatest supporter at Bradford North in 1979. 'I had a dream,' she wrote, 'that a dear friend with whom I worked would some day become an MP. Last election that dream was fulfilled. I always hoped that some day that dear friend would become an important MP of our government. Last night on *Panorama* my idol was toppled from his pedestal into the mud.' That letter in particular was devastatingly upsetting and reduced even Neil to tears.

In Tatton we knew we would have immediate problems because people were still getting to know us. What on earth would they think?

Neil was only 34, brand new to the constituency and this could finish him. He had controversially won the nomination over two sitting MPs whose constituencies had been carved up in a boundary review to make Tatton. Many of Neil's supporters, while outwardly loyal, must privately have wondered what they had done, choosing this man as their MP.

Across the board, the press was lurid and appalling. We did not have the money to embark automatically on lengthy legal proceedings, especially against the mighty BBC, with a billion pounds a year of licence-payers' money at its disposal. Neil was living on borrowed money and dependent on his parliamentary income. But we knew we had no choice. If your integrity is challenged you have to fight.

We have been amazingly lucky in our life, and at this critical moment we were blessed with what we needed most – a very robust constituency chairman. Simon Cussons, ruddy of countenance, stolid by nature, reassuring and strong, was a successful businessman, chairman of Manchester City Football Club and possessed of a splendid sense of humour. He was an immovable rock in the face of *Panorama*'s mighty force. After the initial shock and Neil's exposure of *Panorama*'s tricks, lies and subterfuge, Simon was fully on side and his leadership was crucial. There was no question of Neil resigning, but without Simon it would have been tough. He was resolute and kept the constituency together. Although we were not privy to what went on behind the scenes, we knew Simon had a tough time persuading some local Conservatives to back Neil. With a weak chairman things could have been very different.

I felt completely overwhelmed by what the BBC had done to us. We seemed like tiny grains of sand compared to the mighty sea lashing around us. It did not take long for the hate mail to start arriving, from complete strangers ignorant of the truth and eager to believe the lies. After the first day, Neil refused to allow me to open any letters because a vicious one would reduce me to helpless sobs. Many letters from constituents accused Neil of misleading them and called for his resignation. He had always been a popular speaker on the constituency circuit but suddenly invitations dried up and some were even cancelled. Any prospect of advancement to the first rung of the ministerial ladder, as unpaid parliamentary private secretary to a Minister, went out of the window. With these allegations hanging over his head, there was zero chance of preferment. For the first time in my adult life I was embarrassed to go out because I felt everyone was looking at me, pointing, whispering. So was Lizzie Howarth, who had to steel herself to collect her young children from school – what would the other mums be thinking?

Not everybody was censorious. Neil was sitting on the Trade Union Bill Committee and the Minister in charge was the late Alan Clark MP, the outrageous diarist. Casually wandering over to Neil at the end of a session, he drawled, 'I can't think why you're bothered about that programme. I AM a Nazi. Always have been. Never made any secret of it. It's never done me any harm. I just don't see the problem.' No doubt Neil would have risen further in his esteem if the allegations had been true!

It was amazing how many MPs told us: 'You can't win against the BBC. Just drop it. People will forget it.' But we had to take action or the allegations would haunt us for the rest of our lives. So, we went to the 'King of Libel', solicitor Peter Carter-Ruck, who advised Neil to issue a writ immediately. It was the start of a three-year battle that would eventually cost the BBC more than half a million pounds. As Neil took out his writ we had no idea the financial stakes would be so high, nor how long it would all take or how much it would dominate our lives. We naïvely assumed the BBC would see sense and soon call a truce.

I am often thought to be the dominant, forceful partner, fazed by nothing and nobody. Yes, I am more extrovert and gregarious while Neil is quieter and more reserved. In public I never faltered, but in private I became very emotional, often despairing. In times of stress, I frequently have mega-wobbles and huge dips. This was the first major crisis we faced together and Neil never wavered. He never panics, he pushes the irrelevant or distracting to one side, concentrating like a laser on the issue in question. Without his bulldog tenacity and forensic calm we would never have made it. Feeling the mission impossible, the odds would have intimidated me before we started. If it happened now I would have no hesitation, but then I was new to the game.

As we began to take the programme apart frame by frame, we observed with mounting incredulity the breathtakingly dishonest techniques they had used. Some falsehoods were insignificant but the totality constituted a vicious and poisonous brew. For example, in 1977 BBC Regional News had filmed a gathering at Oxford railway station to re-enact Tsar Nicholas II's stop for lunch in 1895 en route from Balmoral to Cowes. Neil and others, including Count Nikolai Tolstoy, dressed in frock coats and suitable period garb, British Rail co-operated by converting their 'Tasty Bite Buffet' into a Tsarist refreshment room and even changed the platform announcement signs into Russian: 'The next train on Platform 3 will stop at St Petersburg, Moscow and Nizhni Novgorod.' Ironically, the artificial snow to create atmosphere had been provided by the BBC props department. The event was obviously a lark, one of many fun occasions I missed by dumping Neil when I did. The BBC reported it as such in 1977 but *Panorama* deliberately distorted the gathering into a sinister attempt to replace democracy by feudal autocracy!

Although the case was time-consuming and mentally exhausting, real life had to continue. Fergus and Joyce were incredibly hospitable but we needed a house of our own and it took some time to find the perfect nest. Laburnum Cottage had seen better days. It was a dilapidated seventeenth-century cottage, with Victorian extension, where Cromwell reputedly stabled his horses while he stayed at the nearby hostelry. It was charming, bursting with character and had a delightful garden backing on to the village playing fields. It had been on the market for about three years and we subsequently met an alarming number of people who had been tempted by the house but backed away when they saw how much work needed doing. We took local surveyor Raymond Cooper to inspect it and he stepped inside with trepidation, peering anxiously at the uneven roof above him. His subsequent report was half an inch thick and his firm advice was 'don't'. But it was too late. We had fallen in love. We had to buy it. The more Mr Cooper tried to dissuade us, the more determined we became. So, with our meagre possessions, including Perkins the parrot (stuffed), in a borrowed Transit van, we arrived on a bright Saturday afternoon in April 1984. After a quick turnaround, we left in a few hours, holding the hem of my wedding dress above the dust as we departed for a constituency ball.

We were ecstatically happy. The builders took up residence for several months, letting themselves in each morning through tarpaulins covering gaping holes in the walls at each end of the house. They discovered the front was attached to the side wall only by the cement rendering, and props were hastily clamped on to stop the house collapsing into the garden. We gratefully received the old brown Formica units being thrown out by friends, slapped on some white paint and, together with a bright primrose stripey wallpaper, they provided a new kitchen. Neil had the first garden of his own, with cobbled yard, long sun-soaked wall, cherry blossom, apple trees, prolific damson hedge and ground elder, an iniquitous invasive weed. At the front gate, alongside the eponymous laburnum, stood a glorious overhanging copper beech, and a huge japonica climbed up the wall and over the porch, producing a healthy autumn crop of quince. We painted the front door a welcoming canary yellow and padded around on bare boards for months until the glorious day when carpets went down and it suddenly felt like home.

We used the new house as a convenient excuse not to attend the Party Conference that October. Brighton is a long way from Cheshire and we were too preoccupied with builders and home improvements for a week by the seaside, not to mention the cost. We therefore avoided the IRA's devastating attack on the Grand Hotel, which so nearly killed the prime minister and half the cabinet. We were asleep when the bomb exploded and woke to the horrifying news the following day. We watched in stunned silence the scenes of carnage and destruction on our television screen and admired Margaret Thatcher's inspirational determination to continue 'business as usual' on the morning she was not meant to see. The IRA sent a chilling message to us all: 'You have to be lucky every time. We only have to be lucky once.'

We enjoyed playing house but our bitter battle with the Beeb continued. It became easier when we secured some financial support from maverick billionaire Sir James Goldsmith. Jimmy, hugely charismatic and attractive, was a notorious ladies' man and the original Goldenballs, long before David Beckham. The soubriquet was bestowed by *Private Eye* whom he sued in endless libel actions, always represented by Peter Carter-Ruck.

The BBC's tactic was to widen the case and push up the expense, hoping rising costs would force us to abandon our action. Jimmy hated injustice and provided a £50,000 guarantee, giving Peter Carter-Ruck some assurance he would be paid even if it all ended in disaster. Having truth on your side is no guarantee a jury will find in your favour, and miscarriages of justice often occur, as we know to our cost. Jimmy was not the only one to back us. David Davis, a wiry ex-TA paratrooper undeterred by public controversy, unflinchingly stands by friends in trouble. Later to become a leadership contender and Shadow Home Secretary, David was then a director of Tate & Lyle and persuaded them to donate a considerable sum to our cause.

The BBC could easily have saved licence-payers the vast costs incurred by forcing us to a trial. In June 1985 Carter-Ruck proposed settlement terms — an apology and £20,000 each in damages for Neil and Gerald Howarth, terms identical to those finally agreed in October 1986. At that point our legal costs were a modest £40,000. The BBC did not even bother to reply to his letter.

The legal wheels ground slowly on and, in summer 1986, Neil and Gerald tried again. Three times they met Alan Protheroe, the BBC's assistant director-general. Initially, we thought a settlement might be agreed but it was essential the BBC should not misinterpret these approaches as a sign of weakness. Neil and Gerald argued that the BBC had everything to lose by going on, whereas they had little further to lose — *Panorama* had already robbed them of their good names and destroyed their political careers. They also revealed they had financial guarantees should they lose the case. That was pure bluff. Despite the Goldsmith pledge, our homes, careers and livelihoods remained on the line. Jimmy's £50,000 would cover only a fraction of the costs of a failed trial. It was just as well we did not know then the judge's forecast that the trial could last ten weeks, with the loser paying costs exceeding £1,000,000. Unless you have faced the risk of financial extinction, it is difficult to describe the unremitting mental pressure and anguish it creates. Neil and Gerald were very conscious they were not the only ones fighting their battle. Their immediate families, especially Lizzie and I, bore the burden too. For Gerald, the future of his children was an even greater worry. Life was difficult enough for us but, having no children, we had responsibility only for ourselves when taking potentially calamitous decisions.

The contrast with the BBC journalists who had created this firestorm in our lives was stark. We risked everything; they risked nothing. They could fight on, whatever the odds, to the last penny of everybody else's money. Facing different realities, Neil and Gerald desperately tried to convince the BBC to see sense and offered Protheroe a compromise.

We knew the BBC would not want to lose face and its journalists would expect to be protected. If forced into court, though, we would show no mercy. The BBC top brass would be held personally responsible. Protheroe was told, if the BBC wanted out, an apology was essential, but damages could be wrapped up in the costs figure to minimise their humiliation. But false pride came before a fall. Protheroe responded eventually, saying 'no deal'. I then typed Neil's letter to Protheroe on 29 July 1986, telling him to warn his colleagues 'to be aware of the personal gamble they are taking'. They chose to ignore this possibility.

Parliamentary and constituency business kept Neil occupied on the surface, but his mind constantly wandered to the court confrontation that now seemed inevitable. After two and three-quarter years, the crunch was coming. I felt I was being sucked helplessly down a whirling vortex, into a black hole whence no light could penetrate. If we lost, we would lose everything. Neil would be bankrupt, disqualified as an MP, and our lives would be destroyed.

We were due in court on Monday, 13 October 1986. Suddenly, Peter Carter-Ruck rang with amazing news. The BBC had offered to settle with Neil on his terms – apology, full costs and damages. But there was a catch. They would *not* settle with Gerald, whose case was slightly different and for whose trial no date had yet been fixed. Neil didn't hesitate and absolutely refused to settle unless they pulled the dogs from Gerald as well. He would see them in court on Monday. We called a council of war with Gerald and Lizzie. We were all rather awestruck by the magnitude of the decision and Gerald was overcome by Neil's sacrifice. But there could be no question of abandoning him – he and Neil were brothers in arms. Had Neil settled, Gerald would have been left high and dry in a marginal seat, an election looming and the BBC's grotesque allegations threatening his survival.

Neil has always stood by his friends. Loyalty is second nature and it is perplexing to him when others act differently. I admired and wholeheartedly agreed with his instantaneous reaction to the BBC offer but I felt a wave of fear at the public ordeal that lay ahead, from which we could have walked away. What if we lost?

As we entered the Royal Courts of Justice in the Strand the following Monday, Neil whispered, 'I hope we've done the right thing.' I was sure we had.

At the door of the court the BBC again offered Neil a settlement. Perhaps they expected him to crack under the pressure. If so they misjudged the man. Furthermore, he had already made his policy crystal-clear – 'One for all and all for one'! There would be no deal in any circumstances unless Gerald was included. Sacrifice, born of honour and loyalty, was clearly an incomprehensible concept to such grubby little cowards.

Neil positively blossomed when the trial began. Fuelled by adrenalin, in action he immediately began to enjoy himself after the years of terrible waiting. I started to feel almost sorry for Charles Gray, the BBC's QC. This was a political case and Neil was not only a politician but a lawyer, too, which gave him an edge in this courtroom duel. A warrior by nature, Neil loves a good verbal scrap. He prepared and planned meticulously, anticipating Gray's lines of cross-examination. It was his life and opinions they were fighting over and he was bound to know more than his able opponent.

We had over fifty potential witnesses lined up. Norman St John Stevas, MP, was to be Neil's main character witness, in an all-star cast of more than two dozen MPs, but they were never called. Neil's abilities as a mimic were a crucial feature of the case, the BBC claiming his impersonations of Hitler or Mussolini were badges of fascist beliefs. Neil deflated Gray's use of that argument by demonstrating to the jury his ability to impersonate other characters who were somewhat less sinister – like Frankie Howerd! These party japes were simply a bit of fun and it was wicked for *Panorama* to misrepresent carefree tomfoolery as evidence of support for murderous political regimes.

Neil confidently expected questions about some of the fancy-dress uniforms he had donned over the years. He had a photograph from a biography of Robert Runcie, then Archbishop of Canterbury, taken in Germany at the end of the war. When Gray inevitably suggested that giving a Hitler salute was conduct unbecoming for an MP, Neil was looking forward to deploying the photograph of the Primate of All England hamming it up with a Hitler salute, wearing a spiked Prussian helmet and feigning a toothbrush moustache with two fingers. Would Gray and the BBC seriously contend the archbishop was a closet Nazi?

We subsequently discovered that Gray had been horrified at the BBC's decision to brazen it out in court, having advised them they had 'a 40 per cent chance of winning on a good day with a happy judge'. The director-general, Alasdair Milne, ordered the case to be defended at all costs and announced that no journalist would be disciplined, whatever the outcome. After only four days, the BBC were laughed out of court and they capitulated. Neil and Gerald got their apology and damages plus almost £250,000 in costs, but no amount of money could compensate for the hell we had endured for three years.

We were not to learn the true inside story until the memoirs of BBC chairman Marmaduke Hussey were published in 2001, nearly two decades after the offending broadcast. Hussey, appointed just as the trial started, swiftly realised it was a disaster in the making. He rang Charles Gray after three days in court.

'What are the chances of winning?'

'Very unlikely.'

'Why are we fighting it, then?'

'Those are my instructions.'

'Well, you've got fresh instructions now. I have been named chairman of the BBC and am speaking in the company of the vice-chairman, Lord Barnett. We instruct you to settle this case this afternoon for whatever you can manage.'

It was a total humiliation for the BBC. Our own costs ultimately amounted to £237,939.35. The BBC's costs, which we would have had to pay had we lost, were even greater. They had spent recklessly, hoping to dig up some new dirt to throw, to compensate for *Panorama*'s poor research. Cocooned in the arrogance of Goliath, they had refused to compromise. It was a fatal conceit, as they now discovered when our slingshot found its lethal mark. Jimmy Goldsmith was in New York with playboy journalist Taki when news of our ultimate victory came through. He punched the air and said: 'Yeees! I backed those boys, I backed those boys.' He could not have been more ecstatic.

On the day the case collapsed, Neil and Gerald were received on to the floor of the House of Commons like a pair of conquering heroes. It was an amazing scene, with unprecedented cheers, not only from the Tory benches. Only the 'Beast of Bolsover', veteran extreme leftist Dennis Skinner, tried to mar the occasion by giving them a Hitler salute as they passed. Tears of pride and relief mingled as I watched from the Gallery. Later, Neil received a message from Margaret Thatcher saying she would like to see the boys in her room in the early evening and I was invited too. She had been very supportive and was clearly thrilled we had triumphed, recognising the courage and determination it had required. Shortly after we arrived in her room the division bell signalled a vote. Margaret was paired (a regular arrangement whereby MPs of opposing parties can agree not to vote and so cancel each other out) but Neil and Gerald had to rush off, leaving me alone on the sofa with the Great Lady.

She had already been through extraordinary ordeals in her own life, not just at the hands of the press but as the IRA's prime target. Ours must have seemed small beer, but she was wonderfully sympathetic and understanding about the trauma for me in our 'Three Years War'. She knew more than anyone the kind of pressures involved. There had just been a news report of a woman cruelly disfigured when an estranged boyfriend threw chemicals in her face, and Margaret confided her haunting fear of facial disfigurement should anyone throw acid in her face. This is something perhaps more easily understood between women than men. Even though saturated by security wherever she went, somebody could breach it and throw acid as easily as an egg. It could happen in an instant. She told me she always kept an antidote with her for instant application if necessary. So now I knew what was in the famous handbag!

For the first time in the 33-year history of *Panorama* the BBC had to broadcast a grovelling apology on television at the end of the next programme. We gathered to watch it with Lizzie and Gerald in the same Families' Room at the House of Commons where nearly four years earlier I had suffered the original broadcast. It was a sweet moment, for which we had paid heavily in fear, heartache and tears. With some elation we then repaired to the Strangers' Dining Room to celebrate our historic victory.

A few days later, we were taken out by our old friend Andrew Neil, then editor of the *Sunday Times*, for a victory dinner at a fashionable Chelsea restaurant, Sheila Childs making up a foursome. Understandably, we were somewhat exuberant. The restaurant was not full and the few other diners could hardly fail to notice our high spirits. When we reached the coffee stage, I do admit to throwing, gently, a couple of sugar lumps in Andrew's direction as a playful gesture. It was not more than that – well, perhaps three lumps, and maybe he threw one back. We thought no more of it until a couple of days later when, through the internal Rupert Murdoch mail, Andrew received a note from his stable-mate, *Sun* editor, Kelvin Mackenzie. Attached was a letter he had received from one of our fellow diners, reporting the scene in colourful exaggerated prose, assuming Sheila was Andrew's wife and clearly hoping a derogatory piece about us would appear.

'Andrew,' said Kelvin's note. ' Is there *any* truth in this story?!'

'None,' wrote Andrew across the bottom, and sent it back.

The cloud of the BBC allegations had been lifted but a question mark still hung over the path of our lives. On paper, we might have expected a rosy future as a political couple. But Neil had to tread water for most of his first Parliament while others rapidly advanced around him. We had arrived at Westminster in 1983 with high hopes, raring to go, but the *Panorama* lies stopped us dead in our tracks. I did not resent the promotion of others, if they deserved it, but there is always a lot of dead wood appointed to junior ministerial office and it is amazing how long some of them survive and prosper.

The court case generated a storm that changed all normal expectations. Alasdair Milne was rewarded for his arrogant policy and fired by Duke Hussey who confirmed in his autobiography it was because of 'his whole attitude – contempt for the governors and contempt for any normal principles of conducting a business, like the ludicrous and arrogant way we were embarking upon a series of libel actions which our advisers told us we had no chance of winning'. He was 'not up to the job'. Protheroe, too, departed shortly afterwards. Neil's warning in his letter of 29 July, that the BBC top brass ran personal risks if they forced us to a showdown in court, had been proved correct.

After the victory, Neil was offered the job of parliamentary private secretary to the Minister of State for Public Transport. It was the bottom rung of the ladder but it was the only PPS vacancy at the time and a welcome gesture; he was back in the fold. The 'Battle of the Beeb' had been an uphill struggle but our confidence in British justice had been confirmed. Little did we know that faith would be shattered in thirteen years, and yet again twelve months later by one of the most senior legal figures in the land.

Chapter Eleven

No Turning Back – Enter Fayed – Ritz and Whips

Now we had trounced the BBC, there seemed no way but forwards. Tatton was one of the safest Tory seats in the land so as long as Neil's health and enthusiasm held, there was no need to worry about the future. We knew exactly where we would be in five or even twenty-five years' time. We did not have to fret about money; MPs were not paid a fortune but their salary and allowances compared very well with those who had to work for a living.

We worked together four or five days a week at Westminster, and virtually every weekend was spent in the constituency. We were conscious that this was somewhat incestuous and always aware it left little time to pursue other interests. It was politics, politics, and yet more politics. It worried Neil and my mother that I should have sacrificed the opportunity to do something in my own right, choosing instead to remain chained to the secretarial treadmill. There were times when the sheer drudgery of much of the work did get me down and I hankered after new horizons. But not for long. I could have done something completely different, but if I had had a timetable and pressures of my own, we would not have been able to share the close 24-hour relationship we so enjoy. We thrive on togetherness, operating as a couple, as a team.

One of the things I love about Neil is his sense of humour. It makes him a joy to be with and was one of the first things that attracted me to him. He is wonderfully witty and entertaining but occasionally says things in public that should remain unsaid, either because they are in questionable taste or are bound to be misinterpreted. This has frequently got him into trouble and caused friction and rows between us. Quite apart from anything else, when he was an MP these episodes caused an avalanche of mail to pour on to my desk, and it was me who had to administer all the replies. On one occasion, Neil Kinnock, Leader of the Opposition, was at the dispatch box during a debate about a labour dispute at a firm that, *crucially*, made artificial limbs. Kinnock was wind-bagging away when Neil shouted across the chamber, 'Oh, sit down, you haven't got a leg to stand on!'

It was a harmless gibe, albeit somewhat politically incorrect. Predictably, the whole place erupted. Labour MPs jumped up and down, foaming with synthetic outrage, demanding Neil's head on the block – even though many had laughed initially, enjoying a harmless play on words. By the very next day furious letters started to arrive from disabled groups and individuals all over the country. Labour spin-doctors ensured the remark was circulated widely and suitably embellished with inter-pretations of their own, about how it epitomised the hard-faced, uncaring Tories. I had to deal with piles of correspondence I could have done without, thank you very much. Neil cannot stop himself. It was a witty line, not in any way to be taken seriously and, I am happy to say, we received some letters from people with artificial limbs who said it was just a fuss about nothing and they had appreciated the joke. Neil was in the doghouse for quite some time!

Despite our problems with the Beeb it was an exciting time to be in the Commons. Margaret Thatcher was transforming the political landscape and slaying the dragons of the Left. Some timid Tory souls thought the convulsions of her first term called for a period of rest and consolidation. Neil, by contrast, wanted to speed up the pace of change – in trade union reform, privatisation, tax-cutting and slashing away at the constricting tentacles of the 'nanny-state'. He was a founder member of the 'No Turning Back Group', formed in 1984 to fight the consoli-dators, much derided as 'wets'. The NTB were largely contemporaries who had been active in the Federation of Conservative Students in the late sixties and early seventies, nurtured ideologically by the free-market Institute of Economic Affairs under the tutelage of Ralph Harris, later to prove one of the most wonderful friends anyone could wish for. The initial members included Peter Lilley, Francis Maude, Michael Portillo, Michael Forsyth, Alan Howarth (later a Blairite Labour Minister!),

Chris Chope, Eric Forth, Gerald Howarth, Edward Leigh, Michael Brown and Tony Favell.

Being disputatious by nature, no-one could agree on what to call the group. By default it was called after its first pamphlet 'No Turning Back'. I thought then and still think it was a ridiculous name, but the message was clear – we go forward, no weakening, no softening, no turning back. The NTBs regarded themselves as the Praetorian Guard of Thatcherism. Membership was restricted to those who combined revolutionary fervour with intellectual rigour. The NTB met once a month for supper at the Institute of Economic Affairs in Lord North Street. For Neil it was the focus and future. He was in his element, delighted to be part of the driving force of Thatcherism. I would wait up for his news and gossip from NTB meetings, in particular as their influence grew and their ideas became policy and then law.

Only one month after we had been ambushed by *Panorama*, Neil first became directly involved in the 'Battle for Harrods' and the seeds of his downfall were sown. In February 1984, as secretary of the Conservative backbench Trade & Industry Committee, he was invited with the other officers for lunch with Professor Sir Roland Smith, chief executive of House of Fraser, the group that owned Harrods. Lunch had been arranged by Sir Peter Hordern, MP, a paid consultant to HoF and the catalyst for the gathering was the bitter takeover bid for HoF by Lonrho, a worldwide conglomerate led by their buccaneering chief executive, 'Tiny' Rowland.

Rowland had made a vast fortune exploiting his political and commercial connections in Africa and Lonrho, one of the continent's most successful and significant businesses, came under close government scrutiny for some of its business dealings. Famously, in May 1973, Prime Minister Heath had dubbed some of its actions 'the unpleasant and unacceptable face of capitalism'. In 1981 Rowland's bid for House of Fraser had been blocked by the government, on advice from the Monopolies and Mergers Commission. Rowland vented his spleen, in particular when he bought the *Observer* in 1981. The paper made vicious attacks on Thatcher, accusing her of abusing her office, helping to secure Middle East contracts for British companies from which her son, Mark, was allegedly creaming off commissions. Rowland was suave and smooth; a consummate businessman and fixer of deals. Little he wanted eluded him and, most of all, he coveted House of Fraser, because it contained Harrods. He had acquired a 29.9 per cent stake.

Neil was already a partisan for the House of Fraser and against Rowland well before Mohamed Fayed arrived on the scene in October 1985. Fayed had come a long way, from the slums of Alexandria to the court of the Sultan of Brunei. His first stroke of luck had been to marry Soraya, sister of Adnan Khashoggi, in 1952, and start a career that would see him become the Middle East's supreme 'Mr Fixit' who was to make billions on Saudi arms deals. Fayed started as a humble sewing-machine salesman for Khashoggi, but they quickly fell out when Khashoggi discovered his brother-in-law was two-timing him in business deals. Although barely literate, Fayed prospered as a middleman, earning large commissions on deals. Sometimes he took risks and must be the only man ever to have crossed the murderous dictator of Haiti, voodoo practitioner 'Papa Doc' Duvalier, and survive. In 1961 Fayed defrauded the Port au Prince Harbour Board of $100,000 and quickly left the country before he could be fed to the crocodiles. Through the 1960s and 1970s Fayed developed a lucrative business, taking commissions on large construction projects in the Gulf financed by burgeoning oil wealth.

By the early 1980s he had come to the attention of Rowland, who found Fayed's Middle East contacts useful and briefly made him a director of Lonrho. At the end of 1984 Rowland received a tip-off that there might be a way around the Department of Trade's intransigent block on his Harrods takeover plans. If he sold his shareholding, the DTI prohibition would be lifted and a change of government policy on takeovers would later enable him to make a successful fresh bid.

Rowland needed someone to whom he could sell his shares on the understanding he could reclaim them later. It would have to be someone not in a position to mount a successful takeover of his own. Fayed seemed ideal. Rowland thought him worth only £50 million and never dreamt Fayed could or wanted to raise the £600 million necessary to buy Harrods/HoF. He saw Fayed as an 'innocent' on whom to park his shares, who would sell them back immediately on request. The Christmas lights were twinkling, Santa was in his grotto at Harrods and Rowland could enjoy the festive season waiting quietly in the background for his moment to pounce.

But he had reckoned without the treachery of Fayed. On 11 March 1985, in a brilliant and shameless act of chicanery, Fayed snatched the coveted prize from under Rowland's nose. He took control of HoF for a 'cash' price of £615 million. Rowland was incandescent and perplexed.

Not only had he been betrayed by the man he trusted with his shares, but where on earth had Fayed got the money from? Unknown to Rowland, Fayed enjoyed an unlimited power of attorney on behalf of the world's richest man, the Sultan of Brunei. He had used that power secretly to borrow from the banks the colossal sum needed to mount a bid. Astonishingly, someone who had been worth only £50 million was suddenly able to produce twelve times that in 'cash' to buy HoF. Rowland was understandably apoplectic.

In order for Fayed to gain acceptance in City and government circles, his PR machine went into overdrive, disseminating a wholly bogus picture of his family background and the sources and scale of his wealth. The press lapped it up. The *Mail* gushed that the Fayed brothers 'control more than half the shipping in the Mediterranean'. The *Telegraph* enthused: 'The Fayeds are members of one of Egypt's most distinguished families. The origins of their wealth go back to 1876 when their grandfather began business in Egypt shipping cotton to Liverpool. The brothers were educated at British schools in Alexandria.' The *Financial Times* reported: 'The Fayed brothers are fourth generation Egyptian money — their great-grandfather founded the family's financial dynasty growing cotton on the banks of the Nile and exporting it in his own ships to the UK.' This was all rubbish but only a minute fraction of the wave of Fayed lies that engulfed the British media in 1985.

Presaging the credulous media acceptance nine years later of another torrent of Fayed lies about Neil, nothing was either challenged or checked. It was not until 1990 that Fayed was officially exposed by the DTI report on his takeover of Harrods, which concluded: 'The Fayeds dishonestly misrepresented their origins, their wealth, their business interests and their resources to the Secretary of State, the Office of Fair Trading, the press, the House of Fraser board and shareholders, and their own advisors.' But in 1985 an uncritical press had swallowed and regurgitated the fare fed to them by the then unknown Fayed. He was the 'Fabulous Pharaoh' fêted by the financial establishment. Bankers Kleinwort Benson and solicitors Herbert Smith & Co. cloaked him with their prestige. Virtually all of London was at his feet. But not Tiny Rowland. If only we had known then what we know now!

After Fayed had audaciously snatched Harrods/HoF from under Rowland's nose, the latter unleashed a barrage of coruscating public attacks on him. Rowland embarked upon a campaign of unprecedented

ferocity and expense to undo the Egyptian's takeover. He was remorseless and brutal in his personal salvos. A gifted and witty wordsmith, he
dipped his pen in vitriol to produce a series of abusive and apparently
highly defamatory public letters, accompanied by a series of glossy
booklets providing documentary proof, exposing the truth about Fayed's
background and shady business history. These were then regularly
mailed in their tens of thousands to the movers and shakers in public and
commercial life, including all MPs. In addition, through the columns of
the *Observer*, Rowland screamed for investigations, but the government
was impassive. However, Rowland's onslaught was so violent and
widespread that Fayed and his brother Ali became seriously concerned.
They wanted someone to fight their corner in Parliament and the media.
Enter Ian Greer.

In the 1970s, Ian Greer had observed the development of
Washington's vast and highly lucrative political lobbying industry. Well
ahead of others in Westminster's more staid and traditional scene, he
spotted a gap in the market for professional advice on how to influence
political decisions that could vitally affect companies, for good or ill.
Greer had some excellent campaigns under his belt and gilt-edged clients
like British Airways, Thames Water, British Gas, the Newspaper
Publishers' Association, the Royal Marsden Hospital and many others.
He had just fought a brilliant crusade on behalf of British Airways so
when Fayed asked BA's chairman, Lord King, for advice on how to
counteract Rowland's assault, King advised him to engage Greer. He did,
at £25,000 per year.

Greer set about organising a campaign and contacted the obvious
people, the officers of the Trade & Industry Committee. Peter Hordern
was already on side as HoF's paid parliamentary consultant. They all met
with Greer and agreed to help. At the time, Rowland's campaign against
Fayed seemed just megalomaniac sour grapes and Neil was incensed by
his similarly vituperative attacks on Margaret and Mark Thatcher. In
blissful ignorance of the true nature of the beast, Neil had a natural
sympathy for Fayed, who denounced Rowland's claims and sued for libel.
We were still embroiled in fighting *Panorama* and it was easy to empathise
with a fellow victim of apparently outrageous falsehoods. However,
whereas *Panorama*'s claims were all lies, Rowland's were all true.`

Forgive me for emphasising again that Neil had taken the side of
House of Fraser against Tiny Rowland long before Fayed was even in

the picture. He was working for a principle, not a person. Since the gruesome reality of Fayed has become known, many people have asked me how we could possibly ever have had anything to do with him. I completely understand that view. But things were so different then and we were not alone in being taken in by Fayed — so was virtually the entire political and financial establishment of the day.

Over the next three years or so, Neil and the Trade & Industry officers had occasional meetings with Fayed and from time to time Greer asked them to put down a few parliamentary questions or PQs. It is no big deal to ask a written PQ. You scribble it on a printed form, sign it and hand it to the Clerk of the Table Office. Hundreds are tabled every day about everything from local to international affairs. In the mid-eighties they were running at about 40,000 a year. Every day MPs ask PQs prompted by outside individuals. Plenty of people and organisations use MPs to gain information in this way. For example, Gerald Nabarro was chairman of Driving Instructors Limited (DIL), which had regular meetings at the Commons. He was paid as their chairman and occasionally he asked PQs for DIL. That was before MPs had to register interests but everyone knew he was championing these small businessmen. Similarly, trade union MPs have asked thousands of PQs for their sponsors. From the lurid and fanciful press reporting, you might conclude that Neil was doing little else but help Fayed during this period. The mundane truth is that between 1985 and 1989, he tabled just nine written questions and *zero* oral questions on Fayed-related topics. They were just nanoseconds in a busy political life, or so I thought. But these questions were to change our lives for ever.

It may surprise you to learn that, apart from seeing him in court, I have only ever set eyes on Fayed twice. From the way the saga was reported anyone could be forgiven for thinking we had been bosom buddies but, as always, the reality was quite different. For me, the Fayed/House of Fraser/DTI issue was just another item to be dealt with and occasionally factored into the diary. Sensational and exaggerated news coverage, implying a very close relationship with Fayed, has led to my being asked extraordinary questions over the years. I was even asked what the sleeping arrangements were like on his yacht. Thank heavens, I have no idea! My inquisitor clearly thought I had been cavorting on *Jonikal* as though I were Princess Diana, who spent a final holiday on board with Fayed's son Dodi, just before their fatal accident.

Quite apart from anything else, *Jonikal* was only hastily acquired by Fayed especially to foster the 'romance' in 1997.

I first met Fayed in 1985 at the Royal Windsor Horse Show. In those days it was sponsored by Harrods, a privilege long since lost, along with the royal warrants, as an indication of royal disgust. It was a perfect summer's day and he was the picture of bonhomie, beaming as he greeted his many guests in the sunshine. We were ushered into a huge and crowded marquee filled with scores of journalists and twenty or so MPs with their wives or 'wives'. This was when I first met Nigel Dempster, legendary diary columnist of the *Daily Mail*. This was the same 'Pratt Dumpster' (so nicknamed by *Private Eye*) who, many years earlier, had landed me in deep trouble with Lady Nabarro because of his tendentious remarks and veiled innuendos. I was aghast to be seated next to such a piranha, who would write whatever he fancied and make it suitably racy whatever the mundane truth. He was probably just as horrified to be sitting next to someone as lowly as me in the pecking order, unlikely to provide sexy copy. However, I quickly relaxed in his company and had a hugely enjoyable time without my giving any hostages to fortune. I have enjoyed friendly relations with him ever since, united by our opinion of Fayed.

The second and last time I met Fayed was at a Christmas drinks party given by Sir Peter and Lady Hordern, where he was charming and entertaining. The depths of cocktail party conversation are unfathomable and he told me Harrods had its own sausage factory opposite the store, reached via a tunnel under Old Brompton Road. Fayed expressed astonishment that I was unaware of his underground butcher's shop and was even more astounded when I vouchsafed I had never knowingly eaten a Harrods sausage. He appeared mortified and said he would send me some. I thanked him, moved on to chat with other guests and never gave it a moment's thought.

Imagine my surprise a couple of days later when the doorbell rang and there was a green-suited delivery boy from Harrods with a pound of beef and a pound of pork sausages, all beautifully wrapped. I was amazed Fayed had remembered our conversation but thought it very kind, happily unaware of the grotesque indigestion those sausages would cause years later during our libel action when they became the subject of a full front-page headline in the *Sun*.

It was my first experience of Fayed's impulsive generosity, albeit at the other end of the scale from the most notorious – our famous visit to his hotel, the Paris Ritz. This episode has been grotesquely misrepresented, deliberately and calculatingly by George Carman, Fayed's QC, and mischievously by the media. Fayed subsequently claimed, falsely, that we invited ourselves to the hotel. The truth is this. In September 1987 we planned to stay with Joachim Lepelletier (he who had thrown the wine-basket across the restaurant) at his house in Carentan, Normandy, and then call on other friends in Strasbourg, sampling the delights of the Route du Vin in Alsace on the way.

The officers of the Trade & Industry Committee had met Fayed in July and, during small talk, he had asked their holiday plans. Neil told him about our French trip, upon which he insisted we should travel via Paris, which was virtually on a straight line between Carentan and Strasbourg. The point of the invitation was to show us the Duke and Duchess of Windsor's villa in the Bois de Boulogne, which Fayed had recently acquired. The invitation to stay at the Ritz was incidental. He told Neil he always had a suite available for personal use, so it would not matter if the hotel was full. But, as the world now knows, *we* should have had reservations about *his* reservation of Room 356.

What intrigued us most was the chance to view the Duke and Duchess of Windsor's villa. It is relatively small and would never be open to the public. We were being offered a unique opportunity to see a piece of history at close quarters and were to be shown round by Sidney Johnson, who became the Duke's valet after meeting him during World War II when the Duke was Governor of Bermuda.

Our arrival at the Ritz should have been filmed. It was typical *Carry On* material. Although we had moved on from 'Bunny Bobs', our car was not exactly a limousine but a second-hand workhorse and looked it. We pitched up at the hotel rather unexpectedly. We turned into the Place Vendôme, my head firmly down in the map, while Neil concentrated on being on the wrong side of the road, trying to avoid meeting our Waterloo at the hands of manic Parisian drivers.

Suddenly we found ourselves outside the famous façade. I was absolutely horrified but giggling away, 'Darling, for heaven's sake move ahead — we can't possibly arrive in this state.' We had enjoyed a '*déjeuner sur l'herbe*' en route from Normandy and the car was littered with the detritus of provisions. The back seat resembled a Tracey Emin bed — half-eaten pâtés, *jambon*, baguettes, *fromages*, fruit and assorted packaging were sprayed around and we were dressed in very casual holiday gear. At that exact moment an intensely smart and wealthy-looking pair were ascending the small flight of steps to the hotel, following a towering pile of Louis (look-at-me-I'm-rich) Vuitton luggage. For a second the liveried flunkies did not move. Could this dishevelled couple in their broken-down old rattletrap seriously be intending to enter the hallowed portals of their hotel?

Then two of them bore down on us purposefully, as I frantically swept crumbs off the back seat and smoothed the creases in my jeans. The game was up. Hotel staff are used to tips but the car was a tip of a rather different kind. The full horror was revealed when Neil opened the boot. The inscrutable gaze of the doormen alighted on a melée of battered cardboard boxes and carrier bags, with jumpers and other oddments randomly shoved in. I had not totally forgotten we were staying at an hotel. We did have three red Antler suitcases, visibly betraying their age – they had been a twenty-first-birthday present from one of my aunts seventeen years earlier – which the doormen solemnly carried in. They tried not to be overt in their disdain for our appearance and the poverty of our luggage, but their Gallic hauteur spoke volumes – this was not *comme il faut* at the Ritz!

We settled into our room. It was lovely with a splendid marble bathroom attached, though a swimming pool was being constructed in the grounds on our side of the hotel so there was drilling and noise from about 8.30 every morning, which provided an involuntary wake-up call. The day after we arrived the manager, Mr Klein, greeted us enthusiastically as personal guests of *le patron*. He apologised profusely, but it would not be possible to visit the Windsor villa that afternoon as Sidney was unavailable. Perhaps the following day. Then, for the next few days, we were repeatedly told it was not possible because of 'building work'. Initially we were unconcerned and were happy to kill time revisiting old haunts and exploring new areas of the city. Of course, we were also enjoying our fantasy existence at the fabulous hotel.

Yes, we did navigate our way around the restaurant menu and *la carte des vins*. It would have been silly to forgo the pleasures of the Ritz for a backstreet bistro that we could visit any time. When would we return to the Ritz? I was experiencing a great deal of back pain and had to spend some time in our room while Neil went sightseeing. Alcohol dulls pain and I resorted to the minibar for doses of anaesthetic. Some twelve years later in court, George Carman, made us out to be alcoholic gluttons and wallowed in every particular of the hotel bill. Little did we know then that Carman himself could teach us a thing or two about excessive behaviour! We had not expected to stay for six nights. But our visit to the villa was put off to the next day and then the next . . . In the light of subsequent events, this was clearly a ploy to keep us there longer, to compromise us.

The final bill was nominally astronomical, but the Ritz is a phenomenally expensive hotel because of RAT (Ritz Added Tax). Current price lists were produced in the libel trial in 1999, when a can of Coca-Cola from the minibar proved to cost nearly £10. An 'ordinary' bottle of champagne was £70. The actual cost of the food and drink to Fayed was, of course, minimal. The hotel was half empty, so the 'opportunity cost' of our room was zero.

Of course, when we were battling it out in court, George Carman made much of our supposed 'greed' in not paying for stamps on a handful of postcards. I had taken them to the front desk, asked to buy stamps and was told the hotel franked its mail and would take care of it. It was part of the service such a hotel automatically offers and I thought nothing of it. It was only a few francs but, years later, in the mouth of Carman this wholly innocent event became a hanging offence.

I cherish wonderful memories of our time in Paris and do not regret accepting the invitation, despite the fact that we have been monstered as a result by hypocrites in the media, who turn the completion of their expenses claims into a creative art form. It offered us the now unrepeatable experience of exploring the time capsule of the Windsor villa with Sidney Johnson. In 1987 everything was exactly as it had been left by the Duke and Duchess. Their personal memorabilia, photographs and domestic necessities were all there — even the soap in the Duchess's bathroom, half-used on the day she died. I was able to run my fingers along the line of immaculate suits hanging in the Duke's closet, examine the Duchess's fabulous dresses, admire their huge collection of shoes. Neil sat at the desk where the Duke signed the document of abdication, altering the course of history and without which there would probably have been no Charles and Diana, no Princes William and Harry. But undoubtedly the most moving experience of all was to stand at the foot of the bed where the Duke died, while Sidney told us of his final moments. Sidney was the last person to see him alive, fed him a meal of peaches and cream and was in the adjacent room at the end. We were walking through living history, guided by an intimate observer of one of the most legendary romances of modern times.

When he acquired the lease from the city of Paris, Fayed undertook to preserve the contents of the villa for posterity. However, true to form, he broke his word. When his ludicrous fantasy of Dodi marrying Diana and his becoming step-grandfather to the future king was shattered by their deaths, he dispersed the contents to the highest bidders in the four corners of the world, the abdication desk itself going to America.

We arrived home brimming with excitement about our magical experience in France, and made no secret of our stay at the Ritz and visit to the Windsor villa. We were later accused of keeping it under wraps, but nothing could be further from the truth – we were full of stories about the amazing time we had, as many people, including Labour MP friends like Gwyneth Dunwoody, later confirmed. There was nothing to hide. Many MPs and journalists had been to the Ritz but few had visited the villa. There was every reason to boast of our good fortune.

Eight years later, in June 1995, after a politically motivated complaint by Liberal MP Alex Carlile, the Commons Select Committee on Members' Interests judged Neil 'imprudent' not to have registered our stay at the Ritz. But it also had 'sympathy' with him as the rules had been much less clear in 1987. If Neil had registered the visit, he would have been the first MP *ever* to register hospitality of that nature. Coincidentally, shortly before our stay at the Ritz, Tony Blair, no less, was enjoying five-star accommodation in Washington, having flown there on Concorde at the expense of the Unitary Tax Campaign, organised by lobbyist Ian Greer. On his return he signed a Commons motion supporting those who funded the trip. If Neil was wrong not to declare the Ritz, what about Holy Tony? One can only marvel at his hypocrisy in attacking Neil.

I suppose I should not get worked up by the hypocrisy of our critics but it is only human nature. Peter Preston, *Guardian* editor, who acted as Fayed's messenger boy and uncritically published his 'cash for questions' allegations, takes the biscuit. In 1994, a few months before Preston launched his vicious campaign against Neil, Barclays Bank invited us to the Wimbledon men's finals. The invitation included transport, a lavish lunch, coveted tickets for the match itself and a slap-up tea. Fellow guests included Kenneth Clarke, then Chancellor of the Exchequer, and a dozen or so MPs and journalists. The total value of each individual invitation must have been several thousand pounds. Not one MP subsequently registered the hospitality and journalists have no register anyway.

Companies spend so lavishly on mouth-watering invitations to network with people of influence that organising such events is now a major industry in its own right. Newspaper editors have far more power than MPs. They control major organs of propaganda, reaching millions every day. No prizes for guessing that, among Barclays' other guests was the supreme excoriator of politicians accepting capitalist freebies, Mr Peter Preston himself, happily freeloading and tucking in with his wife. Only four months later, Preston was to accuse Neil of corruption for accepting and not registering similar hospitality at the Ritz. If Neil was corrupt for accepting Fayed's hospitality, why wasn't Preston corrupt for accepting Barclays'? Undoubtedly, Mr & Mrs Preston's day out at Wimbledon had cost Barclays more in hard cash than Fayed's hospitality to us at the Ritz.

Favourable coverage in a newspaper is extremely valuable commercially. Perhaps that explains why Preston was invited to other slap-up, all-expenses-paid freebies around the same time. Rocco Forte chartered a private jet to take Preston and a pile of MPs and other journalists to Paris for France's most prestigious horse race, the *Prix de L'Arc de Triomphe*. Again, not one of the MPs subsequently registered the hospitality. If Preston was not 'corrupted' by that jaunt, why assume Neil was by the Ritz? According to Preston's double standards, Neil should eschew such hospitality for fear of compromising his integrity but, apparently, a newspaper editor is wholly exempt from such influences.

Neil was frequently accused, by editors earning many times an MP's salary, of being in Parliament to make money. Quite the opposite was the truth. Neil actually made a big financial sacrifice, quite willingly. He would have earned far more at the tax Bar or as a tax consultant. He is intelligent, talented and would have made a great success of either. He gave up the prospect of private sector riches to fight for his political beliefs. If he hadn't, I would certainly not have had to work as hard as I did throughout all those years as a political wife and secretary. I could have been a lady who lunches! I am not complaining about his decision, far from it. But I do get annoyed at snide criticism from fat cat editors and columnists, who would never dream of making the same sacrifices for themselves.

Although the most publicised, the Ritz was not the only hospitality we received from Fayed. He became a Scottish laird in 1972 when he acquired the derelict Balnagown Castle and its 68,000-acre estate in Easter Ross for £60,000. He then spent £20 million restoring it. In 1989 we planned a ten-day holiday in Scotland staying with various friends. If the weather held, we aimed to drive to Cape Wrath, the only extremity of the UK we had never visited.

Fayed had previously told Neil and others that they should visit Balnagown if ever they were in the area. So we arranged to stay one night on our way to Cape Wrath. The invitation had been issued to various MPs. For example, Michael and Sally Grylls had stayed in the castle with Fayed personally in residence. On our arrival we found Peter Hordern MP and his wife there also. Balnagown is a fairy-tale castle of pink stone with delicate pointed turrets, but neither the Horderns nor we were staying in the castle itself. They were in a lodge in the grounds and we were in a flat above a garage in the converted stables. They were no ordinary stables. Instead of a nosebag of oats there was a bottle of champagne and a side of smoked salmon in the fridge. Frankly, a packet of bran flakes and some milk would have been more useful, though it was a thoughtful gesture and very welcoming. But it was not the castle itself, a point conveniently overlooked by the tabloids in their lurid accounts of our visit.

Staying in the castle at the time was Ali Fayed, Mohamed's brother, who *was* granted a British passport. Ironically he now lives in America. He was there with his wife Tracy and their children. Ali is totally different from his eldest brother, seeming balanced and self-effacing. He invited us all to dinner and we walked across the fields from the stables with Balnagown shimmering in the evening sunlight. We had a pleasant evening and nothing more. The stories peddled later, about boundless and lavish hospitality at the castle with Fayed himself, are utter nonsense.

Back at Westminster, Neil's first proper job was as a junior whip, appointed by Margaret Thatcher in July 1990. Whips have both area and departmental responsibilities and Neil was allocated Northern Ireland. We had to decide how far the need for security was going to intrude into our lives. Neil was a very minor player but, over the years, he had been outspoken on behalf of the Unionist cause. He visited Northern Ireland regularly and, we were told, was on an IRA hit list. We were supposed to check the car every day to make sure nothing untoward had been attached. For a few days we did look in the mornings but one feels a bit daft on hands and knees in the gravel and it also seemed rather self-important — the IRA were not going to bother with a minnow — so we soon gave up. We had all had terrible warnings. Two close associates of Margaret Thatcher, Airey Neave, MP, in 1979 and Ian Gow, MP, in 1990, were brutally assassinated by the IRA. Both brave men, they knew that to have made changes in their lifestyle would have given the IRA a moral victory. Also, if they are determined to kill you they will probably succeed anyway.

CHAPTER TWELVE

Farewell Margaret, Hello John

In 1987 Margaret Thatcher chalked up her third successive general election victory, a feat hitherto unparalleled in modern times. She appeared indestructible – the Iron Lady indeed. But the seeds of her downfall were sown as far back as 1988.

Nigel Lawson resigned to be replaced as Chancellor of the Exchequer by John Major, who many came to regard as the most inadequate Prime Minister in living memory, certainly in the Conservative Party. Early on, he decided to flex muscles other than those used on Edwina Currie. Major led a démarche on Margaret by taking us into the ill-fated Exchange Rate Mechanism. Margaret's intransigent veto on this had been the cause of much of the friction between her and Nigel Lawson. She had just acrimoniously sacrificed him on the altar of Europe and it was impossible to contemplate losing another Chancellor, Major, so soon. She could only rue the day she ever appointed him to a junior job. Major put his pistol to her head and she had no choice but to surrender. It was one of the most catastrophic political and economic misjudgments of the century.

Neil passionately opposed this policy. A long-term opponent of the EEC (now the EU), he had spoken against Britain's entry at the 1971 Tory conference, fought to come out in the 1975 referendum and was one of only nine Tory MPs to defy three-line whips and vote against the Single European Act in 1986. Although he loved his job in the Whips' Office, it was deeply frustrating for him to observe the convention of collective responsibility, forbidden to speak openly, when his private opinions diverged from official policy. Perhaps it was just as well as he would have found it increasingly difficult to defend what he regarded as indefensible.

Michael Heseltine announced he was going to mount a leadership challenge and a whips' meeting was convened. Their main role is to ensure the government maximises its support among Tory MPs. I hadn't thought about it before but naïvely assumed they would pull out all the stops to support the prime minister of the day. Neil was relishing the prospect of being at the centre of the command structure monitoring all the plotting and persuading. How wrong could we be.

I was astonished when he told me after the meeting that, far from acting as Margaret's crack reconnaissance troops, Chief Whip Tim Renton had forbidden them to lift a finger to help her. Just when Neil thought the whips should be at their most useful and busy, Renton ordered them to lay down their arms. His justification was that leaders come and go whereas the Whips' Office is permanent and would have to pick up the pieces and manage the party whatever the result. It had to keep out of the fray. That's nonsense, of course, because a new leader can choose new whips. Neil argued that if Heseltine won, the Whips' Office would *then* have a duty to support him but until that moment their duty was to support the existing prime minister. Renton was adamant and, given his political background and friends, it was not surprising. He was a Europhile, sodden with the sort of Foreign Office wetness that led Norman Tebbit to joke darkly, 'We have a Ministry of Agriculture to look after the interests of farmers and the Foreign Office to look after the interests of foreigners.' Good old Norman and good old Neil. He just ignored Renton's injunction and went his own way, reporting to the Thatcher campaign team every titbit of useful information.

It was a disturbing and emotional time for Neil and his friends who were desperate at what they saw happening around them. They smelt the treachery in the air and feared the eclipse of the dynamic force of Thatcherism, the foundation of their political creed. It was like watching helplessly as someone close to you bleeds to death. Neil had always seen this crisis coming and sank deeper into despair as he saw his prediction, that Europe would break the Tory Party's back, come to awful reality.

I hardly saw him during the next few days of fevered activity, and did my best not to bother him with any daily problems that were arising. I joined the throng of journalists and MPs massed in the corridor outside Committee Room 14 to hear the results of the first ballot. The atmosphere was tense. Everyone knew the future of the country was being decided inside. Neil was there somewhere but far too preoccupied to bother about me. The result was 204 for Margaret and 152 for Hezza. Under the strict rules she had failed by four votes, triggering a second ballot. Margaret was attending the Paris summit to mark the end of the Cold War. She should have been at Westminster where her party was at civil war!

As soon as he heard the figures, Neil rushed to telephone Peter Morrison (her PPS) in Paris, urging her to fight on. With a more vigorous campaign she could achieve a majority. Morrison confirmed she intended to do so. Neil was one of the first to know and delighted that his warrior queen was still in bellicose spirit. The first person he bumped into was Alan Clark, who was characteristically thrilled and outrageous, 'She's not?! She's marvellous. Straight out of *Götterdämmerung!*'

Better an apocalyptic departure than to shuffle off the stage! Next, turning into the Library Corridor, he encountered Norman Lamont and excitedly told him too. His tone was rather different. He also said, 'She's not!' but with a note of alarm in his voice as he scurried off at full-tilt. At the time, Neil was perplexed by this unexpected reaction but, clearly, Lamont's role as Major's campaign manager had already been agreed. The Lady clinging vigorously to political life was a very unwelcome development. Margaret's coffin was ready and some of her Cabinet colleagues could scarcely wait to bang in the nails. Moments later she announced her decision to the world: 'We fight on. We fight to win.'

But it was not to be. Back in London virtually all her Cabinet marched in one by one with the message that the game was up, she could not win. Going into the second ballot would be like the charge of the Light Brigade. Margaret sat in the Cabinet Room, increasingly demoralised as even the likes of Peter Lilley, who she had thought would die with her in the last ditch, acted as counsels of despair.

On that fateful evening the No Turning Back Group had one of its regular monthly dinners. I dropped Neil at the Institute of Economic Affairs. The press had discovered about the dinner and he had to push his way through the pack massing outside. Feeling powerless to influence what I knew to be momentous events, I drove back to Battersea. For the first time ever the NTB drew the blinds so no-one could peer through the windows. The scene would have made good copy. Item one on the agenda was how to salvage the situation. Neil, Michael Portillo, Michael Brown, Edward Leigh and some others vehemently believed Margaret should fight on. But Peter Lilley, as Trade & Industry Secretary the most

Above: Bonny baby – already looking the world straight in the eye.

Above right: Potty but trained.

Below: James, Mum and me – carefree children of the New Forest.

Below right: Happy days at Blynkbonnie, aged 10.

Daddy in his element – at sea.

Below: Neil in brooding Heathcliff mode – I soon got rid of those sideburns!

Below right: The graduate.

At the wheel of NAB 4 with Sir Gerald – he's the one with the moustache.

The newlyweds, 4 June 1983.

Celebrating victory over the BBC with Gerald and Lizzie Howarth, at the flower stand outside the High Court, October 1986.

Electioneering in Tatton, May 1992.

Opposite: Last days as a Minister, October 1994.

With friends at home, Ken Dodd (above) and Razzie (below).

With Dame Barbara Cartland at the Old Rectory – the dog is hers, but who's that man in the white suit?!

With Margaret and Denis Thatcher at our flat for the defamation dinner, 19 July 1996.

Best wishes
Margaret Thatcher   Denis Thatcher

On *Have I Got News for You*, May 1997. © PA/Empics

senior Cabinet Minister there, shook his head resignedly. He said in his quiet, undemonstrative voice that Margaret was finished from the moment she lost the first ballot. Neil was the reverse of quiet and undemonstrative. He was furious, especially when Lilley started talking about John Major in the same breath as Margaret. He threw his chair back, stood up, waved a fist at him and shouted, 'This is Establishment treason. I'm not going to listen.' Clearly, senior political players like Lamont and Lilley were already part of the movement to make John Major the next prime minister.

At the flat, I restlessly padded around, gazing into space, wondering what was unfolding down at Westminster. At last the telephone rang at 10.30 p.m. Neil was in an emotional state, his voice shaking. He could no longer stand the inactivity and was going over to Number 10 to see Margaret for himself. He had no idea when he would be back. He rushed across with Michael Forsyth and Michael Brown. Michael Portillo had already gone ahead.

I didn't fully understand what was going on. Neil was tense, very brief and I could tell he had no time for chat. He told me to get some sleep but that was useless advice. From the balcony of our flat, through the tree tops of Battersea Park, you can see Big Ben and the Victoria Tower. I went out and looked over towards Westminster, trying to imagine what on earth was happening. I knew things were slipping away and felt helpless with a great sense of foreboding that an era was ending. I waited and waited and waited for news. If only I had known what Neil was just learning from Margaret, that all evening she had received a stream of faint-hearts, with wishbones instead of backbones, trooping in to tell her she couldn't do it. By the time Neil saw her that night she had already lost the will to fight.

We had no mobiles so there was no easy contact. I watched the news while intense personal dramas were unfolding elsewhere. I was exhausted but there was to be no sleep. It was after 3 a.m. when Neil finally appeared. He looked like a ghost. His face was drained, his eyes red. He slumped on the edge of the bed and sobbed silently into his hands, 'That's it. It's over. It's all over.' I moved him to a chair, and went to the fridge where there is always an open bottle, but he shook his head to the drink I proffered and tried to describe the scenes of the last few hours when the overwhelming emotion had caused grown men openly and unashamedly to cry.

It was quiet in the Cabinet Room when he arrived. Margaret was sitting, whisky in hand. There were three others there but no-one was speaking. Neil said it was the most pathetic sight he had witnessed – to see this great woman brought so low. He just wanted to hug her back to her former combative self. She was sitting forlornly in her chair, all the stuffing knocked out of her, just repeating that it was all over, all over. She was finished, she couldn't go on. Neil and his colleagues kept trying to encourage her, urging that there was everything to play for. One by one they told her she must continue with the battle for her beliefs, their beliefs, and for her principles, their principles.

After a while people started to drift away. By 2.30 a.m. Neil realised that he was the only one left in the room with her. He still could not accept that she would really give up. He endeavoured to persuade her that whatever her Cabinet colleagues had told her, she could make it, the votes could be got out for her. The first ballot had been a mess with amateurs in control of her campaign team. There had been no direction, no strategy, and too many people claiming to work for her were positively against her.

He tried one last time to urge her into fighting on, though her expression told him it was useless. The time had come. Margaret looked at the clock and decided she was going to bed. She said she would make her final decision in the morning, but it was already made. She would fall on her sword. By early morning we were listening to the radio; it sounded bleak. At about 9.30 a.m. on Thursday, 22 November 1990, Margaret announced she intended to resign. Cecil Parkinson summed up the situation with the words, 'The Labour Party is led by a pygmy and we are led by a giant. We have decided that the answer to our problem is to find a pygmy of our own.'

But Margaret was not quite finished yet. She had gone to see the Queen and returned for her final confrontation in the Commons as prime minister. As luck would have it, Neil was the whip on duty on the front bench that day. His job, ordinarily, was to take notes of what was going on in the Chamber, who was making a good speech, who was dismal, and so on. He had a ringside seat for one of the most brilliant parliamentary performances of all time. I was up in the Gallery looking down on her spellbinding, virtuoso display. Suddenly released from the torment of struggle the Iron Lady was like a medieval knight on the jousting field, sweeping all opposition before her. Her speech was inspired, brilliant, triumphant and she sat down to storming applause with much waving of order papers. Neil noted the reaction in his whips' book: '152 hypocrites cheered her to the echo.' I was enthralled by her show of bravado, which temporarily lifted my spirits. The *Daily Mail* headline next day said it all: 'What Have We Done?'

The Conservative Party was immediately plunged into open warfare. Neil had invested all his political and emotional capital in Thatcherism and was not interested in the succession. The Tories had voluntarily got rid of the best peacetime leader they'd ever had, and the stuffing was knocked out of him.

There was a huge flurry of activity as everybody started madly canvassing for their preferred successor. Douglas Hurd and John Major (miraculously recovered from terminal toothache, apparently so bad it had prevented him coming to London to support Thatcher earlier) announced they would stand against Michael Heseltine. Campaign teams which had been massing underground came into the open. Backbenchers were swept off to be wined and dined, cajoled and persuaded. My overriding concern was that Heseltine be stopped at all costs and the only person who seemed able to do that was Major. Neil would have none of it. He was adamant that Major was not the natural heir of Thatcher, did not have the commitment or beliefs, had already been promoted far beyond his abilities and would be a disaster. His heroine had been fatally stabbed and discarded and there was no credible candidate to replace her.

I now know he was right but I couldn't see it at the time. We had some heated rows, the emotion of the preceding weeks bubbling over into personal arguments. My sense of loss at Margaret's departure was much less political than Neil's. We were both horrified at the tragedy for her but he felt deeply betrayed and was not going to vote for anyone on the second ballot. He wanted nothing to do with it and that was that.

Although I was sensitive to his feelings, I thought he should shake himself out of it and do his bit to stop Heseltine, whose political ideology was so different from his own. Neil had a strong affection for Heseltine, whose buccaneering spirit and star quality he admired, yet, as Margaret's chief assassin and a Euro fanatic, he could not support him for leader. But he was tempted. Major's campaign took full advantage of the fact that Thatcherite MPs had nowhere else to go. I shared Neil's feelings about Heseltine, but was appalled at the prospect of his becoming PM. And so, to Neil's horror, I went to work in a very small way for the Major campaign. I wanted to feel I was doing my bit. He did not try to stop me but was certainly not going to be any part of it himself. We continued to have disagreements as I tried to make him see that, although it was a pretty poor choice, Major had to be the least bad option.

I had a powerful ally. Norman Tebbit telephoned and asked which way Neil was voting. I thought I knew my man and explained that, with zero enthusiasm, he would vote for Major. But Norman was taking no chance, which is just as well because I was wrong. On the morning of the ballot Neil was in the Members' Lobby talking to Chris Chope, then MP for Southampton Itchen and Under-Secretary of state for Transport. Chris is one of Neil's closest friends and his daughter, Antonia, is his goddaughter. Their opinions were identical. They had both just resolved to make a protest vote by writing 'Thatcher' across the ballot paper. Norman, probably the only person who *could* influence them, collared them both. After some blunt exchanges, he bludgeoned them into voting for Major on the sole ground that Margaret was going to, and if she could, they could. So Margaret became history and John Major became Prime Minister.

Chapter Thirteen

Welcome to an Iron Lady, and a Pink Lady

The Latin inscription over our front door read '*Deus nobis haec otia fecit*' – 'God made for us this life of ease'. There were times when I was sorely tempted to paint it out or, at the very least, hit it with my fist or umbrella as we struggled through yet another crisis. The Old Rectory, a gracious Georgian house, nestling next to the ancient St Mary's Church, in the Cheshire hamlet of Nether Alderley, has featured in the pages of myriad newspapers and on countless television programmes. The original window shutters, nailed up in the 1950s, had been restored by us to working order and provided wonderful protection from the paparazzi when things were bad. In times of stress the house was our refuge and strength.

We had been house hunting for about two years but could find nothing suitable. Neil was in America in November 1989 when I saw the Old Rectory advertised for auction with a viewing that afternoon. By his evening telephone call, I had found our dream house, but feared it would be way beyond our means. Auctions are unpredictable, the guide price was more than we could really afford, and we had not yet sold Laburnum Cottage. We had saved hard, our renovations had greatly increased its value, and property inflation had been on our side. However, the market was about to fall and we did not want to be caught with two houses. But we knew we just had to have the Old Rectory and could not wait to begin the process of restoration.

At the auction, I forcibly raised Neil's hand for another £5,000 but, just as we thought it was ours, suddenly, out of nowhere a hand went up and capped our bid by another £5,000. I would have gone on, hang the mortgage, but Neil restrained me firmly. We left the auction in total desolation. I could not believe we had lost our dream. We went to

Cornwall for Christmas with my parents but there was tension in the air. I blamed Neil for not being prepared to take a bigger gamble. I felt we could have coped with the mortgage. We were both despondent and gloomy, feeling we would never find the right house.

And then we received a telephone call from Fiona Roberts, the rector's wife, telling us the purchaser had died and his widow did not wish to complete. Although the auction was in November, completion was not until February because the new rectory was not ready for occupation. There was no time to market it again and the agents invited the various under-bidders to make sealed bids – always a nightmare for purchasers. After much heart-searching, we delivered our bid, held our breath and waited for news. Hooray! The Old Rectory was ours, three months after it had been snatched from under our noses. We borrowed from parents, bankrupted the building society and held our breath again for five months owning two houses on a falling property market. We got away with it and heaved a monumental sigh of relief.

It was the first time the rectory had passed into lay hands, and privatising part of the Church of England fitted in perfectly with Neil's political philosophy! The house was a relic of a more leisured and prosperous clerical life but had fallen into considerable disrepair over the years. One wing and the conservatory had been pulled down during World War II, as Neil discovered when he started to dig over the garden (with his bare hands he disinterred 150 tons of brick rubble) and the stables had been converted into the new rectory.

By 1990 the house had suffered half a century of neglect. Saplings were growing from brickwork and rainwater gushed from broken guttering. The largest of five chimneys leant perilously above the main bedroom and it was only the rector's close relationship with the Almighty that prevented him and his wife being sent prematurely heavenwards, crushed beneath fourteen tons of masonry! Less confident of our own credentials in that quarter, we set about rebuilding all the chimneys immediately.

Nether Alderley is an ancient hamlet. It has no pub because the land owner of a hundred years ago, Lord Stanley, was a devout Muslim and closed it down. He lies buried upright and facing Mecca in the neighbouring wood. The ancient church rises like a magnificent galleon from the garden, the east window being just yards from the house. A handsome stone staircase sweeps up, while stone steps wind down to the all-important and capacious wine cellar.

Over the centuries, the house has welcomed many notable guests. Edward Lear, the Victorian cartoonist stayed, as did Christopher Wordsworth, who composed many of our favourite hymns. Sir Winston Churchill was a regular visitor. His wife was a great friend of the Lady Stanley of the day but Winston preferred the company of the rector. Churchill had also spent many nights at the Leeds Club which, in 1990, was being refurbished and old cast-iron baths were being thrown out. The chairman, John Rae, was a friend of ours. If we could get the baths down and take them away they were ours. And so Neil bowled over to Leeds with a trailer and a couple of strong chaps. With considerable difficulty, several hairy moments and severe risk of multiple hernias all round, the baths were triumphantly brought back to Cheshire. The one magnificent, deep bath that Winston had always used was installed in our bathroom and I drew strength from the knowledge that his venerable backside had slid up and down exactly the same trajectory!

We have welcomed many famous guests of our own, most notably Margaret Thatcher. During the 1992 election she kindly agreed to help Neil's campaign by speaking at a rally in Tatton. Earlier in the day someone had hit her on the head with a bunch of daffodils! We were at home in a great state of excitement about her impending arrival, her minders had near heart failure, but Margaret sailed on unflinchingly. She arrived, with her huge entourage and we rolled out the red carpet through the front door and on to the drive. Margaret, resplendent in purple, hesitated, not wanting to tread on it because it was obviously brand new. Neil explained it had been acquired for this very purpose, ordered her to step on it and she swept in under the motto that was even more incongruous for her than for us. Looking neither right nor left she demanded, 'What are the trade figures? What are the trade figures?' We hadn't the slightest idea they were even out that day, having been totally occupied and absorbed in preparing for our important visitor, so we ignored the question and ushered her on into the drawing room.

Anyone who came to our house could not fail immediately to notice sitting on a chair in the hall my life-size cardboard cutout of Margaret, bought in Carnaby Street in 1975. With its fiery glare, and handbag poised for attack, it has successfully warded off burglars for decades. As a joke, we had placed it on the chair next to hers where she would be sure to notice. It was eerie to see the two Margarets seated next to one another, but the attention of the real one was on higher things. To our disappointment, not to say astonishment, she made no mention at all of her two-dimensional likeness. Perhaps she thought it was perfectly normal to possess such an icon, that every home must have one as an object of veneration. She continued her preoccupation with the trade figures. 'What are they? What are they?' she asked again.

I could not have cared less about the trade figures. I had many mouths to feed. There were ten of us in the dining room and another eight (security, drivers etc.) in the kitchen. I'd spent the entire day running around in circles because, contrary to popular opinion, we did not have endless staff at our disposal.

Margaret was to speak at a big rally that evening in Knutsford so we were eating early. I had organised a light salad buffet, with various meat and fish adornments, in particular my special 'Pâté Marguerite', a wonderful spinach-based pâté that I named in her honour. It has a light texture and is truly delicious. For pudding I had made a large 'death by chocolate' torte because I knew Margaret loved chocolate. Unfortunately, it was Lent and her PPS whispered that she had given it up. I was disappointed but only momentarily.

'I gather you've given up chocolate for Lent – would you like some fruit salad?'

'Certainly not!' she announced loudly to the assembled company. 'I have given up chocolate *bars*. This is quite different. I'll have a large slice!'

We bowled off to the rally where she was mesmerising, speaking for an hour and a quarter without a note, encompassing the whole gamut of national and international affairs. A true *tour de force*. The troops were delighted, we raised a lot of money for the funds, and we have a lasting memory to treasure, tangibly confirmed by her entry in our visitors' book.

As well as the Iron Lady, we also welcomed the Pink Lady, Barbara Cartland, who became a dear friend of ours. One of our closest friends, and certainly our most exotic, is Derek Laud, a public affairs consultant turned businessman, who became the first and, with fox-hunting doomed by Labour, probably the last, black master of foxhounds when he became master of the New Forest Foxhounds in 1999. Derek has a wide circle and Barbara fitted in perfectly with his eclectic and colourful acquaintances and friends. He had not yet met her when we were lunching one day in a restaurant and in wafted Barbara, a vision in pink, escorted by her two sons. We were transfixed. Derek determined he must have a proper introduction, which he quickly effected through her grandson, Viscount Lewisham. He fell immediately under her spell and decided we should meet her too. And so it was that we arrived to take tea with her and she greeted me with the words, 'Come on, come in. I don't like women, you know. But now you're here I suppose you'd better stay. Out of the way, you!' Momentarily nonplussed, I realised the last remark was directed not at me but at the fluffy white blob snapping around my heels as we were swept into Camfield Place, a house built by Beatrix Potter's grandfather. The garden was immortalised in the Peter Rabbit stories but the house now belonged to a modern literary phenomenon, the author of more than 650 novels.

Barbara wanted to redirect government policy and thought Neil was a perfect sounding board. We had been commanded to attend for tea, which was as traditional as Dame Barbara herself. Drop scones, dainty sandwiches of cucumber and paste, followed by walnut, chocolate and lemon cake all cut into tiny squares ready for her to toss to the tiresome Pekinese frothing at our feet. While we tucked into the food, she laid into John Major's government. Major had been invited to luncheon at Camfield Place and it was here, she claims, that his ill-fated Back to Basics campaign was born, causing errant Tory politicians to go down like ninepins. Things, Barbara told me, would have been very different if only Major had put her in charge. 'Never have things been as bad as they are now. People talk about sex all the time and not about love. Good old-fashioned morality is what we want. Good manners, love, love, love.' Major had completely messed things up by ignoring her advice that the campaign should be called 'Back to Romance'.

Undeterred by that setback, the Pink Lady had a new hobbyhorse: mothers should be paid to stay at home with their children. Most modern evils, she thought, boiled down to women abandoning their traditional roles. 'You see, the romance has gone. With a job as well, the gels are just too tired to look after their husbands properly, to love them. They give them food from a tin! Women must stay at home. Then everything will be all right.' In order that she might seek to persuade the government to adopt this policy, we arranged for her to see the Home Secretary, Kenneth Baker, before taking her to dine in the Strangers' Dining Room. We waited, with Derek, at the Members' Entrance as the white Mercedes purred into New Palace Yard. ('I am sorry, Barbara, not even *your* driver can park here.') On arrival at his room, there was no sign of the Home Secretary. 'Only common people keep one waiting,' Barbara acidly observed.

Twenty minutes late, Kenneth Baker puffed through the door, oozing charm to which she was immune. Brushing aside his blandishments, and to his scarcely concealed amusement, she ploughed straight into her argument. He listened, got the odd word in, thanked her politely and bailed out. Without waiting for the door to close behind him, she boomed, 'He's useless. He won't do anything. Come on, where are you taking me for dinner?'

We had assembled an audience of male MPs to join her for dinner including John Patten, then Education Secretary, who was particularly smitten, and Michael Portillo. We conducted her down the 300-yard Library Corridor. What joy to see stupefaction grow on the faces of MPs as a small dot in the distance gradually mushroomed into clouds of vivid fuchsia-pink chiffon, studded with glittering diamanté, make-up apparently applied with a palette knife, magnificent false eyelashes resembling two huge black crows crashing into the white cliffs of Dover. The MPs gaped incredulously as we shimmered past and the chatter was silenced completely as she sailed into the Pugin Room with Neil on one arm and Derek on the other. Eyes popped, jaws dropped and tongues stopped.

Sadly, I did not come to know Barbara until she was ninety and, despite my obvious handicap of being a woman, we got on extremely well. She convinced herself, because my first name is Mary and she had been born Mary Hamilton, that we must be related. Nothing would shake her from this idea that we were somehow Hamilton 'sisters'. Her spirit and drive were indomitable and she became an inspiration to me when the banshees intruded on our lives.

The Old Rectory provided a convenient stopping place on the journey Barbara took each summer up to her estate in Scotland, and she and her two sons came for lunch annually in August. Derek was on hand to greet her, and the red carpet rolled out, when the two white Mercedes swept into the drive, Barbara in the first, driven by son Iain, with son Glen and the fluffy white dogs in the second. On the first visit we hardly recognised her for she looked totally normal, just like anyone's favourite granny. No gravity-defying hair, no false eyelashes. She was in the pink, of course, but just a little Norman Hartnell suit he had whipped up for her in the forties and still wearing well.

We always had a hugely entertaining lunch, with much laughter and mirth, and I overlooked the fact that Barbara constantly fed the dogs with morsels from her plate. She was a life-enhancer and always thought she would make it to a hundred but, sadly, she did not. In death, as in life, she was matter-of-fact and practical. She was 98 when she died in May 2000. There was some controversy when her will was published declaring her penniless. But I can hear her now, 'Look here, I haven't lived this long to give anything to that ghastly Gordon Brown!' It was in that spirit, to the strains of Perry Como singing 'I Believe', that she was buried at her own request in a cardboard coffin: 'No sense wasting wood – everything will rot away quickly enough.'

Chapter Fourteen

Ministerial Red Boxes – a Broken Nose – Sex and Sleaze

Social and political life was never the same for us without Barbara and Margaret. Although Neil was at odds with John Major over Europe and predicted exactly the disastrous outcome of the ERM, he began to prosper within the Party. As a whip he loved being at the centre of the web and I was always riveted by the gossip he brought home, particularly the salacious material about his all-too-human colleagues. He learned valuable lessons about tactics and coping with oversized egos saddled to underendowed abilities. But he found enforced silence in the Commons irksome and longed for an executive post where he could 'get things done' and cut a dash at the dispatch box.

Behind the scenes, however, it was different and he was under no Trappist prohibition. He returned from the whips' annual private dinner for the Prime Minister in 1991 and I was still awake, waiting to hear all the tittle-tattle. He was clearly rather pleased with himself as he had let off some of his pent-up steam and emotion, arguing forcefully with Major, pleading with him to find a way out of the ERM straitjacket. Bizarrely, Major regarded ERM entry as one of his greatest achievements so it was possibly a bit of a gamble to have been so outspoken face to face!

'Crumbs!' I said. 'Wasn't that a bit risky?'

Neil grinned. 'Yes, it did go a bit quiet.'

Apparently a distinct hush had descended on the company in the after-dinner discussion. Neil reminded me that his strong views were no secret to anyone there, and also that Major himself had attributed his staggeringly swift rise through government ranks as 'not inconsiderably due' to the impression he first made on Mrs Thatcher by disagreeing strongly with her at a similar dinner when he was a junior whip in 1984. Neil felt a great deal better for getting it off his chest.

After the 1992 election MPs were anxiously waiting for 'The Call'. The reshuffle started on Friday and continued over the weekend. Appointments were made thick and fast but, by Sunday, we had heard nothing. Monday came and went. By Tuesday we had given up hope. Neil went for a run in the fields to vent his disappointment and was absent when the phone rang. 'Would Mr Hamilton be available later in the morning to take a call from the Prime Minister?' Fortunately, Neil was back when John Major himself rang. 'How would you like to join Michael Heseltine's team at the DTI? I think you will complement each other very well.'

He was to be Minister for Corporate Affairs, a job he would have chosen for himself, reflecting his fields of interest and where he could utilise his legal knowledge and abilities. Neil was tailor-made for the task. His predecessors were Michael Howard and John Redwood so the omens were good – it was a serious job for someone with brains. At last, after nearly ten years, he had something he could get his teeth into. But the meat proved a little tougher than he had bargained for.

At that time, Fayed was waging war on the DTI because of its investigation into the sources of his wealth and his false claims during the Harrods/HoF takeover. Its report branded him a liar and a fraud. Now, as the new Minister, Neil was in charge of all DTI investigations, including this very report. Fayed was seeking to have it quashed by the European Court of Human Rights. Neil had neither seen nor spoken to Fayed for over two years and knew nothing of this. But, crucially, he was now responsible for the DTI's legal work, including the government's defence in Fayed's case. Fayed immediately wrote to him at the DTI: 'You can't keep a good man down for ever! Congratulations on your appointment . . . long overdue . . . remember to spend some of your new salary at the Army & Navy [a House of Fraser store adjacent to the DTI] . . .' The letter was full of effusive good wishes on his promotion and proposed lunch to discuss the DTI investigation and the Strasbourg case.

Do not be fooled by *Yes, Minister* – it is not a comedy but a documentary. Even a humble junior Minister is not allowed to see anything until scrutinised and sanitised by 'Sir Humphrey'. So, Fayed's letter was quite properly opened by Neil's private office and sent to the relevant officials for advice. The first time Neil saw the letter was in a cardboard folder with pages of accompanying documents and comment. The alarm bells rang for him immediately. He told his officials about his earlier support for and hospitality from Fayed and called a meeting with DTI lawyers. They advised that his previous involvement was so long ago that he could now quite properly deal with matters affecting Fayed's interests, but Neil was more cautious. 'Look, these are extremely contentious matters. Whatever I decide will be criticised by the Fayeds or Lonrho. Better to avoid any accusations of partiality by delegating responsibility for these decisions to another Minister.' Michael Heseltine agreed and appointed Edward Leigh, MP.

Neil accepted advice not to reply to Fayed's letter, as even that might be construed as sympathy for his case. Out of courtesy, he asked Peter Hordern, MP, to give his verbal thanks and explain his potential conflict of interest. If only Fayed had written to Neil at the Commons. I would have opened the letter, not civil servants. It would have arrived with hundreds of other congratulatory letters and he would have received a short note of thanks along with everyone else. If only Neil had written Fayed a brief two-liner from the DTI, the course of our trajectory across history might have been very different.

Unknown to us Fayed was angry at the perceived snub and his anger intensified when Neil answered a written PQ from Liberal MP Alex Carlile: 'What assessment has he made of the adequacy of the investigations carried out into the Fayed takeover of Harrods?' Carlile received a standard reply drafted by officials: 'The Inspectors' report reflects a carefully considered and thorough investigation' – anodyne words but not helpful to Fayed.

Fayed regarded Neil's actions, not replying to his letter, transferring DTI responsibility to another Minister and the reply to Carlile, as a gross betrayal. Here was the man, Fayed thought, who could champion his cause at high level and help return him to respectability and acceptance in society. The DTI inspectors condemned him as a liar 'on whose word it would be unsafe to rely on any issue of importance unless confirmed by some independent source'. He wanted this expunged and the record put 'straight'.

In Fayed's warped mind, Neil controlled the levers of power and had only to pull them to give him all he wanted, to have the DTI's critical report shredded and the legal case in Strasbourg abandoned. Paradoxically, if Neil *had* corruptly done Fayed's bidding, he could probably have had cash, not in mythical brown envelopes but by the Harrods van-load. But he behaved with absolute probity and Fayed set out to destroy him. Fayed is a Jekyll and Hyde who can be convivial, expansive and generous. But, when crossed, the smallest perceived slight can turn him into a remorseless enemy. He believed Neil had ignored and betrayed him and so the vendetta began.

Unaware that the die was already cast against him, Neil was thoroughly enjoying his new responsibilities. Many were technical but he had always revelled in the intellectual side of the law and relished mastering a complex brief. However, he did not enter politics to carry on his legal career by other means, and looked for a political issue to focus on. Deregulation was right up his street. The Prime Minister backed him for a 'deregulation initiative' across the whole government, to roll back the 'nanny state', repeal and simplify existing bureaucratic regulations and introduce systems to minimise new ones. Neil was to be in charge with power to go into every government department and audit the costs imposed on business and the public by the accumulation of decades of red tape. Each department would appoint a Minister responsible for deregulation reporting directly to Neil, who would then report directly to the Prime Minister. Among his achievements are two that have cheered the nation: he brought in Sunday racing (squaring the Labour Party by arranging a deal with racing-mad Robin Cook) and made sure there was government time for Gyles Brandreth's Bill to liberalise the restrictions on marriage locations so one can now get married anywhere with a licence.

Neil had sharpened his axe and was longing to wield it to cut away oppressive and pointless legislation, made worse by mad bureaucrats. Unfortunately, the steam ran out of his project because his successor had no political commitment and did nothing, so wasting an opportunity for the Tories to reconnect with core supporters and common sense. But, for now, Neil was still in post. After the ERM debacle there was considerable dissatisfaction at Westminster. Having been sold Major on a false prospectus as Margaret's heir, the Right felt betrayed and angry. The Maastricht Treaty, which greatly extended the EU's powers and led directly to the Single Currency, was a flashpoint and had caused enormous unrest before the 1992 election. Forcing this unpopular measure through the Commons led to civil war in the Party. Neil contemplated resigning at the time but, as a tiny cog in the ministerial wheel, it would have made no difference. Looking back now he wishes he had, but he would only have been replaced by a pro-European. When the Danes rejected the treaty in a referendum, there was Eurosceptic jubilation. If just one country failed to ratify, the Treaty would fall. Here was the answer to Major's problems; he could ditch the Treaty without losing face in Brussels, by blaming the Danes. But Major took the opposite course.

The Danes were bludgeoned into voting 'yes' in a second referendum, which reignited the debate at Westminster. For the next five years the headlines were dominated by splits, plots, and general mayhem, which completely undermined Major and confirmed the public's view of him as a hopeless leader. He tried to walk a tightrope between the two mutually irreconcilable wings of the party and ended up pleasing no-one.

It was a frustrating but exciting time. Westminster was a seething cauldron of internecine strife and recrimination, with huddles and cabals all over the place. Neil was driven to distraction by Major's policy on Europe and twenty or so Ministers shared his view. Unable to speak publicly, Neil persuaded Major to attend a meeting of NTB Ministers so they could express their deep misgivings. He told me in advance he knew it was a waste of time and came back from the meeting in deep depression. It had been clear from Major's body language that he regarded it all as an impertinence, like prefects carpeting the headmaster. But they were all Ministers and, surely, had a right to be heard. The rest of that Parliament would have been a happier experience for Major, and for the Tories, if he had listened.

Aside from the political fracas, we found ourselves embroiled in a physical one of our own. Visiting Harvey Proctor, my colleague at York and former MP, at his shirt and tie shop in Richmond, the three of us were alone when a couple of thugs walked in. Their very presence was threatening, the shop was small, we were cornered, and the atmosphere was tense. After some anti-gay remarks one thug lunged at Harvey, knocking him backwards. Neil leapt forward to defend him, received a huge fist in his face and was also left reeling. My turn next I thought. The thugs looked at me, hesitated and ran! Neil's nose was pouring blood, and I wanted to tend him but was determined they would not get away with this outrage. I charged out of the shop in full cry, running down the street like a demented Valkyrie, lacking only the horns and breastplate. Neil's nose was broken in two places but they got six months.

From 1992 we were all thinking about, and many looking forward to, life after Major. The future of the Right lay clearly with Michael Portillo, and Neil was to be his leadership campaign manager whenever the moment arrived. Soon he began having weekly secret breakfast meetings with Michael and a handful of others. Despite personal friendship and ideological compatibility, Neil would sometimes despair of Michael. He yearned for the strong, decisive, uplifting leadership so conspicuously lacking in Major, derisively known as 'the speaking clock'. To his intense disappointment, Neil encountered early signs of indecisiveness in Michael. The first inkling came on the night of the first Danish referendum, 2 June 1992. We had been at a dinner and were getting into the car when Jonathan Aitken walked towards us on his way home from the Commons, danced a little jig and gave us the tremendous news that the Danes had voted 'no'. Neil was ecstatic and we raced back to the flat at around midnight where Neil immediately rang Michael, hardly able to contain his excitement. 'Michael, it's Neil. This is fantastic news – it changes everything!' From where I was standing I could hear the dead silence from the other end. Then, 'What are you talking about? The Cabinet has decided. We're going on. The Danes' rejection changes nothing.'

Neil simply could not believe what he was hearing. Michael had confirmed that the policy was to back the Brussels Eurocrats. The Danes had shown us the way but here was Michael bottling out, throwing away a unique chance both for him and the Party. If only he had made a stand and resigned, he would have been the acknowledged leader of a huge and growing faction of the Parliamentary Party. Neil and up to a dozen other junior Ministers would resign with him. Major could never withstand that, given the extent of backbench disaffection. Michael would be the heir presumptive rather than merely the heir presumptuous. Isolated resignations among junior ranks were no good. Michael, as a Cabinet Minister, was essential to a successful coup. Neil was dismayed and angry. He got up, threw his hands in the air and said, 'That's it. He's flunked it. He's finished.' Fortifying glass in hand, he rang his closest NTB chums and relayed the dismal news. There was no point in them resigning alone. They just did not carry enough weight and would only be replaced by Europhiles, making the government even more unrepresentative of the views of the British people on this issue. Major had declared war on his own party and consigned it to a generation in the wilderness.

Michael Portillo hungered to be prime minister but it seemed he was just not hungry enough and had completely lost his appetite when on 22 June 1995 Major told his opponents to 'put up or shut up' and called a leadership election. By then, Neil was reconciled to Michael's earlier opt-out, and the circumstances for a contest were perfect. Neil's team were on full alert. Michael was clearly a credible contender. It was not 'disloyal' to take up the challenge that Major himself had invited to clear the air.

However, Portillo was mysteriously 'unavailable' for the crucial few days and it was left to John Redwood to raise the Eurosceptic standard. Of course Neil voted for him but 'The Vulcan' was a far less saleable commodity and lost by 218 votes to 89. If Michael had stood, he would certainly have topped the 100 and Major would have been out. He had flunked it again. Neil was furious and despairing and that was the moment he lost faith in Michael as a political leader, although we remain good friends with him and his wife, Carolyn.

Carolyn is intelligent, witty, vibrant and vivacious. Sensibly, she was never much interested in politics and still has a high-flying career of her own as a head-hunter. She did not relish political life and always shunned the limelight, never wanting to be photographed or commented upon, in which she was successful for many years. Nevertheless, Carolyn always supported Michael in his political ambitions, although her disappointment for him when he failed in his final leadership bid against Iain Duncan Smith in 2003 was significantly tempered by a personal relief that she did not have to enter the maelstrom.

John Major, having ignored Barbara Cartland's advice and promoted his campaign as Back to Basics instead of Back to Romance, began to see his MPs regularly exposed for succumbing to the most basic human instincts. David Mellor, then National Heritage Secretary, was revealed to be having an affair with soft-porn actress Antonia de Sancha. Max Clifford titillated the tabloids and the nation with the snippet that Mellor made love 'in his Chelsea strip'. He now laughingly admits this was merely an invention to add colour to the story and inflate its value. Despite toe-curling appeals on TV and gruesome photo-shoots of family unity, the damage was done and Mellor was soon gone. Other MPs followed in his wake and it seemed no week could pass without another Tory sex scandal.

But some sexual shenanigans never saw the light of day. The most riveting of all stayed secret until recently, which was amazing, considering the female protagonist has a mouth of Amazonian proportions. John Major having sex with Edwina Currie? The improbable in pursuit of the unpalatable! After her revelations about Major were published in 2002, we attended the annual Alan Coren Book Auction in aid of Cancer Research, at the Oxford and Cambridge Club. Illustrious tomes on offer included works by Margaret Thatcher and Winston Churchill. Lot 24 was *Edwina – Diaries 1987–1992*. Alan invited bids. A deadly silence followed, punctuated only by giggles, until a voice rang out, 'Thirty pieces of silver.' Fortunately Alan did not take me seriously and the book was knocked down to someone else for pennies. Sir Nicholas Fairbairn, the MP for Perth, had spoken for many in a debate on the 1988 salmonella-in-eggs fiasco. Edwina was banging on in her usual sancti-monious didactic manner. Suddenly, Nicky could stand it no longer, sprang up and intervened, 'May I remind the Honourable Lady, she was an egg once – and the pity is she was ever fertilised.'

Sex was not the only contributor to an image of Tory MPs as a barrel of rotten apples. A barrage of accusations of corruption and shady business dealings was also flung at Tory Ministers, peers and MPs. Jeffrey Archer was accused of insider-dealing in shares in Anglia Television where the 'fragrant' Mary was a director. Neil was the Minister responsible for such matters, so the papers landed on his desk. Acutely aware of the potential for accusations of bias, he insisted on a written opinion from an independent QC before making any decision about possible action. The QC concluded there was 'insufficient evidence' to be sure of a conviction. Jeffrey publicly announced he had been 'cleared' of any impropriety over the share dealings, but that is inaccurate. It was no part of Neil's brief to decide Jeffrey's innocence or guilt. Mary herself described her husband's behaviour as 'annoying, embarrassing and exasperating'. I should say so – it caused her to resign her seat on the board! Jeffrey had betrayed her again – this time between the balance sheets not the bed sheets.

The Archer scandal was prominent because of who was involved but it was not unique. Allegations of extracurricular sex and sleaze seemed to run through the Major administration like letters in a stick of rock. As the summer of 1994 ended we suddenly found ourselves in the firing line. The passage of time was never going to dim Fayed's lust for revenge – he wanted it hot and cold. Fayed believed Neil had betrayed him. He continued to threaten the government with dire consequences if they did not shred the DTI report and give him a British passport. The then editor of the *Sunday Express*, Brian Hitchen, was Fayed's emissary to John Major. Fayed accused Neil and Tim Smith, MP, a junior Northern Ireland Minister, of accepting payments to ask questions on his behalf in the Commons. Major asked the Cabinet Secretary, Sir Robin Butler, to investigate. On 9 October we were having a lie-in when the phone rang in our bedroom at home; it was the Cabinet Secretary, probably the last person we were expecting to hear from at 9 o'clock on a Sunday morning! He reported the rough gist of what Hitchen had said to Major a few days previously. Neil told him, correctly, he had asked no oral but some written questions on Fayed's behalf in the 1980s but had never been paid to do so. Neil and Butler arranged to meet after the imminent Party conference in Bournemouth to discuss the matter properly. But the dam broke before that meeting took place. Our world was about to be turned upside down and our lives changed in ways impossible then to imagine.

CHAPTER FIFTEEN

Fayed Strikes

My brother James, his wife Fiona and their three children were coming from London and my parents from Cornwall to stay with us in Cheshire for the half-term weekend. I had driven up alone from Westminster early on Wednesday 19 October 1994 to prepare for the invasion. I was carefree, looking forward to a family weekend of fun and frivolity. Driving northwards up the motorways I was happily planning our meals and activities, and spent the rest of the day in frantic activity: shopping, cooking, making up beds, generally getting ready for the onslaught. I had a bath, washed my hair and went to bed early. Perhaps I had a premonition I would be before the cameras at an early hour the next morning.

I was in bed, tired, but thought I would just see the 10 p.m. news. Suddenly Neil telephoned, so, wanting to give him my full attention, I flipped the TV off and snuggled down to enjoy his call. By then he knew what was coming and was desperate I should not watch the news in case there was a mention. He was determined I should have a good night's sleep and not spend the night alone knowing the appalling storm that was about to break around us. He kept me talking until the danger was over. He knew I was exhausted and made me promise to go straight to sleep when I put the telephone down. Darling Neil – he did his best but reckoned without the relentless, unsentimental enquiries of journalists.

The telephone woke me shortly before midnight. A *Daily Express* journalist demanded to know what I had to say about 'these allegations'. I was half asleep.

'What allegations?'

'The ones in the *Guardian* tomorrow.'

I asked what on earth he was talking about and said I wasn't commenting on anything I hadn't seen. He said he would fax the article through to me and so I stumbled downstairs and waited. When the machine whirred into action I simply could not believe my eyes at the headlines rolling out.

I started madly ringing around for Neil, desperate to talk to him. I rang the flat, the Whips' Office, his mobile, but could not find him anywhere. I did not realise at that stage that the massed ranks of the press were also seeking him here, there and everywhere. I finally tracked him down at the flat of a fellow whip who had kindly taken him in to avoid the hue and cry.

Neil's day had started perfectly normally with ministerial meetings at the DTI. At 4.13 p.m. Neil's private secretary received a fax from David Hencke of the *Guardian*. Like Hencke himself, it was a scruffy affair, simply saying he was working on a story about Neil's links with Fayed in the campaign against Lonrho and had many documents. If Neil would like to comment he should call him. There was no indication of urgency. Hencke, of course, was not interested in Neil's comments. His article was already set up for the next day's front page and would be off the presses in a few hours. Hencke had literally taken dictation from Fayed and that was good enough for him, despite the *Guardian* having previously denounced Fayed as an incorrigible liar and fraudster.

Neil read the fax when he ended a meeting at 5.00 p.m., put it on one side, finished his ministerial correspondence and returned to the Commons. On arrival in the Members' Lobby he found a message from the unctuous Liberal MP Alex Carlile, warning that he intended to raise in the House at 10 p.m. allegations in the *Guardian* the next day. This was Neil's first inkling of the avalanche about to engulf us. He had no idea what the allegations were and quickly tried to get hold of Carlile to find out. The Liberal chief whip Archy Kirkwood, MP, said he would get Carlile to talk to him and a meeting was fixed for 7 p.m. Neil understood the tactic immediately. Hencke concealed his story from Neil but leaked it to Carlile to ensure it could be picked up by other media and reported under parliamentary privilege. Neil went to Carlile's room, to find him smugly relishing the power in his hands to cause chaos in our lives, and demanded to see the evidence backing whatever he intended to say.

All Carlile had was a few faxed drafts of PQs and accompanying messages from Ian Greer to Fayed. In themselves, these suggested nothing improper. MPs are primed by outsiders to ask PQs and raise issues in Parliament all the time. Indeed Hencke himself was doing just that with Carlile at that very moment, to advance his own personal interests. Neither of them had any evidence whatever of Neil demanding, being offered or receiving money for asking these PQs. Of course they didn't, because it didn't happen. Neil hit at Carlile in his most vulnerable place. 'You are a QC. You understand the rules of evidence. You know none of this adds up to a row of beans. This isn't even circumstantial evidence. You can see how damaging this will be to me. Don't you think what you propose to do is grossly unprofessional?' Amazingly this seemed to strike home. Carlile promised to consult his colleagues and come back to Neil later. Meanwhile, Neil had to go to the Terrace where he was hosting a reception, exude the bonhomie of the genial host, making small talk over cocktails and canapés, while his mind was racing away on much larger matters. Neil is the consummate professional and no-one had the slightest suspicion of the maelstrom whirling around in his head. Around 9 p.m. he had a call from Archy Kirkwood, saying they had decided not to raise the matter after all, but if the Labour Party raised it they would feel obliged to join in. Neil breathed again. When free of the reception he dashed off to the library for some *Guardian* cuttings, feeling it might be useful to have their own assessment of Fayed as a 'liar and purveyor of cock-and-bull stories'.

Neil took these into the Whips' Office and warned them what might happen. But Neil's success with the Liberals was not enough. Hencke had also tipped off Labour and Neil's ministerial 'shadow', Stuart Bell, MP, was to plunge the knife in public. Bell, now a Church Commissioner, threw Christian charity and natural justice overboard to play naked power politics. Repeating the essence of the story in Parliament meant everyone could now report it under privilege. Neil did not go into the Chamber. He knew it would be a bear garden and, as a Minister, he was forbidden to speak there in a personal capacity.

He stayed in the Whips' Office and it was from there he rang to stop me listening to the news. After the predictable fracas in the Chamber, he had a long meeting with the senior whips to go through the allegations. The *Guardian*'s front-page story was headlined 'Tory MPs Were Paid to Plant Questions Says Harrods Chief'; 'You need to rent an MP like you rent a London taxi' was the memorable subtitle.

The allegations were: First, in 1987–9 Fayed's lobbyist paid Neil and Tim Smith £2,000 a time to ask questions in Parliament on his behalf and we had free shopping at Harrods plus a stay at the Ritz. Second, Greer told Fayed he would be his lobbyist for £50,000 a year but would need £2,000 a time for MPs to ask PQs. Third, Fayed claimed Greer's monthly bills varied from £8,000–£10,000 according to the number of PQs. Fourth, Hencke claimed: 'Documentary evidence shows Mr Hamilton devoted many hours to pursuing Lonrho issues on Mr Fayed's behalf.' Later editions of the paper also said that Neil had been 'notified in advance about the allegations'.

Not a single one of these allegations was checked for accuracy before publication. Having read all this with mounting incredulity, Neil simply could not believe the irresponsibility of publishing such an attack without giving him an opportunity to comment in advance. A few hours' research would have blown the story apart. We discovered, however, during the next few years, that Fayed allegations resemble the Greek hydra: every time one is cut down another dozen appear. But the damage was done. There was no way of shutting the floodgates. Completely ignored in the media feeding frenzy was the immediate catalyst of this firestorm. The European Court of Human Rights had just rejected Fayed's application to quash the DTI report and John Major was refusing to be blackmailed into shredding it or into giving Fayed his coveted British passport. These two events explain both the timing and violence of Fayed's attacks.

Chief Whip Ryder warned Neil pointedly, 'Fayed claims to have evidence to support his allegations – including letters and cancelled cheques. We have to assume he has been trying to set up MPs for some time and conversations may have been taped. Are you completely confident that nothing discreditable can be produced against you?' Fayed's mania for secret video and tape recordings to compromise his staff and anyone who might get in his way is now well known. If Neil had really taken his cash, you can be sure Fayed would have tapes of the event to use for blackmail or revenge. Neil would have been mad to persist in his protestations of innocence, and even more insane to embark on a ruinously expensive libel action, if it could suddenly come unstuck in the event of Fayed producing compromising tapes. Neil didn't hesitate. 'I might have written "thank-you" letters for hospitality. I am sure I did after the Ritz visit. But there can be nothing, nothing that is genuine, more compromising than that.'

Ryder then told him to write a letter to the Prime Minister setting out a detailed refutation of each allegation, which he did immediately in longhand. It was now after midnight and his DTI driver was waiting to take him to the flat. When he saw the massed ranks of cameras and journalists outside they drove on past. He didn't relish being surrounded by television arc lights and microphones. If I had been in London it might have been different. For a start, being practical, I might not have agreed to spend the night elsewhere – women need their 'things'. Together, we would have been prepared to run the gauntlet. But, just when we most needed to be together, by bad luck and timing we were 200 miles apart. All Neil wanted was to shield me from the horrors. All I wanted was to hug him. But we could only talk on the telephone and were, separately, about to be besieged by journalists.

When we were finally able to talk in the early hours, I simply could not believe what he was telling me. What was all this extraordinary business about cash, questions, Ian Greer, £2,000 a time? When you know the truth about something you are optimistic, indeed certain, you can sort it all out. There had clearly been a monumental misunderstanding. We had reckoned (how foolish of us!) without the evil intent of Fayed and the persistence of the *Guardian*.

Next morning I got up early and drew back the curtains behind the front door, to be greeted by a posse of journalists. I explained Neil was in London and making no comment except through his solicitor. I gave them what they wanted, a photograph and brief statement, and dispatched them politely to the end of the drive. I was feeling alone and vulnerable but determined not to show it. I just longed to see Neil, to feel his strong arms around me, assuring me everything would be all right. I wanted us to be able to make decisions together but that was impossible. My mind was buzzing. I had not slept at all since the journalist's telephone call, so I was already feeling exhausted and it was barely 8 a.m. I was anxious about my parents. I did not want them to read or hear anything and then spend a wretchedly long journey worrying. I rang Cornwall to warn them but it was too late. They had heard it all on the *Today* programme. People often forget the extent of the ripples of these momentous news stories. The people you read about in the press are human beings whose family and friends are caught up instantly in a web of worry and concern.

By now Neil was with Richard Ryder and Cabinet Secretary Sir Robin Butler. They produced the bombshell that Tim Smith had admitted receiving undeclared payments from Fayed and had resigned.

Neil was taken aback but this news actually stiffened his resolve not to resign himself. Whatever Tim Smith might have done, Neil had not been paid for espousing Fayed's cause and it was vital to put distance between them. They told him he had either to issue a writ or resign, and then left to attend the Cabinet meeting. Neil told them he would contact his libel lawyer, Peter Carter-Ruck, talk to me and then make a final decision. He was put into a small room with only a desk and telephone for company. He felt that if he opened the drawer there would be the pearl-handled revolver with which he was expected to commit suicide before they returned. Neil rang me immediately. He knew what he wanted to do but was not prepared to drag me through more legal battles without my full-hearted consent. He asked me directly, 'Do I sue? Can you face it? Are you sure?'

Having been through the agonies of the BBC libel, I never thought I would have to face such a nightmare again. Little did I know how much worse this was to be. I was aware of the risks. Truth does not guarantee the outcome. Lawyers take hold and anything can happen. Juries give no reasons for decisions and frequently get things wrong. It could last for years and cost us a fortune. We could lose. Could I cope with it all over again? I took a deep breath, told him I was right behind him, and if that was what we had to do, so be it. He rang Carter-Ruck and instructed him to issue a writ and Ian Greer did the same.

In Cheshire I imparted the news to the waiting journalists, telling them Neil would not be back until the afternoon so they might as well go away until then. These were among the worst few hours of my life. Neil was at the centre of a raging storm and I was not there to support him. Neil was distraught, thinking of me isolated at home surrounded by hostile journalists, without being there to protect me. We had worked as a team for so long and, in our hour of greatest crisis, we were apart. His main concern was to get back to me as soon as possible. Having made his decision to sue there was no point hanging around waiting for Cabinet to end. He called his car and sped for the next flight to Manchester, leaving a note for Ryder telling him the 'good news'. Just as his car was pulling into Heathrow, the mobile rang. It was Ryder in a fury, 'Where the hell are you? What do you mean leaving without permission?'

It was instantly obvious that when he had left Neil to decide, he had expected him to resign, not fight for truth and justice. Ryder wanted the easy way out: Neil hung out to dry and the case out of the headlines as quickly as possible. Neil's decision was extremely inconvenient. Ryder ordered him to turn around and come straight back to Downing Street. But Neil was in no mood to take orders from a man like Ryder, even if he was Chief Whip. He shouted back at him, 'My wife is my priority. She's in distress, and if you can't understand why I'm going to her you're an emotional eunuch. You gave me a choice. I've made it. I'm off and that's that. Anyway, what's the point of my coming back to London?' Ryder slammed the phone down and Neil went for his plane.

The press knew Neil had left London and was coming home so they were swarming everywhere. I could not leave to collect him at the airport without a gaggle following me, jostling and hustling, cameras snapping. So I telephoned our near neighbours, Keith and Nadia McCann, to ask if they could collect Neil from Manchester Airport. Keith's splendid bright scarlet Jaguar scythed through the press pack with scarcely a glance. Before they could realise what had happened, Neil darted inside, depriving them of the photo they had been waiting for hours to catch. James, Fiona and their children, Charlotte, Edward and Henry then arrived for the weekend, soon followed by my parents. Despite having the family to stay, we had several constituency engagements including a visit to Wilmslow High School the following morning, where Neil was opening a new extension. We battled our way through the press at home and were greeted by another huge contingent at the school. We tried to continue as normal and Neil completed the official opening. Afterwards the headmaster took him aside and said Michael Heseltine was on the telephone in his office.

Michael had been out of the country when the story broke. A cold fish, he wasted no time on sympathy or generalities. He had been briefed about the *Guardian* story and read Neil's handwritten refutation prepared for the Prime Minister. As a dyslexic Michael had an aversion to paper – Neil had always been impressed by his capacity to get to the heart of complex technical problems by asking pertinent questions. Neil had written that Fayed had not paid him via Ian Greer or anyone else to ask PQs or do anything else on his behalf. Michael wanted to know if Neil had had any other financial relationship with Greer which might have put him under an obligation to him. Neil, truthfully, replied 'No'. He had received two commission payments for introducing new clients in 1986 and 1988 but they were merely introductory commissions and carried no obligation of any kind.

When Neil emerged we continued our tour including the canteen and kitchens. One of the dinner ladies was leaving after thirty years and they had had a party. Some large, truly delicious, ginger biscuits had been made but were too strong for the children and many were left. I ate one, Neil ate one and a small bag of them was thrust upon us to take home.

Coming out of the school I was staggered by the seething crowd and momentarily drew back, feeling unable to handle the hostile attention. Neil grabbed me by the hand, 'Come on, we can deal with this. Leave it to me.' I did. But I wish I hadn't! As we walked out to the assembled media Neil held up a ginger biscuit and quipped, 'I've just been given this. Of course, I shall be declaring it in the Register of Members' Interests.'

This was a joke, ridiculing those who sanctimoniously criticised his not having registered our visit to the Ritz. The frivolity was compounded by a reporter who asked, 'Is it a Ritz cracker?' Neil was cocking a snook at the hypocrisy of the registration rules, which were full of anomalies, making them a minefield for MPs. Not surprisingly, the government had a collective sense-of-humour failure and, apparently, that sealed Neil's fate. Personally, I think the biscuit episode was a bad mistake and I gave Neil hell when we got into the car. At the time, I laughed and went along with it – what else could I do? – but I was uncomfortable with the flippancy. It was a typical Neilism which, although funny at the time, predictably went down like a lead balloon with the Tory high command. But Neil had made a tactical decision to exude confidence and fighting spirit and this was part of it.

Though our house remained under siege, we continued the family weekend as best we could. It was difficult to explain to a three-year-old why so many people were hanging around with cameras, booms and transmitter vans. Little Henry, although wary at first, soon gained confidence and tricycled up the drive shouting, 'Go away, reptiles! Go away!' before returning to the house beaming with pride at the success of his mission. He had quickly picked up our vernacular! 'Reptile' may sound a hostile word but, of course, we used it tongue-in-cheek, although Henry was serious. We have always recognised that journalists and photographers parked outside are only doing their job and would probably far rather be somewhere else, especially if it is cold or raining. We strove to be courteous and polite, although there were times when I found that hard.

Neil spent every waking hour of the weekend in his library closeted behind shuttered windows, glued to the telephone, drumming up support locally and at Westminster. Each day brought a fresh crop of allegations to be countered, more old files to be disinterred and their facts checked. Fayed's PR machine was embellishing the farrago of lies and feeding 'exclusive' titbits to different papers. Brush fires were breaking out everywhere. Other mischief-makers piled in. Somebody told the *Sunday Times*, falsely, that Neil had been running a business from the constituency offices; a weekend away with my parents at a hotel owned by a personal friend in Cornwall was misrepresented as another undeclared interest, and so on. Each new scare story had to be dealt with and there were not enough hours in the day. By now hundreds of journalists were trawling madly for anything to raise the heat. We felt like hunted animals. The pressure was relentless.

Our long-term objective was to clear Neil's name but, in the meantime, we had to pick up the pieces of life. It was no help to Neil if I dissolved into tears every five minutes. His concern for my wellbeing was obviously distracting him from the task in hand. I tried to keep myself under control. I am very proud of Neil but perhaps never more so than when he is under fire. He is controlled and focused. Many people, including me, would have buckled. He was like a rock throughout.

Chapter Sixteen

Resignation and Making History

Back in London after the weekend, normal life had to continue. We were angry, our friends were angry, but the cumulative stress of the last few days was bearing down on me. Emotionally wrung out and physically exhausted, I was feeling and showing the strain. Neil was resolute and clear-headed, dealing methodically with each problem in turn.

We spent much of the next 48 hours at the home of our friend Patrick Robertson. It was a bolt hole and operations centre, conveniently close to the Commons, and Patrick made it available for endless meetings and cabals despite the obvious intrusion into his own life and work. He never complained, although the repeated arrival of an emotional woman cannot have been easy. As ever, Gerald Howarth was a more steadfast friend than anyone could hope for. Having lost his Cannock and Burntwood seat in 1992, he was having to make a living outside politics, constantly worried by pressures of a mortgage, three children, school fees and so forth. Gerald put his life on hold. If he felt indebted to Neil for refusing, a decade earlier, to settle with the BBC without their settling with him, he now repaid that debt many times over. Later, Gerald jeopardised his own career prospects after re-election to the Commons in 1997 to stick up for Neil, in the face of threats from the whips to back down. No-one could have done more, publicly and privately, to keep us going throughout the unfolding ordeal.

In politics, as in life, you rapidly learn the difference between colleagues and friends. The Commons is a convivial club, awash with daily opportunity to socialise in the canteens, restaurants, bars and corridors. It also teems with testosterone, ego and ambition and, when anyone is in difficulty, public support can be dangerous. Many political 'friendships' melt at the first flicker of flame, others subside when the battle intensifies. Success has a thousand parents but failure is an orphan. Yet we were far from alone. Another staunch ally was Tim Bell, who put the expertise of his world-class public relations company at our disposal. He had advised Margaret and the Tory Party for years and I could hardly believe how much time and trouble he took to help Neil.

By contrast, Michael Heseltine and Richard Ryder couldn't wait to throw him to the wolves. I was surprised to learn later that Ryder has terrible back problems; I sympathise but had always thought him spineless. He was determined to get Neil out. On Monday evening we gathered at Patrick's flat with Gerald and Mark Worthington, Margaret Thatcher's right-hand man, then as now a tower of strength. A press release was drafted defending Neil's position, but ministerial rules required Heseltine's approval before release. A Secretary of State is guarded like a queen bee, every word and move is monitored, every minute of the day mapped out. The Private Office always knows where the boss can be found.

Curiously, on this unique occasion, Hezza could not be contacted. It was growing late, we were in danger of missing the deadline for the next day's papers, so Neil faxed it to Ryder for approval instead. Neil was bailing out his increasingly waterlogged ship with a colander and it quickly became clear that Ryder was going to confiscate even that inadequate utensil. He rang in a cold fury and forbade Neil to send the press release. They had another stand-up row on the telephone. 'What right have you got to stop me defending myself?' Neil demanded. 'The Party's given me bugger-all support over the weekend. I am doing my best single-handedly to turn the tide and all you can do is sabotage me.' Ryder snapped at him, 'Just get back to your department and get on with your job.' As we now know, Ryder had already plotted with Heseltine and Major to sack him in the morning, which explains why Heseltine was unprecedentedly 'unavailable' to one of his ministers.

Despite his fury, Neil felt he had to toe the line when it came to the national papers; after all, he was still a Minister – just. But what harm could be done by sending it to the local weekly papers in Tatton? It was well after midnight and we wanted to catch their deadlines. Although I was dog-tired, I summoned the energy to fax it to our local press including, crucially, the *Community News*, a free-sheet covering rural villages whose most exciting copy usually consisted of reports from WI meetings. I had completely forgotten the editor also ran a tiny press agency. It was Neil's only statement of the day. The nationals didn't have it but the Star Press Agency did!

While we slept fitfully, the damage was done. The press release was to cause a nuclear explosion in Downing Street. They were furious that Neil had said anything at all but, in particular, and *crucially*, the statement pointed out that Neil did not need to resign to fight a libel action. There was an excellent precedent. The Prime Minister himself had remained in office while suing *Scallywag*, the magazine that falsely accused him of an affair with Claire Latimer, the 'Downing Street cook'. Though any man could be forgiven for wanting an affair with such a lovely girl, the story was nonsense. However, there was apoplexy that Neil should dare compare himself to the great John Major, reminding the public of his alleged sexual dalliance.

Scallywag was so near and yet so far from the truth. They made the mistake of naming a lady instead of Edwina . . .! Major was Chancellor of the Exchequer when the whispers began. Norma and the children stayed in Huntingdon and Major found 11 Downing Street a lonely place. As Claire said: 'People saw we were friendly with each other, put two and two together and made five.' The Downing Street machine behaved disgracefully towards a totally innocent girl. Instead of allowing her to defend herself she was told sternly to say 'No comment' and she naïvely agreed. By acquiescing she fuelled media interest – 'No comment' hints 'Yes. It's true.' Mr Nice Guy knew *he* was guilty as charged and Claire was cynically used as a decoy to deflect the hacks from investigating the truth elsewhere. The story was taken up by the *New Statesman* a couple of years later and Claire's situation again became intolerable. With 400 journalists outside her office she asked Downing Street for advice. All she got was, 'We have our own problems. Don't trouble us again.'

Back to *our* own problems. The following day Neil did as Ryder ordered, got back to his department and got on with his job – while Ryder arranged to take it away. Neil had ministerial engagements in Sussex. His driver collected him from the flat at 8 a.m. with his assistant private secretary, Gareth Maybury. Outside he ran the gauntlet of reporters, all shouting, 'Are you going to resign? Mr Hamilton, are you going to resign?' On arrival at Bexhill he ran an identical gauntlet of journalists, all parroting the same question. Neil was to inaugurate the Local Business Partnership Scheme and he dryly thanked the scores of journalists present for taking such a close interest in this worthy project. Needless to say, no questions related to the event; the only issue was Neil. Next, he was speaking to a lunch at Gatwick Airport and the car sped away followed by the cavalcade of journalists. Around noon the telephone rang and he was ordered back to London. As the car diverted at top speed Neil said to Gareth, 'Well! That's that then!'

He called to let me know and I turned on the news to hear he had been summoned to Number 10 to be sacked. Heseltine and Ryder were waiting for him. Neil simply said, 'We all know why we're here. Let's get on with it.' Heseltine had a folder on his lap. He opened it and said they had information Neil had been a consultant to Mobil Oil 'about ten years ago' and could find no mention of it in his entries in the Register. Ryder flicked through the volumes for 1984–6. No mention of Mobil. Of course Neil had registered it and immediately showed them the entry for the relevant year – 1989 – conclusively destroying the allegation. They hadn't bothered with even minimal research; such was their lack of desire to find the truth. Undeterred, they went on to the next point. In 1990, for only a matter of months before he became a whip, Neil had been a director of a gold mining company, Plateau Mining plc. This was apparently connected with another company, Butte Mining plc, which was being investigated by the Serious Fraud Office. Neil had never heard of Butte or the SFO investigation. It had nothing to do with him. What was the allegation? Heseltine applied Catch 22 – the information in his file was confidential so he could not tell him. Without a concrete allegation, how could Neil possibly answer it? Tarzan shook his head and said the continuing flow of allegations, even if unfounded, made Neil's position untenable.

The second story didn't hold up either. Later, it took Neil only a few hours to discover the facts. Butte and Plateau had been spun off from the Robertson Group, in 1987 and 1990 respectively. Robertson had kept a small stake in Butte but none in Plateau. Neil never had any connection whatsoever with Butte. They clearly wanted him out, whatever the pretext.

Rather than argue fruitlessly, Neil just said, 'Look, this is all rubbish. Your minds are made up; there's nothing I can do about it. But, I want the Prime Minister to make it absolutely explicit in his reply to my resignation letter that I was not sacked because he believes Fayed's allegations. It will be very damaging to my case if people think that.' Ryder said he could 'make no promises' and beat a hasty retreat. Neil got in his ministerial car for the last time and made the short journey to the Commons.

I was waiting in his office on the Lower Ministerial Corridor. When he came in I leapt up and we hugged each other while the tears rolled down my cheeks. I was angry at the way he had been treated but a boil had been lanced, the pressure was off and we could get on with life. A gross injustice had been done and I was incensed at the machinations against Neil. Simultaneously, though, it was a tremendous relief. Blood had been spilled, the baying press would disappear and we would have breathing space to gather our wits.

We watched on television as Major confirmed Neil's resignation at Prime Minister's Question Time. Neil's office, where I worked, was directly below the chamber and it was eerie to see the live broadcast and know it was all taking place a few yards above our heads. We had to draw up his formal letter. This was done at Tim Bell's office with expert advice and guidance from Tim himself, and from Gerald Howarth. You might think this would have taken about five minutes, but it took nearly four hours, as they weighed precisely each word for legal implications and media impact. It was an icy letter and did not disguise the controlled rage we all felt.

We were not the only ones. Neil's father was so disgusted by what the Prime Minister had done to his son, he immediately resigned his lifelong membership of the Tory Party. My mother, a dyed-in-the-wool Liberal, immediately cancelled her subscription to the *Guardian,* which she had bought for decades. After a lifetime of loyalty, she felt badly betrayed and transferred to the *Daily Telegraph* – quite a switch!

Neil and I talked long and hard about what lay ahead. We knew the score. The battle against the BBC had taken three years and this would be no pushover. But, together, we were confident that we could take on anyone and anything. We are opposites in many ways but understand how to keep each other going in times of stress and anxiety. We could not always arrange to take it in turns to be depressed or angry, but there is an unspoken agreement that the one least affected at any moment must snap out of it and pull the other one up.

The continual strain and sheer nastiness of it all took a daily toll on me. I often had to summon all my resolve to put on a brave face and charge into what became a daily battle with lawyers, lies and legal argument. Neil's writ against the *Guardian* turned the heat down and we concentrated on gathering evidence to disprove the allegations. Greer's accounts swiftly proved Fayed had paid his company only £25,000 a year (£2,083.33 a month) and this amount never varied over many years, regardless of parliamentary activity.

Quite separately, during the 1987 election campaign Fayed had made, through Greer, contributions to the campaign funds of various candidates. This did not involve Neil in any way. A total of £25,000 was split in amounts averaging £500, not only for Tories but for Liberals and Labour too – including the chairman of the Parliamentary Labour Party, Doug Hoyle, MP. The biggest single dollop was £2,000 for Norman Lamont, MP for Greer's home constituency, Kingston upon Thames. Not even Lamont, then a future Chancellor of the Exchequer, bothered to register these payments. Unlike Fayed, Greer did keep meticulous accounts and could prove exactly where all the money had gone; he had retained all the recipients' cheques, returned to his bank after clearing. None of this money came to Neil – he didn't need it, he had a safe seat. Within days, the facts proved that Fayed's specific allegations, which had forced Neil to resign, were all lies, but the insidious damage to his reputation had begun.

The *Guardian* hadn't even bothered to ask Greer if he could disprove the allegations. They knew Fayed was a congenital liar and had denounced him as such in their own newspaper. They were also well aware of his well-publicised record of intimidation, racism, sexual harassment, secret buggings and recordings. So what motivated these 'high-minded seekers after truth' to behave like tabloids interested only in sensation, regardless of the facts?

Now, though, the *Guardian* was worried. There were no witnesses and there was no documentary evidence to corroborate Fayed's allegations. Indeed their editor, Peter Preston, himself complained to Fayed by fax the day before he printed the allegations: 'nothing in the paperwork proves that Hamilton was doing this for money'. But lack of evidence didn't stop him printing Fayed's words verbatim. The Tory government was extremely unpopular but, in a credibility contest between Neil and Fayed, the *Guardian* could be far from certain a jury would back Fayed. They were desperate to stop the case in its tracks.

Step forward guileful lawyers! They sought refuge in Article 9 of the Bill of Rights of 1689: 'freedom of speech and debates shall not be questioned in any other court or place out of Parliament'. This provision was prompted by Charles I's attempt to arrest for high treason the five MPs who dared to criticise his policies in Commons debates. The *Guardian*'s lawyers argued that newspapers could not, in a court of law, accuse MPs of corrupt parliamentary conduct and, therefore, they would be unable to defend themselves. Talk about Alice in Wonderland! A law of 1689 guaranteeing MPs' freedom of speech was converted in 1995 into a licence for journalists to abuse them as crooks with no legal comeback. How could this dust-covered antique law have any relevance to the modern day? For the first, but not the last, time I was to learn a hard lesson – don't confuse law with justice.

The *Guardian* won a 'stay of proceedings'. To our utter amazement, the judge ruled that Neil could not pursue his libel action. The Bill of Rights became a Charter for Wrongs. It was a very serious setback and there was widespread sympathy for us, but what could we do? We were determined not to be beaten – why should they get away with it? Ever resourceful, Neil set about changing the law of the land! But this requires parliamentary time, of which there is never enough, and a majority in both Houses. We could but try. Neil wrote to John Major who, much to our surprise, invited us to Number 10 to discuss it. I believe he was genuinely struck by the injustice of our immediate plight and the danger this highlighted for other MPs in the future. By coincidence, the government planned a Defamation Bill which could be amended to allow MPs, if they chose, to waive the privilege created by the Bill of Rights. The Defamation Bill would start in the Lords where Lord Hoffman, a Law Lord, agreed to move the necessary amendment. At Committee stage there is no limit on speeches so timing is unpredictable and our amendment was not reached on the day we expected. Next time, events moved unexpectedly quickly and Lord Hoffman was in the gents when it was called! The House moved on and we had to come back yet again. Third time lucky. Our clause was introduced but the crucial vote would come later when we would have to get our supporters out in force.

We could rely on tacit government support, we knew many peers as friends or acquaintances upon whom we could rely, but we needed more. We pulled out all the stops. Margaret Thatcher and Norman Tebbit used their influence, journalist friends like Simon Heffer wrote favourable articles and Ian Greer's firm sent out mailshots and reminders. Other well-connected friends like Derek Laud, who seemed personally to know half the hereditary peerage, persuaded young peers who had never previously voted, and old buffers who hardly ever left their estates, to make a special effort. 'New Labour' unofficially whipped against us but we had backing from 'Old Labour' friends. Lord Harris of High Cross, who was later instrumental in raising the funds for our libel action against Fayed, organised the cross-benchers.

On the day of the vote there was a party atmosphere as hundreds of our supporters packed in. Neil and I watched as opposition came from two sources. Constitutionalists were worried this was the thin end of the wedge threatening parliamentary privilege, and party-political warhorses, sheltering behind shreds of principle, were hellbent on partisan mischief-making at the expense of justice. The last thing they wanted was Neil's vindication, proving 'cash for questions' was all a hoax – it was far too valuable a weapon against the wicked Tories to have the truth exposed. The debate ebbed and flowed but it was clear from the turnout we were going to win. That had been the difficult bit. Clearing the next hurdle, the Commons, would be much easier.

Ninety per cent of Tory MPs, Ulster Unionists and most Liberals would be on our side. Labour would play party games. There would be a strong unofficial whip to vote us down but we hoped some Labour friends would abstain. In the event, the only Labour MP to come into our lobby was Tom Pendry, MP for Stalybridge, who had won a libel action over false allegations of having sex on the Commons Terrace. Neil was very touched by Tom's loyalty but saw he was the sole Labour MP in the milling throng and was anxious he should not blot his copybook. Once MPs are in the lobbies the doors are locked, so Tom could not get out without voting. Neil told him to secrete himself in the gents until the coast was clear.

The amendment was passed and we were elated. No longer could the *Guardian* hide behind ancient laws. We could pursue the case, albeit many months and a lot of hard work after it started. Neil had made parliamentary and legal history as the only person to amend the Bill of Rights in 300 years. That must be a good excuse to break open the fizz! But someone else had grander ideas. Alistair Cooke, a long-time, true and dear friend who ran the Conservative Political Centre, suggested, 'Why not invite Margaret and Denis for dinner?'

'Don't be ridiculous, Cookie!' I said. 'We can't invite Margaret Thatcher for dinner.'

'Of course you can. If everybody thought that, she'd never get invited anywhere. I'm sure she'll be delighted.'

Margaret had been one of our strongest supporters, so why not? I rang her secretary and issued the invitation. As I sat and wondered who else to invite, I began to have second thoughts. Could we really expect her to come to our funny little flat? I tell people they cannot fail to identify our 1960s block, sandwiched between attractive Victorian mansion flats and houses, 'it's the one that looks like a Soviet lunatic asylum'. They unerringly find it. The lift stops one floor below us so you have to clamber up the final flight. Things have improved now, but then the paint in the stairwell was peeling and the carpet was old and threadbare. Cookie told me not to be so silly and Neil assured me she wouldn't even notice. Within 24 hours the message came back: Margaret and Denis were delighted to accept, what about 19 July? Crumbs! We had a date. There was no time to lose. The Celebration Dinner to mark the passing of the 'Hamilton Amendment' and the Royal Assent to the Defamation Bill 1996 was under way. There could be no celebration without Gerald and Lizzie Howarth, and Joanna Trollope and her then husband, playwright Ian Curteis also accepted. I was sure Margaret would be fascinated to meet Ian, who had been commissioned by the BBC to write *The Falklands Play*, which they then refused to broadcast because it was too patriotic and sympathetic to Margaret. Cookie, of course, had to be there and also Timothy O'Sullivan, Gerald Nabarro's former research assistant who was working on a book about Margaret.

I knew I could rely on the guests but how was I going to cope with the food, when I had also to be the perfect hostess? Fortunately, I had a secret culinary weapon up my sleeve in the ample shape of our friend Vanessa Binns, who had been BBC Masterchef in 1992. Vanessa was to be my saviour and instantly jumped at the chance to come down from Cheshire and cook for Margaret. I breathed a sigh of relief, relaxed and began to plan the details.

It was a clear, warm evening so we were able to have drinks and canapés on the balcony, looking out over the trees of Battersea Park. Denis was in tremendous 'Dear Bill' form and the evening rollicked along. The beef was sublime, cheap at twice the price, and as we were finishing the main course Alistair said, 'May we pause and toast the passing of "The Hamilton Amendment to the Defamation Bill".' As I raised my glass, I glanced across at Margaret and commented, 'Well, at least now I'm married to a little footnote in history.' Margaret looked wryly at her husband: 'I'm sure Denis sometimes wishes he was married to a little footnote in history, too.' It was not intended as a put-down and neither did it come across as such. We roared with laughter but the truth was there. Life for both of them would have been easier, but far less exciting, if Margaret had not been one of the major figures of our time.

Vanessa was working her magic. As well as being a hugely entertaining guest, Cookie was busy 'butlering' away, collecting plates and generally ensuring I had nothing to do except enjoy the company of our guests. Denis ate nothing at all after the first course, a delicate ragout of fish with basil. As for the world's most expensive roast sirloin of British beef, he just moved it around the plate and concentrated on the wine! Margaret, of course, sank her teeth into the red meat, as you would expect.

We had been told their car would be waiting around 10.30 p.m. At 11.30 p.m., things were still very much in full swing when Margaret looked at her watch.

'Come along, Denis. We must go.'

'Yes, darling,' he replied, simultaneously picking up the decanter of port and pouring another large glassful!

It was a memorable evening of fun with friends, in what were to become increasingly turbulent times.

CHAPTER SEVENTEEN

Volte-face from Fayed

Neil identified the historical precedent for Mohamed Fayed's assault on Parliament – Guy Fawkes! Having failed to obliterate the DTI report or obtain a British passport, Fayed resolved to 'blow up' the government with his own modern-day Gunpowder Plot. His fantasies were to prove more explosive politically than the intrigues that led to 5 November 1605 so, in justice, he should now be burnt in effigy every year. But, sadly, it was our fingers that got burnt.

Fayed himself never again referred to his original allegations. Faced with incontrovertible proof of his lies, this Ali Baba of deceit simply cried 'New lies for old! New lies for old!' Ignoring the exploded 'money via Greer' story, and without a word of explanation for the change, he now made *completely* new claims. This time, he remembered not to give hostages to fortune by alleging anything that could be disproved by documents or independent witnesses. He now alleged he had *personally* given Neil specific amounts of cash or Harrods gift vouchers on twelve specific dates, in one-to-one meetings, with *no* witnesses or records to substantiate his claims.

This, of course, was wholly inconsistent with his original claim that Greer had made the payments to MPs, not him. Over the years we got used to this syndrome; if a charge was disproved it would be instantly discarded and replaced by others. Fayed had used exactly the same tactic on the DTI inspectors and they concluded: 'One of the difficulties confronting anyone seeking to test the truth of the Fayeds' account of the generation of their wealth is that the story changes as different parts of it are demolished or discredited.'

Fayed's second set of allegations also quickly fell apart. On one day when he claimed to have handed Neil £2,500 in cash at his Park Lane office, Neil proved he was in Tatton 200 miles away, campaigning in the election. On another, when Fayed alleged he had passed him Harrods gift vouchers, Neil had been accompanied by Timothy O'Sullivan, who at the time wanted to write a history of Harrods, so Neil had taken him to meet Fayed. Neil was never out of Timothy's sight and he swore Fayed gave him nothing. Additionally, the dates when Fayed claimed to have given Neil money and gift vouchers as direct rewards for PQs bore no relation whatever to the dates of any parliamentary activity. Furthermore, Fayed could produce no records of the alleged Harrods gift vouchers, despite Harrods' legal obligation to maintain issuing and redemption records for accounting and tax purposes.

Having amended the Bill of Rights, Neil revived his case and the trial was fixed for 1 October 1996. The *Guardian*, having thought it would never have to defend its stories in court, suddenly faced this prospect in a matter of months. Unknown to us, they began a frantic scramble for more ammunition. Fayed's uncorroborated word was less than worthless – yet this was all they had. Action was needed. They were risking millions of pounds to defend their allegations, their reputation and their skins. They were on seriously shaky ground.

Ali Baba rubbed his lamp again. It was time for another opportune swerve in the allegations. There is no moral brake in Fayed's mind. Always surrounded by yes men, their mouths well stuffed with gold, he was used to destroying people without conscience or comeback. In two or three weeks, however, he would face expert forensic cross-examination as the *Guardian*'s sole witness to his alleged 'cash for questions' payments. Clearly, he would be ripped to shreds. Something had to be done and so, nearly two years after Neil's resignation, the famous 'brown envelopes' were born out of thin air. But before we learned anything about them, a far more devastating blow was to fall on us – delivered by our own side.

On Thursday 26 September 1996, Neil was booked to make an after-dinner speech at a British Telecom conference at Althorp House, Princess Diana's family home. Unaware of the impending storm, we set off from Cheshire to drive to Northamptonshire. I was at the wheel while Neil scribbled a few speech notes. Suddenly the telephone rang. It was Andrew Stephenson, the solicitor handling our case at Peter Carter-Ruck & Partners.

Andy is an undemonstrative person, with a quiet ruminative voice, and he is methodical, painstaking, placid and realistic – ideal qualities in a solicitor. Neil was not surprised by the call; the trial was due to start in five days. 'Hi, Andy! All set for Tuesday? How are things going?' Neil did not say very much. Andy was evidently reporting on last-minute details. There was a long gap in the conversation at Neil's end. Then I heard him say, in a matter-of-fact way: 'Oh! Hmm. Yes. OK. We've got to sort this out. What time suits you best?'

I did not pay much attention – calls from lawyers were ten a day, if rather more costly than two a penny. Neil volunteered nothing and, as we were running a little late, I was more concerned about how and where I was going to change into evening dress. Looking back, there must have been something wrong with my usually acute antennae as I had no inkling he had just received totally shattering news. We arrived at Althorp and went upstairs to change, rushing to complete the trans-formation before meeting the conference delegates as they poured into the drinks reception. At dinner in the Great Hall, I sat next to Neil and opposite Charles Spencer. We none of us could know that Charles himself would soon have a significant part in the increasingly bizarre Fayed soap opera.

Although enjoying the splendid surroundings, I began to realise there was something wrong with Neil. He was uncharacteristically subdued.

'What's the matter? Don't you feel well?'

'It's nothing. I'm fine.'

But I could see he was not. His speech was well received with plenty of laughter and no-one else would have known anything was amiss. But I knew his performance fell short of our exacting standards. As we were departing down the long drive, I stopped the car and demanded to know what was up. Neil has always been immensely protective. Until the evening was over and we were no longer on public display, he had been determined to shield me from the dreadful revelation that, for reasons beyond our control, our lives were about to disintegrate yet again. Sitting just inside the gateway of one of Britain's stateliest homes, he told me the awful truth that Andy Stephenson had imparted earlier. There was 'a problem with Greer's evidence'. He had made huge undisclosed payments to Michael Grylls, tens of thousands of pounds, contrary to the evidence they had both given to the Members' Interests Committee.

You may wonder why this mattered – it was nothing to do with us. It would not have mattered had our cases been entirely independent. However, at an early stage, despite our fierce opposition, the *Guardian* applied to 'consolidate' our two libel actions, joining Neil and Ian's two separate cases into one and making them joint plaintiffs; the newspaper argued it would save costs and court time to try them together. Unfortunately, the judge agreed and the die was cast. We were aghast at the time because, as the *Guardian* hoped, any weaknesses in Ian's case would infect our own. How right we had been to try to prevent this happening. We were about to pay a terrible price for the judge's acquiescence.

We did not yet know the details but were obviously in a very serious mess and desperate to learn the full extent. We had intended to return to Cheshire but, clearly, it had to be London. We could not face the drive that night and stayed in the nearest Travelodge, in suitably surreal contrast to the grandeur of Althorp. Sleep was difficult but I knocked myself out with a pill for a few hours while Neil spent the night with his mind in turmoil, trying to fathom how our lives could have taken this ghastly and entirely unexpected turn. More to the point, he was racking his brains for a solution. We had trusted Ian and Michael, never once imagining they might share a guilty secret. Surely it was not true? Please God, let it not be true.

We woke early and sped to London. Andy Stephenson greeted us at Carter-Ruck's office, clearly in a similar state of shock. Throughout he had been Ian's solicitor as well as ours, sharing Ian's confidences, guiding him through the murky legal waters. Not all lawyers are bloodless automatons. Most invest enormous emotional capital in their clients' litigation, especially when cast in terms of Good vs Evil as ours was. Andy, too, had received a major body blow and could scarcely believe the events of the last 24 hours.

He explained what had happened. Ian was seeking £10 million in compensation for the total loss of his business. To verify this claim, he had to allow a microscopic forensic examination of his accounts. Any suspicion of impropriety would undermine his case, but Ian was gung ho and we had no reason to suspect anything untoward. Devastatingly, we were mistaken.

From 1974 to 1983, I had worked closely with Michael Grylls, but never had any inkling of a financial tie-up with Ian Greer. Much more importantly, neither Ian nor Michael had subsequently told me or Neil about any such arrangements, despite Ian's joint involvement in massive litigation. I had enjoyed working for Michael and quickly became part of his lively family. His daughter, Lara, is spirited, entertaining and fun. His son, Edward ('Bear'), born just after I started working for Michael, recently became the youngest Briton to climb Everest and is now a noted adventurer. Michael was a kind and considerate employer, good company and made an excellent speech at our wedding. He appeared on what was my favourite photograph of the most important day of my life. Because our previous relationship had been so close, I was even more shocked to realise what he had concealed from me.

Michael had deliberately hidden the true nature and extent of his financial relationship with Ian Greer. He had not recorded it correctly in the Register but, more seriously, he had misled the Select Committee on Members' Interests when it questioned him in 1990. He admitted receiving three commission payments for introducing new clients to Ian, whereas he had actually received at least six plus a retainer fee, something Greer had always denied paying to any MP. The total payments exceeded £100,000.

Ian's credibility was totally destroyed. Very shocked at his exposure, Ian announced he would unilaterally withdraw, leaving Neil to fight on alone. However, not only had their cases been officially yoked, Ian was also an important witness for Neil on many of Fayed's allegations and he was now wholly discredited, his case high and dry. We were also gasping for breath.

It suddenly became all too clear why Michael had tried to dissuade Neil from taking legal action. In particular, I remembered an incident shortly after the whole saga began. Sally, his wife, arrived unannounced at the grim, windowless little office in the attics of the Commons that Neil had been allocated after losing his ministerial room. In a state of some agitation, she begged us not to proceed with the case. 'Please drop this case. You must. God does not want you to go ahead.' I cannot imagine He had an opinion either way but what Sally failed to say, catastrophically for us, was that Michael wanted us to drop the case for fear of what it might reveal about him. Had Michael been candid about his links with Greer, the course of our lives would have been so different. It would have changed the whole legal approach – the two cases could not have been consolidated because of an obvious conflict of interest between Neil and Ian. If Michael and Ian had admitted the problem, we could have dealt with it in good time. They didn't and we were about to pay the price.

Neil was livid and reacted furiously when Andy explained the true nature of their deception. Ironically, had he been able to react more calmly, shrug his shoulders and carry on, life might have been easier. But he was incandescent with Ian for allowing this time bomb to tick away, while we ran up debts of hundreds of thousands of pounds and risked everything. Like the *Titanic*, we had been steaming in thick fog towards an iceberg. Ian and Michael knew it was there. They could have warned us but for two years chose to say nothing.

Listening to Neil's rage, Andy realised he could no longer act for him either. Law Society rules dictate that where an irreconcilable conflict of interest arises between joint clients, solicitors cannot thereafter act for either. Andy, with whom we had worked so well for two long years, had the difficult job of explaining that he was professionally obliged to walk out of our lives at this supreme moment of crisis. He was choked and could hardly speak, but it was over in a matter of minutes and he left the room. I collapsed on the floor in a corner of the office. Due in court after the weekend, we had no lawyers to represent us and one of our key witnesses was now proved to have lied. Because of the strict rules, Andy had no choice, effectively, but to hand us a copy of Yellow Pages, and leave us to get on with it. How could we continue?

In theory, we could instruct new solicitors and counsel. But it would take weeks for them to read into such a complicated case and would cost us at least another £100,000, which would not be recoverable from the *Guardian* even if we won because they could not be held responsible for our duplicated costs. We were already on our beam ends financially. We could postpone the trial but it would be months before we got another date. An election was looming. With all the prejudice inevitably caused by Greer's withdrawal, how could Neil possibly face that with his own case unheard?

We knew the press would go into overdrive, kicking and knifing us savagely when we were helpless in the gutter, unable to defend ourselves. But even we did not anticipate quite how awful it would be and how low they would sink, led by the *Guardian*; another tanker of poison was to be poured on our heads with maximum publicity, working its vicious way into the national psyche. Could we ever hope to recover?

We had reluctantly agreed that Friday morning, unknown to Fayed, that we had no choice but to abandon the case. It was *after* that decision had been made, and not before – the timing is very important and verified by lawyers – that the 'brown envelopes' emerged. As if the Greer/Grylls problem was not enough, we were also told a few hours later that 'a solicitor' had apparently come forward with a statement supporting Fayed. This turned out to be Mrs Alison Bozek. Bozek had been a hostess on a small private airline Fayed bought in 1981. Obviously satisfied with the quality of her service, he transferred her to his private office where, for thirteen years, she operated as his most trusted gatekeeper and PA. She left Fayed's employ on 30 September 1994. Despite limited academic qualifications, she was awarded a much-coveted training place at top-of-the-range City solicitors. Such firms have the pick of the annual crop of law students with first-class academic qualifications, but Bozek had other important qualifications. This firm had represented Fayed in the lucrative Lonrho litigation. It was unlikely to be a liability to provide sanctuary to one of the closest associates of the fabulously rich, notoriously litigious Fayed, despite his unsavoury reputation.

And so, just three days before our case was due to be heard in court, and virtually two years to the day since Fayed had told the *Guardian* and the world he had *no* witnesses to back up his story, three new witnesses miraculously popped out of the woodwork – all long-serving personal staff. Bozek worked for him from 1981 to 1994 as his most senior, trusted confidential assistant. Her colleague, Iris Bond, has been Fayed's personal secretary since 1979. The third surprise appearance was Philip Bromfield, doorman at his office in Park Lane since 1983.

Their existence was news to us and their allegations were startlingly different from everything Fayed had alleged hitherto. Until that moment, there had been no mention of Neil receiving 'payments in brown envelopes', which is not surprising as it never happened. Indeed Fayed had very specifically and deliberately claimed quite the reverse – that there were no witnesses at all. Very convenient. If no-one was present, if no-one saw anything, if nothing was traceable, nothing videoed, nothing recorded, then it was just Neil's word against Fayed's. That, of course, had been the problem for the *Guardian*'s lawyers. They knew Fayed was a notorious liar and needed a free-standing story where he would not be the main witness.

By immaculate conception the myth of 'brown envelopes' was born. While Fayed spent two years making contrary allegations, Bozek remained invisible. Now, conveniently, she 'remembered' regularly stuffing banknotes into envelopes to be collected by Neil from the desk at Park Lane manned by Philip Bromfield. Bond, equally mute for the last two years, also 'remembered'. No, they could not be specific about dates. Yes, signatures were always required in a book when packages were deposited or collected, but none of these vital records had survived. Sadly also, despite constant video surveillance of the desk, no film footage of Bozek leaving brown envelopes or of Neil furtively collecting them could be produced. Amazing, isn't it?

The new allegations amounted to this: Neil had collected unspecified amounts of untraceable cash on unspecified dates with no records of any kind. If true, Fayed and his staff could have disclosed this at any time in the last two years, but they had all been silent as the grave. Their stories contradicted the original *Guardian* fairy tale of Fayed paying Greer by cheque and Greer then paying Neil. They also contradicted Fayed's replacement allegations of personally paying Neil in cash without witnesses. Cash payments, made in private with no witnesses and no records, cannot be authoritatively proved or disproved and that, of course, was the crucial point. But it was *not* the Bond/Bozek allegations that made our situation impossible. It was the Greer/Grylls revelations, which had come earlier, that forced us to abandon the action.

Our immediate need was for lawyers to represent us while we extricated ourselves from the wreckage. Few solicitors specialise in libel and, as the last service he could offer us, Andy put out a couple of calls to other solicitors explaining the conflict of interest. Neil needed solicitors, could they help? Thus we found ourselves at 5 p.m. that Friday afternoon in the offices of Messrs Crockers at 10 Gough Square, a secluded courtyard off Fleet Street.

We were ushered into the boardroom to await the arrival of the senior partner, Rupert Grey. We had never met this man but were about to place our life in his hands. Andy could accompany us to hand over the files and make introductions but then had to withdraw, professionally, from our lives. He remains a good friend and we shall always be grateful for his unflagging and steady stewardship in both euphoria and despair. Neil's brother-in-arms, Gerald Howarth, once more put his own affairs on hold and rushed to be with us.

I was mentally and physically shattered. Less than 24 hours earlier our lives had fallen apart but here we were, still having to put one foot in front of the other. We had no option but to cope with an impossible situation. We sat round the huge boardroom table and Rupert breezed in, a tall impressive figure in frock coat, with a mane of unruly black hair. He shook hands with everyone, sat down, put his arms on the table and said, 'Well, now, what's this all about?'

I literally slid from my chair and on to the floor in a crumpled heap. I simply could not hold myself upright any longer and the thought of having to start from the beginning and explain everything was just too much. Neil took a deep breath and began to fill Rupert in on the details while I lay in the corner of the room, head on a coat, and closed my eyes against the harsh realities of our world. We would have to settle for the best terms we could get from the *Guardian*.

There were further meetings over the weekend, in particular on Sunday when we had to confront Ian Greer face to face for the first time since we had learned the truth. Having admitted his fault and apologised to us by telephone on Friday, he was now cloaked with a new lawyer on whose advice he had changed his tune completely, seeking to blame Neil for the breakdown of the case. This was a grotesque perversion of the truth, as Andrew Smith, Ian's managing director, has publicly confirmed. Andrew resigned on the spot when he learned Ian had so grossly betrayed him and us. He had had no idea that vast amounts of money were being paid to Michael Grylls.

As the hours wore on, an agreement was thrashed out. We would drop the case, all bear our own costs and that would be that. It sounded so simple but it was devastating. We knew the *Guardian* would now launch a vengeful propaganda offensive against us. That, on its own, would not have been so bad. But it would be just the tip of the iceberg and we would be monstered throughout the media. Not fighting the case to the finish in court would be interpreted as an admission of guilt. The true story of the Greer/Grylls deception would be buried deep beneath the heap of editorial ordure about to be poured over us.

It was the ultimate 'lull before the storm'. It was a strange, unreal feeling knowing something still secret was about to explode over an astonished world, and that we would be caught up in a hurricane of overwhelming immensity. As the hours and minutes ticked away my emotions ebbed and flowed. Part of me refused to accept what had happened. It was just too terrible to be true. Fleetingly, stupidly, desperately, I thrashed around in my mind to find a way to stop the inevitable, to make it not happen, to stop the oncoming tornado in its tracks.

I was mentally drained and physically worn out; it was as though my very entrails were being torn out before my eyes. A brief moment of tranquillity can occur just after waking, with luck lasting a couple of seconds, before the crushing weight of real life resumes. I felt totally inadequate to cope with the terrible ordeal ahead. But there was no choice. After a frantic weekend of legal wrangles, we had to present ourselves at court the following Monday officially to discontinue the action. The frenzied, jostling scrum in the corridor outside the court was indescribable.

The headlines and saturation reporting were brutal, accompanied by the worst archive photographs the picture editors could find. The general line was predictably, 'Hamilton would fight on if he was innocent.' Superficiality ruled the day. Not one paper bothered to scratch the surface of the story. I didn't see any of the coverage at the time – Neil was adamant I should not look at the papers or TV – but it was impossible not to be aware of what they were saying. It was like being broken on a wheel. My battered body could take it no more. I was in despair. But, in public, I was determined to be brave, hold my head up high, stand shoulder to shoulder with Neil. I know him so well but, even as his wife, I cannot imagine what it must have been like for him to read the press, to see himself utterly destroyed and left for dead in the cold.

I just wanted the world to go away and leave me alone. As always, Neil was resolute and lost no time in dealing with the practicalities of our situation. He immediately announced he would ask Sir Gordon Downey, Parliamentary Commissioner for Standards, to investigate the allegations. It was not exactly ideal but it was the only chance we had of clearing Neil's name. We placed our faith in this former civil servant to conduct a full and fair inquiry, if not replicating the procedures of a court of law then at least observing the principles of natural justice. But it was not to be.

Chapter Eighteen

Death of a Career, Birth of a Battleaxe

In May 1997 the Parliament would have endured five years, automatically triggering a general election. Against this deadline, Downey announced he would publish his report in early April. On 17 March John Major announced the long-awaited election for 1 May; Parliament was to be dissolved. Downey would just be able to publish and the stress would be lifted from our lives. We were very unhappy indeed about the way he had conducted his inquiry. Downey was not a lawyer and the QC drafted to help him lacked experience of cross-examining witnesses in criminal trials. The inquiry was held in secret with no-one on oath, despite Neil's request that they should all be. Neil was not allowed to see all the evidence against him nor was he allowed to cross-examine witnesses. All he could do was send written suggestions of questions and hope Downey used them to good effect. Downey flatly refused to hear evidence from ex-Fayed employees whose testimony would have contradicted that of Bozek and Bromfield. Despite that, we were confident he would come to the right conclusion and Neil would be exonerated before the campaign began. Needless to say, it was not as simple as that. Yet another shock was in store.

Neil was in the Chamber for the weekly Business Statement. To his utter amazement, he heard the Leader of the House announce Parliament would be prorogued at the end of the week, leaving us in limbo. There would be no Parliament for Downey to report to. It was the kind of legal nicety with which we had had to grapple for so many years, but nothing could be done. Downey was being kicked into the long grass. Neil rushed to the Whips' Office. Were they mad? How could we be expected to go into an election with this issue unresolved?

No answers, just embarrassed shrugs. So, despite earnest efforts on our part, Downey's report remained under lock and key and we had to fight the election with the allegations suspended like a guillotine above our heads.

Ironically, had the report been published Neil would never have been able to fight the election, the 'Battleaxe' would not have been born and I would certainly not have written this book. Another example of the inscrutable workings of Providence! What seemed yet another devastatingly unfair hammer blow was a blessing in disguise. But the comfort of hindsight was still some way ahead.

Now the gloves were off. Major had decided on the most protracted campaign of modern times – six weeks instead of the usual three. The outcome nationally was a foregone conclusion to all but the purblind in the Downing Street bunker. The Tories had lagged well behind in the polls since the ERM debacle in September 1992. Tony Blair had positioned 'new' Labour several miles to the right of Margaret Thatcher in 1979, so there were few policy controversies to divert the media. Personalities were bound to dominate – not exactly the hapless Major's strongest suit. Added to which, Labour's media manipulators, Peter Mandelson and Alastair Campbell, had resolved quite ruthlessly that Tatton should occupy centre stage.

With some trepidation but reasonable optimism, we began the campaign to retain the fifth-safest Conservative seat in the country. Neil's majority in 1992 was 15,860 and boundary changes had improved his position. It should have been a walkover, however unpopular the government. Yet the media had found Neil guilty already; no-one was interested in the mundane detail, only in lurid headlines.

In January, this feeding frenzy had been aggravated by a Channel 4 *Dispatches* programme made by two radical-left journalists, Richard Belfield and Christopher Hird of Fulcrum Productions, in cahoots with the *Guardian*. Interestingly, as graduates of the Fayed Academy of Propaganda they went on to make *The Secrets Behind the Crash* for ITV, which propagated Fayed's preposterous claim that the royal family and MI5 had conspired to murder Princess Diana to stop her marrying a Muslim, Fayed's son, Dodi.

Dispatches made no pretence of objectivity. It opened with a voice-over intoning that John Major's government depended on a number of MPs 'fighting to save their reputations'. In a darkened room a grainy photograph of Neil appeared. Another earnest voice-over introduced him: 'Neil Hamilton, former Minister for Trade and Industry and the man who dropped his libel action in the "cash for questions" scandal. A man battling to be believed.' Fayed was wheeled out with his allegations of free shopping, gift vouchers and free holidays. 'If he is innocent, why did he run from the court case?' No explanation was given of the true reason.

A variety of axe-grinders then appeared disguised as impartial witnesses: Brian Basham, who (undisclosed by the programme) was paid by Fayed as his PR guru; Liberal MP David Alton, who (undisclosed by the programme) had presided over a bogus campaign against 'Tory sleaze' funded by Fayed to the tune of £1 million; Andrew Gifford, founding partner of lobbyists GJW, which (undisclosed) was one of Greer's main rivals. Gifford was (undisclosed) a significant shareholder and director of Fourth Estate Ltd, publishers of *Sleaze*, a vile propagandist tract against Neil, written by David Leigh (undisclosed as a *Guardian* journalist and brother-in-law of *Guardian* editor, Alan Rusbridger). Fourth Estate was (undisclosed) half owned by the *Guardian*, whose editor Alan Rusbridger delayed submitting his written evidence to Downey to coincide with the programme.

Rusbridger wrote to Downey asking him to watch the broadcast and denying *any* personal involvement in it. Yet, named in the programme's credits, was Jamie Wilson, one of the *Guardian*'s 'cash for questions' team. And this hypocritical crew were accusing Neil of undisclosed conflicts of interest! The programme, a hatchet job as vicious and dishonest as *Panorama*'s 'Maggie's Militant Tendency' thirteen years earlier, generated huge attention and press comment. It subsequently formed the basis of our libel case against Fayed himself but, at the time, it merely added petrol to the flames licking around our funeral pyre.

Additionally we had to cope with two weekly local papers distributed free to every house, the *Wilmslow Express Advertiser* and its Knutsford sidekick. By sheer bad luck they were owned by the *Guardian*, who used them mercilessly to attack us in the most tendentious manner for months on end. The *Guardian* also owned the *Manchester Evening News*, our main regional daily, so we did not get a fair run from them either. In Knutsford a rival paper, the *Knutsford Guardian* (confusingly, no relation to the enemy) was balanced and fair. But, in Wilmslow and Alderley Edge there was no competitor to counter the weekly dose of vitriol in the *Express Advertiser*. Neil demanded the right of reply but the editor (a *Guardian* puppet) refused to print it, claiming it was libellous to Fayed.

Fortunately, it was not all doom and gloom. As when the BBC had struck in 1984, we were blessed with an amazingly resolute constituency chairman in the solid and dependable shape of County Councillor Alan Barnes. Indeed we were twice blessed because Alan's wife, Joan, was equally loyal and determined. They are a formidable and wonderful pair, very well known through charity and local government work. Alan had endured far worse pain than us in life – having survived a horrific car crash as a result of which he lost an eye and had to have his face entirely rebuilt. We could not have wished for greater support, guidance, leadership, loyalty and friendship throughout the most difficult and tempestuous times. And, of course, there was still the amazing Peter McDowell, Neil's agent, who battened down the hatches and calmly dealt with the media storm and the divisions that broke out within the Conservative Association.

We tried, with difficulty, to have a normal Easter. My brother and his family were staying, together with our dear friend Diana Rasbach. 'Razzie' had already been a tower of strength and support and was destined to be with us on many critical occasions in the future. We could not even attend church on Easter Sunday without a rabble of photographers. After Easter the family departed and we heard rumours of an 'independent' candidate standing. Various names canvassed in the press included Terry Waite, who had been born in the constituency at Styal. However, Terry Waite, an honourable man, refused to be exploited in a cynical electoral ruse. Several others also ruled themselves out and it began to appear that this balloon was deflating when, suddenly, on the Sunday after Easter, we heard someone had taken the bait. The Ego had landed.

I had, of course, seen Martin Bell on the BBC News. I knew little and cared less about his private life, his politics or his disenchantment with the BBC. Foreign correspondents are supposed to report the view from all sides. But in Bosnia Bell had become a Reporter-with-Attitude who could no longer cover issues dispassionately. While there he had bonded with *Guardian* reporters and, in particular, celebrated photographer Tom Stoddart, partner of Labour MP Kate Hoey, and Tony Blair's official photographer in the 1997 election.

Bell was having one of several midlife crises. In 1996 the BBC had given him hardly any decent stories to cover and, the last straw, was refusing him a starring role in its national election coverage. He was being dispatched for the duration to a Scottish backwater. Demanding centre stage, he threatened to walk out in a huff. On 3 April he opened an exhibition at the Royal Festival Hall of Stoddart's photographs from Bosnia entitled 'Edge of Madness'. Afterwards, at dinner with Stoddart and Hoey, he lamented his fate at the BBC. According to Bell, Stoddart said, 'Martin, we're looking for someone just like you. You would be perfect for the job,' and outlined the plot that was to transform his life and ours. The 'job' was to stand as 'Independent Anti-Corruption' candidate for Tatton. Labour's candidate would stand down and they would get the Liberals to do the same, giving Bell a clear run. In the normal party dogfight Tatton was unwinnable for either of them. With the demonisation of Neil and the Tories' record unpopularity, it might just work to combine the anti-Tory vote in a 'whiter-than-white' candidate standing for 'motherhood and apple pie'. The idea appealed to Bell's self-image as a moralistic white knight fighting for Good vs Evil. Although he knew nothing of the detail of the controversies swirling around Neil, he had imbibed the headlines and superficialities. This would give him the starring role he craved and which the BBC had denied him.

This Machiavellian plot was the product of two fertile but cynical minds: those of Peter Mandelson and Alastair Campbell. Its success depended on finding what Lenin called a 'useful idiot' of no known political views likely to upset people. Bell fitted the bill. Amazingly, he had never voted in a British election. Immediately after dinner, Stoddart phoned Campbell with the news. Cock-a-hoop, Campbell instantly rang the Liberals who, equally cynical, jumped at the wheeze. Next day, Campbell called Bell; later, none other than Paddy 'Action Man' Ashdown, Bell's old soul mate from Bosnia, telephoned offering full support and urging him to take the plunge.

Curiously, if Tatton had been a less safe Tory seat, Neil might have been less vulnerable. Neither Labour nor Liberals had any chance of winning so neither had anything to lose by 'giving it away' to Bell. His intervention would keep media focus on Tatton, turn the national spotlight on to what would otherwise be just a local issue, put 'sleaze' on the national agenda and implicate the whole Tory Party. It was a spectacularly powerful publicity stunt.

On Saturday 5 April 1997, Bell had dinner at his Hampstead home with another chum from Bosnia, Colonel 'Bonking Bob' Stewart, former commander of the Cheshire Regiment. Stewart made Bell's mind up for him and by Sunday morning the decision was made. Bell was rushed north to meet the Tatton Liberals, who agreed, by just six votes to five, to pull their candidate out. 'New Labour', predictably, proved much more malleable. Bell was driven to a rendezvous with a Labour activist in a car park. In classic cloak-and-dagger fashion, he switched vehicles to go to another car park to meet the Labour candidate and then on to the pub where the local Labour executive was in session. They had already been squared by the intellectual force of John Prescott at an earlier meeting, the result was a foregone conclusion and only a handful dissented. Bell headed back to Hampstead for dinner at his favourite restaurant, La Gaffe.

All these machinations were kept very quiet indeed. The following morning, on his own admission, Bell felt like a fugitive as the enormity of the enterprise was borne in on him. But the bandwagon was now rolling so fast, it was impossible to jump off. A complete ingénu politically, he phoned both Labour and the Liberals for advice on what to do next. He was told to make it clear he was standing for one term only. Tory voters would be far more likely to switch. It might be worth another 10,000 votes.

Just four days after his dinner with Tom Stoddart, with little idea what the allegations against Neil were and no knowledge of or curiosity about Neil's side of the story, Bell found himself holding a press conference to announce his candidature at the Institute of Civil Engineers in Westminster. The room had been thoughtfully booked and the £375 cost paid by the Labour Party. What price his much vaunted 'independence'? Disingenuously, Bell declared he was 'not trying to prejudge Mr Hamilton over the issues still under investigation by Downey'. Well, if not, what was he doing there? He didn't care whether Neil was guilty or innocent. He cared only about the self-aggrandisement of Martin Bell.

Bell's intervention increased the media pressure still further. We were besieged and battling away before the cameras on the front lawn. Bill Roache telephoned. The veteran *Coronation Street* star and his wife Sara live in Wilmslow and we first met them at an event just before the 1987 election, ten years earlier. Lining up for a press photograph, Bill whispered furtively, 'We've got to keep that lot out – how can I help?' I had no idea he was even a Tory. We quickly roped Bill into the campaign and into a walkabout in the pedestrian precinct in Northwich, Labour's stronghold in Tatton. People were astonished to see him and queued up for autographs which, cleverly, he wrote on Neil's leaflets. I chuckled at the likely reaction in Labour households when children came home proudly bearing Bill's signature blazoned on Tory propaganda. Once Bill had cut his political teeth, he went to marginal seats all over the Northwest, as Neil did not need the support.

Ten years later, however, things were very different. Bill was appalled by the Bell caper and rang to ask how he could assist. What a friend in need! 'If you could just turn up at the house and show support in front of the cameras, that would be tremendous.' Not only did he arrive but he brought his young son, William, providing the press pack at the end of the drive with some extra 'colour' for that day. I fell into his arms for a great warm hug, gaining strength from his presence. His *Corrie* glamour generated much positive press, his endorsement giving us a tremendous morale boost. By sticking his neck out he risked upset with his bosses. Bill knew Granada would not be happy to see him taking such a public stand in our favour, as they discourage their stars away from controversial politics, but he didn't care.

As fate would have it, the following morning heralded the first day of the rest of my life as a Battleaxe. It was Tuesday 8 April. Bell had scheduled a press conference for 1.30 p.m., at his hotel overlooking Knutsford Heath. Back at the Old Rectory I was trying, as politely as possible, to get the press to shove off from our driveway. An ITN crew presented themselves, hopefully, at the front door. When I said 'no comment' for the umpteenth time, they helpfully told me they would all be off shortly because Bell was holding a press conference at his hotel. I went back inside and relayed this news to Neil, feeling relief that we would be spared media attention for a few hours at least. Neil's reaction was the diametrical opposite and much more positive. 'Is he indeed! Well, I'm going along to ask him a few questions. Let's see if he can answer them.'

He raced upstairs to put on a suit and tie. It was a perfectly normal and modest Prince of Wales check suit, later described by a sketch writer as his 'Terry-Thomas outfit, in bounder's check'. I did not want to go, indeed argued against it for purely selfish reasons. I did not want to launch into the limelight. I had had enough of the press. But, togetherness and solidarity won the day, so I tagged along. It would have looked odd had I not been there in the background and wrong conclusions might have been drawn. If only I had known the images would be on every news bulletin, beamed around the world and appear in every national and many foreign newspapers next day, I would have smartened up a bit and tried to look more like Mrs Tory MP. Instead, I rushed out in what I happened to be wearing – garish bright orange jeans and a truly multicoloured cotton sweater, my hair only half-brushed.

I quickly telephoned Peter McDowell, and told him of our plans. His office backed on to Knutsford Heath and Peter was with a small group of envelope-stuffers who would come down and support us. Neil's intended doorstepping of Bell was just the sort of jape Peter adored. It was a glorious sunny day. As soon as we were spotted, pandemonium broke out among the hundreds of journalists massing outside the hotel – there were too many to accommodate inside. It seemed as though we were surrounded by a seething mass of locusts, but we managed to get out of the car and made it on to the Heath. Questions were fired like cannonballs. What in heaven's name were *we* doing there? I pointed out sarcastically, 'Unlike carpetbagger Bell, we live and vote in Tatton. As constituents, we have a perfect right to come and question any candidate at his own press conference.'

After a few minutes, unaware he was about to be ambushed, Bell crossed the road through his own media scrum on to the Heath, accompanied by 'Bonking Bob' Stewart. The mob parted as Bell pushed through cameras, microphones and notebooks towards this unexpected confrontation with his uninvited guests. Neil and Bell faced each other like prizefighters in a ring, totally surrounded by an impenetrable crowd of journalists. Photographers standing on stepladders, giving height to the spectacle, shouted out their names, trying to turn them in their direction. After perfunctory handshakes Neil spoke first: 'I'd really like to know what act of corruption you think I'm guilty of.' Bell was flummoxed. 'I'll give you my answer,' he floundered, 'I don't actually intend to talk about you at all, though people are going to ask me about you . . . I want you to run on your record, against your record or whatever it is. I want a clean election. I may talk about trust. I think the issue of trust is important. And if, at the end of the day, the electors of Tatton feel they can trust you more than trust me, then, my goodness, they should elect you.' The candidate of probity had told the most stupendous porky in the opening words of his campaign: 'I don't actually intend to talk about you at all.' What else was he there to do?

I certainly hadn't planned to say anything. Neil was the candidate. I was merely the loyal wife. But we all have our breaking point. The sight of that sanctimonious little prig in his grubby white suit posing as the political equivalent of Mother Teresa was just too much. I could not keep quiet. I rudely interrupted Neil and demanded. 'Do you accept that a man is innocent unless proved guilty?'

'Yes, of course I do,' said Bell.

I fixed him with what Neil calls my 'gimlet stare'. 'So you accept that my husband is innocent?'

'I think there's a lot . . .'

I was not prepared to let the squirming fish off the hook. 'Do you accept that my husband is innocent?'

There was panic in his eyes now. Blinking like a rabbit caught in the headlights, Bell stammered, 'No! I'm not going to be facing ambush here . . . let's just . . . let's just see . . . let's just see what I have . . . I don't know! I don't know! . . . I'm standing here because a lot of local people have asked me to stand here . . . and the impetus comes from local people . . .'

'I thought it came from a dinner party in London,' I snapped back acidly. Goody-Two-Shoes had told his second giant porky.

Neil then cut in, 'I would just like to know that you are prepared to give me the benefit of the doubt on the allegations that have been made against me.'

'Absolutely,' said Bell firmly. 'Absolutely.'

Clearly, he had not been scripted by Labour HQ to deal with a Battleaxe. It was a blatant lie for Bell to claim he was standing because 'the impetus came from local people' when he knew the entire stunt had been dreamed up by Alastair Campbell and masterminded by Peter Mandelson. All I did at Knutsford Heath was stand up for my husband and the truth. I was burning with the injustice of it but my outburst was totally unplanned and spontaneous. Bell said later that nothing he faced in Bosnia had prepared him for the shock of meeting Mrs Hamilton. What a wimp!

The myth was born. When I saw myself on the television news later that day I was horrified. There I was booming on and on. I dissolved into tears. I had let Neil down. Christine, the virago, had ambushed and savaged Bell while Neil paddled along in her wake, unable to get a word in. I was the 'wife from Hell', the 'bossy termagant', the 'monstrous liability', 'to compare Christine Hamilton with Lady Macbeth is to insult Lady Macbeth' – that last one was from the *Observer* who, wisely in the event, sent their war correspondent to cover the election in Tatton! Actually, of course, he was there as a war-zone pal of Bell's, hardly independent.

The media delighted in portraying Neil as weak and inadequate, whereas nothing could be further from the truth. Without him I would have crumpled months earlier but, because I am noisier, extrovert and more voluble than he is, the press went to town portraying him as a downtrodden mouse, hiding behind my skirts. It was thoroughly unfair but it was all my fault. I was desperately upset. Neil, typically, would have none of it. Not only did he totally reject that I had, however innocently, done the wrong thing, he positively exulted in my steamrollering Bell, demonstrating his political ineptitude live on prime-time TV. He is very phlegmatic about these things, but it must have been excruciating for Neil to see the way my strength was used against him, to portray his imaginary weakness, not only in insulting cartoons but also editorial columns of serious newspapers.

Having not even been a household name in my own household, I was suddenly thrust into the nation's psyche, catapulted into the 'love her or hate her' category. I was totally unaware at the time, too absorbed in our survival, but opinions on my performance, as my brother told me, 'divided dinner parties'. I had been touched, never to recover, by the double-edged sword of celebrity. The Battleaxe had been conceived and born in a few short minutes on Knutsford Heath, with Bell the unwitting midwife.

My onslaught had thrown up Bell's total hopelessness for the task in hand. He was in deep water, not waving but drowning. Labour could not risk another exposure like that. We now know, from their own records of events, that Mandelson's storm troopers were immediately dispatched from Party HQ for the duration of the campaign, to control Bell's every written or spoken word, and mastermind his every move. There was to be no talk about policies, which is just as well as he had none, and nothing must be said that could be challenged in any way. It was to be all bullshit and blather.

Labour had to get Bell's show back on the road. Later that day he received a fax from Alastair Campbell. It contained a carefully worded open letter from Bell to Neil for Bell to release as if it were his own composition. Bell dutifully parroted it to the press waiting on the steps of his hotel that evening. It stated that he gave Neil the benefit of the doubt on the 'cash for questions' allegations and concentrated on a highly tendentious misrepresentation of the Ritz episode and Greer's commission payments, which were described as 'breaching the rule that MPs should not be for sale'. This statement was based on a completely misleading account of the allegations against Neil, printed in that morning's *Guardian*, which Bell had clearly not read before our encounter earlier in the day.

Bell's pathetic performance on the Heath caused consternation at the *Guardian* as well as at Labour HQ. The following day Rusbridger dispatched northward his brother-in-law David Leigh and another *Guardian* acquaintance from Bosnia, Ed Vulliamy. Their mission was to explain to Bell the allegations they had taken so much time concocting which, despite his obvious ignorance of them, were ostensibly the *raison d'être* of his candidature. They would ensure he would not be so humiliatingly unprepared a second time.

We were misguided enough to think Bell might just have an open mind. Perhaps, despite appearances, he might be a decent chap, possibly out of his depth. How naïve! He was too cowardly to dare debate the real issues, taking refuge always in the voluminous skirts of generalities and platitudes. As to 'open mind' and 'decent chap', suffice it to say that in thirty years of active politics I have never encountered such a fraudulent campaign. Politics is a dirty business but Bell and his acolytes plumbed new depths. Having served their purpose, Labour quickly dropped him in the sleaze, revealing (after the election) his breathtaking duplicity about the true extent of their and Liberal financial support, which included a staggering £9,000 in legal fees, blowing asunder his bogus claim of independence.

As if the Knutsford Heath confrontation were not enough for one day, we still had Neil's adoption meeting to surmount that evening. Press speculation that the Tatton Tories would not readopt Neil as their candidate had risen to fever pitch. We had been beleaguered at home for more than a month and our footsteps were dogged whenever we left. I don't think anyone camped outside overnight, but they were in place by 7.30 a.m. and there was always someone still waiting, hoping, when we finally retired, exhausted, to bed.

Joan and Alan Barnes drove us to the packed meeting at the Dixon Arms in Chelford and, although we expected a crowd, I have never in all my experience had to push through quite such a mass of photographers and journalists. The atmosphere was intensified because it was dark. Arc lights illuminated everything and cameras flashed madly from all sides as we got out of the car and tried to enter the building. I genuinely could not believe the intensity of the interest. Surely there were more important things going on, more pressing issues at stake? This was a general election for heaven's sake. The future path of the country was being decided. Why all this focus on one candidate in one constituency? I had reckoned without the Mandelson/Campbell propaganda machine, in overdrive to ensure all attention was beamed on Tatton. It suited them to have sleaze, sleaze, sleaze in the headlines. We were but pawns in their game.

Journalists were not allowed into the meeting itself, which was solely for paid-up Conservative Association members. Several unsuccessful attempts were made to bribe staff at the Dixon Arms to allow some press to slip into an empty adjacent room to listen through the door. In a tense and crowded meeting, there was both vocal support and unspoken dissension. I felt very uncomfortable sitting on the platform, my emotions whirling between intense gratitude for those who were supporting Neil so strongly, and disappointment that some erstwhile friends were not. Many sat silent and I could only wonder at their thoughts and voting intentions. When the vote was taken, Neil was adopted, with only 35 out of 282 actually voting against. As the result was announced, one or two of the minority burst out of the room to vent their fury to the waiting cameras.

Clearly, it would have simplified matters for the Tory Party high command if Neil had fallen on his sword and crawled away from the fight. Despite public murmurs of support, Conservative Central Office were not exactly helpful behind the scenes. Regular unofficial briefings were taking place to try to destabilise Neil and prevent his adoption, which again fuelled media speculation. By contrast, Michael Portillo was outspoken in his public support on television, for which we were very grateful indeed.

It was a tough time. We were constantly in the spotlight, under relentless pressure from the media, and desperately worried about what lay ahead. My weight fell away effortlessly as I just could not eat. And I could not sleep either. Pills and alcohol would knock me out at first but I would always wake in the early hours, my mind racing, tormented by our multifarious problems. Awake for the rest of the night, I was constantly exhausted during the day, which made it harder to cope. And so the vicious circle continued. Media interest seemed insatiable and its full extent was inexplicable. TV crews from Australia, France,

Germany, the USA, Japan, Italy and Denmark pursued us, all wanting their pound of flesh.

Clearly prompted by my performance on Knutsford Heath, I received a fax next morning inviting me to appear on *Have I Got News For You* (*HIGNFY*). I could hardly have swanned off to London to do a comedy show in the middle of a serious campaign. The opinion polls were unremittingly negative for the Tories and Neil was bearing much of the brunt of national media attention. *HIGNFY*'s producers had to be content with a promise to appear after the election. I was genuinely surprised that, whatever the outcome, they thought I would still be regarded as news.

I have always tried to conduct myself with dignity, whatever the pressures I am faced with. However, there is one incident that mortified me at the time, but that I can now laugh about with the cameraman in question. The strain was beginning to tell and it was a challenge to maintain good humour in front of the unrelenting pressure from the media. Things were bad inside the house, Neil and I were snapping at each other, needing an outlet for our turbulent emotions. I saw a posse of people with equipment coming, yet again, down the drive. I stormed to the front door and found not one but four camera crews. Given my real feelings, I was remarkably restrained but told them to get lost in no uncertain terms. Then, suddenly, I did the one thing I knew you should never do. With arm outstretched, I put my hand firmly over the lens of a television camera and pushed it backwards. However intense the pressure, that sends out all the wrong signals and is not dignified. They backed off. I went inside knowing I had, momentarily, lost control. Shots of my hand coming aggressively towards the camera would be on the evening news somewhere. Neil, as always, was understanding, comforting and totally without censure. There was nothing on the news and I later learned that Sky News deliberately chose not to use it, which was pretty decent of them. They've shown it since, of course!

HIGNFY were not the only people who took notice of my performance at the Battle of Knutsford Heath. The following day the house resembled the set of the farce *Boeing, Boeing*, with journalists running in and out of doors, the central characters – Neil and me – trying to prevent them discovering each other. We hoped for positive publicity, so I agreed to many interview requests. But we felt it advisable to keep the scribes apart so they did not feel they were on a conveyor belt. I was the one on the conveyor belt, as Neil isolated the competing journalists behind the scenes, but our timetabling efforts were undermined by the unpredictable length of the interviews. I was in the drawing room finishing an interview with the late Lynda Lee-Potter (*Daily Mail*), while Jane Moore (*Sun*) was waiting in the kitchen, Rosemary Carpenter (*Daily Express*) was on the telephone and Robert Hardman (*Daily Telegraph*) was in Neil's library. Jane Moore ended up writing her piece on my computer while I posed for her photographer back in the drawing room. Fortunately, the *Yorkshire Post*, Sky and *Richard and Judy* were scheduled for the following day!

The Hamilton saga became an industry of its own. In the hot weather, an enterprising ice-cream van would park in our little country lane providing ice-cold relief for the press, its childish chimes sounding an incongruous note of reality. At election meetings, the police turned up in case of a scrum. Bell, having nothing to say and no policies, had no organised public meetings of his own. It was impossible to carry on a normal campaign but we had to try. Canvassing was out of the question – who wants to come to the door to face a dozen cameras and notepads? We received a welcome from most places, but not all, and there were some thoroughly unpleasant moments. One nutter would turn up at meetings with a banner reading: 'Behind Every Bad Man There Is a Wicked Woman.' The Labour/Bell campaign was ruthlessly efficient. Hundreds of volunteers were brought in. Neil's posters were routinely torn down or defaced with brown envelopes and pound signs. It was devastatingly hurtful but we had to soldier on.

Needless to say, once Bell had thrown down the gauntlet, other bizarre cranks, crackpots and publicity-seekers followed suit, making the campaign a farce. The most extraordinary candidate was 'Miss Moneypenny', an already tall man wearing a garish flounced frock who, when dressed in transvestite gear, with high platform shoes and birdcage atop his head, reached the alarming height of about seven foot six. Unlike Bell, who ran a mile, I took the trouble to talk to him – as best I could from my more modest five foot eight. He was actually rather amusing and provided some welcome light relief and diversion for the press. He turned out to be a highly educated science graduate, taking advantage of the media spotlight to have a bit of fun and advertise a gay nightclub. Tragically, he died a few years later.

About halfway through the campaign, Neil was reading the morning papers in bed and announced that unless there was some movement in the opinion polls we were going to lose. With a unified opposition, we could possibly survive the personal attacks or government unpopularity, but not both. As we drove along a quiet lane, the neat Cheshire countryside which had been 'ours' for the last fourteen years and that should have been 'ours' till retirement, looked perfect in the brilliant spring sunshine. Neil stopped the car and, tears welling in his eyes, said imploringly, 'Surely, those bastards can't take all this away?' But the polls were unforgiving. The sheer weight of hostile propaganda sealed our fate. We toured the committee rooms on polling day, 1 May 1997, knowing the election was lost. It was obvious from the detailed returns that the votes were not going into the boxes. Bell polled 29,354 votes and Neil trailed with 18,277. The 'Hamilton factor' probably accounted for half the difference, the national swing accounting for the rest. If all Tory candidates had had a combined candidate against them, only twelve would have been elected that day. We had made superhuman efforts to swim against the torrent that washed us away but, even with all our stalwart supporters, a couple of individuals simply could not match the firepower of money and propaganda ranged against us in the most unpropitious climate.

The count itself was a surreal experience but something we just had to get through. There was, as always, saturation media coverage and we arrived in the sure knowledge we would be leaving empty-handed, without the initials MP after Neil's name. It was bad enough having to cope with our personal situation and emotions, but we also felt we had let down our supporters who had worked so hard against what proved to be impossible odds. If only we had not been so optimistic. If only they had not been so loyal to Neil, when it would have been much easier to dump him and choose someone else, they would still have had a Conservative MP. Many were in the hall that night. It was very hard for them to bear the exultation of local Labour and Liberal activists, disguised behind white Bell rosettes, and the derisive cheering of interlopers, parachuted in from London for the campaign, who would melt away now their marionette was in place.

In a peculiar way I felt relieved. After all the fighting, the battles, the hopes and the fears, the pressure was gone. The decision had been made. We could do no more. We had been bucked off. Although I did not realise it at the time, that particular horse was one I would never wish to bridle again. We had no idea what the future would hold or what a big, bright and often brash new world was opening up before us.

CHAPTER NINETEEN

Unemployment – Objects of Curiosity – Downey

We awoke on 2 May 1997 to a new world of unemployment. I couldn't bring myself to get out of bed. There were no tears; I just lay in total numbness, staring at the ceiling, unable to comprehend the enormity of what had happened to us. How could everything have ended like this? I wanted to crawl away from the limelight for ever, away from the prying lenses, away from the endless stupid questions, away, away, away from life itself. But that was not an option. There was no alternative but to press on, to put one foot in front of the other, and the first step had to be to drag myself out of bed. With Neil's eternal patience and encouragement I got myself going and together we prepared to begin the rest of our lives.

The outlook was bleak. Shoulder to shoulder with our loyal supporters, we had fought long and hard against a dishonest campaign. Mandelson and Campbell had won and we had lost. Such is democracy. The *Telegraph*'s Robert Hardman asked me if I had considered counselling. He might as well have asked about a flirtation with CND. 'Counselling?' I replied, in pure Lady Bracknell. 'Tosh!'

It was tempting – and it would certainly have been easier – to stay inside, lick our wounds and keep out of the eye of the storm. But, although down, we still had plenty of fighting spirit and there were things to do. The traditional Royal May Day celebrations were taking place on the Saturday, culminating as always in the parade arriving on Knutsford Heath for the crowning of the queen. Hundreds of children take part in a pageant unchanged down the years. The whole town turns out for a day of fun and frolic. Battered and bruised, we were in no mood for any of that but I suddenly realised we had to go. Neil was a patron of the event, we had accepted months ago and I felt we had more right to be there than Bell the interloper. Although it was my decision, when the moment came to walk on to the Heath I felt nervous and hugely self-conscious. Absolutely no-one would have been expecting us to turn up and I was very unsure of the reaction we would get. I need not have worried: we received an overwhelmingly warm reception. We had made our first tentative steps back into public life.

There were immediate and pressing problems. Having been DINKYs (Double Income No Kids) we were suddenly NINKYs (No Income No Kids), which, as my ever-resourceful mother pointed out, 'Well, darling. It's better than being a NISKY (No Income Six Kids).' What on earth were we going to do? We had both lost our jobs overnight in the most public way imaginable. Instead of income, we had huge legal bills and many more battles to fight.

We sat down like any unemployed couple and decided our priorities. What did we have to spend and where could we save? Some budgets could not be cut — the mortgage, insurance, car and, of course, alcohol! My prop through all the stress and strain was essential — I would starve first. Yes, we lived in a large and valuable house but, despite the popular misconception, we do not live extravagantly and have relatively modest tastes. We were amazed to discover we spent around £1,300 a year on the printed word, much of which went unread and sometimes even unopened. Newspapers and magazines, part of the old job, were cancelled instantly. We haven't taken regular papers since and don't miss them at all.

Defeated MPs get six months' salary, a welcome cushion that gave us a breathing space to find alternative employment. But there were dozens and dozens of ex-Tory MPs after the meltdown of 1997. There would be few takers for any of them, especially one pilloried for years on the front pages of the national newspapers. Or for his wife. Unexpectedly, it was precisely that predicament which kick-started our new lives, although we did not know it at the time. We were high-profile and unemployed. One of the topics on *Kilroy* the following week was 'unemployment' and Robert Kilroy-Silk asked us to take part. I didn't particularly relish the prospect of being savaged by a studio audience on live television, but it was work and a chance to put our side of the story.

The studio was packed with the unemployed, from bankers to builders, including some moving hard-luck stories. I felt very uncomfortable and sensed we were in for a bad time. Robert wished us luck and then we were off. The questions and accusations came thick and fast. 'How can you claim to be unemployed? . . . Your pay-off is more than I've ever earned in a year . . . How do you expect us to identify with you? . . . You deserve everything you've got – hope it gets worse.' Robert tried to broaden the discussion but, inevitably, we were the main focus. We did not seek sympathy ourselves, but could readily sympathise with and understand something of the distress and trauma faced by the others. For once people were able to see the real Hamiltons. Afterwards one of the cameramen approached Robert: 'What the hell was that – a promotional puff for the Hamiltons?'

Yet, all we did was be ourselves. One unemployed man, who had been sitting opposite me in the semicircle, saying almost nothing, approached me afterwards and said, 'I came on this programme really to have a go at you but you're obviously so warm and genuine I completely changed my view.' I hugged him with tears in my eyes. We had been allowed to talk for ourselves, something impossible in the animal frenzy of the election, and people had responded positively. Perhaps there was a life for us away from politics after all.

Originally issued in direct response to my savaging of Martin Bell, the invitation to appear on *Have I Got News For You* was now also extended to Neil. It was the first and last time in the show's history that 'one' guest has been two. I was delighted I would have his support and, also, by the very practical consideration that we would now each get a fee of £750. Neil had never seen the show but was about to appear in one of the most watched and oft-repeated episodes in its history. Friends expressed concern at what Ian Hislop, Paul Merton and Angus Deayton might say and do, but we had already had so much excrement dumped on our heads from the lofty heights of the editorial columns of serious newspapers, there was little the trio could throw at us in jest that we had not already suffered in deadly earnest. We both have a good sense of humour and are not afraid of laughing at ourselves. As for the editing, we just had to trust to their sense of fair play.

It had already been agreed that I should be on Paul Merton's team. Ian's guest was the brilliantly witty actress Maureen Lipman, who had come hotfoot from Falmouth, where she had campaigned hard and successfully for Labour against Sebastian Coe. Our paths were destined to cross again later, when she told me she had been a little unsure what to make of us. She had slightly wished for a more 'normal' guest on the other side and was amazed to hear me say: 'Are we supposed to have read the papers?' I knew we would be hopeless at the 'silly stories' round. We had been far too busy making our own news to have much time to read about anybody else's.

HIGNFY is recorded on Thursday evening, and before the audience arrives you take your position in the studio to be shown the photographs for 'odd one out', the pictures to be captioned, the newspaper headlines to fill in the missing word. You then have about an hour in the dressing room to scratch your head, think up some clever lines and wonder what act of madness led you to pit your wits against the professionals. In theory, you discuss the basics with your team captain. Not that Ian or Paul have any intention of sharing the glory of their sharp lines, but it does help to sort out who recognises whom in the photos and identify any mutual gaps in knowledge. Paul was in the middle of his divorce from Caroline Quentin and spent all his time on the telephone to solicitors, completely eliminating any chance of preliminary conferring. Researchers had reassured me Paul would know all the 'silly stories' so I need not worry about any of them. With no Paul to ask, however, Neil and I were floundering in confusion with extraordinary tales of pigs falling out of aeroplanes over Cornwall, and so forth. Angus Deayton wore a white suit, a satirical nod to Bell's trademark attire. During the show I incautiously mentioned that Margaret Thatcher had sent us a supportive message, saying how sorry she was Neil had lost. Ian cut in immediately, 'That's the first time she's ever shown compassion for anyone unemployed.'

We knew we were the human sacrifice for the evening and took the barrage of cutting barbs and one-liners in good part. Most were very funny and, fortified by a few liquid 'stiffeners' in the dressing room, we had no difficulty laughing genuinely. I positively enjoyed the programme. It was pacy, racy and fun. The only moment when Neil felt really uncomfortable was right at the end when Angus handed him a huge brown envelope. Ostensibly containing our fee, it was filled with scraps of paper – I checked just in case! We took it in our stride. We could hardly do anything else in the context of the programme. In retrospect, it was an obvious gag. We should have seen it coming and thought out a humorous response. We don't mind people making jokes about us and the things that *did* happen, like the Ritz visit; indeed we often make such cracks ourselves. But we never jest about the things that didn't happen, like the brown envelopes. We suffered seriously as a result of that lie and would hate to give an impression of treating it lightly.

I think we handled a potentially difficult situation reasonably well and gave as good as we got. We certainly presented the editors with a task because we recorded ninety minutes (instead of the usual sixty), which had to be cut to thirty. The final programme was well balanced and we had no complaints. Ian Hislop was between a rock and a hard place. He loathes Fayed (as editor of *Private Eye* he had christened him the 'Phoney Pharaoh') but he wasn't exactly a fan of the Hamiltons either; as a hardened cynic, I am sure he still isn't. He said later that he thought we had come out of it too well. Perhaps he had expected me to burst into tears like Paula Yates.

The programme proved highly popular, and people frequently tell me how much they enjoyed and admired our performance. Coming in the same week as *Kilroy*, various other smaller programmes and two large double-page spreads in the tabloids, *HIGNFY* confirmed us in our new role as 'professional objects of curiosity'. Not exactly the career path of choice, but it was keeping the wolf from the door.

In the second jobless week we were still in high demand as television fodder. So much was happening it was sometimes difficult to think straight. We were booked to appear on Sky. Halfway to London, we pulled in to Warwick service station on the M40 for petrol. Neil filled the tank with diesel instead. He had every reason to be distracted but it was a disaster. The car could not be moved and we had to be in a Westminster TV studio in a couple of hours. Luckily, at the adjacent pump Neil espied a familiar face – Tory peer, Lord Inchyra. He had never previously spoken to him but explained our plight, hopped into his car and left me to sort out the wreckage!

A few days after the election we received a letter from Jonathan Hunt, a TV journalist who had produced a highly regarded series of investigative reports for Granada TV called 'On the Hunt', exposing idle and inefficient bureaucrats for wrecking people's lives. He realised during the election media circus that he wasn't hearing Neil's side of the story and wondered if we would be interested in a TV programme taking an objective view. We did not know Hunt, but could lose nothing by exploring the possibilities, so we agreed to talk.

A few days later he sat in Neil's sprawling, untidy library.

'I expect you're sick of being interviewed by the media about the Fayed allegations.'

'No,' replied Neil. 'Not at all. No-one has wanted to discuss my case in any depth.'

Jonathan was incredulous. 'What? In all the time the story has been running not one national newspaper reporter has been to see you to hear your side of the case?'

'None. They've stood at the gate in a pack, demanding denials and not giving me a chance to explain, but no-one has actually asked for my version of events.'

I could see Jonathan was stunned but intrigued. He was concerned about investing time and money in a TV programme, only to be overtaken later by one of the bigger companies muscling in.

'What makes you think anyone else will want to speak to me?' asked Neil.

'Surely someone will? The man who lost his seat, the pain he went through and so on.'

'If no-one's been near me in three and a half years, I don't think they'll be around now there's a new government to concentrate on.'

With that Jonathan began what became several years' hard labour, sifting, reading, analysing every single piece of evidence from all sides. We gave him a free run of our files in a project that eventually expanded to PhD proportions. In due course, Jonathan's book *Trial by Conspiracy* gave the full picture, but that was still years ahead. After an initial trawl through mountains of documents, Jonathan decided he needed extra help and persuaded a film editor, Malcolm Keith-Hill, to assist. An avid anti-Tory and no admirer of ours, Malcolm's natural scepticism would be ideal for critically assessing our evidence. Throughout June, the pair pored over the paperwork and held dozens of Q&A sessions with Neil.

Meanwhile, we still hoped to turn the tables and vindicate Neil. The difficulty was to persuade the media, obsessed by triviality and sensation, to take a serious interest in the true story below the mendacious superficialities of brown envelopes and Ritz dinners. After Greer's case collapsed, the *Guardian* had damned Neil in a self-serving and highly biased account, totally misrepresenting his case. It had done the same during the election, publishing a hatchet job of the then confidential and unpublished evidence to Downey. Even the hapless Sir Gordon condemned this as 'selective quotation, a gross breach of faith and contrary to the principles of natural justice'. Occasionally, the *Spectator* had allowed Neil to write a few articles refuting Fayed's allegations as they mutated and the *Telegraph* printed some helpful editorials and articles, but no-one was interested in a serious investigation to discover the truth behind one of the biggest political stories of the decade.

Daily life continued and we had the gruesome job of clearing Neil's office at Westminster. A tiny, airless, windowless box, it resembled the Black Hole of Calcutta, except it was in the roof rather than the cellar, and we had absolutely no pangs leaving it behind. They don't give you long to scoop up 14 years of your life (in Neil's case; 26 in mine). We did a preliminary sort-out in the week after the election and returned the following week to find everything had been dumped in cardboard boxes and binbags in the bowels of the Palace, along with the belongings of the other electoral casualties too slow to remove all traces of their existence. How quickly one becomes a non-person. At the Commons I received the warmest possible welcome from one of the security men. A big hug and, 'Cor, I wish you were back here Christine, this lot's dreadful.'

I still miss the camaraderie of the place. Whether you worked as a secretary, police officer, in the canteens or restaurants, the post office or wherever, it was a big happy family and, after 26 years, I was one of the senior members. But there was no time to be maudlin about the old days. With no guarantee of regular employment from the media once we ceased to be news, we had to manufacture fresh sources of income. We talked endlessly during journeys up and down the motorway, turning over and over in our minds what we might do. Suddenly, about three weeks after the election, Neil came up with an idea: 'Look, the press has cast you as a Battleaxe, let's turn a potential liability into an asset.'

The title popped out of his head fully formed – *Christine Hamilton's Bumper Book of British Battleaxes.* It was the beginning of the rebranding of Mrs Hamilton. I told him not to be ridiculous but, a few minutes later, took out a pen, started scribbling down potential candidates and by the time we reached Cheshire we had a gallimaufry of gutsy girls. But nothing could be achieved without a publisher and we had no idea where to turn. Our good friend Gyles Brandreth, who had just lost his seat in Chester, put us in touch with Jeremy Robson, whose company Robson Books had many big names on its list. We prepared an A4 sheet to sell the idea, sent it to Jeremy and he telephoned by return, 'I like it, let's talk.' We subsequently learned that it was his wife, Carole, who had been so instantly positive. A meeting with Jeremy sealed the deal and my career as an author was about to begin. The distraction of *Battleaxes* gave me a positive focus through many subsequent days of great despondency, when nothing seemed to be going our way.

After the election we were begging for the Downey Report to be published, looking forward to our vindication and resurrection. By then both Jonathan and, more surprisingly, Malcolm, were firmly of the view that Neil was innocent of Fayed's allegations. Finally we were told the report was due out on 3 July 1997. Neil was to be allowed to look at it privately for a couple of hours in advance of its release to the press. Gerald Howarth, newly re-elected as MP for Aldershot after five years in the wilderness, collected Neil and took him to the House. We had arranged to meet at Razzie's flat in Westminster for a celebration lunch before the good news was announced. Jonathan and Malcolm paced the floor while I answered the incessant telephone calls, each time hoping it would be Neil.

Jonathan wanted exclusive footage and had hired a crew to film my elation when Neil phoned to say he had been cleared. Every time the phone rang the camera started rolling as I picked up the receiver. Each call was a false alarm, just another media enquiry. What on earth was taking Neil so long? I waited with mounting apprehension and foreboding. I rang Razzie. Neil was there, but she said he could not come to the phone.

'Jonathan, you talk to him. Find out what's going on.'

Neil did come to the phone. 'Don't let your facial expression betray anything, Jonathan, Downey has found the evidence against me . . . well, the word he used was "compelling". Don't say anything to Christine; just bring her here so I can tell her myself. Don't let her drive.'

'What is it?' I demanded. 'What's happened?'

'Nothing, let's go to Razzie's.'

Jonathan's bluff failed. I went to the bedroom and called Razzie again, demanding Neil came to the phone. He was quiet and composed. 'I didn't want to tell you over the phone but Downey found against me. It's pretty grim, I'm afraid, you'd better come over here straight away.' It is a cliché to say I felt numb; but I did. How could Downey possibly have come to this conclusion on the basis of such flimsy and obviously flawed evidence? I returned to the sitting room to find the camera rolling to catch my immediate reaction. I was in a turmoil of disbelief and despair and the camera was the last straw. They were supposed to be there to capture my joy, not my anguish.

'Just say something, Christine,' Jonathan coaxed. 'Something for the record. We may need it.'

Drained of emotion I could only say, 'Downey's got it wrong.'

'So what happens now?'

'Well . . .' I raised my hands and shrugged. 'We just have to carry on. Life goes on.'

Later, that snippet of film appeared on ITN News but the brave face belied utter desolation. How could we recover from this?

Downstairs we squeezed ourselves into our old Rover. The electric window was jammed half-open but nobody cared. The air was warm and we were lost in our own thoughts. I was too stunned to cry. As I went into Razzie's flat Neil came over, kissed me awkwardly and led me to a sofa, where we hugged each other silently. Gerald spoke in hushed tones to Rupert Grey, our solicitor. Razzie was distraught and shocked, self-consciously fussing with the buffet she had prepared for the celebration that had turned into a wake. None of us could understand what had gone wrong. What was so 'compelling' to Downey? How were we going to weather the deluge of recrimination about to engulf us?

It was horrible, nightmarish, incredible but true. Downey, after presiding over a kangaroo court, found so-called 'compelling evidence' that Neil had taken payments from Fayed to ask questions in Parliament. Despite the gravity of this finding, and the profound impact on our lives, he could not say when any money had been paid, how much, or by what method, but concluded it must have been between £18,000 and £25,000. This was a cavalier attitude to figures for someone who had been Comptroller and Auditor General, responsible for auditing the nation's accounts.

Downey had sat in private with no-one on oath, so nobody could evaluate the evidence or credibility of witnesses as things proceeded. Fayed could not be believed unless independently corroborated, so it all boiled down to his employees. Downey could produce no findings of fact – of course not, there were none – and resorted instead to the 'broad thrust', which is exactly what Fayed intended. The inconsistency of the detail did not matter to Downey as long as the allegations against Neil were of the same 'broad thrust'.

Neil was not even allowed to *hear* Fayed's witnesses giving evidence against him, let alone *cross-examine* them. Their credibility was absolutely crucial to Downey's findings. It was clear from the transcript that Nigel Pleming, Downey's QC, had made no serious attempt to cross-examine them nor to evaluate the weight of their evidence. Neil had written with suggested lines of questioning which Pleming either wasted or didn't use at all.

Downey even had a tape recording of a conversation between Fayed and Rowland (recorded secretly by Fayed) in which he confirms he gave Neil no cash — it all came via Greer, an allegation that had already been disproved. But Downey had simply reversed the legal burden of proof, leaving Neil to disprove Fayed's allegations. Yet how could he prove a negative, i.e. that he didn't take unspecified amounts of untraceable cash, offered for unspecified reasons on unspecified days, spent in unknown ways, with no records of any alleged payments? Downey gave no reason or justification for his decision, nor did he make any analytical refutation of Neil's cogent and forceful criticisms of the inconsistencies and gaps in the evidence of Fayed and his employees. Downey ignored the fundamental principles of natural justice and would not answer any questions about how he arrived at his flawed conclusions.

Downey even withheld evidence from Neil so that he could not comment on it; one glaring example will suffice. Neil's telephone conversation with Michael Heseltine, while under siege at the Wilmslow school, had been reported to Cabinet Secretary Sir Robin Butler, who made a *very* misleading note about it: 'Mr Hamilton has given Mr Heseltine an absolute assurance that he had *no financial relationship* [my italics] with Mr Greer.' Neil had not used these words — and that question was not asked — but he did not see Butler's note until three years after the conversation. If only he had seen it at the time, or if Downey had been sufficiently fair and open-minded to show it to him when it was tendered as evidence against him, he would have immediately corrected the mistaken impression. Butler had neither overheard the conversation nor shown his inadequate minute to Neil or to Heseltine for confirmation that it was accurate. Hence, a damaging myth had arisen that Michael had asked Neil a catch-all question, whether he had ever received *any* payment for *any* reason from Greer, rather than his specific question about payments 'obliging' him to provide assistance to Greer or his clients.

Michael had actually confirmed that the minute was misleading in a letter to Downey: '... my concern was to ascertain whether Mr Hamilton had had any financial relationship with Mr Greer *which might have put him under an obligation to him.*' [My italics.] Despite the fact that this letter clearly proves Neil did not lie to Heseltine (of course he didn't), Downey conspicuously failed to tell Neil of its existence. When questioned afterwards Downey said it was 'not relevant' – although he had treated the issue as crucial to Neil's reliability as a witness. Perhaps it was just not convenient for Downey's conclusions.

Downey also refused to hear evidence from other ex-Fayed employees whom Neil wished to call as witnesses and whose testimony would have contradicted that of Bozek and Bromfield. Flying in the face of the most fundamental principles of the law of evidence, he illogically found 'strong support' for Fayed's allegations against Neil in the fact that Fayed *had* paid Tim Smith. But the fact that A (Fayed) has paid B (Smith) is obviously no proof he has paid C (Neil). No-one denied Fayed's infinite capacity to make corrupt payments to anyone; but that did not guarantee he had made them to Neil. Guilt by association is a feature of primitive societies. It was disgraceful that Downey gave it a moment's credence.

Later, in our libel action against Fayed, his QC George Carman sought to use such evidence in court but the judge refused to allow him, calling it 'irrelevant, and highly prejudicial'. Fayed's witnesses had contradicted themselves and each other and their evidence was peppered with inconsistencies. Yet Downey commented on none of this and simply passed over all Neil's reasoned arguments in silence. Months of work wasted.

At Razzie's flat we had about an hour and a half before the report would be released and the missile explode. We could see it coming towards us, knew exactly when it would hit, but were powerless to change its trajectory or avoid its path. We could have escaped from the media: they had no idea where we were and the storm would eventually die down. But that is not our style. We had nothing to hide and nothing to be ashamed of. And so we walked, hand in hand, the few hundred yards to Millbank studios, where we knew the scrum would be waiting. As we approached we encountered a pack of starving wolves falling on and fighting over their prey. They pushed and shoved each other to gain prime position, following us from one studio to another. We sat together in one soundproof cubicle as Neil did a radio interview, while the hacks outside dementedly tried to snatch photographs through the tiny window. Physically cornered, we could scarcely move around the building. It was a savage and brutal two hours.

We had just begun to pick ourselves up after the election defeat when, yet again, we had been bloodied. I kept telling myself life goes on. But how and in what form? Despite the obvious shortcomings of the process, of which we had been well aware and which have now been changed by Parliament so no-one else has to suffer the same injustices, we had made the mistake of pinning our hopes of justice on Downey. What now? Sound bites and headlines are seductive. Although Neil was permitted to make a written response published a fortnight later, no-one in the media could have cared less about the detailed criticisms. Memorably, Neil appeared on *Newsnight* and was answering a question from the then political editor, Mark Mardell. After half a minute or so, Mardell interrupted, 'But, Mr Hamilton, that's all detail.' Surely a programme like *Newsnight* should have been interested in detail. The truth was simple but proving it was not. It required careful analysis of the credibility and evidence of Fayed's witnesses, and understanding the tangled mass of Fayed's changing allegations, plus others made by political opponents and the media. If one could not rely on *Newsnight* for an intelligent approach, it was tempting to give up.

People ask me what were the worst moments of our various trials and tribulations. Despite later disasters, those post-Downey days were among the worst. Many may think, if that's all she's been pretty lucky. I know I am. I have been spared the tragedy of terminal illness, untimely death and other real human sufferings so many have to cope with. But, nevertheless, it was pretty grim.

Chapter Twenty

The Queen – Battleaxes – Fighting Back – the Mothers' Union

Life goes on and it was time to see the Queen. All MPs, even republicans, are invited annually to her garden party. Her Majesty cannot predict the date or outcome of an election, so invitations go out months ahead to all sitting MPs. Half of me did not relish another very public outing, but we presumed this was the last time we would be going. They are heart-warming occasions, where the Duke really does rub shoulders with the dustman. We knew we would come across numerous friends, but also some who would avoid meeting our eye. By then, I had developed very sensitive antennae and could feel black looks and veiled comments from a hundred yards away. But I didn't care. We had a joyous afternoon, saw many old friends and made new ones too.

One magnificent feature of the garden, slightly off the beaten track, is the 'Waterloo Urn'. We headed over for a little peace. Standing there was a slender, statuesque, beautiful woman, wearing a magnificent pearl choker, accompanied by a short, fat, balding middle-aged man (his own description) who greeted us *con brio*. It was serendipity in the form of Emma and Julian Kitchener-Fellowes. Julian was then best known for his part as Kilwillie in *Monarch of the Glen*, but has now swept to international fame with his Oscar-winning screenplay for *Gosford Park*. Emma, but for the regrettable oversight of her parents in producing a daughter, would be the next Lord Kitchener and it was she who taught me the immortal phrase, 'Christine, we don't do negative.'

Their instant, effusive response to us was hugely morale boosting when we were feeling especially vulnerable. I shall never forget the generosity of spirit of this life-enhancing pair at a time when we were discovering the meaning of true friends, as the fair-weather variety vanished into the mist. Julian knew all about our case. He was able not only to learn his own lines as an actor but to read between the lines of the actors in our real-life drama. Theirs, of course, was not the reaction of the tabloid press who predictably carped, 'How brazen can they be?'; 'Hamiltons flaunt themselves'; 'How could they embarrass the Queen?' But we were determined to carry on as normal, holding our heads high. We were certainly not going to allow Sir Gormless Dopey and his illogical report to stop us attending upon our Sovereign as loyal subjects. Besides, it is a jolly good tea!

Social events can be daunting if you have just attracted screaming tabloid headlines of the type normally reserved for child-molesters. Eyes seem to burn into the back of your head and every whispered comment must be about you. We were instantly recognisable and, to anyone naïve enough to take newspapers at face value, Public Enemy Number One. In an effort to cheer us up, a good friend gave us tickets to Glyndebourne, pretending he was unable to attend at short notice. I love opera but absolutely refused to go. Buckingham Palace was one thing, but I could not even face the local supermarket without headscarf and dark glasses and knew I could not cope with Glyndebourne if we were on our own. I could see the press gossip, 'Hamiltons have no friends . . . Hamiltons alone' etc., etc. It was just too predictable. In my fragile state, I was not going to walk into that trap. Neil told me I was being ridiculous. I was adamant but had reckoned without Cookie who, on hearing of the situation said, 'Christine, I would be honoured to be seen in public with you.'

Goodness knows how he obtained two extra tickets for that sell-out performance, but he did. On a glorious summer afternoon, we sped off, together with Brigid Utley, widow of the great T E Utley, the blind Tory sage and long-time pillar of the *Telegraph*. We shimmied into evening clothes in a lay-by, obtained the perfect picnic spot near the ha-ha, imbibed operatic quantities of champagne and salmon and wallowed in the music and spectacle. I was scarcely aware of the opera itself as my mind kept returning to our own horrors. The make-believe scenes on the stage seemed just a part of our own unreal world. For a while, though, I did forget our troubles and realised that nothing could take away from the warmth and comfort of genuine friends.

Meanwhile, *Battleaxes* had given me something constructive to do. Neil helped me with the research and his ready wit was always at hand as he risked life and limb touching up the individual Battleaxes. It was easy to find subjects. Margaret Thatcher, of course, the Battleaxe of the Century, followed by Joan Collins, Queen Victoria, Barbara Cartland, Elizabeth I, Boadicea, Nancy Astor, Cynthia Payne, Ann Widdecombe, Barbara Woodhouse . . . Thirty-two belligerent British belles to cheer us all up.

I had been working hard for a month and the book was well under way, when the Downey bombshell exploded. I was convinced the torrent of bad publicity would seriously undermine the potential success of *Battleaxes* and might make it unworkable from Jeremy Robson's point of view. Would he even want to continue? Would anyone want to read it? Neil and I went to see him in his office in the shadow of the Post Office Tower.

'Well?' I said nervously. 'Is there any point in going on?'

He could easily have taken the soft option and backed out. I would have understood. Jeremy, as always, was totally honest. 'I don't know,' he said. 'But we *are* going on. I believe in you and want to publish your book. So hurry up and finish the manuscript!' Jeremy and Carole have since become close and dear friends, and his support at that crucial moment helped restore my faith in human nature and brings a tear now as I write.

A few weeks later, *Marie Claire* asked me to take part in a feature about shoes. I laughed and said surely they were on the wrong track. They can be the sexiest things imaginable, but not for me because I am the horrified possessor of large feet. *Marie Claire* persisted. There were only two other people in the feature, Shirley Bassey and Mandy Smith, erstwhile teenage lover of Rolling Stone, Bill Wyman. Emily arrived for the interview. Going through my shoe cupboard, she gave the game away with her question, 'Where are the shoes you kicked Martin Bell with?'

I roared with laughter. Now I knew why they wanted me for the article. 'I didn't kick Martin Bell, I didn't touch him, thank you very much!' If that was the basis of the article they were under a mis-apprehension. Emily wrote an amusing piece and the photographs looked fabulous, but my shoe collection seemed pathetic alongside Dame Shirley's vast array.

As the weeks rolled by, we did an extraordinary range of press features and television programmes, even appearing at the Edinburgh Television Festival. Cautiously we began to sense things were changing. Gradually, as we received a positive response from strangers when out and about, I began to feel less self-conscious in public. Perhaps we were not the pariahs we had feared? The more inquisitive were starting to take a closer interest in what had happened and began to realise all was not what it seemed. It was dawning on people there might be more to it than blinkered Downey had wanted to see.

Then, on 31 August 1997 came the shocking news that Diana, Princess of Wales, had been killed in a car crash together with her companion of the moment, Dodi Fayed. Once the full horror of the tragedy had sunk in I wondered whether it would have any repercussions for us. I feared the death of his son would bring a wave of public sympathy for Fayed generally. Little did I suspect that he would soon dissipate that sympathy by his ravings that the Duke of Edinburgh had conspired with MI5 to murder Diana, fuelling the flames of a conspiracy theory.

We went for a welcome break in the Adirondack Mountains in upstate New York, where Neil was speaking to the National Center for Policy Analysis, an important free-market think-tank. Their gatherings are always convivial and stimulating, with speakers from around the world. It was therapeutic to enjoy anonymity. Meeting people who knew nothing about us or our problems enabled us to stand back from the minutiae of our own lives, and restored our perspective.

But a fortnight soon passes and we returned to reality in early October. Neil demanded the right to put his case in person to the Parliamentary Standards Committee to whom Downey had reported. Neil knew the now Labour-dominated committee would not seek justice and would just play politics, and rubber-stamp Downey's flawed findings — to admit Downey had cocked things up would undermine the new self-regulation system on its first major test. The advantage to Neil was that his appearance would be televised and shown live on Sky.

The secrecy of Downey had been disastrous. If people had had the chance to see the evidence unfolding they could have made up their own minds. When Downey published, everyone parroted his headline conclusions without even opening the thick volumes of evidence from Neil who had been denied the opportunity, afforded to every other MP investigated under previous inquiries, to see and comment on a draft of the report before it was published. Neil had only been allowed a couple of hours to see the *final* version before it was released to the press, when it was far too late to make any representations or point out any inconsistencies or factual inaccuracies. Once something is set in print the damage is done. A direct televised appeal might help to change public opinion and expose Downey's shortcomings.

Neil started his speech by referring to the death of Princess Diana and Fayed's invention of her last words, implying she was pregnant by Dodi. 'In the last few weeks we have been once again reminded of Mr Fayed's infinite capacity for invention. There are no depths to which he and his acolytes will not stoop to achieve his ends, even to exploiting one of the most poignant tragedies of modern times.'

He then set about demolishing Downey with devastating effect. Was Downey merely inconsistent or biased? When examining Fayed's bribery allegations against Michael Howard, Downey decided Fayed's employees were *not* independent and could *not* corroborate Fayed's claims. But, with Neil, he *did* treat them as independent and convicted Neil solely on their evidence. By contrast, he refused to hear four ex-Fayed employees who wanted to contradict their testimony. Downey had relied on highly prejudicial evidence, inadmissible in a court of law, and found Fayed's witnesses 'reliable', despite manifest contradictions and inconsistencies. Critically, he failed to investigate why Fayed made a complete volte-face in his allegations on the eve of the *Guardian* libel action coming to court, when he suddenly made totally new claims after two years about the 'brown envelopes'.

Neil also exposed the Fagin's Kitchen of Fayed's office and personal entourage. Tiny Rowland had told him that Fayed ordered his staff to break in to his Harrods safe-deposit box. Tiny's documents were illicitly copied and priceless emeralds and other personal and valuable items stolen. This was confirmed by Bob Loftus, head of security at Harrods, who received his orders from ex-Scotland Yard Detective Chief Superintendent John Macnamara, his immediate boss and one of Fayed's closest cronies. When Loftus protested it would be illegal, Macnamara bluntly replied, 'If the Chairman [Fayed] wants it done, we do it.'

The scene, had it not been criminal, would have been pure Ealing comedy. A locksmith was taken down to the dungeons where the safe-deposit boxes were stored. Once Rowland's had been illicitly opened the contents were taken upstairs to Fayed's office. In his presence, and under the supervision of former Metropolitan police officer Macnamara, using plastic gloves from the food hall the contents were removed, emeralds and other items stolen, everything copied and returned. Neil denounced

Macnamara thus: '. . . in charge of arresting shoplifters by day, in conspiracy with the chairman to break into safe-deposit boxes and rob their customers by night. If the head of security can behave like this under Fayed's orders, why should Fayed's personal secretary and personal assistant offer any resistance? The relationship between Fayed and his employees renders them suggestible to his improper suggestions.' Fayed hotly denied all this but, after many years of litigation, he paid several millions to Tiny Rowland's widow in costs and damages, implicitly admitting it was true.

Neil challenged the MPs: 'Each of you will have to decide whether your conscience will be clear if conclusions are endorsed which are so grave, based on procedures so flawed and evidence so flimsy as in this inquiry. It is not just my reputation at risk, but the reputation of Parliament itself.' As he fully expected, the majority remained impassive, but Quentin Davies and Ann Widdecombe refused to see injustice done. The chairman, veteran Labour apparatchik and chum of Downey, Robert Sheldon, had prepared a draft report endorsing all Downey's conclusions. Having heard Neil, Quentin and Ann refused to go along with this. They shamed the committee into *not* endorsing Downey's view about 'cash for questions'. Neil's performance had been electric and spellbinding. It was the beginning of the fight back.

The following week saw the launch party for my book and I invited all living Battleaxes. Cynthia Payne, Lady Moon, Jean Trumpington and Teresa Gorman all came but, sadly, Barbara Cartland was ill. The launch was to have been at Mary Sumner House, HQ of the Mothers' Union. Neil and I inspected the premises, Robson Books confirmed the reservation in writing and paid the deposit. A few days before the event, Jeremy telephoned to say the MU had reneged on their contract and left us high and dry. I was both perplexed and furious. Why had they landed us in this mess? All the invitations had been sent and the catering arranged. Suddenly, we had no venue for no given reason. I was also very upset, suspecting some MU high-up had decided Christine Hamilton was not a person they wished to be associated with. I happened to be in the area when Jeremy called, so I went personally to the MU to see the conference manager who had taken the booking. She haughtily declined to give me any explanation for the cancellation and said I should speak to the chief executive. It took some time for this panjandrum to descend from her heavenly cloud. She asked me to go with her into the chapel, perhaps thinking I would be overawed by the religious surroundings. I was not, and I did not think it appropriate for a business meeting. I was sweetness and light. With the Virgin Mary looking on, I proffered a copy of *Battleaxes*. She refused even to look at it, let alone touch it. Her mind was made up. I must not confuse her with the facts.

'What's the problem?' I asked. 'Is it because it's "commercial"?'

'No.'

'Is it me?'

'No.'

'Is it the presence of the media?'

'No.'

'Well it can't be the book – you haven't even looked at it.'

'No.'

'Well, why can't we hold it here?'

She held out a cutting from the Peterborough column of the *Telegraph*. It was a silly gossipy item but it transpired she was offended by the reference to the 'camp comedy' of the juxtaposition of *Battleaxes* and the Mothers' Union. It was the first I had heard of it; it was trivial and innocuous. But Mother Superior had decided. She declared the publicity might be 'unacceptable to members of the Mothers' Union worldwide' and was miffed the *Telegraph* referred to the 'Mothers' Union' rather than 'Mary Sumner House' – she being their founder. As if any of that was my fault! The deputy chief executive (male) rang down and ordered me off the premises immediately. Clearly, he hadn't the balls to do his own dirty work, preferring to hide behind the skirts of the women.

We were well shot of them. Not only did the MU have to compensate Robson Books but we transferred to the St James's Court Hotel who came to our rescue, even allowing us to do our own catering, unheard of at a major London hotel. The room was light and airy, far better than the MU dungeon, and the undoubted highlight of the party was Lord Longford and sex-madame Cynthia Payne in animated conversation together on a sofa. Such an incongruous pair looked like a game of 'Consequences' made flesh!

Cynthia's notoriety arose out of a quintessentially English sex scandal. The entire nation has been chuckling for years over events at The House of a Thousand and One Delights, a.k.a. Cynthia's home in Ambleside Avenue, Streatham. Her novel idea was to charge men for twenty-year-old luncheon vouchers, which entitled them to sandwiches made by

Cynthia, wine and a trip to bed with a willing woman. Cynthia was arrested and accused of running a brothel. In court, she insisted they were parties not brothels and the jury agreed with her. Eventually, bored with sex and looking for a career move, Cynthia turned to politics under the slogan 'Vote for me or I'll give you ten of the best.' As leader of the 'Payne and Pleasure Party', she did well in the 1988 Kensington by-election on a platform of legalised and wholesome prostitution! The first time we met she handed me her visiting card, a luncheon voucher on which she had naughtily scribbled 'To Christine -so sorry to lose one of my best girls.' She also gave one to my husband which said 'To Neil – so sorry to lose one of my best customers.' She is a life-enhancer!

While researching and writing *Battleaxes* was therapeutic, I did not realise quite what a financial lifesaver it would prove to be. I had been booked for several literary luncheons and began to receive increasing numbers of invitations to speak at lunches, dinners, conferences and events of all kinds, and *Battleaxes* provided excellent material, both humorous and serious, on which to draw. Neil and I went all over the country promoting *Battleaxes* and having fun. At a public school in the Home Counties we learned a useful lesson in salesmanship. The master in charge told us, 'Bring plenty of books. All the boys will have a copy.' My faint protestations that all two hundred boys were unlikely to purchase were swept aside. 'Of course they will. It goes on their parents' account for books.' The boys duly obliged and I happily dedicated copies to their mums who were blissfully unaware, on receiving them at Christmas from their devoted sons, they had paid for their own present!

I was invited to speak all over the place, including at both Cambridge and Oxford Unions. In Cambridge I spoke to a packed chamber with no mishaps. The Oxford Union was even more crowded; they were hanging from the rafters. During questions, a young man seated at the far end stood up and said loudly and clearly, 'Mrs Hamilton, why have you come here to lie on behalf of your husband, when he's perfectly capable of doing it for himself.' There was a mixture of applause and boos as the various sides supported their champion. I stood up and smiled, picking up the decanter of water. Walking towards him across the floor of the Union, in full Battleaxe mode, I boomed, 'First of all, that is slanderous. Second, if you come here and repeat it, I will pour this water over you and smash the decanter on your head.' As the place erupted, he quickly came forward and solemnly allowed me to drench him. The undergraduates loved it. It was a sharp question, I gave better than I got, and they enjoyed the spectacle.

Derek Laud whisked us off for a cheer-up dinner at Le Caprice. As we stood up and prepared to leave, a man came over and stopped me in my tracks. 'Mrs Hamilton, you cannot leave without saying hello to me.' Say hello to whom? I had no idea who had accosted me. He introduced himself as Nicky Haslam. I knew about this acclaimed interior designer to the 'stars', all-round party animal and social butterfly, but he had recently entered his 'Liam Gallagher' phase and was totally unrecognisable with 'punky' dyed hair, leather outfit and designer stubble. Nicky was fascinated by 'La Hamilton', and had moved places at his own table the better to observe this phenomenon. He is utterly charming and I was bowled over; he wrote his contact details on the back of a menu and has been a good friend ever since, regularly scooping us up to treat us for dinner at The Ivy or inviting us to lavish parties in the company of his 'A-list' celebrity friends.

His 60th birthday party was an amazing affair, the venue decked in white and gold, with semi-naked dancing girls and boys gyrating on a central circular bar top. The dress code was '*tenue sumptueuse*' so we went over the top. I festooned the hem and neckline of a bright pink silk ball gown with tiers of purple and white feather boas and, from the local Wilmslow Green Room Society, Neil hired a splendid seventeenth-century outfit, complete with knee breeches, buckled shoes, opulent velvet jacket, ruffled collar and sleeves. We looked superb, or ridiculous, depending on your viewpoint. Nicky's address book is second to none and an amazing array turned up to wish him Happy Birthday. Every time I turned there was a famous face – from Mick Jagger, Jerry Hall, Jemina Khan, Kate Moss, Ringo Starr and Barbara Bach, to Elaine Page, Anna Ford, Anjelica Huston, James Hewitt, Michael Heseltine and Tom Parker-Bowles.

Amid the fun and frolics there was also sadness. In July 1997 Jimmy Goldsmith who had so generously supported our fight against the BBC, died after a long and courageous battle with stomach cancer. He had stood at the election for his Referendum Party, securing David Mellor's defeat in Putney. Outside Jimmy's immediate circle no-one knew he was dying and he confronted death as impressively as he lived. A fighter to the last, his election performance, only weeks from death, was a superhuman rally to preserve the integrity of the United Kingdom. In another typical display of bravado *in extremis* he preserved the integrity of his fortune by decamping to Spain on his deathbed, to stop the new Chancellor, Gordon Brown, grabbing a large slice of it. His memorial service in November was a fittingly magnificent occasion at St John's, Smith Square. Neil went, but I could not face the hordes of press. Jimmy had been so good to us. I knew, with the innate sadness we felt at his death and the sorrowful nature of the occasion, I would be overwhelmed. Jimmy would not have been impressed.

CHAPTER TWENTY-ONE

Fighting Fund – Hospital – Snogfest – Battling Fayed in the Lords

After the Downey debacle the only way forward was to take legal action. But we had no money and no income, beyond 'odd-jobbing' in the media, which was spasmodic and precarious to put it mildly. We had spent everything on lawyers. Financially gutted, there seemed no way we could even contemplate funding a court action against Fayed. But we had reckoned without the friendship and loyalty that continued to surround us. Two stalwart supporters in Tatton, Robert and Heather Craig, totally unsolicited, offered £10,000 to help Neil fight the case. They were incensed, and remain so to this day, at the injustice that had been committed. They were the inspiration for what became the 'Neil Hamilton Fighting Fund', which Lord (Ralph) Harris and Norris McWhirter, founding editor with his brother, Ross, of the *Guinness Book of Records*, picked up and ran with. They sounded out friends and political figures for guarantees that would cover the costs in the event that we lost. When quizzed by the media, Ralph shrugged it off as 'a little whip-round among friends'. That was a fiscal understatement worthy of Gordon Brown; the total amount finally raised was nearly half a million pounds! This was not just a punt with other people's money. We paid huge sums of our own, as our income allowed, and signed away Neil's share of our house to guarantee our lawyers would be paid as much as possible if the unthinkable happened.

The Fund is one of my warmest memories during a deeply troubled and traumatic time. It was agreed, and strictly adhered to, that Neil and I should be very much at 'arm's length'. It would have been invidious for us to know that someone had been approached and declined so we were not to know who had contributed, unless that individual told us themselves. One who did, and made a point of helping Ralph and Norris with some of the administration, was Julian Gibbs. Julian has to be experienced to be believed. He is a timeless relic of the 1960s. While his brother, Chrissy, a renowned antique dealer and interior designer, cavorted with Marianne, Mick, Keith et al., Julian dined at the Carlton, Pratt's, Whites and Brookes's. His big, deep, throaty voice is equalled only by the depth of his heart. After an initial wave of letters to individuals he felt might be supportive, Ralph wrote to the *Daily Telegraph*, inviting anyone who felt so inclined to contact him at the House of Lords. Ralph asked only for 'pledges' which could be called upon when needed to pay the legal bills.

The response was very, very humbling. Some people wrote to us direct, sending £5 and £10 notes. People who will never have as much in their lives, financially, as we will always have, whatever happens, felt moved to join the fight. They were in good and august company. We did not know it at the time but the Duke of Devonshire contributed, only concerned, we learned later, in case his wife found out! So did Taki, the Greek multimillionaire, playboy journalist, *Spectator* columnist and all-round defender of the truth. Lord Hanson, business tycoon extraordinaire, dug into his pockets. We had never met any of these people. They had no personal 'Hamilton' reason to contribute, but something moved them to enter battle against Fayed.

Perhaps it was not surprising. He had, after all, made allegations against five former Prime Ministers, four Cabinet Ministers and half a dozen other MPs. He claimed the Duke of Edinburgh was a closet Nazi who had masterminded a secret service plot that led to the death of Diana and Dodi. He even invented Diana's 'dying words' ('Please look after the baby'). No wonder people were incensed and wanted to see him brought to justice. One letter was so moving Ralph sent it to us, removing the identity of the sender. I simply could not believe what I was reading.

Dear Lord Harris,
I have seen your letter in the *Telegraph* and I want to contribute £37.50 towards Neil Hamilton's fighting fund. You may wonder why not £35 or £40? Why £37.50? I am disabled.

> My wife is disabled. Our daughter is our carer. We have sat
> down together at the kitchen table and agreed we would like
> to donate ten per cent of our total weekly income.

This family received but £375 a week between the three of them and they wanted to donate ten per cent to help us fight Fayed. Can you imagine how I felt when I read that letter? We have since come to correspond with our friend from South Wales, delighting in his letters, which tell of outings and escapades with his wife and family. He was glad to back us; he wanted, and is proud, to have been part of the crusade.

Some months later and, crucially, after Fayed's allegations following the death of Diana, Ralph and Norris sent out letters asking donors to send a cheque to the value of half their pledges. Our 'friend from South Wales' immediately sent £50, despite having pledged £37.50 and only being asked to send half of that. He explained in his letter that he was sending it all at once, and had 'upped it to fifty', because he was so angry about Fayed's recent outpourings and absurdities. Gestures like that, from the heart and the salt of the earth, reduced me to rubble and tears, but also gave me the backbone and courage to fight on. While there were decent people out there who could see through Fayed and who supported us, not only those who had offered money, but also those who were with us in spirit, we had to continue. We could not let them down.

I had even more personal and worrying problems in the weeks and months that followed. My mother had a heart attack in early August 1998 and was rushed into hospital. My father, unable to look after himself, came to stay with us. His hips were so bad he could walk only a few yards and needed a wheelchair for all practical purposes. We made up a bed for him in a corner of Neil's library, from where he could watch the comings and goings without having to move. Every morning and afternoon I would take him to see my mother, wheeling him to her bedside where she lay with all the tubes and drips that accompany intensive care. I could not fight back the tears, but fortunately Daddy was unable to see them, his sight having failed almost totally. I felt desperately low and miserable, seeing both my parents so frail and vulnerable, but I had to try to keep Daddy's spirits up. He was a darling man, universally loved, and constantly asked me, 'Is Mum going to be all right? Is she going to be all right?'

'Of course she is Dads, she won't let us down.' I didn't believe it but had to pretend. Yet she rallied, the original Battleaxe pulled round, and we were overjoyed one day to find her propped up in bed, taking an interest, and about to be moved to a normal ward. It was all too much for Daddy. We were chatting in the sitting room with two of their dear friends, when he suddenly glazed over and slumped forward in his wheelchair. He was quickly admitted as a patient. I felt like a yo-yo, rushing from one end of the hospital to the other, visiting them both and wheeling one to see the other. I was in need of cheering up.

The launch of the new regional Century Radio did the trick. They threw a huge party on the waterfront at Salford, attended by hundreds of people, including many 'celebs' and some amusing lookalikes. Comedian Ken Dodd was there (the real thing, of course) and I was determined to meet him. I threaded my way towards him and his face broke into the famous toothy smile. I started to introduce myself and he interrupted. 'I know who you are. You're that Battleaxe!'

I was delighted at the success of the branding. Neil and I had much in common with Ken and his partner Ann. They had been through the media mill with his income tax case, when he had been successfully defended by our impending opponent, George Carman. They knew exactly what we were experiencing and had every sympathy. But it was impossible to have a serious conversation with Ken for long and he was soon entertaining us with the one-liners and witticisms that fell so easily from his lips. A few months later, during a hilarious speech at an Arthritis Care event I was involved in, he told everyone that he had a pair of ducks in his garden at Knotty Ash and he called them Neil and Christine — because they are devoted to and look after each other. It was a charming thing to say, although I didn't believe him for an instant!

My mother was able to leave hospital a week or so later, and I brought her home, pale and shaky, until she was well enough to look after herself. My father was still in hospital. While my mother, now universally referred to as Granny, was settling into her bedroom the telephone rang. It was Cynthia Payne — one of my best-loved Battleaxes. She was in the area for a speaking engagement with time on her hands — could she call in?

'Of course — we'd be delighted to see you. Where are you now?'

'I'm in Alderley Edge.'

Help — that was only five minutes away! I raced upstairs and explained to Granny she would find Madam Cyn installed in the drawing room. I didn't want her to have another heart attack. When she came down there was Cynthia sitting on the floor, legs curled under her. It was August, so we lit the fire, and I found some crumpets in the freezer which I thought would be appropriate fare. Cynthia is a breath of fresh air and was in great form when Granny appeared, unable to resist meeting this icon. They got on famously.

Talking of sex, much to my astonishment and distress, I found myself filling the front page of the *Sun* in May 1999. Neil and I had been asked by the Oxford University Conservative Association to speak at their annual dinner. Their letter had said, 'We'd love you to come because you're such fun. We don't want a boring old fart from the Shadow Cabinet!' That was such a sensible view we accepted. However, unknown to us, the invitations promised not only 'the Hamiltons' but also 'the most alcoholic dinner ever'. We gathered for drinks. The natural exuberance and gaiety of youth were bubbling over. And why not? Exams had just finished, for some only that afternoon, so they had much to celebrate, and so did we. Only two days earlier we had heard the joyous and highly satisfactory news that Labour had decided not to give Fayed a British passport. Yippee!

It was a convivial gathering but nothing out of the student ordinary. Also present were a vicar and three Fellows. We were introduced to a rather jolly drinking game, similar to the kind my father had played for years in the Navy. Someone starts by putting a five-pence piece in his neighbour's glass and saying, 'The Queen is drowning, save the Queen.' Well, there is only one way to save the Queen! You drain the glass quickly and rescue the five pence. You, in turn, pop it into your neighbour's glass or a glass across the table, preferably of someone who is unaware that the game is approaching them. And so it continues. We entered into the spirit of the evening; only a 'boring old fart' would refuse to play along, at least once. The survival trick is to make sure your glass is never very full and, preferably, cradle it in your hand out of harm's way. Not much was required in terms of speaking. Neil went first, gave a few rousing words and I followed and said even less. It was perhaps a little riotous and one or two undergraduates, unused to drink, were somewhat the worse for wear. We repaired back to the president's room in Balliol.

A young man I now know to be Will Goodhand suddenly turned to me and asked, 'Go on, please, give us a kiss.' It was no big deal. I leant forward, our lips met for a nanosecond, and that was that. I thought nothing more of it. There *was* nothing more. Having been the focus of attention all evening, we were glad to escape to our room in the college in the early hours and the next morning we set off back to Cheshire.

Driving to London on Monday we received a call from Peter McDowell, who said a reporter from the *Sun* had been on the phone — 'Something about you kissing a student in Oxford. He says they've got photographs.' Peter was laughing. Nothing flustered him and, by then, he was used to taking 'Hamiltania' in his stride. I thought for a moment and then remembered Will. But there had been no photographs — was this a set-up? When we arrived at the flat, the inevitable reporter was waiting. I politely said I had no comment.

'You should know we're running it on the front page, half is the photograph and the headline is "My snogging session with Mrs Hamilton".'

I tried not to show my horror. 'Look,' I said. 'If he thinks that's a snog, he's got a lot to learn.'

To my dismay, that quote went everywhere. I would never have volunteered the word 'snog' but he used it first! That evening we were dining with Julian and Emma Kitchener-Fellowes. By the time we arrived on their doorstep in Chelsea, I was highly emotional, as I began to realise what I would have to face the next morning. A national newspaper? The front page? The world had gone bananas. Julian was horrified when he opened the door to find me in a state of collapse. Ever practical, he sat me down, gave me a hug and a talking to, and told me to put things into perspective and not to worry.

The next morning there it was, but not just the front page. There were several inside pages too. You would have thought we had participated in a drug- and drink-fuelled, week-long Roman orgy! I was portrayed as a 'Mrs Robinson', lusting after young students, with all the attendant innuendo and make-believe that is part and parcel of a *Sun* 'scoop'. How had this come about?

It later emerged that a latter-day Judas Iscariot had betrayed not just Neil and me but also her fellow Tories. She had been taking clandestine photographs and saw the main chance. Later, she claimed they had been 'stolen' but I have yet to find anyone who believes her. The photos were hawked round the tabloids, and someone I know was present at the *Daily Mirror*, to which they had been offered, when the news came through that a deal had been struck with the *Sun* for £6,000 — quite a ransom for a little peck on the lips! Other garish photographs were accompanied by 'quotes', clearly thought up by *Sun* hacks, but put into the mouths of conveniently nameless students. Among the worst: 'It was a real tonsil tickler – we wondered when they were coming up for air.'

There was nothing I could do. It was damage-limitation time and I had either to laugh or have an uncharacteristic sense-of-humour failure. I hastily rang my parents. Obviously they did not take the *Sun*, but even Daddy would have been able to see the enormous photograph covering half the front page displayed on the racks in the newsagent's. Needless to say, my mother was robust, assuring me they were not going out and none of their friends read the *Sun* so that was fine.

The *London Evening Standard* picked up the story and photograph but they did print my robust denial of the wilder shores of fancy reached by the *Sun*. I had put the record straight and thought that was over. Wrong. Don'tcha just love the *Sun*? They went for it all over again. Apparently, Will had lost his 'street cred' for kissing a woman older than his mother. So they dispatched a Page Three girl to Oxford to rescue his reputation, photographing them punting on the river and canoodling at dinner. Will's 'cred' was rescued. I didn't blame him, he was having a good time, but I could have done without everyone being reminded of the original story and photographs.

I had recovered my sense of humour and readily fell in with a *Big Breakfast* stunt. Will did not know I was also in the studio. He was sitting with Johnny Vaughan when I marched in. He had been hugely embroidering our little encounter, in particular saying it was *me* who had asked *him* for the kiss! Smiling broadly, I boomed at him, 'Will Goodhand. You are an Olympic-class liar!' We re-enacted the 'snog', it was all good-humoured and we both played along with it.

My good humour vanished when I saw the *Telegraph* as I was leaving the studio. They had printed the story as a news item and taken the opportunity to reprint a huge photograph. The *Sun* is one thing, the *Daily Telegraph* quite another. Apart from anything else, this was Granny's newspaper! I quickly rang her; she was upset but at least it had not come without warning. As night follows day, the photograph appeared again at the end of the week, this time on *Have I Got News For You*. Neil just laughed the whole episode off and we now affectionately call it 'the Oxford Snogfest'.

After the frivolity, it was back to the usual with legal wrangles and mounting bills with which to contend. Fayed was still trying to stop us bringing the libel action with an appeal to the House of Lords. The case was heard in the magnificence of the main Chamber; Fayed's QC, Michael Beloff, was droning on at interminable length when Lord Longford walked in. He wanted to give his support. His eyesight was very poor and as he searched around, his clear voice rang out, 'Where's Mrs Hamilton? Where's Mrs Hamilton?'

It broke the solemnity of the occasion and there were suppressed smiles as everyone saw the humour of the situation. I slipped out to Frank Longford who had retreated to the lobby. He was an incongruous sight, with his white hair, thick glasses, shabby suit and, the crowning glory, a pair of trainers on his feet — for comfort! He said earnestly, 'What can I do to help? I want to help you and Neil.' I explained that we were cautiously optimistic about the appeal.

'Can I take you to tea?

'Frank, we'd be delighted — if we finish in time.'

Just after I went back, the senior Law Lord turned to our QC Desmond Browne. 'I don't think you need detain their Lordships with your arguments, Mr Browne.'

We were all astonished, no-one more so than Desmond, who had prepared a *tour de force*. Highly articulate and with a brilliant mind, he was a little disappointed they had already decided in our favour and did not need the benefit of the arguments he had carefully prepared! But it meant we did finish in time for tea with Frank — just. We found him, already tucking in to the cucumber sandwiches, anxious not to miss tea even if we did. He was a very sweet and gentle soul and his concern for our welfare was touching. After pushing the sandwiches and cakes in our direction, he turned to business. 'I know Lord Harris is trying to raise money for you,' he said. Putting his hand in the pocket of his jacket, which, like him, had seen better days, he pulled out two twenty-pence pieces. 'That's all I've got, Elizabeth doesn't let me have any money.'

I felt the tears welling up at the sight of this once strong and healthy man, now reduced by age to a shadow of his former self, but still earnestly solicitous for the wellbeing of others. I squeezed his hand over the coins. 'Elizabeth is quite right,' I said firmly. 'You'd only go and spend it!'

In between all the legal shenanigans, Neil found time to write a book. The idea had come from Jeremy Robson and it instantly appealed. Neil beavered away whenever he could spare the time from knotty legal problems and *Great Political Eccentrics* – a cornucopia of curious and colourful characters from more than 250 years of political life – was born. The trouble with political jokes is that too many of them get elected, and here were some that did, some that didn't and some who didn't need to, as they sat in the world's most eccentric legislative chamber, the House of Lords. The book deftly and hilariously illustrates why Britain is the world's leading political asylum.

Eccentrics was launched at Politico's bookstore in early November, and chosen by the *Mail on Sunday* as their 'Book of the Week'. Away from political eccentricity, reality was waiting just two weeks ahead of us. What the press called 'one of the most sensational libel actions of recent times' was finally scheduled to be heard in Court 13 at the Royal Courts of Justice on Monday 15 November 1999.

The Battleaxe, October 1997.

Low point at the High Court, December 1999. © PA/Empics

Opposite: Glamour girl – make-over by *You* magazine, June 2000. © Tim Winter

Below: Arrest and detention, August 2001. © PA/Empics

Happier times relaxing at home. © OK! Magazine

Would you Adam and Eve it?!
January 2002. © Donna Francesca/GQ © The Conde Nast Publications Lt

Safely out of the jungle – with Ant and Dec, September 2002.

I'm a celebrity, run me a bath!

With the original Battleaxe! © *OK!* Magazine

Barbara Windsor visits Bossy Fairy Battleaxe in her dressing room, Yvonne Arnaud Theatre, Guildford, Christmas 2003.

Strutting our stuff in the *Rocky Horror Show*, October 2003.

Above, right: Returning to Swinton Castle in 2004, where we first met thirty-seven years earlier.
© Nicky Johnston/Katz Pictures Ltd

With James and Granny on her ninetieth birthday, April 2004.

Delighted and amazed to have completed the Flora Light Women's Challenge in Hyde Park, in aid of Breast Cancer Campaign, September 2004.

Chapter Twenty-Two

Trials and Tribulations

For 'personal security reasons' Fayed asked permission to enter the courts via the judges' car park. No doubt he feared the Duke of Edinburgh and MI5 might be waiting at the main public entrance to bump him off. The Court pandered to his pompous whim and felt bound to offer us the same facility. Not likely! Fayed may have had reason to hide but we did not. We would use the public entrance like everyone else. Subsequently he was shamed into doing the same. A couple of days later he made an even more outlandish request, which we discovered only through a mistake by the judge's clerk. In error he telephoned *our* solicitors, instead of Fayed's, to say the judge had refused his request for six bodyguards to be with him in court at all times. What is good enough for Her Majesty's judges would just have to be good enough for the self-important Fayed.

My fiftieth birthday arrived on 10 November 1999. I had a terrible cold and felt pretty miserable about life, particularly what was lurking around the corner. We had been invited by the Bond Street Traders to the early evening switch-on of Christmas lights by Victoria Beckham. The reception afterwards was at Asprey's where I could only gaze in awe at the glittering displays. You could, for example, buy a pack of six silver covers for your party poppers for a mere £245! Asprey's MD, Guy Salter, asked if I was tempted. I explained our predicament: 'Don't worry, when we've won the case I'll send Neil around to get several little somethings for my birthday.'

A little later I was astounded when he presented me with a beautifully wrapped box, with a card reading 'Christine, Happy 50th Birthday!' Inside was a solid silver straw (well, it has a hole up the middle) with

'2000' in large silver letters attached to the side. This attractive novelty is, apparently, an absolute must-have for supermodels to avoid smudging lipstick. It was a splendid gesture and let Neil off the hook for yet another year!

The next day we were to meet the Earl of Portsmouth, who had just contributed £100,000 to the Fund. We did not know him and were open-mouthed at his amazing donation. He invited us to lunch at San Lorenzo and explained he did not like people being denied justice for lack of funds. He had a history of supporting impecunious litigants. I was overwhelmed that a total stranger should suddenly appear and so selflessly involve himself in our problems. His support was a great boost of confidence. We toasted victory. Right was on our side. What could possibly go wrong?

On the way home I went shopping for some sombre clothes for court. I was determined that my outfits would not become a matter of comment but I would have to ring the changes a bit and genuinely needed some additional items. It was an hour well spent. At my brother's for family supper, it was brought home to me how out of touch with real life I had become. His elder son, Edward (then eleven), had weekly homework questions based on the news. He needed some help but I couldn't answer a single question. Encouragingly, I told him, 'Don't worry. I bet you'll know some of the answers next week!'

We had lived against the background of Fayed's lies for so long, it had become a way of life. We were desperate for the case to begin but I was apprehensive, nervous, dreading the very public ordeal. We had moved heaven and earth to get here, and there was so much at stake. Suddenly a bombshell exploded. The day before the case began, we were preparing to attend the Remembrance Day ceremony at the Cenotaph, when our QC Desmond Browne rang at 9.30 a.m. I knew immediately from his voice that something was badly wrong. It was, and Neil spent the day surrounded by lawyers, grappling with the latest unfounded allegations, which concerned Mobil Oil. Fayed's QC, George Carman, was arguing that the perfectly legitimate tax consultancy Neil had with Mobil in 1989 advising them, with his joint expertise as a tax lawyer and politician, on opposition to a retrospective change in tax law, was another 'cash for questions' deal of the kind Fayed was alleging. It was nonsense, but we had to deal with it.

There is a solemn duty on lawyers to reveal their hand well in advance, to give the other side time to prepare its reply or encourage a settlement.

Carman had a well-deserved reputation for underhand tricks, and I am convinced he knew well before about the Mobil allegations but deliberately chose to withhold them until the last possible moment so as to wrong-foot us at the start of the trial. He even delivered the crucial information to the wrong address. Rupert Grey had moved his firm from their old offices in Gough Square, a fact well known to Fayed's lawyers who were regularly corresponding and liaising through the new address. But they carefully delivered this particular envelope to Gough Square late on Friday afternoon. Fayed's lawyers denied this was intentional, but either way Rupert/Crockers did not get it until Sunday morning. Neil had done nothing corrupt or wrong in relation to Mobil but we knew this could be viciously misrepresented. His dealings with Mobil were ten years earlier, and all the paperwork was in the attic in Cheshire 200 miles away, effectively inaccessible with the case due to start the next day.

We had to get to court every day. Driving ourselves was out; there is no parking. I could not face the tube or the twenty-minute walk to the nearest station. A taxi would be hugely expensive. The problem had been solved a few weeks earlier when Sheila Childs rang to say, no arguments, she was driving us in every day and she had arranged for Derek Laud's driver, Clive, to stand in if ever she couldn't. I protested, but to no avail. It's pointless arguing with Sheila and I was so relieved to have the problem solved. Normally in London only three days a week, Sheila would frequently leave her home in Herefordshire at 9 p.m. on a wintry Sunday evening, purely to be there for us on Monday, and delay her departure for us at the end of the week. It became so important to have her with us for that dreaded daily journey. We could share the triumphs, the despair, the agonies and the fear with someone unequivocally loyal, who understood.

We had not given our actual arrival a second thought when Mark Lloyd from ITN called on Sunday evening. It would be helpful to them and, he thought, to us if we approached from the far side of the Strand, across the pedestrian crossing, giving TV and press cameras longer shots. There would be less of a scrum. His call brought home the awful reality of the intense media scrutiny we were about to endure. We never resented the omnipresence of the photographers, but there were days when it was hard to maintain dignity and patience in the hurly-burly.

Interest in the case was intense. The judge ruled that only journalists could sit in the court itself and this meant that even Neil's sister, Lindsay, and close friends were excluded. Lindsay had to stand in line with everyone else for the gallery. This seemed outrageous and I felt the judge had got his priorities wrong. Queues formed at the main doors, the first people arriving before 6 a.m., several hours before even being allowed inside where they faced another long wait outside the gallery itself. I was deeply touched by the loyalty of so many friends standing in the freezing cold for hours, returning for more the next day. At lunchtime the gallery was cleared and they would immediately start queuing again for the afternoon. There were no chairs, no refreshments, nothing. Several people came from Cheshire, staying overnight in hotels. Peter McDowell, Neil's agent, had remained steadfast through all the horrors of the BBC case and the long years of the Fayed struggle, keeping the constituency together while internal battles raged. Although terribly crippled with rheumatoid arthritis, he was determined to be there. His eternal optimism kept me going on many occasions. David Davis, MP, who had supported us against the BBC all those years ago, was also there to stand by us in court. Such loyalty is rare in politics. Another friend who was unwavering was Geoff Yeo, an antique dealer, who would sometimes catch a train from Wilmslow at 5 a.m. to join the queue. Richard Clay, one of our benefactors, and his wife, Heather, travelled from Shropshire and stayed for the duration. Jeremy Robson and his wife Carole were often first in the queue outside. Perhaps Jeremy already had this book in mind and wanted to witness a chapter in the making!

Fayed employed a phalanx of lawyers – three QCs (one to advise on the criminal implications of his own evidence), two juniors and countless solicitors. George Carman, QC, was his main gladiator and we wondered what it would be like to face this legendary but diminutive giant of the Bar. Despite his towering reputation, Carman was surprisingly small (a Napoleonic five foot three inches) and, in the quaint Victorian garb of QCs, he was a *Spy* cartoon made flesh. His tubby tummy gave the impression of a minor landslip under his waistcoat. With a curious little concave mouth and receding thin lips, he resembled a geriatric cherub. We knew he would be anything but cherubic in court – squirting inky jets of half-truths over us like a malign squid, ruthlessly twisting our words, turning any ambiguity against us.

Carman never raised his voice, and spoke more in sorrow than anger. Master of the art of playing to the jury, he clearly broadcast on their wavelength and, to be sure of their reactions, constantly looked at them, even in a fast-moving and complicated cross-examination. He was a famous phrase-maker, always with an eye for headlines. Defending Ken Dodd against allegations of tax fraud, he memorably observed, 'Some accountants are comedians but comedians are never accountants.' Against David Mellor, accused of sexual impropriety, he had the court in stitches and Mellor hugely discomfited when he said, 'He behaves like an ostrich and puts his head in the sand, thereby exposing his thinking parts.' He was no genius on legal technicalities, but his sound bites were guaranteed to resonate with a jury. Margot Asquith said of Lloyd George that 'he could not see a belt without hitting below it'; she might as well have been speaking of George Carman. He and his team expected their client to lose. Carman was hellbent on conveying a general impression of corruption, regardless of truth. His misrepresentations and distortions infected the whole trial. The judge said later that if the trial had relied on Fayed's evidence alone, 'I very much doubt I would have allowed the case to be put to the jury.'

The jury were sworn in. We scrutinised every face, trying to weigh the jurors up. These twelve people had our life in their hands. What were they like? What prejudices did they bring to the court? Beyond their names (which are given in open court), we knew nothing except what appearances might reveal. One young man, clearly almost illiterate, had to be helped through the words of the oath on the card. How was he going to assimilate the complex issues about to be unfurled? The jury were immediately dismissed while legal argument raged and when they did come back one was missing – he had collapsed and been taken to hospital. The judge ruled we should continue with the remaining five men and six women.

Fayed's team were keen to divert the jury's attention from Fayed, and on to Mobil. Desmond Browne, ably supported by his junior Adrienne Page (now herself a QC), argued powerfully throughout our battles that Mobil was a red herring, had nothing to do with the case and should be excluded. But the judge decided it was 'similar fact evidence' and allowed it in. It seemed to us that Mr Justice Morland made every decision in Fayed's favour. If we wanted something in, he said 'no'; if Fayed wanted something in, he said 'yes'. For example, we thought it relevant to bring to the jury's attention the very close relationship we had been told Fayed had with Alison Bozek, his PA for fourteen years, who had suddenly appeared with the 'brown envelopes' story, two years after Fayed's original, and different, allegations.

Bozek, formerly an air hostess, became Fayed's personal assistant. According to Brian Dodd, who worked as personal security for Fayed after being in the parachute regiment in the SAS, they were very close indeed. He was our witness and, among other explosive details, wished to give evidence that he drove Fayed to be Bozek's first visitor after her son was born. Bozek was unmarried at the time and, according to Dodd, when Fayed returned to the car, he innocently asked who was the father of the child? Dodd was astonished by the vehemence of the response he got to his casual question.

By the nature of his job, Brian Dodd had to be physically close to Fayed and had intimate knowledge of his behaviour. He accompanied Fayed on a business trip to Malaysia with Bozek and another young female employee. His evidence would have been that walking behind them in the hotel grounds he noticed Fayed had his hands inside the undergarments of both girls at the same time; Bozek would have denied it. It would have been his word against hers. We had no means of knowing who was telling the truth. But in view of her bizarre but convenient late emergence with the 'brown envelope' allegations, Dodd's evidence was highly relevant to her credibility and we felt the jury should have had the opportunity to hear it. But the judge refused, on grounds that the case was about alleged financial not sexual impropriety. When Bozek and her sidekick, Fayed's secretary Iris Bond, arrived at court they looked like a pair of harpies, expensively dressed in near identical lavish black coats with large fur collars. Gerald Howarth instantly summed them up as 'ageing crumpet'.

So the jury were not to hear any 'side issues' from us, but the 'side issue' of Mobil Oil was fair game. I was not alone in thinking the judge bent over backwards to be 'fair' to Fayed. Not only did our lawyers agree but no fewer than five separate journalists, representing the whole spectrum of the media, speaking to me individually, all said the same – the judge is against you. I am sure he was striving to be just, but that was my perception. One man was overheard coming out of the gallery muttering, 'How many hampers has the judge had?'

We could have appealed against his decision on Mobil but concluded we could not afford to. It would be months before we got through the appeal process and a new trial could be a year or more away. Delay would be fine for millionaire Fayed, but was simply not an option for a shoestring litigant like Neil. Despite the generosity of the Fund, we were already way over budget and simply could not afford to stop the case in its tracks. We took the view that once we explained Mobil to the jury our case would remain rock solid. We naïvely assumed that everybody connected with the Mobil issue would tell the truth in the witness box.

The case became very complicated and confusing. In the fifth week, after endless examinations and cross-examinations, the jury were presented with issues involving baffling complexities of parliamentary privilege, double taxation treaties, claims and counterclaims. Understandably, it went over the heads of many people in the court, which may explain why one gentleman of the jury became absorbed in playing noughts and crosses with himself instead of listening.

Carman wasted no time in his examination of Fayed and wanted him out of the witness box as quickly as possible. When Desmond Browne cross-examined him it was like pushing jelly uphill. Fayed's favourite response was, 'I don't remember', interspersed with, 'It's a possibility. Yes, definitely that's a possibility.' Or, 'My lawyers do that – you have to ask them.' Or, 'I don't understand.' Among his wilder assertions were: that former Home Secretary Michael Howard had been bribed a million pounds to set up a government inquiry; that Dominic Lawson, editor of the *Sunday Telegraph*, was working for MI6; that the Duke of Edinburgh was a Nazi and had masterminded the deaths of Diana and Dodi; and that Neil was a 'homosexual prostitute and supplier of rent boys'. When tackled about the European Court ruling against him, he dismissed the European Court as 'fourteen old farts'. Perhaps his choicest response, which gave the *Evening Standard* a marvellous headline, was 'Mind your own bloody business.' Desmond had merely been enquiring about his finances. The journalists amused themselves by counting his absurd replies and it was reported to me one morning that he had said 'I don't remember' fifty times and 'It's a possibility' thirty times before lunch! At one point the judge became so exasperated he started cross-examining him himself.

At the end of the first week I was totally exhausted, mentally and physically. The long hours in court were very draining and afterwards we returned to Crockers, our solicitors, for consultations, discussions, searches through documents and more documents, trying to fill the gaps, and meet the distortions and lies thrown up by the other side. Neil and I were not the only ones under pressure. Rupert Grey had been miraculous throughout, working incredible hours, always putting us before his family and home life. Unlike Fayed, we did not have unlimited resources to put countless people on the case; everyone was feeling the strain.

My morale had been shattered because of the unexpected upset about Mobil, exactly as Carman had intended. If anyone had told me we had another four and a half weeks to go I would have collapsed on the spot. I had not been eating properly and the weight was dropping away. I was living on a cocktail of drugs: pills to sleep, pills for my cold, pills to keep me going, pills to calm me down, and alcohol for all-round suppression of the awful reality surrounding us – no wonder my body was rebelling. We reached the first weekend. Neil was immersed with lawyers when the telephone rang in the flat. It was Gerald Howarth with the news that Jeffrey Archer had been rumbled. Ted Francis, a friend of Jeffrey's, had come forward to say that the vital alibi he had given him, on oath, which enabled him to win record damages against the *Star* in 1987, was a lie. The stage was set for Jeffery's trial for perjury and subsequent imprisonment. We instantly knew this was disastrous 'mood music' for us. There was no connection whatever between Archer and Neil, but following Jonathan Aitken's case, where he was convicted and imprisoned for perjury, the sensational story of Jeffrey's lies and deceptions in court would undoubtedly intensify public perception of Tory 'sleaze'. It could not have come at a worse moment.

We had to get to Cheshire over that weekend so Neil could find his papers relating to Mobil Oil. We finally left London at 8.30 p.m. on Saturday, had a dreadful journey, and did not arrive until the early hours of Sunday morning, but it was good to be home. I had my first decent night's sleep for ten days. I was in no mood for going to church, I just didn't want to see or talk to anyone. Neil found the Mobil papers he needed in the attic and we drove back to London that evening not knowing when, or under what circumstances, we would return home.

Court 13 became a way of life, but I frequently sat in my place on the front row feeling alien and lifeless. Occasionally I could not remember why I was there. Carman was on the row behind, only feet away from me, and my loathing of the man steadily increased as the weeks wore on. He grunted like a geriatric bear from behind his piles of cardboard files and, in the corridor outside, disgustingly stubbed out his interminable cigarettes on the floor of the Royal Courts of Justice. He looked like a little turkey cock, with multiple chins cascading over his stiff collar. He spun everything out at great length. Of course he did. Not only was he salivating over every detail, trying to make sure the jury did the same but, on top of this his fees mounted staggeringly for each day the trial lasted.

At the end of one particularly taxing day, when the blows had rained down thick and fast, I felt as though I had been punched in the solar plexus. I was physically winded from the verbal onslaught, the distortion and the character assassination. We held our heads high but internally I was collapsing in mind and body. Neil had to go to Crockers but I couldn't stomach any more lawyers, lawyers, lawyers and legal speak. I went straight to the flat. Such a grossly distorted picture had been built up by Carman, mainly of Neil but also of me, that it seemed impossible to recover. I was convinced now we would lose the case because of a side issue: Mobil, a red herring cunningly added at the fifty-ninth minute of the eleventh hour. Then what?

The prejudicial press coverage we had endured for so long was bound to have an impact on the jury. After all they had read and heard – the initial allegations, Neil's resignation, Bell's campaign, election defeat, Downey, saturation coverage – we had an impossible uphill struggle. It was all slipping away.

Fortunately, that evening Nicky and James Stafford scooped us up for dinner. Nicky had shared the House of Commons office with Debbie and me and now worked for Lord (Cecil) Parkinson. Their enchanting little daughter Jessica greeted us excitedly and their neighbours, Lucy and Nicholas Gormanston, soon arrived. Lucy is the daughter of actor Edward Fox and half-sister to Emilia Fox and Nicholas represents all that is best about the Irish peerage. They are a highly entertaining pair and I could not have asked for better company to jolt me out of my despair. Nicky Haslam called round for a drink, on his way to the first of what were probably half a dozen parties that evening, and brought me a very spoiling bottle of Jo Malone cologne. I began to cheer up, dried my eyes and realised that, whatever happened, our friends would always be there for us.

The following weekend was my father's 89th birthday. Daddy's health and strength were failing fast and I was determined to get back to Cheshire on such an important day. I managed to catch the 08.45 from Euston to Macclesfield not relishing the thought of sitting in a crowded train by myself. It was packed with Manchester United supporters but I just managed to find a seat and slumped, head down, trying to look as inconspicuous as possible.

Icy wind and rain greeted me in Cheshire. Granny had been in and put the heating on at the Old Rectory, bringing one of her famous cottage pies. We settled down to a birthday lunch in the kitchen and spent the afternoon round a roaring fire. It all seemed so normal, so far away from my daily routine in Court 13. The journey back was ghastly, the train again full of Man U supporters celebrating their win with all the attendant lager cans and exuberant boisterousness. But it had been well worthwhile, my parents were so thrilled to see me that my effort was amply rewarded.

Neil spent Sunday in conference as always. I ironed 25 shirts and blouses before going for lunch with James and Fiona. Family normality, in particular eight-year-old Henry's hilarious 'concert' on the trombone, which he had just begun to learn, made me feel almost human again. There was no talk of The Case. By evening, though, it all came flooding back and poor Neil was greeted on his return from eight hours with lawyers, tired and embattled, by me falling sobbing into his arms. With another week to face, I flopped into bed taking two pills to blot out the world.

When the time came for Neil to give evidence, I knew he was positively looking forward to the chance to put his side of the story. All too aware of his tendency towards flippant witticisms, which he hugely appreciated in normal life, Rupert was anxious Neil should be very careful. He passed him a note:

Rules of Engagement:
1 Eyes on jury
2 Hands still
3 Voice even
4 NO speeches – save on rare occasions
5 NO jokes or quips – none, NONE!
Best of luck – Rup.

Desmond Browne examined Neil first, taking him step by step through the saga. Two days later came the moment I had been dreading, when Carman was let loose. He quickly focused on our stay at the Ritz as Fayed's guests, with graphic descriptions of our alleged excesses. Even the manager, Mr Klein, was brought over from Paris to 'confirm' what Carman described as 'uncontrolled greed and unbridled extravagance'. We did, at least, extract from Klein the astonishing news that a can of

Coca-Cola from the minibar cost £10 and, as Desmond pointed out, in 1987 it would have cost a dog £47 to spend a night at the Ritz – the bone was extra!

Carman's sound-bite phrases made good headlines, as he intended, for he always had an eye on the media. Desmond, although not as flamboyant, was intellectually far superior to Carman and described as such by the *Daily Telegraph*. On hearing this Desmond commented ruefully, 'It's like being described as better looking than Bernard Manning!' Neil was also more than a match for Carman intellectually but on several occasions he had to suppress his natural wit and repartee. This was no time for jokes. This was deadly serious. Remember Rupert's note. Generally he did, but the court liked this exchange:

'Mr Hamilton, do you have difficulty in paying close attention to anything you find disagreeable?'

'I'm paying very close attention to you, Mr Carman.'

Neil impressively held his own against the barrage, yet he seemed so alone, so vulnerable, so isolated in the witness box. I was longing just to hug him, but when giving evidence strict rules apply and, during the hour-long lunch break, he was not allowed to talk to anyone and had to eat his sandwiches alone, like an outcast. I needed a diversion and heard the sound of heavenly voices. I wandered to the gallery overlooking the Gothic vastness of the great hall, and there below was a charity carol concert. It was ethereal to watch and listen to 'normal' people doing 'normal' things when my whole life seemed so surreal, so not normal, so totally out of this world.

It was back to reality in the afternoon. Carman was labouring over and over the Mobil issue. The jury looked bored stiff. Was it too much for them to take in or had they already made up their minds? They were inscrutable but I feared the worst. The man playing noughts and crosses was more absorbed in the game than usual – as my friends in the gallery could see very well.

One of Carman's gibes that angered me the most was his allegation that Neil cared and worked more for Fayed and his own interest than for his constituents in Tatton. How dare he? We should have anticipated this line of attack but we had not thought it necessary to obtain character witness statements. Of course an MP is 'paid' to help constituents but Neil had worked long and hard beyond the call of duty, in particular putting his immense legal skills and knowledge at their disposal. Now, the grotesque idea that he had somehow neglected his constituents had been put into the minds of the jury and we had to try to defuse it. There were many we could have approached but we contacted two individuals and one organisational representative, Colin Cook, MBE.

Colin had put his heart, soul, family and whole being into setting up and running the Mid-Cheshire Sheltered Workshop, which trained 'special needs' school-leavers in basic tasks and helped them into employment. We had become involved immediately when he was operating from a couple of Nissen huts on wasteland, and the workshop is now a huge enterprise.

I contacted these witnesses on my mobile from a corner of the corridor, and each wanted to come straight to London and endure the rigours of the court in support of Neil. But there was a catch. The judge announced he would hear *no* character witnesses in Neil's defence. All we were allowed to do was put in statements which were not shown to the jury. The judge merely told them he had seen the statements and could assure them Mr Hamilton had not neglected his constituency duties. After Carman's spiteful attack, that was pretty inadequate. I was livid, hurt and disappointed.

However, it was not all doom and gloom. The judge did begin, at last, to make some decisions in our favour. Carman wanted to describe the Fighting Fund in detail, telling the jury Neil was supported by wealthy individuals, so he had nothing personally to lose, which was untrue. The judge restricted him to saying Neil was supported by 'members of the general public' – no more. Obviously that was no use to Carman, quite the reverse, so he said nothing.

It was Friday afternoon and I was the next witness. To my great relief, the court rose so I had a couple more days to prepare myself. But Neil was worn out after being in the box from Tuesday to Friday, with still more to come on Monday. I was very proud of him. He had conducted himself admirably, proved equal to Carman, and patiently endured constant attempts to denigrate and smear him. Although pleased to be able to speak for myself at last, I was also apprehensive. I knew my every word, every gesture, every eye movement would be analysed by Carman, the jury and the press, to be fed to the outside world. After his own strong performance, I must not let Neil down. I must keep my cool. Desmond and Rupert had both lectured me. No histrionics. No speeches. Just answer the questions.

I did, but was totally unprepared for the first question from Desmond. Once I had sworn to tell the truth, the whole truth and nothing but the truth, and confirmed my name, he suddenly said, 'I don't think it's any secret, Mrs Hamilton, that you were born in 1949?'

'Well,' I retorted, 'It certainly isn't now!'

Desmond did not detain me long and Carman started his cross-examination before lunch. He was not at all sure what path to tread and stepped carefully on the minefield. He hinted there was an option; I could be in it up to the last brown envelope or it could all have happened behind my back. I told him sharply there was a third option – that nothing had happened at all and Fayed and his minions were lying. Carman asked me to suppose Neil had received all this money, what would he have done with it? Well, he would have given it to me. He simply wouldn't have known what to do with it. Anyway, I told the court, I empty his trouser pockets every night – of course I do, I don't want to mend endless holes. There was no way I was going to allow the jury to think anything had happened of which I was unaware. Carman would not get away with trying to divide us in their minds.

I had to spend the lunch hour alone, as Neil before me, but I couldn't eat. I felt I was doing OK but I did not know what tricks Carman had up his sleeve. In the afternoon he once more salivated his way through the food and drink we consumed at the Ritz, reminding the jury again of what he regarded as our 'excesses', feigning surprise when I said it was perfectly normal for me to consume two bottles of wine a day on holiday. We now know from his son's biography that Carman himself was no stranger to excess, having narrowly escaped death while driving blind drunk, and drinking so much at night he was often still inebriated in court the following morning.

We got on to the business of the sausages delivered from Harrods, which occasioned the splendidly vulgar *Sun* front page next day, 'I Never Had Your Sausage Mr Fayed'. I certainly did not but, by Fayed's own admission, plenty of women did! In spite of his legendary lack of physical endowment (in his own words, 'my b**** are big, my c*** is small'), his 'sexploitation' had already been well documented.

Despite Carman's hard-hitting attacks on our integrity, and the grotesque way he exaggerated things out of all proportion, I kept calm and controlled, while the anger and rage seethed inside. Having described the confrontation as 'Hairdo puts Wig to flight', the *Times* reported the end of my cross-examination:

> No vouchers, no money, no couriers, no calls, and no envelopes. Nothing. She barked. The Hair had decided to end the cross-examination. Meekly, the Wig sat down.

Carman's son later confirmed he kept my cross-examination to the minimum, thinking too much pressure on me might backfire with the jury.

It was Desmond, the friendly wig, who reduced me to tears in my re-examination following Carman. It was impossible to fight them when he asked about the impact of having to discontinue the libel action against the *Guardian* and when I described our valedictory visit to Neil's DTI office after his resignation in 1994. I had formed a close relationship with his Private Office and recalling the deep sadness I felt when trying to say goodbye was more than I could bear.

The case continued. Fayed's tactic had been to comb his diary, identify dates that indicated a meeting, and claim he had handed Neil money each time. Fortunately, on one date, Neil was with Timothy O'Sullivan, Gerald Nabarro's former research assistant, who was hoping to write a history of Harrods; the meeting was to introduce him to Fayed. Timothy confirmed he was present throughout and Fayed gave Neil absolutely nothing.

Then followed Fayed's former head of security, Brian Dodd, whose evidence about the closeness of Fayed and Bozek had been ruled out by the judge. But Dodd had plenty more to say. A very large, tall man, he seemed a positive giant when raised up in the witness box. Towering over the diminutive Carman, he exploded like a rocket, bellowing and roaring, waving his arms dramatically as he detailed the outrageous things he had seen Fayed do. His parting shot was: 'Mr Fayed? He's the biggest bloody crook in town.' Dodd's performance was electric and the whole court was riveted by the passion and ferocity of his outburst. Here was a man speaking from the heart. Even the judge failed to calm him down and had to order him to leave the witness box. As he did, Dodd looked across at us, 'I apologise, Mr Hamilton. I don't think I've done your case any good.'

Goodness knows what the jury thought but it was a fine display and gave rise to the spectacular headline, 'Biggest Bloody Crook in Town'.

That evening Sheila came round for lasagne and frozen peas on our laps. I suddenly realised I *could* cope. Even if the jury found against Neil, millions of people would never believe it. Sheila summed up our thoughts.

'We're on the edge of something colossal.'

'Yes,' said Neil. 'Either way.'

Desmond began his closing speech on Thursday. His summing-up was masterly and as he described Neil, his actions and motives, the tears forced their way out and rolled down my cheeks as the emotional highs and lows of the previous five weeks were encapsulated. Desmond dealt with every aspect of the allegations, not shying away from the awkward and difficult bits: 'A saint might have turned down the invitation to the Ritz. He is not a saint but he was not a sinner.'

Carman began on Friday and was, of course, horrendous. His closing speech was short, but long on carefully contrived sound bites and he put the knife in at every possible opportunity. He knew Fayed had lied and behaved like a buffoon but Neil and I had to sit and listen while his words rained down on us. My anger and frustration mounted and I became so incensed by Carman's outpourings, I could barely restrain myself from turning round and punching him. I could feel and see my hand shaking as I poured a glass of water, banged the carafe on the table and swallowed two more beta-blockers. I simply didn't care whether, in excess, they were damaging me.

Jeffrey Archer and Jonathan Aitken's cases were totally irrelevant but Carman took maximum advantage of their misdemeanours. Pointing dramatically to the witness box where they also gave evidence in their trials, his disgraceful last words to our jury were, 'Neil Hamilton would not be the first ex-MP to lie in that witness box.' The judge instantly rebuked him. But it was too late. Scandalously unfairly, he had made the prejudicial connection in the minds of the jury, exactly as he intended. Surely they could see through him and were loathing him as much as I was? We would soon find out.

CHAPTER TWENTY-THREE

The Verdict

The judge began his summing-up on Friday morning. He explained the law, brought together the threads of the case and reminded the jury what they had heard and seen. He tore Fayed's evidence to shreds. Fayed has 'a warped appreciation of what is fact and what is fiction, what is truth and what is falsity'. His evidence was 'inconsistent and unreliable'. He had made 'wild and unsubstantiated allegations'. The judge suggested they might feel Fayed's 'obsessional attitudes and beliefs have distorted his perception of the truth'. He 'strongly advised' them it would be 'very dangerous to accept even those parts of Mr Fayed's evidence you find credible . . . unless you are satisfied that evidence *independent* of Mr Fayed . . . confirms his evidence in a material way'. He spent time guiding the jury on how much to award Neil in damages if they found in his favour, indicating a ceiling of £150,000. When considering damages he also said they might bear in mind whether Fayed and Carman had rubbed 'salt in the wound' by their vicious and gratuitous attacks on Neil, for example, calling him a 'homosexual prostitute and supplier of rent boys'. Clearly, he thought they had.

Just before we broke for lunch the judge explained to the jury that, because of Christmas postal pressure, they would be getting their allowance 'in cash'. Huge guffaws all round and a welcome relief from the tension.

When we returned, the judge continued, suggesting the jury might feel Bond, Fayed's personal secretary, had been under the influence of drugs to embolden her to say what she did in the witness box. He was not alone in that observation and Bond's demeanour had already been commented on to me by several journalists. She had indeed appeared totally spaced-out but no-one, least of all me, had expected the judge to comment. I cannot second-guess the judge, but many interpreted his comments as indicating he believed Bond was lying. Together with Bozek she was crucial in replacing Fayed as a source of allegations – suddenly popping up after more than two years with a new story contradicting much of what Fayed had alleged hitherto. After five long weeks it seemed pretty obvious what Mr Justice Morland was thinking, but legal alarm bells rang immediately in Neil's mind. He whispered straight away, 'This is disastrous. There are Carman's grounds of appeal.'

The judge had not finished when court rose for the weekend. Sure enough, hardly had the jury left the box when Carman was on his feet objecting, with veiled threats that he would appeal if the judge did not change his tune by Monday. The judge said he had not made his original comments lightly and had carefully considered them before speaking, but promised to ponder them over the weekend. Outside court we were greeted by the *Evening Standard* headline: 'Hamilton Set to Get £100,000'. The money was not the issue. We had already irretrievably spent much more than that. We hardly dared hope but, after Fayed's ludicrous performance, the obvious deficiencies of some of his witnesses, and the judge's comments, we had every reason to be optimistic. It was a view shared by the press.

Sunday dawned icy but sunny, and we had lunch with Rupert and his family in Hampshire. There was a splendid story in the papers that the Duke of Edinburgh was to withdraw his royal warrant from Harrods because of Fayed's lies about him in the witness box. A journalist friend rang to report that Tom Bower (well-known investigative journalist and biographer of Rowland and Fayed) had changed his mind about Fayed's allegations after seeing me in the witness box. I had convinced him they were untrue. If even Bower, previously so hostile towards us, had been persuaded then surely the jury would also see the truth? We wallowed in a joyous family lunch party. Rupert's wife, Jan, and two of his daughters had been in court for the summing-up. Seeing them there had brought home to me the gross intrusion we had been and how much we had taken Rupert away from what mattered most in his life. This was confirmed when Jan said to her two younger daughters, without reproach, 'We'll have to adjust to having Daddy back, won't we?'

We returned to Court 13 on Monday. It was cold, Father Christmas was waiting for us outside in the Strand, but I could not have felt less like seasonal cheer. Carman was still bristling with objections to the judge's observations about Bond, and his threats had worked. When the jury came in, he rowed back from his remarks, telling them he should not have spoken as he did on Friday. Worse was to come as he went into overdrive to redress the balance.

Of course I am not objective. I was, am, seeing, feeling, reacting as a partisan but also as one of only three people in this world who really *know* the truth; the other two being Neil and Fayed. I was not alone in feeling the judge went too far on the Monday, and as the jury left to consider their verdict, his final remarks were ringing in their ears. His coruscating comments about Fayed and his witnesses were the other side of the weekend, diluted and weakened by the passage of time.

It was not warm in court but I was shivering with more than cold as I walked down the corridor past the mass of journalists and the public. I managed to keep back the tears until the door of the conference room closed behind us but then the floodgates opened. I was frightened, but also deeply wounded by the judge's remarks about Neil, which I knew had been inflamed by Carman's tactics.

We waited for the rest of the afternoon but there was no verdict and we had to sweat it out overnight. What was taking them all this time? Back again on Tuesday 21 December, for what must surely be the last time. It was raining. We arrived at court with Sheila and Gerald to find the posse of press had been swelled by the addition of a dozen policemen. Peter McDowell was waiting for us. It was his 43rd birthday and he was hoping for a present from the jury. There was more delay. One member of the jury had to take her daughter to hospital and could not be there until 11 a.m. So we had to kick our heels in the cold empty vastness of the courts. I had taken the precaution of wearing a vest. Like Charles I at his execution, I did not want to be seen shivering.

Just after 2.30 p.m. we were called into court. The jury had decided. I sat in my place on the front row next to Neil, hardly able to breathe. He held my hand tightly as we waited for the foreman to rise. We were not surprised when she emerged – we had guessed it would be her. A journalist told me afterwards he was standing next to Tom Bower when the foreman revealed herself. 'That's it!' said Bower triumphantly. 'She's a leftie, they've lost.'

I felt I was standing on the scaffold, waiting to be executed. The axe fell. An audible gasp went up from the public gallery and the press box;

even the hard-nosed journalists could not believe the jury had found for Fayed and against Neil.

The faces of the jury will haunt me for ever; I searched them for clues as, one by one, they left their box, passing only feet away from me. Not one even glanced in our direction. Not one would look us in the eye. To this day, I cannot understand. If I had condemned anyone I would have acknowledged my decision. Members of a jury cannot give any reasons for their verdict. They cannot be questioned to discover whether they have fully understood the evidence. I wanted to ask each one of them, 'Why, why, why? Why haven't you seen through Fayed? Couldn't you see he was lying, lying, lying? Carman knew. The judge knew. Why didn't you?'

I sat motionless, staring at the floor. I wanted to scream, to bang my fists on the table. It could not be true. It could not be true. It could NOT be true. I had to escape, but how was I going to get out of this hellhole? Our lives had just been shattered in the most public way imaginable. Yet I now had to face the waiting hordes, both the hundreds outside court and the millions watching their televisions at home.

We had fought for five long years through the Court of Appeal, the House of Lords, even changed the law of the land to get to the High Court. Against all the odds we had surmounted all the legal obstacles put in our path, but ultimately we had lost. Neil looked pale. He had shed nearly two stone during our ordeal. But, as always, he held his head high, inspired me with his discipline, gripped my hand and gave me strength. The judge had graciously agreed that Neil's sister, Lindsay, could sit in the body of the court for the verdict, instead of having to clamber up to the gallery. Lindsay has always been such a stalwart support and strength throughout our various tribulations and there was nothing either of us could say as we hugged each other.

Fayed's lawyers were unable to conceal their glee, their relief, their surprise. They had expected to lose. Fayed had been told to expect defeat and stay safely out of sight at Harrods, but was quickly summoned to perform like a clown outside the court. Rupert, Desmond and all our team were as stunned as we were. They had fought long and hard on our behalf and were aghast the jury had decided for Fayed. The journalists thronged around the door of Court 13 itself and Rupert went out to speak to them. I could hear him as we stood behind the glass door, steeling ourselves to face the world and some of the most testing minutes and hours of our lives. 'This verdict has clearly been a great shock for Mr and Mrs Hamilton, indeed for all of us. I ask you, please, to respect their need for a little privacy, for some time to themselves. I know they will make a statement shortly.'

The journalists parted without a word to let us through their ranks. I don't know how I got down that corridor, lined with people who had come from the public gallery. They stood in silence like mourners at a funeral. I faintly remember familiar faces, a few hands stretched out to squeeze my arm, to touch my shoulder, and then we reached the privacy of the conference room at the end of the corridor. A small windowless room, the 'home' where we had lived out our highs and lows for five and a half gruelling, brutal weeks.

We were all stunned, the whole team. I dimly remember the hushed tones, the disbelief, the gentle sympathy, the tears, as the wreckage of our lives lay around us. There was no point delaying. We went to talk to the throng of reporters who had, unusually, been allowed to mass inside the great hall itself, at the foot of the stone staircase. As we stood on the bottom step, I clung to Neil's hand, composed, but dying inside. My mind would not acknowledge the injustice and the awesome consequences for us.

Instead of the usual quick-fire questions, the hacks waited in respectful silence for Neil to speak. He said later he felt like a corpse speaking at his own funeral. He told the reporters he was convinced the jury had not believed Fayed's claims but had come to their decision because of the last-minute allegations about Mobil. The newsmen who had covered the trial throughout were as amazed by the verdict as we were. Many had understood the complex twists and turns of the Mobil saga and had seen it for what it was – a diversion and distraction. Someone asked for my comments. I had determined to say nothing, but just said quietly, 'The jury are wrong. The jury are wrong.'

We came out of court, dignified and composed, to find more reporters, cameras, police and onlookers; the crowd was immense. I was in shock and disbelief, despair and defeat. Neil hid the newspapers from me the next day, saying they could hardly be worse if he were a paedophile. The messages of support, sympathy and incredulity poured in from friends and strangers alike, among them an e-mail from Michael Portillo:

> The news has shocked us all and the consequences are chilling. When Mrs T was booted out, Neil and I went to

Number 10 for lunch and we wept. I remember Denis saying,
'We're not dead, you know!' Neither are you.

No. But I felt as if we'd been buried alive.

Christmas was looming. Our legal team needed to get home, back to
their families, off on holiday, in particular have a rest from the
Hamiltons. We would regroup and take stock in the new year. After 24
hours besieged in the flat, we tried to set out for Cheshire. We needed a
police escort to clear a path through the mob as we walked to the car,
laden with bags, boxes and flowers. They had to block the traffic while
we drove away, in case the chaos and struggle caused an accident.

We arrived at the Old Rectory at about 7 p.m. Waiting in the
darkness were a dozen loyal friends and neighbours. They knew the press
would be there and wanted to welcome us with a public display of
loyalty and support. They brough flowe   1 ch   '
wife had put one of her deliciou
came in. They knew we were exhausted and jus.   .ap   ...
house was warm and welcoming.

The next day, Razzie, James, Fiona and the children arrived for what
was certain to be our last Christmas in the house we loved and had lived
in for a decade. It would have to go to pay the legal bills. We had put
our all into it, not only money but blood, sweat and tears. The thought
of parting with it was heartbreaking. For the first time I began to count
the cost of what we had suffered and were about to lose.

Everyone was determined to have a good Christmas. Granny had been
gradually shopping for all the necessities, putting things away in the
freezer. Fiona came armed with her delicious home-made everything,
and Razzie had piled smoked salmon and other delicacies into her car.
The fire was roaring away, we put up decorations, retrieved the tree from
the cellar (Neil is allergic to real ones), opened the cards, and enjoyed the
ritual trappings.

The family and Razzie departed and it was New Year's Eve. The
whole world was partying for the Millennium but we stayed at home
alone. We were not without invitations, but I pretended to everyone we
were going to another party. I knew I could not cope with the jollity and
merriment when, inside, I was feeling so wretched. Despite Neil, family
and friends, I felt lonely and isolated as the enormity of our plight
overwhelmed me. We went for a celebratory drink with my parents and

left their flat pretending we had to get ready to go out. In fact, we just came home and Neil spent the evening assessing our financial situation. We had made gross earnings of £16,000 in 1999. We were hardly entering the twenty-first century as high-flyers. After a bowl of soup and some cheese, we went to bed early and watched some of the celebrations on television. It seemed everyone in the universe was happy and laughing except us.

Perversely, the good wishes of friends made it worse. Several had left cheery messages on our answerphone just after midnight. The noise of the partying in the background merely amplified our lonely despair. I sat listening to them on New Year's Day, the dawn of the new century, in floods of tears. Keeping a stiff upper lip in court and in public was not easy but the kindness of friends was overwhelming.

We had lost the last great libel action of the twentieth century.

New Year. New century. New beginning?

CHAPTER TWENTY-FOUR

Bankruptcy Looms – New Horizons – a Little Red Sofa – Bin-bags

A friend had e-mailed us: 'You are people of talent, personality and resilience, and somehow you will make a new way in life.' But how? Despite spending so much time on legal battles, we had managed to earn a living of sorts from writing, TV and the media, but who was going to be interested in us now? We were advised not to appeal. The cost, both financially and emotionally, was beyond us, we already owed our lawyers a small fortune, there was just no money. Much as we yearned for justice, it seemed 'get a life' was the more practical view.

We began to realise that not everyone had been duped by Fayed. Despite being monstered by the press, it was obvious from the reaction we received that many people felt we had suffered a miscarriage of justice. The letters rolled in from total strangers. The envelopes them-selves were a joy to read, 'Neil and Christine, Cheshire' found us easily, as did 'The Fighting Hamiltons, somewhere in London, please, please find them!' The oft-maligned Post Office did us proud! One, in particular, amused us greatly, 'To the Hamiltons fighting the evil Fayed. Mr Postie, please, please find them.' Mr Postie did find us and in the envelope were £5 worth of stamps from an anonymous well-wisher. Yet again, I sat at my desk in tears as I opened the mail. One envelope even contained, anonymously, a lottery ticket, sadly unsuccessful. It was deeply humbling and overwhelming.

Meanwhile Fayed festered with revenge. The instant after the verdict, Carman was demanding the names of Fighting Fund contributors. As Neil could not pay Fayed's costs (running into millions) they should make up the shortfall. I experienced a new wave of horror that those public-spirited people would now be subjected to Fayed's vicious attacks. They had given us, by their support and faith in our cause, not only the financial means but also the moral strength to carry on. We did not know all their identities but knew the Fund was a pyramid, with hundreds near the bottom contributing modest amounts, some as little as £5, with the Earl of Portsmouth at the apex. The legal argument had volleyed back and forth and the judge decreed we were only obliged to reveal the names of those who contributed £5,000 or more — a total of eighteen people. I felt sick for Lord (Ralph) Harris and his noble army — it was now their turn to face the brutal onslaught of Fayed-funded legal vultures.

In the new year Fayed pursued his threat. As he engagingly put it, 'I go for the bastards who think they are members of the Establishment, who pay his fees and want to bring me down. I am going for the people who encourage him like Lord Harris and that . . . Earl of Shit.' The latter title is unknown to *Debrett's Peerage* but was apparently an allusion to the Earl of Portsmouth. Fayed demanded £3 for every £1 the eighteen had contributed, totalling one million pounds of flesh. I had never expected to concern myself personally with the concept of 'maintenance', a term associated with the pains of divorce, but it has another legal meaning. Fayed's lawyers argued that Neil's action had been 'maintained' by the contributors. Our own legal costs amounted to £1.3 million, of which the Fighting Fund contributed nearly half a million, but we had to find the rest. In addition, as costs were awarded against us, Fayed claimed roughly £1.5 million, plus interest at £321.66 per day.

Without the 'maintainers', he argued, we would never have been able to fight the case. It was their fault he had spent so much money and they should make up his loss. He was incandescent with rage but the backers battened down the hatches to fight him tooth and nail. The likes of the Duke of Devonshire, the Earl of Portsmouth, Lord Hanson and Taki were not likely to bend the knee to the Egyptian guttersnipe. Nevertheless, the protracted legal battles, the worry and uncertainty, took their toll on dear Ralph Harris, the moving force behind the Fund, following the initial £10,000 pledged by Robert and Heather Craig. He was now under intense threat and it was particularly difficult for his wife, José, who became ill with strain and worry. With a billionaire client, manically intent on vengeance whatever the cost, there was little incentive for Fayed's highly paid solicitors to make him see reason. Quite the contrary. It made sound economic sense to indulge his whims, however fanciful, and pile on the pressure.

The 'maintainers' were determined to oppose Fayed's demands, not only to avoid putting money in his pocket but also to establish the principle that charitable individuals should not be penalised for helping impecunious litigants obtain access to the courts. It took three years and it was not until February 2003 that Fayed finally lost in the Court of Appeal. The Hamilton litigation had made yet another useful contribution to English law. Happily, far from the 'maintainers' having to pay him, he had to pay their costs.

Before that legal battle got under way, new opportunities were presenting themselves that led us to hope some of our fears were perhaps misplaced. Almost immediately after the trial, Quentin Portsmouth invited Neil to speak the following November at the annual dinner of the Basingstoke Agricultural Society, of which he was president. This amazing man had just lost £100,000 because of us and his gesture of continued support was deeply affecting.

Marc Granger, then chief executive of the Children's Wish Foundation, invited us to their annual ball. I was surprised that a big charity, so dependent on public goodwill and support, actually wanted us to be associated with them. Three years later, I was able to repay Marc for that kindness by nominating the Foundation as my charity when I took part in *I'm a Celebrity . . . Get Me Out of Here!*

Gyles Brandreth invited me as a guest on his LBC radio programme, *Stairway to Heaven*, an engaging format where he chatted to guests about what they would take with them in the afterlife. What drink? Certainly not champagne — in heaven it must be on tap! My personal angel? Dame Edna Everage, of course, who would look stunning in the outfit and let me get away with anything without silly lectures. Who was I looking forward to meeting? Jesus — there were a few things I wanted clarified. Could he really turn water into wine?

Invitations to speak at events did not dry up. Quite the contrary, I had a flood of them. Perhaps we could bounce back after all? Then, amazingly, Stuart Murphy, boss of BBC Choice (now BBC3), asked me to make a series of programmes interviewing celebrities who had 'been through stormy waters'. It was Stuart's wife, Polly, who had the idea after seeing me being so positive. She told Stuart to grab me for BBC Choice.

Stuart, only 28 at the time, later told me he had got so far, so young, by taking risks. Now, I was one of them!

The programmes were made by Princess Productions and, apart from stipulating a few people I was *not* prepared to interview (e.g. Martin Bell, Max Clifford), I left the choice to them. *The Christine Hamilton Show* was born. The trademark was my 'little red sofa', a copy of the ones in our flat, upon which I perched with a host of fun and interesting people in relevant and quirky locations.

For James Hewitt we sat in a large window of the Hyde Park Hotel with Kensington Palace in the frame over his shoulder. We later went riding together in Richmond Park – without the sofa! An open and engaging subject, he reflected ruefully that it would have been easier for everyone if he'd been killed in the Gulf War. The sofa also looked fabulous against the green of the Aston Villa turf where I flirted with Paul Merson and John Fashanu, but I was nervous when the great bulk of Bernard Manning sank down. The sofa held up, but as I gazed at his impressive belly I couldn't help saying, 'Bernard, I can't imagine sex with you! When did you last see your willy?' Nothing fazes Bernard. He told me, 'This morning. In the shower. And, on a good day, I don't have to bend down.'

Bobbing on the deck of a Thames river boat off the House of Commons was the perfect location for former MPs Piers Merchant and David Ashby, both caught up in sex scandals. We also chose a boat, this time an expensive 'gin palace' at St Katharine's Dock, for Greg Martin, son of the legendary Beatles producer, George Martin. After a whirlwind courtship, Greg had briefly been engaged to Tara Palmer-Tomkinson, then betrayed her, temporarily breaking her heart. The sofa perched precariously on the edge of the swimming pool at the top of the Berkeley Hotel for Tara, who arrived in regulation tottering heels. We finished with a shopping spree where TPT spent about £3,000 on clothes in five seconds flat. I liked her. She was entertaining, direct and frank about her battles with addiction and continual failures with men.

The longest journey was to Monaco to see Ivana Trump on her yacht. We flew, the sofa came overland and we met on the quayside. That was a different world and the sofa had to put its slippers on before being allowed on deck. It was the Grand Prix and Monte Carlo was heaving. It was hot, I was tired and feeling rather dizzy. It was a difficult interview for me and I don't know why Ivana agreed to do it. She gave nothing and merely went through the motions.

Taking the sofa to Longleat, home of amiable, aristocratic fruitcake Lord Bath, was a headache. It rained hard, the sofa came on an open trailer and the covers blew off. By the time we arrived, it was sodden and we conducted the interview on one of His Lordship's magnificent antiques instead. The team badly wanted to drive the sofa and trailer through the lion park, with me sitting aloft, to get some amusing footage. No way! Not that Lord Bath worried about my welfare — he feared only that his lions might nibble the sofa and swallow a nail or some other upsetting roughage. Neil was concerned I might become seventy-third 'wifelet' of the 'Loins of Longleat', but I resisted.

By far the most difficult subject for me was Jonathan Aitken, who had only recently finished his prison sentence for perjury. He was reluctant to do the interview and only agreed as a favour to me. I had not known him particularly well in the Commons but had written to him regularly while he was in prison and developed a fondness for the man. I found it incredibly hard to ask him searching and, what seemed to me at the time, impertinent questions. We had a common enemy in the shape of the *Guardian*, I had an overwhelming sympathy for what he had been through and, in particular, an admiration for the way he had coped. It was a moving interview and Jonathan talked candidly about his failings, both in marriage and life in general. I was very grateful to him and admired his nobility and humility in the wake of his sufferings.

I interviewed Michael Cole, former royal correspondent who had been fired by the BBC for leaking secrets of the Queen's Christmas broadcast. As he had only just retired as Fayed's PR supremo, and for all I knew was still retained, it was sporting of him to agree. We perched the little red sofa in a large bow window immediately opposite the corner of Harrods with the column of royal warrants in-shot over Michael's shoulder. I was tempted to shin up with a screwdriver and remove them. I thought the Duke of Edinburgh should have been more vigorous and ripped his down without delay — perhaps his wife was restraining him! Afterwards I wandered across, cameras in tow, and went into the emporium. The first time I had crossed the threshold for nearly twenty years. Immediately, the green-suited doormen accosted me, 'You can't come in here, you can't come in here with those cameras.'

Fair enough. We had been anticipating that response. The doormen were perfectly friendly and were aware who I was; I wanted to know exactly where I stood personally. 'So, there's no problem with me, it's just the cameras – is that right?' The situation was confirmed, I shooed the cameras away for effect and we retreated with some fine footage. Within 24 hours two identical letters, one each for me and Neil, arrived from Harrods. Starting with a load of pompous blather, they continued, 'If you attempt to enter the store it will be regarded as an act of trespass and the police will be called.' A dangerous strategy for Fayed I would have thought but what fun to have annoyed Fayed. He could have saved the stamp – I have no intention of putting any money into his pocket, the only people I would encourage to go to Harrods are shoplifters!

The reviews for my programmes were good although, true to form, the *Guardian* described me as a 'monstrous bitch'. It was good of them to confirm quite how much I was irritating them by still being alive and, even worse, making a success of life after death.

At the same time, I had been approached in early January by Ed Hall, a friend of Derek Laud and managing director of a new digital channel Simply Money, to interview women who had successfully seized the financial reins in businesses, from fishing and farming to fashion. Ed invited us to discuss the details with him at Le Caprice. No thanks, I said immediately. I knew our presence in such a chic restaurant, only a fortnight after losing the case, would attract adverse press comment. Le Caprice, like its sister the Ivy, is stalked by photographers as a 'celeb hang-out'. But my protestations were waved aside by Neil, Ed and Derek who all told me not to be so ridiculous.

So there we were, much against my better judgment, and the evening was drawing to a close. The manager came over, said the cameras were outside and there was no-one else in the restaurant they could possibly be interested in. Through the semi-darkened windows, I could see the outline of the group waiting to pounce and instantly felt trapped with a panic rising inside me. We had only just dropped out of the headlines and I could see the tabloids – 'Brazen Hamiltons, have they no shame? Blah, blah . . .' We had to deny them a photograph, but we were cornered. Our car was parked a few yards away; there was no escape. I was furious with the boys for getting me into this trap.

Never underestimate human ingenuity in a crisis! Ed wandered out and the cameras flashed madly just in case. He got into our car and nonchalantly reversed it down the ramp of the adjacent underground car park. Derek acted as second decoy and while the cameras flashed at him, Neil and I dropped on all fours and crawled out of sight into the kitchens. The management had tipped us off — past the dustbins and down the back stairs we would emerge in the underground car park where Ed was waiting with the car revved up on the ramp. Lying flat on the back seat, we swept away totally undetected within feet of the cameras. Outwitting the press in a James Bond manoeuvre was a simple but satisfying pleasure.

We were living in a strange twilight zone. One minute we were at the Brit Awards, in the company of Robbie Williams, Geri Halliwell et al., as guests of BBC Choice; the next moment we were watching ourselves portrayed in *Justice in Wonderland*, a courtroom TV drama. This had been widely trailed and, despite the encouraging ring to the title, I was dreading it. I was played by successful actress Belinda Lang, and Neil was amused and flattered to be played by heart-throb Charles Dance.

Justice in Wonderland had to be very careful and use only the exact words spoken in court, but the editing and choice of words would be all-important. We sat down to watch with trepidation. It is an eerie experience, seeing yourself played on the screen. Despite being totally unlike me in real life, Belinda Lang was excellent, but Charles Dance's portrayal of Neil was too arrogant and smug — a pity he had not had the benefit of seeing him in court. By the end we had relaxed — no sane person watching could have understood how on earth the jury had reached their verdict. Julian Fellowes, a friend of Belinda Lang, later told me the BBC had filmed two endings, leaving open the final choice of which to use. The first had 'me' just sitting and staring at the jury uncomprehendingly as they left, which is accurate; the alternative had 'me' shaking my fist at them. Fortunately, they chose the right one; the other would have been a travesty.

It was all very encouraging, but Fayed was lurking. Back in Cheshire, a bailiff in seedy overcoat arrived with a 'statutory demand', the first step towards bankruptcy and the loss of our home. Fayed demanded an interim payment of £501,000, giving us 21 days to pay before further action, in other words, seizing our possessions. I was distraught but, suddenly, we were delivered a miracle.

In early February I was by myself in the house when I saw a man coming down the drive. I froze motionless in the stairwell, hardly daring to breathe. He rapped menacingly on the door. I ignored him. I simply could not face 'the enemy' on my own. The telephone rang but I couldn't move to answer it as the man might see me through the window. Someone started shouting through the letter box. This was the last straw. I was alone and frightened, not physically but mentally for what lay ahead. I put my head in my hands, refusing to listen. Then a few shouted words began to pierce my subconscious – 'Fayed' and 'thief'. I went to the door and found Andrew Chapman, a reporter from the *Mail on Sunday*. He wanted our reaction to the revelation that Fayed had paid £10,000 for documents stolen from our barristers before and during the trial. What?!

As the story unravelled over the weeks ahead we were flabbergasted. We were not surprised at Fayed – it was totally in keeping with his character – but how could it have happened at all? Amazingly, not all our confidential documents had been shredded. The case had produced three million pages, many drafts becoming redundant when superseded. These had been put out in waste bags each evening to be collected for disposal but 'Benjy the Binman' gathered them up instead. A weirdo *extraordinaire*, Benjy rummages through, steals and sells interesting documents, and had profitably plundered the refuse of lawyers acting for James Hewitt, Jonathan Aitken, Elton John and others. Instead of being prosecuted for theft, Benjy was regarded as a harmless eccentric. He was such a familiar sight, in his battered old Transit van, the security men at Gray's Inn had merely waved him through. It was all so incredible it could only be true.

It transpired that Mark Hollingsworth, a freelance journalist closely connected to Fayed, acted as Benjy's 'fence'. Hollingsworth, a sanctimonious Leftie, who had written a book accusing MPs of impropriety for having paid parliamentary consultancies, was now revealed in his true colours as a dealer in stolen goods. He negotiated a deal with Fayed, handed over 'Benjy's documents' – *our* documents, stolen from *our* barristers – in exchange for £10,000 cash in a white envelope.

These bizarre revelations helped explain a lot. One of the mysteries had been how Fayed's witnesses, Bozek in particular, had delivered such pat replies to certain 'surprise' questions we had prepared. It had seemed at the time as though she knew what was coming – was this the explanation? We never discovered exactly which papers had been stolen but it became clear that Carman had had advance notice of our cross-examination strategy and had almost certainly seen confidential memos between Neil and his lawyers. Fayed had behaved like a common thief and dishonestly denied us a fair trial. Can you imagine the impact if this had been revealed during the trial? The judge would have stopped it in its tracks, Fayed would have been totally discredited and it would have been impossible for him to defend a second trial. If only this had come to light earlier!

And so it was straight back to court, where we succeeded in getting Fayed's costs order against Neil stayed, pending an appeal. Despite their pathetic denials on his behalf, Carman and his crew knew perfectly well Fayed was guilty as hell — no-one will ever convince me Carman had not seen our documents with his own eyes. In the corridor outside, Carman tried to stop me talking to the press. What business was it of his who I spoke to? I wasn't taking orders from him. Carman had accused us of being 'on the make'. His fees were as big as he was small — £125,000 brief fee and £3,000 for each day in court. I towered above him. 'You work and take money from the biggest liar and crook in town! How dare you tell *me* what to do!'

He waddled away in a puff of smoke and I skipped off to meet the delightful Richard Bee, my producer for *The Christine Hamilton Show*. We had headed off immediate bankruptcy.

Life was breezing along in the first year of the new century. We were busy and well received when out and about. More and more people had seen through Fayed and there appeared to be much sympathy for us in the wider world. Neil was preoccupied with legal matters but, although anxious about the outcome of the appeal, my overriding concern was my father. He had collapsed after a stroke in July and was in hospital for two months. It seemed unlikely he would make his ninetieth birthday in December but, after an anxious few months, he rallied and we had a weekend of family celebration, which he hugely enjoyed. I knew in my heart it was probably his last.

Whatever the outcome of the appeal, the loss of our house seemed unavoidable. Rupert Grey was understandably concerned about rising costs which, together with the outstanding bills from the trial, had soared to over £1 million. Without his friendship and support, persuading his partners to keep faith, we could not have continued. The appeal was to be heard over five days and was led for us, *pro bono*, by Anthony Boswood, QC, one of the most able commercial silks. He did not want a 'no win/no fee' agreement. He simply did it for nothing because he believed it was right. He was masterly, as was his junior, Tom Lowe. The case was heard by Lord Phillips of Worth Matravers, Master of the Rolls, Lord Justice Sedley, human rights lawyer, and Lady Justice Hale, since appointed the first woman Law Lord.

Neil and I sat at the front of the court. Fayed's QC this time was not Carman but the interminable Michael Beloff. Buried in copious notes, he never used one word where fifteen would do. A Beloff performance exhausts time and begins to trespass on eternity. According to him, even if Fayed *had* bought our stolen documents it didn't matter. Beloff, understandably, tried to avoid the prospect of Fayed giving evidence, saying he had a charity engagement in Liverpool. Lord Phillips was unimpressed that the mayor of Liverpool should take precedence over him. Finally, Fayed took the oath. Starting as he meant to continue, lying as he swore to tell the truth, his 'evidence' was a joke. Boswood made dog meat of him, and Beloff did not even bother to ask him questions as he knew the less his client said the better.

Yet again, it was blindingly apparent that Fayed was telling lies. Surely the Court of Appeal must penalise such a blatant attempt to pervert the course of justice? We came back on 21 December to receive judgment, one year to the day since the jury's devastating verdict. The shortest day, would we again draw the shortest straw? Lord Phillips' opening remarks set the tone. He began with a pathetic joke, with which he seemed unduly pleased. Lady Justice Hale smirked and the lawyers tittered sycophant-ically. A judge's 'joke' in court, like a rich man's elsewhere, is always funny. 'This case,' said Lord Phillips, 'is about a load of rubbish.' Well it might have been rubbish to him but it certainly wasn't to us. Full marks for insensitivity, making light of the evil lies that had wrecked our lives.

We won but we lost. The court accepted Fayed had paid £10,000 in cash for the stolen documents but considered his conduct merely 'discreditable', and proposed to do absolutely nothing about it because he had not 'initiated' the theft. He 'merely' sought to profit from Benjy's entrepreneurship. Hell's teeth! Why should that distinction matter? Fayed knowingly bought stolen property and secretly used privileged and confidential documents to tilt things to his advantage in court. What about the fairness of the trial? What would the jury have thought had they known? What would the judge have done had he known? Fayed would have been holed below the waterline, the case would have been instantly dismissed, we would not have lost and would not now be facing financial ruin.

Their Lordships just shrugged their shoulders, like hopeless parents unable to control a wicked child. Fayed had got away with it again – first the jury and now the Court of Appeal. I wanted to scream with disbelief.

I felt betrayed by the whole legal system. For three of the most senior legal figures in the land to be so indifferent to such crookery in their own courts defied everything I thought this country stood for.

Lord Phillips of Worth Matravers? Worthless Matravers more like! Perhaps he caught mad cow disease during his 1999 inquiry into the BSE fiasco! No-one expected this bizarre result. We did not think they would overturn the jury verdict — that almost never happens — but even Fayed's own lawyers expected the costs order would be quashed. This would have sent a strong and necessary signal to others that such criminal behaviour cannot go unpunished. Instead, nothing, sweet bloody nothing! No wonder Fayed's lawyers were exultant.

As the full implications sank in, I realised our hopes of averting financial disaster had been destroyed but I was determined not to show my inner turmoil. I felt physically sick but, yet again, it was stiff upper lip time. I knew many of the press were sympathetic and equally amazed at the judgment. But it was hard to tough it out yet again when all I wanted to do was curl up in a ball and wail about the unfairness of life. Later, Ralph Harris called and commended our dignity outside court. As so often, a kind word opened the floodgates but Ralph admonished me, 'Come on, keep going — you can't let your friends and supporters down.' He was right. I vowed that I wouldn't.

So it was back to Cheshire for another Christmas that, surely, really would be our last. Razzie, yet again, provided a broad shoulder to lean against and an ample bosom to cry on, acting as cook, housekeeper and everything else while we coped with yet another legal knockout. James and the family arrived and the children took our minds off our own problems. We had spent the last year pinning our hopes on the British legal system. Never again will I confuse law with justice but there was nothing we could do but soldier on and prepare for the inevitable. Fayed had got away with criminal behaviour while all we had done was stave off bankruptcy for a year. I could only hope Worthless Matravers choked on his turkey.

Yet again we had to pretend nothing was spoiling the festivities. Three days later the snow arrived and the family departed. I went out with Neil as he set off for his early morning run and walked a short distance across the crisp, firm fields. The sunlight, watery and hesitant, was trying to penetrate the mist and the Old Rectory stood ethereal and beautiful in the refracted light. I was overcome with the thought that soon we must leave all this behind for an uncertain future.

New Year's Eve saw the arrival of Sheila and Jean from Herefordshire and Michael and Christopher from Brighton. After a simple but splendid dinner we went next door to the churchyard, carrying bottles of fizz and glasses, to hear the bell-ringers heralding the new year. There, sitting in the church porch with his arm around his teenage son, was a man in his forties staring at the flagstones. I fell into conversation and he explained, tears welling in his eyes, that he had come to visit the grave of his seven-year-old daughter who had been killed that year. He gladly accepted my plastic glass of champagne and, as we talked about his tragedy, it put my own problems firmly into perspective.

Chapter Twenty-Five

Fayed Pounces – Farewell to Daddy – I Take to the Stage

On Thursday 4 January 2001 the telephone went mad. George Carman had died. What were our comments? Neil's immediate reaction, fortunately only to a friend, was witty but tasteless and is best forgotten. I made sure I grabbed the phone thereafter so he would not get caught by his acid wit. We made no comment, but I didn't change my view just because he had died.

We knew Fayed would not wait long to pounce. A couple of days passed without a visitation but, just after New Year, Neil was out while Razzie and I were taking down decorations in the hall, thick velvet curtains drawn across the glass of the front door. Suddenly we heard a determined knocking. Tired boughs of holly in hand, we froze, our eyes met, we both held our breath. We knew instinctively who it was. I peered round the curtain to find a pleasant-looking man in his late thirties.

'Mrs Hamilton?' It seemed a rather unnecessary question.

'Yes.' My heart was pounding but I tried to keep calm.

'Is Mr Hamilton in?'

'No. Who are you, anyway? What's your name?'

'My name is Colin Naylor and I think you know why I'm here.'

'Yes,' I said. 'You are Mr Fayed's arsehole.'

The tension immediately eased. Despite his best endeavours, a smile creased the corners of his mouth. 'Look. I'm only doing my job. I want to go home as much as you don't want me here. I've come all the way from Stone and I'm bursting to go to the loo.'

I opened the door slightly on the chain, not knowing if he had accomplices who might force their way in, but there was no point playing cat and mouse. I said I would call Neil on his mobile to arrange a convenient time for an appointment. Meanwhile, he could go to the Little Chef a mile away to relieve himself. It seemed a suitable place for the emissary of the owner of the Paris Ritz.

The papers were duly served and there seemed no way of avoiding the inevitable. Neil appealed to the House of Lords, against the Court of Appeal's decision, so Fayed had to wait. We bought a little more time for which I was grateful, because my father's grip on life became more tenuous with every week and I was dreading having to sell up and move out of the Old Rectory while his own future was so uncertain.

Daddy was almost blind and his hips were so bad he could only stagger from chair to chair indoors and needed a wheelchair for all other purposes. My mother had been his full-time carer for years but never complained. Daddy bore his sufferings stoically although physical disability was a constant source of frustration as he had always been so active. It was easy to shield him from the worst of our nightmare; routine chores were struggle enough and he lived from day to day. As long as I greeted him with a cheery smile and a hug, and answered his invariable question with, 'No, Dads, no problems,' he was happy. Almost daily I wiped tears from my eyes, and forced my voice to stop wobbling, perversely thankful that his blindness and general ill-health prevented him realising his darling daughter had all too many problems.

On 28 January he had a stroke and was rushed into hospital. We pitted every hope against reality but he died the following weekend. His funeral was on 12 February in Cheshire and, considering he was ninety, there was a remarkable turnout. Many of my parents' elderly friends from Cornwall and Hampshire made the long journey. I chose the first reading, by Joyce Grenfell:

> If I should go before the rest of you
> Break not a flower, nor inscribe a stone,
> Nor, when I'm gone, speak in a Sunday voice
> But be the usual selves that I have known.
> Weep if you must, parting is hell,
> But life goes on, so sing as well.

We did. 'Eternal Father Strong to Save' was a particular favourite of my sea-loving father. As he requested, he was cremated and his ashes placed in a wooden casket for us to fulfil his wishes later that year.

I became even more depressed, drinking far too much and sleeping only with sedation. I tried to hide my state from my mother, who had enough on her plate as a new widow, but I was at my lowest ebb and full of aches and pains. I underwent various medical tests to try to ascertain what was wrong. The outlook was bleak. How would we earn a living? How could we possibly claw back from such losses? I felt isolated, without intellectual stimulation or sense of purpose. I had lost my beloved father and was worried sick about my health and my mother's future as well as ours.

For some people, bankruptcy is an easy way out of debts. It wipes the slate clean and many never look back. Bankruptcy forced and funded by a vindictive billionaire is something else. We knew Fayed's main aim would be to see us turned out of our house and flat with minimum delay. The house had been quietly on the market since the previous autumn through agents, Gascoigne Halman, handled by the very capable Tim Jackson. Journalists would frequently ring him with only two questions: 'Are the Hamiltons moving?' and 'Are Posh and Becks moving?' — possibly in reverse order! P&B had lived for some time in an apartment in a large Victorian house in Alderley Edge, a popular haven for Manchester United players. As Brooklyn grew up, needing more space and their own garden, they moved to a converted barn in Nether Alderley, just across the fields from us. It focused media attention firmly on our little hamlet.

I was very concerned we might find journalists posing as prospective purchasers, to gain access by false pretences. We could rely on Tim to screen everyone carefully to ensure only genuine viewers and, suspicious of anyone not already on his books, he foiled several such attempts.

As each new couple came round, some several times, we hoped against hope they would drop out. We had some near misses but we remained lucky and life continued as normal. But what is normal for the Hamiltons? The House of Lords refused Neil leave to appeal on preordained technical grounds, the Court of Appeal having deliberately ensured there was no further avenue. We could not allow imminent bankruptcy to overwhelm us and normal life had to continue, however difficult and futile it seemed at times. Of course, it was only Neil who was bankrupt and, in addition to TV and radio work, I was in demand as an after-dinner speaker and my earnings kept the wolf from the door while Neil battled with Fayed's hyenas. He began to enjoy being a kept man! Yet he was far from idle. He hates officialdom and injustice and helps others, as others have helped us. He has always done *pro bono* legal work for friends and those who cannot afford to pay and now, as well as helping me keep the show (literally) on the road, he took on several more cases. He was absolutely *not* going to earn any money for Fayed!

My breadwinning took a new turn. Tony Benn was enjoying great success with his one-man show, *An Audience with Tony Benn*, on stage with an armchair, cardigan, pipe and pot of tea. He had long complained about the media trivialising Parliament, reducing politics to the cult of personality. Having 'left Parliament to devote more time to politics' he set out to revive the public meeting. Inspired by this, I took to the stage too, swapping the pot of tea for a bottle of champagne. I took my one-woman show to theatres all over the country from Windsor to the Wirral, from Bath to Bournemouth. Like Benn's, my evenings were interactive with audience participation in the second half. Iain Dale, founder of the politicos.co.uk website and now Conservative candidate for North Norfolk, acted as ringmaster, introducing me and fielding the questions, and Neil made a surprise appearance after the interval. The evenings were pure entertainment with no hint of politics.

In April 2001 I received a letter from Jeremy Paxman inviting me to lunch. He was writing his book *Political Animals* and said he wanted to tap my experience of the beasts as a close observer for many years. I subsequently discovered, when his book was published, his motive was altogether different. Our paths had crossed at parties over the years but I was interested to meet him properly. I presented myself at fashionable Clarke's restaurant in Kensington, where I also espied Lucien Freud and Jamie Oliver. I found Jeremy surprisingly shy, not at all the *Newsnight* Rottweiler.

He made no mention over lunch but, at the beginning of his book, he recounts his experience as a sixth-former when Gerald Nabarro spoke to his class. I appear then as Christine Holman, whom Sir Gerald 'bequeathed' to the political world. Later, in a chapter entitled 'The Price of Fame', I am 'wife of disgraced MP, Neil Hamilton'. That is a maddening phrase I encounter from superficial hacks too idle to scratch the surface of stereotypes. I also resent his highly selective quotation of my words about Neil, which I have used many times publicly: 'If he is a liar, then I am a liar. If he is a crook I am a crook.' 'Well,' he continued, 'she said it!' Yes, Jeremy, I did, but you deliberately chose to ignore the end of my remark because it did not suit your purpose: 'He is not and I am not.' His book disparages evasive and mendacious politicians. Pots and kettles come to mind.

He did attempt to flatter by saying, 'She still exudes the sort of sexual charge which used to send Conservative MPs weak at the knees in the presence of Margaret Thatcher.' Too shy or repressed to mention sex over lunch, he later e-mailed me, bewailing the omission, asking to talk about it on the telephone. No thanks, I told him, I don't do phone sex. Before we could arrange another meeting, Neil and I were engulfed by sex of a totally different nature.

Chapter Twenty-Six

Ischia – Farewell to Peter – Enter Fish-Face and Slug – Lurid Allegations

In May 2001 various things happened which then appeared unremarkable, but assumed monumental importance when we were later to be accused of sexual impropriety. On Saturday 5 May (the date is important) we went to Snappy Snaps, Waitrose and Marks & Spencer in the King's Road. We were giving an informal dinner party that evening and needed film for a trip with the BBC the following week. Coming to dine were our old friend Tony Tucker and his daughter, Lucy. I knew Tony when he worked for Central TV, which covered Gerald Nabarro's constituency. He was at the Institute of Directors when Neil arrived in 1982 but later moved to the Scotch Whisky Association in London and then Edinburgh. We had also invited Razzie and Derek Laud, but the only entry I had made in our diary was 'Inkpen'. Nearly twenty years earlier, while Neil and I were preparing for the 1983 election in Cheshire, my mother was receiving acceptances for our wedding.

'The Inkpens are coming,' she told me one day on the telephone.

'Inkpens? We don't know anyone called Inkpen!'

My mother would not be moved, insisting the name was 'Inkpen'. When I saw the handwriting I realised her mistake. 'Tucker', in the florid hand of Tony's wife, Corinne, could indeed be interpreted as 'Inkpen' and we have known them as such ever since.

Contrary to popular opinion, Neil and I are not habitués of expensive hotels, but an American friend, Lorie Karnath, had just e-mailed us. She and her husband Robert were passing through London and invited us, with other of their friends, to join them for a drink at Claridge's at 6 p.m.

It was short notice and I put nothing in the diary. We were delighted to see them briefly and then raced back to the flat where I had prepared my magnificent Jellied Bloody Marys for a starter; I forget what else I gave them, after a good JBM nothing much matters!

On Monday we departed very early from Gatwick. I was to present a BBC *Summer Holiday* programme and had suggested Ischia, an island in the Bay of Naples. My choice had nothing to do with *The Talented Mr Ripley*, which was filmed there. It was far more serious — a daughter's pilgrimage. I was tremendously excited about visiting the island that had meant so much to my father, who had spent the latter part of the war there. It was three months since Daddy had died. We enjoyed a full life together and I am rich in happy memories, but I ruminated on the things we failed to do — shared experiences we missed through the pace of my life and his failing health. I always regretted I had never gone to Ischia with him, but here was a chance to savour its magic for myself.

He rarely talked about his assignment and it was only now my mother produced contemporary documents, including a translation of the mayor's eulogy when he left, which I had not seen before. In November 1945, the mayor, with operatic Italian brio, spoke of *il dottore*'s

> fine qualities of heart and mind . . . our consoling angel, with a nobility of heart dedicated the best of your scientific acknowledgement and accompanied your activities with such a gentility and delicacy of manner to conquer us in heart and soul. You have performed a mission with the highest human sentiment and with full efficacious results. It is indeed beautiful and honorific for Ischia to count you among her best souls, benefactor of everlasting memory.
>
> Destiny has ordained that the honour to preside this memorable ceremony be reserved to me, who among the few, even when the flashing Teutonic victories astonished the world, and when the Hun hordes seemed to submerge everything, I always kept faith in the destinies of Great Britain, for the saving of civilization and the eventual triumph of liberty and justice.

The obvious sincerity of the mayor's exuberant rhetoric moved me across the years from the printed page. Tears of pride trickled down my face at my father's legacy. The mayor continued,

We are comforted by the thought that you will feel a beat
of longing for our island as you may feel certain of our
lasting gratitude.

That 'beat of longing' surfaced in me. I felt ashamed I knew virtually
nothing about 'Daddy's island'. This was my chance to pay homage to
his memory. We had a hectic schedule of filming. Ischia is renowned for
its natural thermal waters and the healing qualities of its volcanic mud.
Under the eye of the camera, I was slathered from head to toe in warm
mud, with only a small towel to preserve my modesty. It was unnerving
to be at the mercy of an overenthusiastic Italian matron who could not
understand my concern not to be overexposed for the cameras. She was
all for ripping the towels off and getting down to serious business.

Sitting on the sea wall in Ischia Ponte, sipping glasses of chilled Casa
D'Ambra – my father's favourite local wine – I watched the moonlight
shimmering on the rock walls of the castle. The world of war and
suffering seemed far away. I was supremely glad I had come to Ischia
and, in a small, inadequate way, felt I had helped bridge the gap between
the end of my father's life and the rest of mine.

We returned home, and on Saturday evening Neil participated in a
debate about privacy and the press. He was gathering material when I
answered the entryphone at the flat. It was a *Sunday Mirror* journalist
asking if he could come in. You must be joking. I asked what the devil
he wanted. He 'understood' we had attended a party in Ilford where
'sexually explicit material was exchanged'. I told him not to be
ridiculous and put the phone down. He buzzed back immediately, 'I've
got evidence you were there . . . with your former chauffeur, Barry
Lehaney.' I told him not to be idiotic. He buzzed again; could he come
in and talk about it? Certainly not – there was nothing to talk about.
He rang yet again and I began to get upset. What game were they
playing? What headline were they planning? I called Neil, who told him
in no uncertain terms that if he did not stop harassing us he would call
the police. Little did we know how ironic that remark would turn out
to be, but it did the trick.

Neil was jotting a few notes and, on a scrap of paper, wrote 'Sunday
Mirror' and 'sex' – a titillating trio of words, which later greatly excited
Scotland Yard. During the debate he jokingly lamented the only thing he
had not yet been accused of was a sex scandal . . . He described the usual

tactic of Sunday papers, calling you late on a Saturday afternoon to comment on a story already in print. He referred to our earlier caller and said he had no idea what might be published the next day. In the event nothing appeared, but that Sunday brought other truly dreadful news.

Neil's former agent, Peter McDowell, had been gravely ill as a result of medical incompetence during a laser operation to deal with internal stones, and had taken a dramatic turn for the worse. The doctors had given up hope. His life-support machine was to be turned off in a few hours. His wife, Alison, stoically brave as they had both been throughout his long years of illness, called us that morning from his bedside. 'If you want to say goodbye to Pete, it has to be soon.' To our eternal regret, we were not able to make it up the motorway in time. We had been out of the country at just the wrong moment.

Peter was modest and quiet and never pushed himself forward but fought fearlessly for his beliefs. Politicians are reliable in different ways. Someone said of Randolph Churchill you could always rely on him – to let you down. Peter was the exact opposite and his absolute loyalty and calmness in a crisis saw us through many dramas, not just the ones that hit the headlines. What malign fate inflicts such suffering on some, while others sail through seemingly unscathed? From an early age Peter endured daily arthritic pain that most of us can scarcely imagine. He never complained, although sometimes it took him an hour or more to get his joints moving in the morning.

With a wicked sense of humour Peter could be highly mischievous. At the height of the furore in the 1997 election, he was at home with us, surrounded by the usual mob. We were watching the BBC news in the drawing room when Peter espied Jim Hancock, the BBC's excellent chief political reporter in the Northwest, standing in the middle of the field about to do a live broadcast. We could also see him on television.

'I bet he hasn't switched his phone off,' chuckled Peter as he dialled the number. Sure enough, an instant later, Jim appeared to suffer an attack of St Vitus's Dance as he searched desperately to silence the phone in his pocket!

Peter and Alison were made for each other and devoted to their two boys. It matters not how a man dies but how he lives. We were distraught and angry at the manner of his death but cherish his memory. Neil gave the address at Peter's funeral. It was probably the most difficult speech he has ever had to make but gave him the opportunity to pay his personal tribute to one of his closest friends, one of the most remarkable and admirable men he ever met.

The day before Peter's funeral, Tuesday 22 May, we had presented ourselves at Macclesfield County Court where Neil was officially declared bankrupt. As we walked out of court into the arms of the press, I felt at an all-time low. How would we get through the statutory three years with a trustee on our backs, monitoring Neil's every move, trying to make life hellish? Three years seemed an eternity. Would we ever emerge on the other side? Neil, more robust as always, regarded the bankruptcy as a challenge with which he was well qualified to deal. Not only was he a tax lawyer with a sharp brain and wide knowledge but he had also been in charge of insolvency as Minister for Corporate Affairs at the DTI.

The humiliation and indignity began in earnest. Fayed had appointed as Neil's trustee-in-bankruptcy Colin Haig of accountants Baker Tilly, who was charged with stripping Neil of all his assets and handing them over to Fayed – minus his astronomical fees. Haig, as Jonathan Aitken's trustee, had grotesquely tried to sell Jonathan's personal papers by public auction, including medical records and confidential constituency correspondence. He even tried to seize his daughter's computer to sell for the benefit of Jonathan's main creditor, the *Guardian*. In Jonathan's court case against this, Mr Justice Rattee rightly described Haig's behaviour as 'repugnant and a gross invasion of privacy'. The man was a vulture. No wonder Fayed wanted him to act against Neil.

In due course Haig arrived at the Old Rectory with his sidekick Louise Brittain, who was to control Neil's bankruptcy day to day. I deeply resented their presence and had to brace myself to let them in. I could barely control my anger and was icily polite – but only just. Neil dealt with them in the dining room, the table spread with our financial records, while I had to show the accompanying valuer round to make a detailed inventory of our possessions. Haig claimed the right to inspect my computer files because some might relate to Neil's finances and be relevant to his bankruptcy. I was not going to allow Fayed's lackey unbridled access but Neil persuaded me it would be sensible to open various files at their request to prove there was nothing relevant to their sordid enquiries.

Despite their bullying tactics, Haig and Brittain made little progress against Neil's vastly superior knowledge of the law and he became the 'Bankrupt from Hell', frustrating them wherever possible. Knowing now the tactics these people use, it is no wonder bankrupts with inadequate legal knowledge are bludgeoned into submission. For example, a trustee can seize a bankrupt's earnings only where they exceed an agreed amount for reasonable living costs. Neil was told to hand over anything above the small agreed sum. He instantly replied, 'I think it very unlikely my earnings will exceed that by a single penny.'

'Oh, but you have a duty to earn as much as you possibly can for your creditors.'

'Do I?' said Neil. 'Which section of the Insolvency Act says that?'

Awkward glances between Haig and Brittain accompanied their complete silence. Round one to Neil.

Ms Brittain quickly became known as 'Fish-Face'. Probably unfair, inspired by her glasses and quickly adopted by all our friends. Childish it may be, but it helped me get through. She set about her task with zeal. Money was no object as Fayed was paying. All Neil's financial records were scrutinised in microscopic detail to find his bank accounts in the Cayman Islands, yachts in Mediterranean harbours, New York apartments, etc. They didn't find them because they don't exist. But fruitless enquiries for creditors can be very fruitful indeed for accountants and lawyers on £300-plus an hour.

Fish-Face demanded access to my flat, unable to accept it did not belong partly to Neil and, even if it was mine, it must contain something of his. I resolutely refused to allow her across the threshold, signing tedious, lengthy letters over many months, full of detailed legal argument. I wonder who wrote those for me! The fact remained, I bought the flat before we were married. It had always been mine, I owned everything inside and however long she banged on the door, it would get her nowhere. Eventually, after endless correspondence she let the matter drop 'for the time being'. She could not bring herself to admit defeat. My ownership of the flat was a life-saver for us and deeply annoying for Fish-Face and Fayed.

But life goes on. Just when you feel it cannot get any more serious, frivolity breaks in. Martin Bell realised he could not win in Tatton once normal party politics resumed, and announced he would stand against Eric Pickles, MP, in Brentwood and Ongar where a rump of disgruntled Tories were alleging that the Conservative Association had been taken over by religious fundamentalists. There was also speculation that Frank Bruno would enter the fray. One morning the telephone rang in the flat.

It was Frank, wanting to speak to Neil and ask his advice about Bell — was he really as pompous, humourless, and egocentric as he seemed?

'Good heavens, he's even worse!' I told him to ring back shortly, when Neil would be free to talk.

'I gather you want me to be your agent!' was Neil's opening gambit and they continued to josh each other in a hugely entertaining manner. The penny wobbled when Frank asked Neil which party he should join and finally dropped when he asked whether Neil knew Sven Goran Eriksson had been the victim of a spoof interview. It wasn't 'Frank Bruno' at all, but a local radio 'shock jock' having a bit of fun. The call received widespread publicity, the radio station played it repeatedly and we hugely enjoyed the joke.

In June, while many of our former colleagues busied themselves with an election, we took my mother to Cornwall. As we traversed different constituencies, seeing endless posters along the roadside, I realised how thankful I was to be out of politics. Together with my brother, we stayed at Housel Bay Hotel, a regular haunt when my parents had lived in Cornwall. High on the cliffs above the Lizard, the most southerly point in England, the hotel affords incomparable views of the sea, rocks and birds. We felt at home.

By design, the holiday coincided with our wedding anniversary and we pilgrimaged to St Anthony-in-Meneage, where we had married eighteen years previously. The church nestles by the beach and my father's navy blue fishing boat, *Lady Mary Anne*, still bobbed at anchor in the little bay. She had been sold to neighbours who kindly lent her to us to chug past the Nare Head in Falmouth Bay on a warm, sunny day. My brother calculated the exact spot where the water was deepest and we lowered Daddy's casket near the Manacle Rocks, where he had spent so many happy hours fishing for mackerel and laying pots for crabs and lobsters. As we turned for the shore, the flower heads we had strewn floated in the sparkling water and the melancholy toll of the bell in the Manacle's buoy reminded us of our own mortality.

It gave me a great sense of completeness and peace to lower Daddy into the waters he had so loved. It seemed very much the right thing to do. I feel powerfully he is still with us and time will never dim my cherished memories. After we returned to the shore, Neil and I walked up the beach to St Anthony church and I recalled how my father and I had shared a swift but strong gin to stiffen any nerves as we set out for the wedding — 'Come on, Blossom, let's go.'

'Blossom' was later approached by the BBC for us to make a fly-on-the-wall documentary with Louis Theroux — *When Louis Met the Hamiltons*. We had never seen his documentaries but, after viewing tapes of previous programmes, we thought it would be a laugh. We liked Louis' wacky style. We had nothing to hide; he could go anywhere and ask anything. Contracted to film for fourteen days, the only problem we foresaw was finding enough to film. The summer holiday period was virtually upon us and our diaries were not overfull with opportunities. Many of our engagements could not be filmed — for example, media commitments with rival TV companies who would not allow the BBC anywhere near.

Day one, 9 July, Louis arrived at the flat with cameras rolling, determined to miss nothing! We chatted, we sparred, and we bonded. On day two Neil took Louis with him to Battersea Park for his morning run and a little work-out on the Trim-Trail. This produced the hilarious scene of the pair of them going up and down on either side of a vaulting bar like pistons in a steam engine. It was young Louis who got puffed! Next day he was in a state of collapse but did just manage to push the supermarket trolley for me.

From his initial remarks, it was clear Louis arrived believing all the usual guff about us. Within minutes, I had a light-hearted showdown with him in the bathroom, when I made it plain that if he really believed all that rubbish, he might as well pack up and go; there was no point continuing the programme. He protested an open mind but we thought exposure to some Hamilton propaganda in the form of Ralph Harris would soon sort him out! So down we bowled to Eastbourne for lunch with Ralph and José. The Rt Hon the Lord Harris of High Cross opened the door of their seafront apartment. 'Eccentric' is an overused word but Ralph really is a true example of the breed, and wonderfully politically incorrect. A cross between Magnus Pyke and Frank Muir, he was decked out in white flannels, striped blazer, crewel-work waistcoat, sandals, cotton sunhat, pipe in hand, dead straight, mid-grey hair plastered down on either side of a centre parting and moustache browned from decades of pipe smoking. Even Louis was impressed.

After a pub lunch we took the glorious summer air on the front and played a round of golf. I whacked the ball in a desultory fashion for the benefit of the cameras, then chatted with José, looking out to sea while

Ralph and Louis putted further and further away. When they returned Ralph had clearly given Louis an ear-bashing and corrected some misconceptions.

'Well,' he said, 'that's sorted a few things out.'

Louis remained inscrutable.

My mind was fully occupied by other, greater distractions – for once, not our legal and financial affairs. I was not well and was seriously worried about my health. When planning the filming schedule we had to work round dates for a series of medical checks. I knew I was stressed, suffering bouts of depression, but this was more – terrible burning pains in my stomach and cramps lower down. My throat was seriously irritated and I had painful glands under my arms. My imagination ran riot, although my doctor tried to reassure me that physical symptoms of stress take many forms and, after all I had endured, it might be no more than that. But he wanted to be sure.

The strain over recent years had certainly been appalling. We kept going, telling ourselves everything would be all right in the end. But when? I suddenly felt I just couldn't cope any longer and collapsed in floods of tears in the surgery, feeling completely overwhelmed. I had no energy at all and felt dreadful. My doctor tentatively suggested anti-depressants. What, me? I couldn't believe it had come to this. What sort of mental and physical mess was I in? He explained how they worked and, slightly reluctantly, I agreed.

It had been a bad year. We had lost in the Court of Appeal, I had lost my beloved father, we owed millions, Neil was bankrupt, we would lose our house and we had no secure income. On top of all that, daily threats and intimidation from Neil's trustee were taking their toll. I hated and deeply resented the legally sanctioned invasion of our lives, home and privacy and the attempts at humiliation. One of the worst moments came early in the bankruptcy. Speaking engagements had kept us away from Cheshire for five days and, as we were then to be in London for over a week, I asked my mother to forward the post. We arrived in Battersea and found no letters behind the door. We received little there so didn't even think about it. But there was nothing the next day or the next. The following morning I commented on this to Neil and his sensitive antennae instantly detected the enemy. He knew, as I did not, that a trustee can intercept a bankrupt's post. A quick call to the Battersea and Macclesfield sorting offices confirmed his suspicions.

'Oh, yes, the post is being forwarded to Crawley, as you instructed.' Our instructions? We had given none. Neil understood immediately. Crawley was Fish-Face's bunker. She had obviously applied to the court ex parte (without telling the other party) for an Order to intercept our post, a device normally used in emergency cases, like drug-running or international money laundering. I was screaming, literally screaming, with anger. How dare they? That these bastards, Fayed's lackeys, were opening and reading my personal letters was more than I could bear. How could we combat such underhand, devious behaviour? I felt utterly defeated, battered and bruised but as always, Neil remained calm and lawyerly. 'Look,' he said. 'You're not bankrupt. It's only me they can seek to control. What's the point, anyway? They already get my bank statements directly and there's nothing else of interest to them in my post. They can't legally open anything addressed to you.' That was some consolation at the time but I soon learned otherwise.

After a quick telephone call, we rushed to the High Court, where Neil made an emergency application to quash the Order. He rang Fish-Face, hauling her out of a meeting to tell her bluntly to get down to court without delay. She protested she could not come that afternoon but a hearing was arranged for two days' time. In court, the usual phalanx of Fayed-fuelled lawyers occupied three rows on the right; on the left, just Neil, with me sitting behind him at the back. I had taken my pink pills to keep calm; without them I knew I would not be able to keep my hands from their throats.

Neil was correct. They could not interfere with post addressed solely to me but, of course, they already had. The Order related only to Neil and although that gave them permission to redirect items jointly addressed, it absolutely did not allow them to redirect or open anything addressed to me. They had done both. They had opened everything including my bank statements and a letter to me from my father-in-law. The judge took a dim view of their behaviour, ordered them to hand back all post and the Order was quashed immediately. Game, set and match to Neil, justice and common decency.

Fish-Face's solicitor was Paul Gordon-Saker, senior partner of Stephenson Harwood, an expensive City firm. We quickly christened him 'the Slug'. He was incredibly supercilious, rude and bullying. But, his terror tactics ultimately rebounded. Finally he went too far. One day, we received a letter from our mortgagees, the Yorkshire Building Society:

'Following the release of the title deeds to Solicitors acting on your behalf, a deeds production fee of £38.50 has been debited to your account . . .' What! The deeds of our house, of which I was joint owner, sent to the enemy — unknown to me! Neil immediately contacted the building society. Gordon-Saker had written them a deliberately misleading letter: 'We are instructed in connection with the sale of the above mentioned property. Please would you let us have the title deeds on the usual undertaking.' This wording naturally implied I had consented, whereas he had not even bothered to ask me. The YBS subsequently confirmed, 'all solicitors must have the consent of all the borrowers to apply for the deeds'.

The YBS immediately realised they had been duped and told Gordon-Saker to return the title deeds. I gave the Slug the chance to apologise, to admit his mistake, but he was far too arrogant to countenance that. His charming reply: 'The arrangements between us and the Yorkshire Building Society are not your concern.' Not my concern! Was I not joint owner? It was very much my concern. But, of course, this thug had acted previously for Colin Haig in Jonathan Aitken's case when the judge described their demands as 'repugnant and a gross invasion of privacy'.

Neil and I had had enough of Gordon-Saker's bullying so I reported him to the Law Society. After months of bluster but still no apology, the Slug was officially reprimanded in a damning four-page judgment. They found him guilty on several charges of unprofessional conduct, describing it as 'extraordinary', 'high-handed', 'ignorant', and 'arrogant'. Most seriously, for a lawyer supposed to uphold the truth, he was found guilty of deliberate deceit in correspondence. Neil had proved, once again, we were no pushovers. When provoked we would fight back with all guns blazing.

And so, against this extraordinary background, we were acting normal with Louis. I had thought it would be interesting for the viewer if I took Louis behind the scenes when I recorded two episodes of *Quote, Unquote* for Radio 4 on 19 July 2001. Despite it being a BBC programme, however, they did not want the cameras in there. If only they had, Louis would have been in at the very beginning of our 'sex scandal'! It was the day Jeffrey Archer was found guilty of perjury. After recording, we switched the mobile back on and it went into overdrive with the press wanting Neil's comments on the verdict. We were in the right place to meet requests from the BBC and then went by taxi to Millbank for Neil to do a broadcast for Sky. As we were rounding Trafalgar Square a call came in from Michael Coleman, the solicitor who kindly, free of charge, had been assisting Neil with his bankruptcy.

'Where are you? When will you be on a land line?'

I could tell instantly something was wrong. 'Michael, what's the matter?'

'I can't talk on a mobile. When will you be on a land line?'

'Why not? What's happening? What's wrong? Tell me.'

'Well, let's just say there seems to be another challenge you and Neil have got to face.'

'What the hell do you mean, Michael — tell me, for heaven's sake just tell me.'

He refused and we had to wait while the taxi threaded its way through London traffic, down Whitehall, through Parliament Square to Millbank. Neil went into the studio for his interview and I called Michael from a land line in the corner of an open-plan office, surrounded by journalists. He wasted no time with pleasantries.

'Have you and Neil ever been to a sex party?'

'Of course not, don't be daft.'

'Have you ever been to a party in Ilford?'

'No. What in heaven's name is all this about?'

'Christine, I have to ask you. Have you ever been to a wife-swapping party, a sexually explicit party?'

I was becoming exasperated with his ludicrous line of questioning. 'Michael, look, whatever the question, the answer is No, No, No, No. What on earth is this all about?' I was conscious that my end of the conversation could be overheard by Sky journalists. And then he explained. The police had told him they had 'sufficient evidence to arrest us on charges of sexual assault'. Sexual assault! I was both speechless yet voluble.

He kept telling me, 'just listen', 'It's not a question of *if* they will arrest you but *when!*'

'But they can't. This is ludicrous. Michael, the whole thing is nonsense on stilts.'

He was adamant. 'Listen, Christine, just listen. This is not a wind-up. You and Neil are to be arrested for alleged sexual assault. Either you give yourselves up for arrest by appointment or the police will come for you at a time of their choosing. And, let me tell you, that will be in the middle of the night, with the press alerted.'

Yet again, we were plunged into a Hieronymus Bosch nightmare. I simply could not take in what I was hearing. I could see Neil in his glass cubicle broadcasting to the nation about Jeffrey Archer while here I was, at the other end of the long room, with perhaps twenty journalists in between, being told we were to be arrested for non-specific sexual crimes. Wake up, girl, you're dreaming!

Neil came out of his studio and, while we rushed from Sky to ITN, I had time to relay the gist of my conversation with Michael. Walking down the corridor, we suddenly remembered the man from the *Sunday Mirror*, two months earlier. When, finally, we had a sensible conversation with Michael, some of the facts emerged.

The 'incident' (we still did not know what it was) allegedly happened at a flat in Ilford on 5 May at an unspecified time. It all seemed so preposterous, so absurd, but Michael made it plain this was serious, yet more trouble for the Hamiltons. We would be arrested. There was no way out. Before arresting somebody the police should have reasonable grounds to suspect that the 'offence' itself actually happened and, secondly, that those arrested were actually involved. We had no idea whether any offence had occurred in Ilford on 5 May but we did know we had nothing whatsoever to do with one. So there would be no problem.

But, despite our categoric denials, we faced charges of 'sexual assault'. We protested to Michael, 'Why can't we just go and explain to the police there's been a misunderstanding, perhaps mistaken identity?'

'It's too late. This has gone too far for that and you *have* to be arrested. In the meantime, you say nothing, nothing, nothing. They must lay their cards on the table. Give nothing away. It is none of their business now, where you were on 5 May. They have decided to arrest; they must prove the allegations.'

Reluctantly, I had to go along with his sound advice. We were busy, Michael was busy and also abroad. We alighted on Friday 10 August as the first available date when we could 'conveniently' be arrested. Frankly, I wanted to march round to Scotland Yard, break the door down and tell them exactly what I thought of their ludicrous time-wasting nonsense. It would have taken Noddy only two minutes to check the facts and come to the right conclusion. Why had Mr Plod taken nearly three months and come to the wrong one?

That said, we were worried, seriously worried. We didn't know what the allegations were but knew only too well that if the girl claimed an 'assault' had occurred in the middle of the night, we would have difficulty proving our whereabouts. How could we establish we had been safely tucked up in bed alone, fast asleep, miles away? We had already experienced injustice at the hands of one jury. It could happen again and this time we could find ourselves in prison for seven or eight years.

It was against this background that I went to see the consultant gynaecologist. I had already had tubes inserted into my stomach, my throat and nasal cavities and I was apprehensive. I was particularly anxious to keep my health problems from my mother. She already had quite enough worry because of me, was recently widowed and did not need any more concern. The consultant said he could not rule out the 'C' word. I passed out on the floor of the consulting room, all the stress exploding and imploding at that one moment. He ordered more investigation under anaesthetic and I had to stay in overnight. It transpired I had ovarian cysts, which were causing the pain. Nothing more than millions of women experience every year, but it felt like the last straw for me then. We discussed the possibility of a hysterectomy; not an appealing prospect anyway and certainly not with everything else on my plate. There was also the continuing underlying fears about cancer. But there was no time for self-pity and wondering what might be to come. We had to deal with the here and now and that meant Louis! I told his producer, Will Yapp, that he must book Louis in with us on Friday 10 August.

'I can't tell you why. You've just got to trust me. You know I won't let you down. If you miss this you will never forgive yourself.' By then, the bond of friendship with Louis and Will was already strong. Our shared experiences over the days ahead were to strengthen it even further.

CHAPTER TWENTY-SEVEN

Arrest and Detention

Frank Longford had died and his funeral was to take place in the morning; our arrest had been scheduled for noon. On Wednesday, we had asked to move the arrest to 3 p.m. so we could attend the funeral. We began the day at Westminster Cathedral. The cavernous space was crowded but we were shown to a seat near the front, an unexpected privilege. The service was profoundly stirring, with powerful hymns and eloquent addresses, which left me acutely conscious of my own mortality and inadequacy. I left the cathedral in a tearful state. I had been so moved by the music and the tributes to a great man, husband and father.

As we walked out of the cathedral with the awful realisation of what we were about to face, I could not keep my composure any longer. I tried to avoid the cameras, not because I thought my tear-stained face would be of any interest in the context of the funeral, but because I was desperate not to draw attention to what was about to unfold. If only the press had known as we slipped round the corner, that we were linking up with Louis and Will, still completely in the dark about why we had insisted on filming that day.

We drove in convoy to Michael Coleman's house in Upper Wimpole Street where, on the steps, Neil revealed to Louis we were going to Barkingside Police Station to be arrested on suspicion of serious sexual assault. When Louis had recovered, we climbed into Michael Coleman's 4x4 and, discussing our predicament while edging through the traffic, predicted the odious Max Clifford would be involved somewhere.

We were at Barkingside rather than the main station at Ilford for our 'convenience and protection'. It was far from convenient and, in the event, offered zero protection. Apparently, it was not normally used for these purposes so we would not have to line up with everyone else being arrested that day. We drew up 50 yards beyond the police station and clambered out. The street was deserted. The camera crew filmed discreetly as we walked up the steps and disappeared inside with Michael.

Louis told us later, journalists began arriving within 45 minutes. One can only wonder how they found out we were there, when the details of our appointment were known only to a handful of police officers. By then we had been greeted by Detective Inspector Terence Summers and shown into a small interview room to be formally arrested. It was here I heard the word 'rape' for the first time and was told that our house, flat and car would be searched and our computers seized for forensic examination. We had to arrange immediately for someone to let the police into our home in Cheshire at 5 p.m. or they would break the door down. As for the flat and the car, I was to hand over the keys at once. I was horrified, desperate, and furious. I sprang up from my chair, banged the table and yelled, 'This is outrageous. You can't do this! You can't do this!'

DI Summers told me that they most certainly could and, looking into his eyes, I realised we were powerless. I was in a police state and had been formally arrested as a suspected accessory to rape! Me? Michael and Neil tried to calm me down as we moved into the back of the station for the next part of the process. I could barely contain my rage and frustration.

This draconian invasion of our privacy had been sanctioned under section 18 of the Police and Criminal Evidence Act 1984. This authorises searches merely on the signature of a police inspector and is there for emergencies, when surprise is vital to prevent evidence being destroyed by drug-dealers and other serious criminals. We had known about our impending arrest for several weeks; if there had been any evidence we could already have destroyed it. This was a deliberate ploy to enable the police to turn our house, flat, car, computers, and our very lives upside down. Why? Who was behind it all? Who would have an interest in gaining access to our private affairs, hoping, just hoping for something incriminating or humiliating? To me, the answer was obvious.

In the custody area I came across Sergeant Robinson and sensed he was going to enjoy his moment of power. He dealt with Neil first and, when I tried to intervene and make a comment, he pointed and barked, 'Go and sit in that corner.'

I looked at him in total disbelief. He repeated his order and I moved to the corner but remained standing.

Sergeant Robinson glared and pointed again. 'Sit down.'

'No.' I had asserted my independence and felt better.

Neil's paperwork was completed and I was allowed out of my corner.

'Name?' demanded the sergeant.

'Address?' He was painfully slow, laboriously writing the details, which only added to my irritation with the whole process and him in particular. But I kept my cool.

'Occupation?'

'Housewife.' He hesitated, unsure whether I was taking the mickey.

'But what do you do?'

'I *am* a housewife.' I fixed him with an unblinking glare, daring him to challenge me. He didn't.

We moved at snail's pace through the bureaucracy. Sergeant Jobsworth even had to check I could speak English and thus understand the questions. Eventually it was time to confiscate the contents of my pockets and handbag. I should be grateful he did not demand a strip-search in case I carried an offensive weapon. If only! I was being treated like a convict.

There was nothing in my pocket, beyond a tear-stained hanky left over from the funeral, already a distant memory. Then came the matter of my handbag. I didn't see why it had to be confiscated and questioned this calmly and politely, but in an acid tone. Sergeant Robinson shrugged and said my solicitor could retain it. 'All right,' I said, 'give it to Mr Coleman, then.'

'Too late,' he said triumphantly, 'I'm taking it into police custody.' He bobbed under the desk and came up with a large polythene bag into which he sealed the handbag. The atmosphere was tense. I was seething, but tried to keep cool. Neil, outwardly composed, was quietly noting with Michael everything that was going on.

Having done reasonably well so far I was beginning to feel very emotional, not just about the arrest but about the totally unwarranted invasion of our home and flat. I would have to steel myself to telephone my mother and put her through all the upset and strain of the police search. Sergeant Robinson wanted to know about my health. I did not see why I should answer his impertinent questions. He pulled another trump card. 'I'm calling a police doctor to check you are fit to be interviewed.' That might generously be interpreted as concern for my welfare but it was just another attempt to bully and humiliate me and did not improve my mental state.

The sergeant asked me to sign a form in exchange for my handbag. Under the circumstances, I was not prepared to sign anything I had not read. He had ticked a box at the top of the form to indicate that no cash had been handed in. I pointed to this, saying, 'But there is cash in my handbag. I can't sign that.'

Perhaps I was being unnecessarily pernickety but we were about to be swamped with a deluge of lies and I was not prepared to sign an untrue statement. That was the sergeant's signal to go into overdrive. 'Right, Mrs Hamilton, I will list the entire contents.' He then ripped off the polythene, slammed the bag down and emptied the contents all over the desk. How utterly ridiculous, how stupid. I exploded, quietly, but it was an explosion.

'If you don't keep quiet I'll lock you in the cells.'

I couldn't believe my ears. Where was this all going to end? The sergeant solemnly listed every credit card, banknote, lipstick, pen, pencil, perfume, all the detritus of a handbag. Imagine how long that took. I was drumming my fingers on the desk, still astonished at the treatment we were receiving.

I couldn't visit the lavatory without being accompanied down the corridor and someone standing guard outside the door. I was starving. I had had no breakfast and, somehow, lunch had not been on the agenda. Cheese rolls were procured but my request for a gin and tonic, which would have been more use, was refused. The police doctor took an hour to arrive although he was, apparently, only coming from Ilford. I was then subjected to detailed questions about family history, operations, medication – the lot. I could see no earthly reason why I should tell a total stranger my medical details with a policewoman listening in, but I was under arrest and had no choice.

After Robinson had laboriously noted her name and number, I was allowed to telephone my mother, not privately but standing at a wall-mounted telephone, surrounded by policemen. The moment was not without humour. I was poised to speak to her, idly playing with the dado rail running round the room. Suddenly, the alarms started ringing loudly all round the station. Now what? It transpired I had touched an electronic strip running at waist height round the entire building, in and out of every room!

'Hello, Granny, it's me.'

'Good. Are you on the way home yet – the cottage pie is waiting?'

'I'm afraid we won't be coming home this evening . . .'

I had to tell my mother we were under arrest on suspicion of rape.
Neil was currently being interviewed, I was next and, by the way, would
she pop round to our house and let the police in within the hour
otherwise they would break the door down. Then, please, give them free
rein to rummage and pillage wherever they liked. Oh yes, and they would
be taking away our computers and anything else they fancied. It was
beyond my wildest nightmare. Granny, of course, rose magnificently to
the occasion and, at the age of 87, jumped into her car and drove to the
Old Rectory to lie in wait for the police.

I pointed out it was a bit much to expect her to manage on her own.
Also, I was anxious to have someone else there because I wanted more
supervision, thank you very much, if our house was going to be rifled.
After giving his name and number, I was allowed to telephone Geoff
Yeo. Geoff lived nearby in Wilmslow and had always been kindness
itself, a dear friend who had worked closely with Jonathan Hunt to try
to expose the machinations behind the Fayed allegations. He was exactly
the reliable, unflappable, sensible chap I needed to hold Granny's hand,
give her a whisky and keep a keen eye on the police activities. With the
flat I had no choice. I was appalled at the thought of strangers combing
through my belongings with no friend around but there was no-one I
could ask on a Friday afternoon to go and supervise.

I know now that, even as we arrived at the funeral, six Ilford
policemen, including a computer expert, were charging up the motorway in a hired minibus, with a warrant to crawl over everything in our
home. Another six were dispatched to the flat and another six, yes six,
searched our car, parked in the underground car park near Michael
Coleman's house. His wife kindly supervised that and confirmed how
many descended, checking every nook and cranny, grabbing the laptop
in the boot.

The hired minibus, which, Geoff told us, had a broken exhaust making
it unfit for road use and probably illegal, duly arrived. Cheshire police,
headed by an inspector, had been drafted in to keep journalists at bay. The
search took three and a half hours, plus travelling time, Cheshire police time,
the time spent by the six in the flat with Battersea police in attendance,
another six searching the car – possibly 150 police-hours in total.

My mother was phlegmatic. She had, after all, been through the war; this was nothing. She had seen off Hitler and could take half a dozen coppers in her stride. But she, too, was angry about the invasion and Geoff was concerned at one point that she was hyperventilating. He tried to persuade her to sit down but she had no intention of letting any of them out of sight at any stage. It was difficult for two people to oversee six, though, and Geoff could see it would have been very easy for something to be planted.

The officers looked a little surprised at the size of the task and made the mistake of going into Neil's library first. We were in the process of packing up, in preparation for a sale. Chaos greeted them – piles of packing cases, each filled with dozens of books. They managed to be both thorough and sloppy. They opened every drawer, cupboard, filing cabinet, fridge, oven, microwave, deep freeze. They moved every cushion, looked under every mattress, even, God help them, picked up Margaret Thatcher and looked under her! In our bedroom they opened my chest of drawers. On seeing all my knickers and bras displayed, Granny, ever practical, thought, 'Good girl, it's tidy!'

Yet they ignored the door to our capacious cellars – our bondage dungeon could have been down there! They forgot to search the garden sheds and missed an entire bedroom. Geoff was in no mood to point this out. They were largely silent, making it surreal and spooky, except when their mobiles rang and the conversation centred on repairing the exhaust and how eventually to get home.

My mother finally retreated from the fray and went to sit in the drawing room nursing a large whisky. A WPC was instantly on her tail.

'You're following me, aren't you?' She wagged her finger.

The policewoman admitted she had to keep an eye on her, so she did not hide anything. My mother snorted, 'Don't be so ridiculous. I was here for an hour before you arrived. If I was going to hide anything I would have done it by now. And in a place where you wouldn't find it.'

Her guard looked embarrassed. It was obvious from her demeanour she didn't believe a word of it either and was just obeying orders.

Meanwhile, back at Barkingside, Neil was reaching the end of his hour-long interview, and I was waiting my turn. As he came out, he said, 'I'm not allowed to talk to you but guess who is involved – just as we thought!'

We now know that the girl, Nadine Milroy-Sloan, had visited Max Clifford a few days before the alleged 'rape', telling him she had saleable information, sexually explicit e-mails about the Hamiltons. He asked for proof, explained she needed to do a bit better than that and soon after contacted Fayed, who had employed him for media advice. Fayed was to offer £100,000 if it were true and could be proved. Four days later she called with the news that she had been 'raped' – and guess who were accessories? Clifford advised she should go to the police and she told him she already had. The whole fiasco was set in motion. Clifford must have been extremely disappointed when we were not arrested immediately.

So, three hours after arriving at the station, I entered the room where DI Summers and DS Richard Rees were waiting. The police recorded the interview but we were leaving nothing to chance and had borrowed a BBC recorder. I was very tired, and many of the questions were laughable. Except that this was no laughing matter. We started at 18.02, finishing after three changes of tape at 19.35. The tape is fascinating and a child could see immediately the inadequacy of the police 'evidence' and their so-called 'case' against us. Anyone hearing the full two and a half hours of both interviews might wonder if they had taken leave of their senses. Remember, to make our arrest lawful, they needed reasonable grounds to believe the offence had been committed and reasonable grounds to suspect we were criminally involved. We didn't know whether Milroy-Sloan had been raped but we did know they had no reason whatever to arrest us. I will spare you the whole transcript; an edited version will give the flavour.

DS Richard Rees (RR): I'm going to ask you questions about an allegation of indecent assault and rape. A lady, by the name of Nadine Milroy-Sloan, alleges that on the evening of Saturday 5th May 2001, at [address], she was raped and indecently assaulted. She states she had conversed via the internet and e-mail with yourself and Mr Hamilton, and another man by the name of Barry Lehaney. Some of these e-mails stated you were in the process of getting a divorce. She alleges she was held, naked, with her back to the living room floor and raped by Mr Lehaney . . . Mr Hamilton was kneeling on her left side and masturbated over her . . . you, wearing a blue dress, knelt over her face trying to force her to perform oral sex . . . Ms Milroy-Sloan identifies you and your husband from media and television pictures. I would ask you to account for your movements on that day if you can remember.

I was aghast at what I was hearing. This girl had made very serious allegations against us as long ago as 6 May — why had the police not come straight to the flat to ask where we had been on the Friday night? We would have had total recall, proof readily to hand, and the whole thing would have been finished in five minutes. If they hadn't believed it then, what had changed in the intervening three months to justify our arrest now? Michael Coleman tried to pin them down.

Michael Coleman (MC): Before we do that officer, does this woman say what time the incident took place?

RR: Not precisely, no. The best I can tell you is that it's on the evening of Saturday 5th May, and I think the latest time was around 5 p.m.

MC: When did she first make an allegation to the police about the incident?

RR: I think I'm correct in saying it was Sunday 6th May at Peckham police station. The time of 5 p.m. is the best we've been able to establish through our enquiries.

MC: Bearing in mind the severity of the allegation, I would suggest you clarify precisely how she came to be at this apartment, how long she was there, how she came to be naked, and how, or at what time Mr and Mrs Hamilton took part in this incident. Timing in this kind of case can be quite important. It does say that she remained there overnight and went home the following day.

We later discovered that the police had known for three months, from CCTV footage, that Milroy-Sloan was not in the flat at 5 p.m.

RR: Sorry, just to go back, can you detail your movements for me on that Saturday 5 May.

CH: We had people for dinner that evening so I went shopping and in the afternoon I was preparing dinner, laying the table . . .

MC: Can I guide you if the officer doesn't mind? Do you remember where you went shopping?

CH: I can't, but I'll have the receipts somewhere . . .

RR: What did you give them to eat?

CH: I can't remember . . . they might.

RR: You can't remember what you gave them to eat?

CH: No.

RR: So you've gone to the supermarket . . . bought supplies for that evening. Can you remember what you did next?

CH: I would have gone back, unloaded, got on with cooking, preparing, tidying the flat . . .

RR: What time would you have started preparing the meal?

CH: Well that depends what I was giving them. I really don't know.

RR: Would it have been a full cooked meal?

CH: It would have been three courses and cheese. I might have done Jellied Bloody Mary, one of my specialities. If I'm having people for dinner, I take some trouble.

RR: Do you send out invitations?

CH: No! It was a friend of ours . . . coming to London, to see his daughter . . . could we meet up? Because they were coming we invited two other friends of ours, Derek Laud and Diana Rasbach.

RR: Who arrived first, and at what time?

CH: Well, they would have arrived half past sevenish. My guess would be the Tuckers arrived first . . . but I'm not certain. They might remember.

RR: That's fine. I've got to deal in facts. So if you can't remember. What time did they leave? Can you remember that?

If only they had been dealing in 'facts' — we would never have been there!

CH: I think the Tuckers probably left — I'm guessing, but around midnight. The other two stayed on later.

RR: Can you give us a time everyone had left by? What time did you go to bed?

CH: They would probably have gone by 1 a.m., but then we would have cleared up.

RR: Did you leave the flat at any time during that night?

CH: No.

RR: Did you leave the room for any noticeable length of time? I understand you probably went into the kitchen and back.

CH: Of course I left the room! To go to the loo I should think . . . anybody would have done.

RR: I'm talking about for half an hour . . .

CH: Lord, no.

RR: If I speak to all these people, they're going to say you were there throughout the whole evening?

CH: Absolutely.

Did they honestly think we had popped out after the first course, rushed to Ilford, raped someone and come back for the meat and two veg? It was surreal.

RR: Do you know anybody by the name of Barry Lehaney?

CH: No.

RR: He uses other names, James Hamilton?

CH: I know Lord James Douglas-Hamilton. I imagine it's not him.

RR: Have you ever employed Barry Lehaney or any of those other names that I've given you?

CH: No.

RR: Do you have access to the internet?

CH: Yes.

RR: Do you visit chat rooms?

CH: No.

RR: Have you ever visited a chat room or been present when someone's been in a chat room?

CH: No.

RR: Do you have a computer in London or Cheshire?

CH: I've got one in London, currently in the boot of the car, and two in Cheshire.

All three, by then, were in the swag bag.

RR: Do you visit internet porn sites?

CH: No, I do not. Sorry!

RR: Have you ever conversed about sending images like that to other people?

CH: No.

RR: Do you know a female by the name of Nadine Milroy-Sloan?

CH: No.

RR: I'll show you the picture . . .

CH: No. I don't recognise her at all.

RR: Have you ever seen her before?

CH: No. No.

RR: Have you ever used on the internet or otherwise, the names Sir Barry, or Lady Joan?

CH: No, I haven't.

RR: Is there anything that the officers attending your home will find relating to Nadine or Barry?

CH: No. Nothing at all. Unless something's been planted.

RR: Are you in the process of getting a divorce?

CH: Certainly not!

RR: Have you been contacted . . . by the press or Max Clifford in relation to this allegation?

CH: By the *Sunday Mirror*. Not by Max Clifford.

RR: Do you have a working or personal relationship with Mr Clifford?

CH: Certainly not.

RR: You are obviously aware of who he is?

CH: I've had the misfortune to meet him in television studios. I'm not surprised you mentioned his name.

RR: Why are you not surprised?

CH: Because this has all the hallmarks of a Max Clifford set-up job. Of course, he works for Mr Fayed.

RR: When you say a 'set-up', what do you mean?

CH: Well, I don't know how it's been set up. The allegations are preposterous and untrue. I don't know whether the girl has or hasn't been raped, but the idea that we had anything to do with it is nonsense on stilts. Whether Clifford has put the idea into her head that it was us I have no idea. All I'm saying is that the whole thing stinks and has all the hallmarks of Max Clifford. I'm not remotely surprised that you mention his name.

RR: I'll go over the allegations. You, along with your husband and Mr Lehaney got this female, Mrs Nadine Milroy-Sloan in this flat. She had been raped by Mr Lehaney and indecently assaulted by yourself and your husband. What is your reply to that?

CH: Completely and utterly false. In every particular. No truth in it whatsoever.

We had been asked to take our diary along with us. Rees honed in on an entry for 12 May.

RR: Could I ask you to read the entries for that day. There's one word which says, if you wouldn't mind reading it for me.

CH: It says, 'Lust'. Lust is the nickname of a friend. It was his 52nd birthday.

RR: It says Lust – 52.

CH: It means it was Lust's 52nd birthday.

RR: That's the only words written on that page?

CH: Absolutely.

It could only happen to the Hamiltons! We are being accused of sexual assault and the police find the word 'Lust' written in my diary! It is just as well there was no mention of our friend Gerald Rand, who goes by the nickname of 'Randy'.

RR: Can I ask what you were wearing that night as well.

CH: Not a blue dress.

RR: Why did you say a blue dress?

CH: Because I understand that I'm alleged to have been wearing a blue dress . . .

RR: Did either of you leave the flat after 3 p.m. that afternoon?

CH: No. Once we got back with the shopping I would have needed all the time to get organised.

Only the Hamiltons could have forgotten they were at Claridge's – see more later!

RR: Did anyone see you bringing all that back? Neighbours? Didn't bump into Mr Jones from next door and say hello, nice weather?

How could I possibly remember whether I had bumped into a neighbour while puffing and panting with carrier bags of food, three months ago. If only they had cross-questioned Milroy-Sloan with this degree of detail.

CH: It's three months ago – I don't know.

RR: Is there anything else you can think of that would be of assistance to us in investigating this matter?

At last – questions were being asked that might get us somewhere.

CH: Well, I don't know what questions you've asked this woman, but how does she know it's me? What did she think I looked like for a start? I've changed my appearance quite dramatically.

RR: How have you changed your appearance quite dramatically?

They'd been on the case for three months – he should have known.

CH: Well, there's the classic pictures that everybody remembers . . . me coming out of court. My hair was swept back. I've had it fringed and layered and shortened. It looks quite different.

RR: Have you got any distinguishing features that would not be immediately apparent to me looking at you . . . any scars or tattoos or anything? Birthmarks?

CH: No.

RR: Would you feel it appropriate for your client to consider an identification parade?

MC: Unless we can have half a dozen Christine Hamilton lookalikes, with a variety of hairstyles, I cannot see any benefit in there being an identification parade.

CH: I just think she could be nailed down a little bit as to what she thinks I look like. Dress, what sort of blue dress? . . . Shade, style, length, sleeves. . .?

MC: Did this girl give any description to the shade, colour, style, length, cut, sleeves?

RR: She couldn't give a description; all she can recall is that it was a blue dress, that's her recollection.

CH: She must know whether it was light or dark.

RR: There are issues around this and obviously she's given us a statement and has been interviewed. We can only record what she recollects.

MC: She can't recollect whether it's warm, woolly, silky or man-made fibre.

RR: It's a blue dress. We haven't put that to her.

CH: I don't wear blue . . . I'm associated with red not blue. Blue is a Tory colour . . . it could be autosuggestion. Mr Clifford should have done his homework. He knows I wear red.

Towards the end of the interview we got on to the question of the computers that I thought were merely being 'examined' at our house and flat. Far from it; they were being seized.

DI Terence Summers (TS) to Sergeant Rees: I think we've adequately covered the areas that need to be covered. They will want their computers back very promptly, so we're happy for you to take a scan, or whatever your computer people need.

CH: Computers haven't been taken, have they?

RR: Um.

CH: They haven't been taken from the house?

TS: They will physically remove the computers.

CH: Well, I must have it back. I can't operate. I need it, I'll need it.

TS: Well, this is the point I've just, Christine . . .

CH: My whole life is there!

TS: This is the point I am making. [To Sergeant Rees] So, can you promptly have your people take a copy of the material . . . can you ensure that copy does not at any stage leave police custody and, assuming, um, er, that this inquiry takes the course that I would expect it to take, you will require a swift destruction of your copy of that material together with certification that no further copies of it have been made.

CH: You mean the computer in the boot of the car and the two from Cheshire have gone?

RR: Yes. They go to our technical department and they download the information.

CH: They'll do that tonight . . .

RR: Well, they won't, they won't download it tonight, no . . .

CH: But it's Saturday tomorrow, I can't live without that until Monday, I just can't, I can't . . .

RR: Unfortunately, we will not be able to do it over the weekend.

TS: It will, it will not be. I'll be realistic; I'll be honest with you . . .

CH: I can't do, I can't e-mail anybody, I can't . . . access all the information I need.

TS: I'm not a computer expert . . . they have to do things . . . the reason your computer is taken is so that its integrity is intact. It is unplugged in situ. . . brought to our computer lab and the specialist there will download it in their own specific way.

CH: When is that going to be? Can we not be lent a computer?

TS: Them facilities, to be, got, we'll be, I'll be, bluntly honest, we, no, that does not sort of happen . . . We have got to pursue every avenue in this inquiry . . . it may prove to be to your advantage for us to have your computer, I know it doesn't feel like it now . . .

CH: This is the final straw . . . [sounds of ripping paper and crying]

TS: I think it's probably appropriate to conclude this interview. Do you have anything else you want to deal with?

CH: No . . . except the whole thing is a monstrous lie.

TS: Thank you. Time by my watch is 7.35 p.m. and we conclude the interview.

I looked at Summers through my tears, 'You don't believe any of this, do you?' He was silent.

It was not, of course, DI Summers alone who had sanctioned our arrest. Because, to date, the police have declined to come clean with us, I still do not know where the line divides between a shambolic cock-up and a deliberately perverse decision. Our arrest cost the taxpayer a still unrevealed sum, probably running into millions. All because of an idiotic decision to arrest two people who, on the most elementary enquiry, could be proved totally innocent. Why? Who was really behind it? Were these senior police officers stupid or was it something else? Perhaps we will never know because we cannot get answers to our questions.

    Back to Barkingside where, earlier, Neil had been asked similar questions.

DI   Terence Summers (TS): Do you attend sex parties?

NH: No.

TS: Do you know Mr Max Clifford?

NH (laughing): Oh yes, we have come across him many times . . . I did wonder if his grubby little paws are on this one. I know Mr Clifford very well. He is employed by Mohamed Fayed as his chief public relations supremo. I suspected he was the intermediary between your complainant and the *Sunday Mirror*.

TS: Have you ever had any direct contact with Mr Clifford?

NH: Yes, I have spoken to him in television studios.

TS: I have got to put it to you, sir, that we have received this allegation that you have indecently assaulted this young lady and that you, along with your wife, an unknown man and a named man have got her in this flat and whilst there you have assisted in restraining her on the floor and performed an act of indecent assault upon her. Have you any comment?

NH: Well, it is wholly false and the girl is either hallucinating or it is part of a malicious fabrication.

I do not know what underhand and shadowy forces were responsible for it but, clearly, the police had no grounds whatsoever for arresting us. Why had they done it? We still have no answer. She said it happened and we were involved. Barry Lehaney, her alleged 'rapist' said it did not, he had never met either of us and we had never been to his flat. Lehaney was sixty, hugely overweight, a chronic asthmatic and so arthritic he had to be carried from his flat when arrested.

'The suggestion of me kneeling on the floor to have sex is ridiculous. I can barely stand, let alone kneel. I told them from the start it was just rubbish.'

Furthermore, within a couple of days of Milroy-Sloan's complaint, the police amassed CCTV evidence from three separate locations proving that she and Lehaney were not in his flat at the time of the alleged rape. She was recorded laughing and joking with him elsewhere.

The girl came from Grimsby and the Met had not even taken the elementary precaution of checking with Lincolnshire police who could have told them she had a record of sexual fantasy, including allegations against her own grandmother. They had had months to trawl for 'evidence'. They found nothing whatsoever to corroborate this girl's wild lies but some evidence that contradicted them. They knew arresting us would create headlines hence the presence of their press officer when we were at Barkingside. At the time of writing, well over three years later, we have not had the results of the internal police enquiry; the original copies of the information on our computers have not been returned to us; we have had no confirmation that all copies have been destroyed and no apology from the police for the way we were treated.

Having been immured in Barkingside for five hours, we were finally released on bail. Michael and Neil were hopping up and down, having been waiting for an hour and a half while I was interviewed. It was gently explained that an army of journalists and banks of cameras were waiting outside. Sergeant Robinson, deprived of the fun of locking me into a cell, informed me, 'There is a tunnel. You can use that if you like.'

I stared at him with incomprehension. Clearly, we lived on different planets. 'You must be joking. You tunnel if you want to. I'm not sneaking away. I don't care how many are out there, we are leaving by the front entrance, the way we came.'

I was not feeling anything like as brave and gung ho as I must have sounded. I was suffering from lack of food and five hours spent on an emotional roller coaster, battered by police questioning. All I wanted was a large stiff drink and then another.

Neil and Michael had decided they would tell the press all details of the allegations. This news was imparted to me as we were walking towards the glass door, behind which I could see the seething mob. I stopped in my tracks. 'You can't. You can't . . . It's grotesque . . . you can't . . .'

Neil grabbed me by the hand, 'Trust me. It's the only way. Look at all the press. Who told them we were here? Much better to give them the true story now, otherwise there will be endless speculation for days on end, with even worse things being alleged.'

By then we were about to burst through the doors. I had no choice but to go along with it. I was mesmerised as we went out into the flashlights. It was utterly humiliating and degrading, having to stand and listen to Michael Coleman detail the sordid allegations. Despite having had my share of public controversy and being in the spotlight in traumatic circumstances, nothing, nothing, had prepared me for the awfulness of those few minutes.

Through the barrage of cameras and reporters, I could see the familiar faces of Louis and his team. They had been waiting outside for five hours. We sped back into central London, with Louis' cameras rolling. I hardly registered they were there. The mobile was ringing madly. We were all hungry and stopped for takeaway pizzas. When we arrived at the flat we were greeted by another posse of cameras and microphones. 'Christine, how do you feel?'

'I'm feeling innocent, as always,' I barked, as I marched into the block, pizzas in hand. Upstairs, only minutes later, I saw that very retort reported on the TV news. Surely something more important was happening in the world?

That weekend 'Hamiltons on Sex Charges' dominated the headlines and many inside pages. Determined not to sink under a tide of false allegations, we tried to ensure our denials became the dominant theme, not Milroy-Sloan's squalid lies. We were besieged. At one stage – remember we live on the seventh floor – a 'cherry-picker' camera (one on a crane) reared its head at our level, trying to peer through our windows.

My mother had been waiting in Cheshire on Friday evening with the cottage pie, expecting just Neil and me. Instead, she had had to endure a police search, two days of waiting until Monday and then got Louis as well! By then, she was fed up with the delay and the journalists parked on the lawn. She all but hauled us into the house. Having said our piece yet again for the cameras, we put up the shutters, drew the curtains and sat down to supper – four-day-old cottage pie! Granny had had the odd nip of whisky and was in full flow about the dreadful journalists; why did we spend so much time talking to them?

Turning to me she exploded, 'Now you've got here, at last, what's *he* doing here?'

I reminded her about Louis and the programme. She looked extremely doubtful about the wisdom of the whole thing, so I told her Louis was an award-winning journalist. Granny had some carrot on her fork, midway to her mouth. Stabbing the fork, carrots and all, in his direction, 'Award-winning! Him? I *don't* believe it.'

It was a magic moment!

I was beginning to recover my perspective. We were assembling our alibi, the pieces of the jigsaw were fitting and we were confident of sorting the matter out in a few days. The saga had its funny side. Neil went into the local newsagent the following day to be told an elderly customer had announced, 'All that stuff about Neil 'amilton, I don't believe it – he 'asn't got it in him!'

It frequently happens when people are in the news that others crawl out of the woodwork to make a fast buck. As if the Milroy-Sloan allegations were not enough, a 'kiss-and-tell' bimbo quickly emerged to seek publicity and, no doubt, money for her mucky little lies. Emma Padfield, noted only for her romps with famous footballers and appearing without knickers on *Blind Date*, claimed in the *Daily Star* that Neil and I had propositioned her for a four-in-a-bed frolic with her 'boyfriend'. According to Padfield, I said, 'How about the four of us go somewhere afterwards?' Apparently, this was done 'in a really sexual way.

It was obvious she meant she fancied more than a quick drink. It was done in such a suggestive way . . .' Then I was alleged to have come back a few minutes later, this time with Neil in tow, asking 'What do you think about it?' Padfield was 'gobsmacked' and 'couldn't wait to get away from the party'.

The article, with the usual innuendo, fabrications and bimbo photographs would have been laughable but for its timing. Coming just three days after the allegations from Milroy-Sloan, it added fuel to the fire, encouraging people to believe we were up to sexual shenanigans of all kinds. We had to rack our brains to think who Padfield was and why she should make these absurd allegations. Suddenly we remembered. We had met her a couple of years earlier, as members of the studio audience in a Jackie Mason television special in London. His theme was 'the Media' and we had been invited along, together with the usual suspects from both sides, both the hunters and the hunted, including Max Clifford.

Also present was Greg Cordell, whose claim to fame was winning a bride in a contest organised by a Midlands-based radio station. Greg picked up £50,000, a flat and an all-expenses-paid honeymoon in the Bahamas, within weeks of which they had split up. Padfield, who said she was a model and had been treated 'appallingly' by the media, put on a convincing show of nerves, sidled up to me and asked for some tips on being in front of the camera. I tried to relax her, telling her not to worry, to ignore the cameras and be herself – the usual friendly advice. After the show, she approached me again, said she was getting on well with Cordell and did I think it all right if they left together? She was worried that it might be reported in the press. I commiserated about the press and said that all they had to do was leave separately and meet up later. She said she wanted to stay in touch in case she needed any help or advice. Like an idiot I gave her my mobile number. Hindsight is a wonderful thing! At the time she seemed nice enough, appeared genuinely worried and I had no reason to suspect anyone was pulling her strings.

Later, she called on the mobile, saying the press knew she and Greg had teamed up. It was all very stressful; could I give her some advice? I had no idea of her history of scandalous under-the-duvet-exposés and claims to have bedded more than thirty footballers and TV stars. She asked about selling her story. I told her if she wanted to plant or sell a story she should probably go and see Max Clifford. It is amazing she did not burst out laughing – Clifford was probably standing right beside her at the time!

About a week later, she called again. Her story now was that she and Greg were at a hotel in London, still worried about the press, could we meet them for a drink to talk about it? I had had enough, said I really could not help and told her again if she wanted advice about selling her story she should consult the expert tripe-pedlar.

Against that background, imagine my feelings on reading the *Daily Star* garbage. I realised in a flash that she had been trying to set us up two years earlier. Just suppose, sympathetic to Padfield's entreaty for help, we had gone to that hotel and, because she wanted privacy, met them in their room? Photographs would have been taken and produced as 'evidence' and Padfield's lies and fantasies would have appeared much earlier, earning vast amounts of money for her. How disappointed she must have been that it didn't work.

There were other surprises too. *Coronation Street* star Bill Roache and his wife Sara were close friends. I was staggered, therefore, in the middle of the furore, to receive a call from a journalist I knew and trusted.

'Christine, have you anything to say about Sara Roache's comments?'

I had no idea what he was talking about so he read her quote from the *Daily Express*, 'I think their behaviour is absolutely disgraceful.' He confirmed she did say exactly that. But I kept my counsel and confined myself to the well-trodden path of 'No comment'.

Neil and I were amazed and upset. Whatever she felt in private, how could Sara make such a comment in public? Sadly, we have not heard from either of them since. I regret the rift and looking back, it seems so foolish to have allowed a wicked fantasist to kill a friendship.

Sara could not possibly have believed the allegations; it must have been our very public rebuttals she found objectionable. She was not alone in that, and cynical commentators described us as 'enjoying' and 'milking' the publicity. But it would have been folly to remain silent and allow a torrent of lies to gain credence. We had to fight our corner, to prove our innocence.

Our problems were compounded because Milroy-Sloan continued her assault, through her solicitor, repeating her heinous allegations. Police 'sources' claimed they had to arrest us because we had earlier refused to be interviewed informally – another monstrous lie that had to be nailed.

Daily, we amassed more detailed proof of our whereabouts and expected the police to admit their mistake. There was also the extraordinary business of Claridge's. We had completely forgotten we had joined our American friends for a quick drink in the bar before dashing back to host the dinner party. But someone else remembered. We had not met Barry Moss before but he recalled the occasion. Reading his newspaper the morning after our arrest, he immediately telephoned Barkingside police to say he could confirm our whereabouts. What did the police do? Telephone our solicitor and report this development? Dear me, no! They did nothing. With zero response from the police and reading nothing in the press about Claridge's, Barry Moss decided on further action. He contacted Michael Coleman the following Tuesday. Michael wrote to DI Summers – his fifth letter since the arrest, all unanswered for many more days – giving details about Claridge's plus names and numbers of others present.

We gave Milroy-Sloan every opportunity to admit she might have been mistaken about us. Instead she continued to throw petrol on the flames, selling her story the following weekend to the *News of the World* for £50,000, brokered by Max Clifford. Unbelievably, the headline included the words 'Christine's Lesbian Lust'. Milroy-Sloan had sold her precious right to anonymity, given by Parliament (voted for by Neil) to protect 'victims', not to enable sluts and fantasists, egged on by publicists, to profit from their lies.

With all the evidence – Lehaney's denials, the CCTV footage, information from the Lincolnshire police, shop receipts, mobile phone records, testimony from our dinner guests, witnesses at Claridge's – still the charges were hanging over our heads. Is it any wonder we kept up the public denials? The police finally capitulated, releasing us from bail at 4.45 p.m. on 28 August, nearly three weeks after our arrest. It took even longer for them to admit the whole thing should never have happened. The London *Evening Standard* billboards and newspaper ran the banner headline:

POLICE: WE SHOULD NOT HAVE ARRESTED THE HAMILTONS

The paper attempted to cost the whole fiasco, millions of pounds to the taxpayer. The story, however, appeared only in the early editions as it was overtaken by terrible events thousands of miles away in the USA – it was 11 September 2001.

CHAPTER TWENTY-EIGHT

Adam and Eve – *Millionaire* – Make-overs

Life lurched from the ridiculous to the ludicrous. While Neil was dealing with Fish-Face and Slug, and I was coping with doctors, consultants, scans, prods and probes, we were approached by *GQ* magazine and asked if we would do a feature article with them. Yes, no problem. Then came the question of the photograph. Tim Lewis telephoned and I said cheerily, 'Do you want to do it at home or in the flat?'

'Well, um, in a studio.'

Blast, I thought, that takes longer – glossy studio shots can last all day. 'All right, I suppose so, what sort of thing do you want?'

A long pause from Tim, 'Well, um, er, well, you know Lucas Cranach's painting of Adam and Eve . . .'

'What! *You are joking!* For heaven's sake!'

I did know the painting, a famous and beautiful sixteenth-century oil of Adam and Eve in the Garden of Eden, under the Tree of Knowledge, surrounded by beasts and animals, with the serpent descending temptingly from the branches. 'Oh, Christine, come on, it would all be done very tastefully . . .'

'Look, Tim, I'm 51, I wouldn't have done that when I was 21! Don't be daft . . . sorry . . .'

Neil, of course, considered it a highly amusing idea. He would! He put me under no pressure but it was clear he thought I was silly to object. With body stockings, Lady Godiva wig, strategically placed leaves etc., everything would be left to the imagination. It would need to be! Eventually we were persuaded to go to Vogue House. In editor Dylan Jones's office an image of the painting was laid out – very splendid, muted colours, soft focus – it would make a wonderful photograph. My mischievous side wanted to do it – what fun, what a jape, what a laugh! My sensible side cautioned against. I knew the photograph would cause consternation in certain quarters – for a start what would Granny think?

We were not being paid for the article itself but I didn't see why *GQ* should get it all for nothing. I told Dylan he would have to pay a charity a really good figure, if I was going to expose, however camouflaged, my own less than perfect one! He nodded, that was fine and we agreed a sum. He also granted my request that I have total veto if I wasn't happy with the photo.

The photo-shoot was fun. I had stipulated an endless supply of champagne to relax my inhibitions and it did. The serpent arrived deep-frozen and gradually defrosted as the day wore on, becoming more and more droopy. Against a lush backdrop of trees, leaves and apples, with assorted stuffed animals, we posed on a soggy forest floor. I wore a ghastly nylon, platinum blonde, thigh-length wig (which looked silky and fabulous in the photograph) and we both wore flesh-coloured underwear on to which the stylist had to pin the fig (actually it was a spray of ivy) leaves. It was a happy and memorable day.

I had planned my Granny strategy. She doesn't read *GQ* so I would get an advance copy, sit her down and explain the whole thing was a bit of a laugh, tongue in cheek and she mustn't take it seriously. She had been to stay with friends in Oxfordshire and clambered on the train home, clutching a copy of the *Daily Mail* because the *Telegraph* is just too big to cope with under such circumstances. Imagine her horror when, as she settled into her seat, she saw a banner headline across the top of the front page: 'Would you Adam and Eve it!?' together with a small photograph, clearly recognisable to a mother as her daughter, despite the wig. There on page three was the whole photograph, taking up most of the page. *GQ* was delighted but Granny nearly had terminal heart failure! They had circulated the photograph in advance to all the press. Of course they were going to, they have a magazine to sell, but I genuinely hadn't thought about it – I was too busy fending off trustees and lawyers and dealing with medical problems.

It was not the best way for Granny to find out; she had to face the whole journey on her own, horrified by what was in the paper and wondering what I was going to do next! At least the *Mail* stuck vaguely to the facts. The *Mirror*, of course, had to put the knife in. They devoted an entire editorial to the item, 'Naked Greed – Is There Nothing the

Hamiltons Won't Do for Money . . .?' They knew perfectly well all the thousands were going to charity, and we had received nothing, but it didn't suit their purpose to make that fact clear.

Sadly, charitable causes did not do so well when we appeared on a 'Christmas Celebrity Couples' edition of *Who Wants to Be a Millionaire?* It was clearly a golden opportunity to win some serious money for charity but I was worried about our combined lack of knowledge of 'popular' culture, which is essential to get through the first rounds. We would probably know the answers to many of the 'serious' questions, largely thanks to Neil's wide knowledge, but how were we going to reach them? Easy — ask the audience, go fifty-fifty, phone a friend and Bob's your uncle! What you also need, of course, in total absence of knowledge, is a little bit of luck. Not knowing whether we would be dividing a million pounds or nothing, we nominated the Children's Wish Foundation and the Mid-Cheshire Sheltered Workshop.

I was very nervous indeed, unusually so for me. While we waited in the green room we watched the others ahead of us. Jimmy and Liza Tarbuck did very well and then Frank Skinner and David Baddiel did brilliantly. Time was ticking away, the tension mounting, together with the pressure on us to succeed. It is, of course, easy sitting at home or watching in the green room! I know everyone says this but we really did seem to know the answers to most of their questions. Even the one Frank and David finally baulked at, not risking their £125,000 for the possibility of £500,000. 'What is the national flower of Japan?' Neil gave the correct answer, 'chrysanthemum', before the options had even appeared on the screen.

By the time we came to be perching on the stools in the middle of the familiar horseshoe audience, expectations were high but I was a bag of nerves and not focusing properly. It had been a bad year — Daddy had died, we had been arrested, Fish-Face had been reinforced in her assault by Slug, and I was still very worried about my unresolved health problems.

'Well,' says Chris Tarrant. 'What are your weak spots?'

'Gosh, everything, popular culture, sport, soaps, pop music, films . . .'

Chris was incredulous. 'Christine, what on earth are you doing here?'

That was my cue to flee the studio right then but we were off. After a couple of utterly daft questions to get things going we had 'Which of these was a 1983 UK Number I single for UB40? "Red Red Wine", "Black Black Coffee", "Orange Orange Squash", or "Pink Pink Gin"?'

We hadn't a clue although, clearly, it was not coffee or squash. Remembering 'Lily the Pink' from the 1960s I thought it just could have been the gin. We could not afford to fluff such an early question so we asked the audience, too hastily. We should have taken more time, thought it through and, I think, we would have come to the right answer without 'wasting' a lifeline. But I was not thinking clearly. We climbed with two lifelines intact and faced the £8,000 question.

'Who won a Best Supporting Actress Oscar for her role in the 1988 film *The Accidental Tourist*? Meryl Streep, Geena Davis, Jessica Lange or Whoopi Goldberg?' I knew it was not Meryl Streep. We went fifty-fifty and were left with Geena and Jessica. We phoned our 'film' friend; he gave us the wrong answer. As we crashed back to £1,000 and out of the contest, the whole year of horror just welled up in me. I had to get away and out of the limelight. I slid off the stool and rushed out of the studio in floods of tears; on prime-time television, watched by millions. Everyone, including Chris Tarrant and all the crew, were wonderfully kind and understanding but my sense of failure and disappointment was profound.

Just before that disastrous performance went out at Christmas 2001, *When Louis Met the Hamiltons* was broadcast. The programme achieved record ratings and millions were fascinated to see behind the scenes as the saga unfolded before their eyes. There was probably a bit too much Hamilton on the television but viewers saw, many for the first time, that we were just normal, ordinary human beings; I drink too much and flirt with anything in trousers, while Neil tells rotten jokes and gets into trouble! My overreaction on *Millionaire*, even the awful fact of our arrest, helped to change many people's perceptions. We were suddenly seen as vulnerable, a word not previously associated with the Hamiltons; people began to notice the human side.

Seeing yourself as others see you is not easy. I am not obsessive about my appearance, far from it, but, in the public eye, how you look is noticed and my look had been noticed. In particular by the *Mail on Sunday*'s *You* magazine, which was longing to transform me, as they put it, from 'Battleaxe to Babe'. I would have been daft to turn that down! Their make-over changed my appearance for ever and I will always be grateful to their beauty editor, Jo Fairley, who was responsible. She was determined to alter my hairstyle. Instead of being 'clipped back and lacquered into submission' it would be softer and more flattering. I had never really bothered with hairdressers, apart from the odd cut and I even did that for myself on many occasions, with predictable results! I was nervous at the shoot, especially when I saw the lady from Michaeljohn wielding her scissors with a vengeance, and sheltered behind the excuse that I needed continuity for my BBC TV series. Things could only be rearranged, not cut. Nevertheless, the results were spectacular. I looked and felt totally different and even Neil noticed! But Jo was not going to let me off so lightly. A few weeks later, when the series was completed, I was summoned back for the full chop and another article. I should have done it decades before. My fine hair is now a triumph of mousse, magic and the lovely Matt Harrison at Michaeljohn. The fringe is flattering and usefully covers the furrows in my forehead, the result, Neil says, of my 'overenthusiastic' face.

You had less long-term success with my clothes. Looking back, my affinity with red started as a child, although as a weight-conscious teenager I swathed myself in navy to look slimmer. I soon gave up the unequal struggle and reverted to my passion. Henry Ford's customers could have any colour they liked as long as it was black and I take the same view of red. My wardrobe is a cornucopia of bright primary colours, somewhat akin to the contents of a child's paintbox. Why wear one colour if six will do? I love colour and panache and have no intention of becoming frumpy. I am 'realistically' sized, have spent my entire life wanting to be slimmer and smaller, but I've now reached accommodation with my body. Actually that's *not* true, but let's not draw attention to defects!

Sometimes you receive a jolt from an unexpected quarter. In 2000, in my 51st year, I was asked to take part in a charity fashion show in Cheshire, the organisers approaching different shops to dress each 'model'. 'I'm sorry, but we cannot consider dressing Mrs Hamilton. She is too old.' Too old! What for? Benetton, Top Shop? That would be understandable. But this was dear old Jaeger pronouncing me over the hill because, apparently, their policy was now to appeal to those on the 'right' side of the great Five-0. Forgive me for not having realised when looking at some of their clothes!

We all like compliments and I am certainly no exception, especially after my experience with Jaeger. I am not vain, but my appearance is important to me. Growing old with someone you love is a joy not given to everyone. Neil and I find great mutual support in facing physical deterioration together. We are virtually the same age and understand (if

Venus can understand Mars!) what each is feeling as things sag, bag, wrinkle and decay. Women have the advantage of make-up whereas the poor chaps have to make do with nature – well, most of them do! With them, what you see is grim reality. But for us, bliss to have been born female; what you are is what you see after half an hour's reconstruction. Not even your life's companion should be allowed to gaze for too long on the grisly truth!

I am reasonably happy with the way ageing has treated me but others have seen scope for improvement. A couple of years ago, whenever the media wanted a middle-aged face to 'improve' they thought of me! Gloria Hunniford persuaded me to have infill injections (polyfilla, according to Neil!) live on her *Open House* programme. They were great; plumped up my nasal-labia lines and lasted about six months. Then the *Daily Mail* asked me to have NewFill, which plumps up the face with collagen, the effects lasting up to a year. Before my natural lines began to reappear, *Tonight with Trevor McDonald*, investigating the Botox controversy, overcame my initial reluctance and persuaded me to have that too – again on camera. Heavens alive! I was going to be a human pin cushion! There are apparently two sorts of line or wrinkle – expression and gravity – and different treatments deal with different lines. So I had the lot, was delighted with the results and, by the time you are reading this, I am sure I will have ventured back for more!

Age has a wonderful way of compensating. As your wrinkles arrive so your eyes begin to fuzz over and you simply don't see the cracks. I use a 5x magnifying mirror to ensure the make-up goes in the right place. So I either see my wrinkles like huge crevasses (they can't be that bad) or I just glance in a mirror during the day (without reading glasses) and am agreeably surprised. I really don't know exactly what I do look like. My glasses are 2.5 magnifications so does that mean I am seeing my hips bigger than they are? Or does it mean, when I look without them, I am seeing myself smaller? Either way, do I ever see the real me? Thank goodness, probably not!

I'm not obsessive, but I am conscious of what I eat both for health and weight reasons. We all know how to stay eternally young – lots of water and exercise, plenty of sleep, no sun, smoke or drink. Some are easier than others and I do, of course, fall down heavily on alcohol. On the roller coaster of life, if things are good I want to celebrate, if things are grim I need support – either way, alcohol fits the bill perfectly. I refuse to feel guilty about my wine consumption. Life is too short and we should all be free to go to hell in our own way.

Just as *You* were getting to grips with my appearance, I was on *Any Questions* with Norman Fowler, MP, Michael Cashman, MEP, and Jonathan Porritt, the environmentalist. There is always a warm-up question, which is not broadcast. On this occasion it was, 'In times of stress what authors and passages of their works do you turn to?' The others gave serious answers but I couldn't think of anything and simply said, 'I don't bother with authors. I turn to gin . . .'

Gin was our cocktail of choice in Spain. After a bucket-shop flight out of Luton, we stayed with Razzie and another dear friend, Patsy Baker, at charming, old-fashioned Villa Fuz, just yards from the sea. We had a glorious week, totally relaxed and happy except for my one *big* concern. The tabloids love to print unflattering paparazzi pictures of ladies in bathing costumes and I did not want to be caught out. The villa was delightfully private, with secluded balconies and inner courtyard. But the beach, deserted in the morning and evening, filled up a bit in the middle of the day. I never ventured forth without hat and sunglasses, sensible anyway but also essential for anonymity. Spain is crawling with Brits and I was determined not to be the subject of one of those awful sneak photographs. Razzie was dismissive: 'For goodness sake, Christine, who the hell do you think you are? Joan Collins? Nobody's going to be interested in snapping you.'

'I do not want my cellulite blown up all over the *Mirror*.'

Razzie roared with laughter, 'It wouldn't need blowing up, darling, it's all there!'

Sure enough, back home in the *Daily Mail*, there was a large photograph of a near-naked Hamilton. Phew — it was only Neil, looking surprisingly athletic, stripped to his shorts out running, but you can't be too careful!

Chapter Twenty-Nine

It's a Jungle, Get Me in There!

Little did I know, my years of coping with reality in life were but a rehearsal for an altogether different kind – reality television! Here frustration, sexual tension, hunger, tiredness, fear and boredom combine to create friction, feuding and the whole gamut of celebrity emotions. This cavalcade of tantrums and tears became compulsive viewing for millions. 'Reality TV' – what a misnomer! It is difficult to imagine a more artificial situation. Eight people, carefully selected for contrast, are plonked in a goldfish bowl while millions watch their antics and sadistically select them for 'Bushtucker Trials' of manipulated horror and humiliation.

I was approached by LWT to take part in the original *I'm A Celebrity . . . Get Me Out of Here* early in March 2002. I turned it down with hardly a thought. Feeling out of sorts with the world and weighed down with my own problems, I didn't need to be dropped into the Australian rainforest with goodness knows who, deprived of creature comforts and under 24-hour surveillance. Also, it was nigh impossible for us to plan ahead, with uncertainty over the sale of the house and the constant demands and intrusion of the bankruptcy. We feared they might get up to dirty tricks if we left the country, probably break into the house and impound everything while our backs were turned.

I thought no more about it while the months ticked by. The dynamics of the group were all-important and LWT had not found their 'mother hen' so approached me again in the middle of July. By then, I was feeling better about life generally and I agreed, but insisted they had to fly Neil out to Australia with me, otherwise I would have to put him into care!

We were to spend a couple of days in a splendid hotel and then be dumped in the jungle to fend for ourselves, against not only poisonous snakes and spiders but the far more deadly machinations of the programme-makers. We were to be skewered, grilled and served up as nightly fare for the millions back home.

We were asked to see a psychiatrist. I said thank you very much but I didn't want, or need, to see a shrink. I was perfectly sane, balanced and normal and knew exactly what I was doing. No choice – requirement of the programme. So I was bundled off to see Dr Sandra Scott, who would be accompanying us to Australia. Sandra asked if there was anything I was afraid of.

'Well, I don't particularly want to share my bunk with one, but it's not the snakes. Only one thing concerns me – the editing.'

Sandra was worried in case I took another pasting. How would I feel if the public didn't like me, if I had a bad press?

'Well, there's nothing I can do about it. I'm me and that's that. Look, I'm not doing this to prove anything either to myself or to the great British public. I'm doing it for fun!'

Granny snorted when she heard I'd been to see a shrink but was not at all happy at the prospect of losing me for three weeks and was very dubious about the whole escapade. As we jetted off to the tropical rainforest of Northern Queensland, her words were ringing in my ears: 'You've got yourself into the hands of a bunch of sadists!'

I was certainly in motley company: evergreen DJ Tony Blackburn, spoon-bending psychic Uri Geller, former boxing champ Nigel Benn, singer/actor Darren Day, Scottish left-wing gay comedienne Rhona Cameron, glamorous model Nell McAndrew and former 'It girl' Tara Palmer-Tomkinson. We flew out in first-class luxury to Sydney, connecting flight to Cairns, an hour and a half's drive down the coast and checked into the Mission Beach Hotel where Neil was to spend more than a fortnight, free from old Bossy Boots, making life-changing decisions – should he swim in the ocean or the pool?

The hotheads were warming up before we even left the hotel. Nigel Benn, a born-again Christian, wanted to take his Bible as his luxury. Rhona, who had already dismissed him as 'thick' exclaimed, 'Oh, we're not going to have all that religious crap, are we?'

Later, as we talked round the pool, Nigel looked soulful and shook his head. 'I can't believe she said that. She doesn't understand what the

Bible has done for her. Our Lord saved my life, gave me my wife and my family. She must understand the Bible says "Man shall not lie with man, woman shall not lie with woman."' He pointed dramatically across the pool to where Rhona was lying, her voluptuous figure enhanced by a black bikini. 'She is a sinner!' He said if there was 'any more from her' he would denounce her on television as a lesbian who would be sent to hell. We were in for a stormy time!

Our kit was not particularly flattering. I was delighted with my red trousers but the T-shirts, emblazoned with our names and our voting telephone number, were grey, gloomy and prison-like. It didn't really worry me, we were not entering *Miss World* but Rhona hated it and was giving the wardrobe lady a hard time. She's a good-looking girl, with a heart-shaped face, huge brown eyes and wonderful skin. She had had a tough start in life, adopted as a child, brought up in a modest Scottish household and was now a proselytising, Leftie lesbian. We have an eclectic group of friends, including left-wingers and lesbians, but I didn't want any strong opinions rammed down my throat for a fortnight.

Tara was doing the programme to try to shake off the perception that she was merely a spoilt brat, incapable of anything but snorting drugs and partying. A reformed cocaine addict, she told us her mother had said, 'Darling, if you can get every drug addict in the country to vote for you, you're bound to win.'

She was trying to cram in as much nicotine as possible before the fortnight's deprivation began. Teetering around in her regulation stilettos, she was a lively and entertaining presence although I knew I would have difficulty putting up with her juvenile behaviour for the duration. We could each take one luxury. I opted for my diary, which proved a life-saver, somewhere private to vent my feelings when things got tough.

We all arrived with varying degrees of antipathy towards the creatures of the jungle and were introduced to those we were likely to meet, including a deadly Taipan snake. It was young and only three feet long, but they grow to eight or nine feet and move very quickly indeed. Once you have been bitten, the venom enters the lymph system, causes respiratory failure, blood pours from every orifice and you are dead in six hours. As I looked at the Taipan thrashing around in its glass tank, darting its head towards us, I swallowed and wondered whether I had made the right decision to come along. I challenged our guide nervously,

'Come on, you've cleared the area of those, you must have – haven't you?'

He smiled enigmatically. 'Don't worry, they'll have other things on their mind – it's the mating season soon.'

Finally we were off. After an exhilarating open-sided helicopter ride over the immense rainforest, we were dropped into a clearing and left alone trying to decide what the hell to do next. Then the foliage moved and cameras appeared. Trekking in single file, we tumbled into the jungle like boy scouts at first camp; it was all new, exciting and fun. Would the novelty wear thin when the rain poured down, the bunks were soaking, food was scarce and the trials horrendous?

I've led an active life and enjoy 'roughing it' from time to time. It was liberating not to have to bother about hair and make-up. Flopping unwashed into a bunk would be no problem; it would be more comfortable than relentlessly crashing up and down through ocean waves at an angle of 45 degrees! But would the irritating habits of my jungle-mates assume gigantic proportions? They must have been thinking the same about me!

I was shocked at how small the camp was. Millions now know exactly what it's like but before we arrived the details were deliberately kept hazy. This was the first show. We marched into the jungle in total innocence of what awaited us. I had assumed we would each have our own area where we could retreat, but there was no hiding place – not even the loo! We girls were instantly concerned about this extremely basic wooden throne, about twenty yards from the camp, totally exposed on all sides, but soon made private with a bit of hessian and rope. We were busy finding our way around, choosing bunks, unpacking rucksacks, when suddenly a female voice boomed over the Tannoy, startling us all, 'Will Christine please come to the Bush Telegraph.' I hurried to the little hut and sat down. An anonymous voice announced, 'Hello, Christine. You are the leader for today.'

This, frankly, was the last straw so early in the game! I had been trying to follow my friends' advice not to appear bossy, and here I was, having to give orders to everyone within minutes of arrival! Responsibility for tasks, fire, cooking, water was allocated. We found some utensils lying around: buckets, billycans, cooking pots and the ubiquitous rice and beans, plus a few basic essentials including half an economy loo roll to last eight people for two weeks. As leader I went straight back to the Bush Telegraph to demand more.

We were all worried about the first Bushtucker Trial that one of us, chosen by the viewers, would have to face the following morning. Tara was convinced viewers would want to see 'toff totty showered with maggots'. She was apprehensive and already desperate for a cigarette; by the end of the day they had to send in patches to calm her down. We were bonding as a group but the tensions were already bubbling away. I was happy with my day as leader and wrote in my diary, 'I feel really at peace – left the world behind. To hell with all our problems. I can cope.'

We had been up since 3 a.m. and turned in early. Rhona had been feeling unwell all day, so I made up her bunk. She snuggled down, 'I cannot believe I'm being tucked into bed by Christine Hamilton!' Nor could I! We were from different worlds and both appreciated the irony of our current pairing.

I clambered into my bunk (a piece of canvas stretched between two poles) fully clothed, carefully placing my mess tin upside down on top of my boots to ensure nothing crept inside during the night. Contented, I listened to the jungle. The creatures were not as noisy as I had been warned but I could hear the crickets all around and the river in the background. The dappled light of the waning moon filtered through the trees high above my head, the campfire flickered and the Tilley lamps glowed softly as we settled down in our little cocoons, like eight covered wagons in the Wild West corralled around the fire, each occupied with our private thoughts and fears. Suddenly I heard a rustle in the under-growth a few feet from my head. Crumbs, what was that? Reminding myself sternly that, whatever it was, it was probably more frightened of me than I of it, I wriggled threateningly to create a noise and it slithered, crawled, or scampered away.

The presenters Ant and Dec arrived early every morning, infuriatingly immaculate and sweet-smelling in their crisp, laundered shirts, in stark contrast to our crumpled dirty selves. Every day the prospect of the Trial hung over us, each of us praying not to be chosen but, equally, not wishing it on anyone else. I was feeling sorry for Tara, clearly struggling with nicotine and worry about the Trial. The moment Ant and Dec announced her name I felt a wave of relief it was not me but instantly felt sick for her. When she returned to camp we listened in horror as she described how she had had to stand under eight different 'showers' containing maggots, dung beetles, spiders and who knows what else. Each one she endured won a star – a meal for the camp. In a sadistic twist

(Granny was right!) she had to pull the levers herself one by one to release the torment. I felt a terrible foreboding about what else they might have in store.

We were slowly revealing more of ourselves. I had known little or nothing about the others and was interested to listen and learn. I knew Darren had provided the tabloids with much copy, was generally known as 'Love Rat' and had an impressive history of conquests and liaisons. He was endearingly open, admitting his faults and weaknesses. 'Too successful too young', he had topped the bill at the London Palladium, hailed as the new Jason Donovan, the new Cliff Richard. Outside the stage door, hundreds of young girls were desperate just to see or touch him. It went to his head; the drugs and women followed. He claimed now to be a reformed character, totally in love with his current girlfriend, and had come into the jungle to attempt to dispel his tarnished image.

Rhona's face was a picture of astonishment as Tara described how Bessie, her maid, did everything for her. Rhona asked if she'd been to university.

'No, I went to finishing school – it almost finished me off!'

'What's a finishing school?' said Rhona.

'It's where you learn to get in and out of a Lamborghini without showing your knickers.'

A fascinating collision of worlds in the Australian rainforest!

Nell was a trooper, a lovely uncomplicated girl. She is not only the body most beautiful but a delightful person as well. She had nothing to prove, either to herself or to the public. She was looking forward to the total experience and did not want to be involved with any disagreements. Whatever the task, however menial, she never had to be asked. She just got on with it and, dammit, looked fabulous all the time!

Like Nell, Tony Blackburn doesn't have a nasty bone in his body and didn't want a row with anyone, although sometimes his jokes made it tempting to start one!

It was impossible to be private; 'they' made sure of that by restrictive rules. Thou shalt not go down to the river alone. Thou shalt not leave fewer than four people in the camp at any time. Thou shalt not be able to sit quietly anywhere. Thou shalt not have enough to do. Thou shalt get bored. Thou shalt get on each other's nerves. It was classic manipulative television and it worked. The cameras covered every last inch of the camp, from all possible angles, and you couldn't escape at the river either. A couple of roving crews were permanently down there, following everywhere, probing with questions about the latest argument in camp.

Rhona and Nigel were at loggerheads not only over religion and sex but also over that third great staple of life – food! They both enjoyed and wanted to do the cooking; neither could stand back and let the other get on with it. It was going to be tricky enough anyway with two veggies on board, Tony and Uri, but that was nothing compared with two mighty egos battling over the billycans. Tara won us a splendid basket of goodies, our first proper food for two days. Rhona took charge and prepared a delicious-looking vegetable concoction in which the chicken breasts would be cooked. She wanted them in chunks. Suddenly, without warning, Nigel picked up all six breasts and threw them, whole, into the stew. For a moment I thought Rhona was going to hit him – she's a good boxer – but she just exploded into a magnificent Shakespearean tirade lasting a good fifteen minutes. All her pent-up feelings about Nigel and life in general poured out. She stood her ground, waving the wooden spoon, refusing to let anyone eat before she'd had her say, which was probably just as well as the breasts, being whole, needed to cook through. I was absolutely on her side on the basic issue, the wretched chicken breasts, but the atmosphere was wrecked for the evening and more trouble clearly lay ahead.

Uri said he would not use his 'psychic powers' in the camp as it could give him an unfair advantage. I am not sure about that because he got Michael Jackson's birthday wrong and had us all 'teleporting' messages to him on the wrong day! He spent considerable time meditating cross-legged on a large rock in the middle of the river. It must have been very calming and I marvel at his ability to switch off so completely. Seeing we could all do with a bit of calm, he instituted regular 'thought sessions'. While I tended to ignore his guidance, they were welcome and blissful moments of peace when the whole camp was silent, eyes closed, round the fire.

We had been warned that ticks were prevalent and could attach themselves anywhere. In particular, they were attracted to warm, moist, hairy parts of the body. Uri was taking no chances and wanted someone to examine his pubic area. Why he couldn't do it himself in the privacy of the loo, I don't know. Arguing that he couldn't expect the men to do it, or any of the heterosexual girls, he asked Rhona and she obliged. Uri suddenly enquired if any of the chaps had had an erection while in the camp. Nigel said nothing, Tony was aghast, while Darren admitted he hadn't had one for two weeks and was getting concerned. Uri said he had read that in Darren's mind and thought it better to ask the question in public rather than in private. I couldn't see the logic, but I suppose it made good television. He asked me one day why I thought we were all there.

'Because, Uri, LWT invited us. We're making a television programme.'

'No. Christine, listen to me. We are all brought here by cosmic forces. Cosmic forces have brought us together.'

Tony started to argue the toss but I couldn't face it and escaped to the river to breathe some sanity.

Tara's preoccupations continued to be sex and nicotine. She did her best to secure the former from Darren but he was not obliging. The patches were having no obvious effect and she was beginning to shake. She had survived her Trial but could she survive without nicotine? Wanting to keep her in, 'they' provided cigarettes for her. Though the rest of us were sympathetic, in varying degrees, to her addiction, we were all supposed to be there on equal terms and were all missing different things. If Tara was getting cigarettes to keep her in the game, what about my wine?

Nigel, with a terrible, real phobia about snakes, had been voted to do 'Snakes Alive', to pluck stars – meals! – from a tank of curling snakes. He overcame his fears, won dinner for us all and should have been allowed to cook it. Instead, Rhona elbowed him out of the way and our evening was wrecked by yet another stand-off. I like Rhona. She is feisty, engaging, positive, and I admire her spirit. But she always seemed to be at the centre of the axis of argument. It was Darren vs Rhona, Nigel vs Rhona, Tara vs Rhona – always Rhona. The camp would definitely have been more peaceful without her – but duller!

I took a sleeping pill (smuggled in) as I just wanted to crash out and forget the disputes and tantrums erupting all around. Tara and Darren were scrapping and bitching, Rhona and Nigel were on the brink of nuclear war and I just wanted out for a few hours. The next morning I had slept in a bit and woke blearily to the sound of the Tannoy. I looked at Tony sitting on the next bunk. 'Who are you? Where am I?' I knew perfectly well who he was and didn't give it a second thought, but after Ant and Dec had been and gone, I was summoned: 'Would Christine please go to the Bush Telegraph.' Psychiatrist Sandra Scott was sitting there waiting for me. 'Christine, we're a bit concerned. You seemed disoriented this morning when you woke up. You didn't know where you were, or who Tony was.' I couldn't believe they had taken it seriously but, with so many people flaking all over the place, they couldn't risk that I was also going bananas in this extraordinary environment!

We had three days of rain, intense tropical rain, saturating everything. It started gradually, with enormous drops landing, almost in slow motion, from the canopy of trees. Despite a gimcrack canvas sheet that 'they' rolled out high above to shelter us from the worst direct downpours, the place was soon a quagmire, logs were getting scarce and what remained were now wet. Things were becoming grim and tempers fraying. It suddenly seemed less of a holiday camp and more of an ordeal. Despite that, I welcomed the rain. I've always been fascinated by it, loving a downpour at sea or watching it cascading from rooftops. It gave the forest a whole new fresh feel, its very lifeblood returning. There were problems, of course. Who left the loo roll, a precious commodity, out of its little wooden box so it was sodden and useless? When we turned in for the night we discovered the outer canvas sleeping bags were not waterproof and the inner bags were damp. Yuck! At least it gave us something to do the next day – drying, drying, drying around the fire.

In the middle of the rain, the public voted for Rhona to be 'Buried Alive'. She suffers from claustrophobia, and when Ant and Dec made the announcement I could see the emotion in her face and eyes. What sadistic pleasure the British public take in voting from the flabby comfort of their armchairs. Rhona warned us not to expect dinner that evening. Put in a 'coffin' at the bottom of an animal trap, totally dark and soundless, she would win one meal for every two minutes she endured her underground prison. She had lasted twelve, and was doing well, too well for 'them'. Suddenly something grabbed her in the darkness. She was petrified and shrieked, 'Get me out of here.' We subsequently learned that the cameraman who was recording the ordeal was told through his earpiece, 'She's coping too well. Give her a fright.'

'I can't. She's terrified.'

'Do it or you're fired.'

His hand had grabbed her like an unknown animal in the underground darkness. She came back with six meals but had clearly been scared. They learned from that experience; when Jennie Bond had to face a similar trial in the third series, the water and rats were already on hand! Each succeeding series sees the trials getting progressively more sadistic and humiliating — they have to, to keep the viewers.

The next day Rhona was leader and thrilled. She came back from the Bush Telegraph, baseball cap askew, brandishing the 'rifle' she had made from a branch of wood. If she had asked us to line up in ascending order of height and chant the 'Red Flag' I would have done it. It was her day, why not? But her gung-ho attitude annoyed others. Tara was feeling unwell. Darren was hung over from the night before. He had had enough of Tara, Rhona and the whole blinking lot. His 'Frank Spencer' impersonations had been annoying Rhona intensely, she called him a 'dickhead', he exploded, said he was leaving and stormed off. 'They' had been right to send in a wine box the night before and were now getting their reward!

Nigel couldn't take Rhona in any position of authority. Rhona is articulate and has a good command of language. Nigel is more of a man of action than of words. 'Why don't you swap your Bible for a dictionary!' she swiped at him, dealing a double blow at both his religion and lack of education. But that day he had the upper hand. Rhona seemed to crumple before our eyes. Her day as leader proved untenable before it began. I was furious with Nigel for beating her, metaphorically, into submission. Without laying a finger on her, he had used his brute force to subdue her spirit. She retreated to her bunk.

Uri had been voted to face the 'Jungle Feast'. It was obviously going to be one of the veggies — the voting public knew what they were doing! Needless to say an argument erupted between him and Tony. Tony thought Uri's vegetarian code ought to be more important. Uri said he could not deprive us all of food just because of his principles. He ate the lot and returned triumphant. Tony felt betrayed but I didn't notice him refusing food that evening! There had been another mega-row about cooking. Nigel and Darren wouldn't eat if Rhona cooked and Rhona wouldn't eat if Nigel cooked. It was tempting to tell all three to starve. I was appointed neutral chef. I had been keen to cook all along but, with those two slugging it out, had not wanted to inflame things further and contented myself with chopping and slicing. The raw material was potentially delicious and I was looking forward to rustling up a great meal for everyone.

After making irritating interventions from her bunk ('That has to go in last you know . . . I wouldn't put that in there'), Rhona retreated to

the Bush Telegraph wanting to leave the show. Nigel started to help with
the cooking. I tried to suggest he should desist but was not forceful
enough and allowed it to drift. I didn't want any more spats; I just
wanted some tranquillity and harmony. After dinner Uri accused me of
being 'double faced'.

'What on earth are you talking about?' I demanded to know. It
transpired it was all to do with the flaming cooking. I should not have
allowed Nigel to help me when the agreement was neither he nor Rhona
would be involved. Uri was right but I was furious at what I saw as his
pedantic intervention and shouted at him, 'I'm not taking that from you,
Mr Geller.'

The problem was the wine we had been allowed that evening. I was
possibly a little volatile but Uri, after a glass or two, had become a tad
aggressive. I burst into tears. Why couldn't he just let it ride? The whole
thing was so pointless and futile – why couldn't we just get on with the
evening, enjoy the food and the environment. Silly me! 'They' had
worked hard to get a volatile mix of people and were rubbing their hands
with glee as they twiddled the 'edit' knobs.

After dinner I sat on my bunk with Tony, chewing over the
explosive events of the day. Suddenly I saw a ten-foot python wending
its way under his bunk, slithering in our direction, forked tongue
darting in and out just three feet away from our legs. That brought us
thudding back to reality, put our petty squabbles into perspective and
reminded us where we were! The timing seemed impeccable. Had it
been deliberately planted to jolt us back to jungle life, to stop us
becoming obsessed with trivialities?

Rhona decided she would stay another night but the atmosphere
remained tense. Half of me was genuinely delighted she had triumphed
over her desire to bolt but I knew that more strife would inevitably
follow. We immediately had a wonderful row over feet. Darren and
Uri had gone to search for the chest. Tara announced she would
personally administer a pedicure to anyone who wanted one. Rhona
immediately said yes, please, using the pedicure as an olive branch to
get back into the group. Tara was horrified. Rhona was the last person
(possibly excluding me) to whom she wanted to minister. When
Darren returned to find Tara caressing Rhona's feet, he went berserk,
felt she had betrayed him and told her to f*** off. I just wanted to bang
their heads together.

That evening, having managed to avoid snakes and spiders all week, I trod on a huge hornet's nest. We had not been warned about those! Rhona had retreated early to her bunk, battered and bruised from Nigel's onslaught. I tried to explain that it wasn't anything personal but, as a born-again Christian, Nigel regarded the Bible as gospel truth. I assumed she already knew his views on homosexuality and knew, therefore, he regarded her as a sinner. She must understand, it was not antipathy towards her personally but towards what she represented. She looked across to where Nigel was lying propped up reading his Bible. 'So he's a f****** homophobe then!' I realised immediately I had lit the fuse and it could only be a matter of time before the bomb exploded in my face.

The following morning, Ant and Dec arrived as usual and I was convinced it would be my turn to face the Trial. All dutifully assembled round the fire, I hardly dared move while Ant and Dec played their psychological games: 'Christine, it might be you.' I held my breath. It had to be me. But no: 'Darren, it's you.'

The pleasure of my relief was momentary. I looked across at Darren and saw he was devastated. He didn't move. It wasn't the actual trial but the fact that the public wanted him to suffer twice in succession. He felt he was being punished. As soon as Ant and Dec had gone, but while we were still live on ITV2, Nigel turned on me. 'You are so two-faced . . . and a liar . . . get away from me . . . stay away from me you foolish old woman.'

I couldn't believe his attack. I knew why he was doing it, but the charge was totally without foundation. I refused even to discuss it with him. We would talk rationally later but, right now, this was Darren's moment and we had to help him through, not canter off on a ridiculous sideshow of our own.

Despite my display of bravado, I was terribly upset about Nigel's allegations and that he should think I had deliberately stirred things up. Contrary to what some might think, I do not relish confrontation and tend to shy away from argument. I went down to the river to escape – not just from Nigel but from the whole flaming game. As I sat on a rock looking at the clear, crystal water of the river, the tears flowed freely in a release of tension and pent-up emotion. Nigel and I had got along well and I wanted him back as a friend but he would not speak to me or acknowledge my presence. This was the first time I had personally felt such animus in the camp.

By then I had spent nearly a week cooped up with explosive beings, the atmosphere artificially and deliberately heightened by the demands of television. I needed an outlet.

It came in the unlikely form of the camp lavatory! The area was beginning to smell pretty vile, despite our daily applications of ash from the fire. Action was urgently required. I boiled up several billycans of water, poured them all over the wooden throne, pulled up some large clumps of foliage and decorated the cubicle with jungle plants. It was transformed. Apparently many viewers were amazed – Christine Hamilton cleaning the lavatory! Well I don't know who they think cleans it in our house, but it sure isn't Neil!

That evening was to be our last as a group – someone would be going. We were bonded by the common thought that no-one wanted to be first. We all bravely said we could handle being second, but not first, please not first. Although we had been disintegrating emotionally all week, there was an uncharacteristic degree of harmony. I held out my hand to Nigel, 'Are we friends again?' He took my hand, pulled me towards him and embraced me silently.

Darren and I brought back the celebrity chest and we were faced with the question, 'What is the name of Posh and Beck's new baby – Romeo or Juliet?' We thought long and hard, chewing this momentous question round and round for about ten minutes! Surely no-one would really call their child 'Romeo'? Even for P&B that was not possible, was it? No, of course not. So we opted for Juliet. How sad is that? We had now been isolated for a week and the *only* thing we knew of events outside was the name of the Beckhams' baby.

First out was Uri. Then we were seven. The press had been having a field day with us all but Uri had taken some hard knocks, the *Mirror* in particular describing him in terms that were grossly unjust and probably libellous. I was summoned to the Bush Telegraph. No longer were we to be at the mercy of the public's whims. We now had to nominate one of ourselves to face the trial. I was to be the leader again. I had not yet done a trial so I nominated myself. By then, I was seriously annoying Tara. Unheard by me, when I came back into the camp, she muttered, 'Get off your crucifix, Christine.' I wasn't feeling remotely like a martyr. Quite the reverse. Being voted by the public was one thing, putting myself forward was totally different psychologically.

I crossed the bridge in good spirits but my heart sank when I was asked to put on a waterproof battery pack – what were they expecting me to do? With Ant and Dec I walked a few hundred yards to a large corral. I would have to get in it – but what was in there already? I could hear animal noises and nervously peeped over the side. Instead of snakes there were eight black piglets snuffling and charging around in mud. Clearly, this was going to be a bit smelly! I had three minutes to catch each pig in turn, grab the star on its collar and stick it on a board. Obviously everyone was hoping I would go head over heels in the mud but I was determined to remain upright and I got all the stars!

We had passed the halfway mark, the days were moving swiftly but home still seemed a long way away. I dared not think what difficulties were stacking up while I was incommunicado on the other side of the world. What was Fish-Face up to? What nasty little tricks were being plotted, planned and perhaps put into effect while our backs were turned? I pushed it all out of my mind. I was enjoying an experience of a lifetime.

We all had our problems. Tara was suffering dearth of sex and nicotine and surfeit of Darren. She wanted out. Nigel wanted out. He got his wish the next morning when the public voted him out. Tara went AWOL and disappeared into the jungle. She was eventually found, given much cosseting in the Bush Telegraph by Sandra, came back to the camp and told me to 'F*** off and stop bullshitting.' I wasn't aware I had been. She later apologised and I thought we were back on an even keel. I liked Tara. She is a spirited girl, inventive and lively but, for me, not easy to live with for a fortnight. We had deliberately been picked for our differences, to make explosive television. It would have been a nightmare if there had been another one in there like me – Tara would be the first to tell you, one Christine Hamilton is too many!

I found her inability to do anything practical somewhat infuriating. She was always losing everything and never saw what needed to be done, let alone do it. I was doing my best, enjoying her antics but also finding her exasperating. A defining moment, for both of us, came over the question of the cafetière. We had won this delicacy – fresh coffee was to be ours – Wow!

Less than 24 hours after we had acquired it, she broke the precious artefact. I said nothing but my look spoke volumes. I was speechless at her clumsiness. Being Tara, of course, she used her artistic and inventive talent to good effect, turning the plunger into part of a hat that would have graced Ascot! I didn't realise how her resentment of me was building up and the climax arrived when she was closeted in the Bush Telegraph for hours as they tried to persuade her to stay. Was it deliberate or a genuine mistake that a switch was flipped? Sitting alone, trying to work out what to do, Tara could hear the comments from the camp? Needless to say most of it was about her. I described her as 'a few sandwiches short of a picnic' and 'a spoilt little rich kid'. I wasn't exactly alone in my view and others were voicing similar opinions. Rhona had previously described her as 'not shuffling with a full deck' and Uri had wondered 'what's she ever done in her life except happen to know Prince Charles'. None of us had an idea then that she had heard our comments. Probably they impelled her to stay – she would show us!

The next morning Darren was voted out, leaving Tony with four girls. That evening we did impersonations of each other. Rhona did Tara, Tara did Rhona, Tony did Nigel, I did Uri and Nell did me. They were all very funny. It is salutary to see yourself as others see you.

I woke next morning utterly convinced I could not survive another vote. But Rhona was out. Although there were times when all I wanted was for her to leave the camp, I had actually grown fond of her. She has great character and I was genuinely sorry to see her go.

I was amazed to have survived. It was day twelve with no news from the world outside. We had no clue how massive the show had become, dominating the tabloids, occupying well over 50 per cent of the viewing public. I was beginning to look forward to getting out, back to Neil and civilisation, a feeling I had not previously experienced. But I also wanted to stay to the end. Most of the personal friction had been dissipated; the camp was quieter, softer and probably far less interesting. Nell was the next out. But why was anyone voting for me?

The remaining three, Tony, Tara and I, were summoned for the day's trial. We knew it was water and Tony opted out – he is not a good swimmer. I could swim before I could walk, so quickly volunteered. After trekking for three-quarters of an hour, I was hungry, tired and hot by the time we reached our destination, a large deep pool of water into which cascaded an impressive waterfall. Tara suddenly announced she would like to do the trial. I didn't like to point out that I had already volunteered before seeing it and reluctantly stepped back. 'OK, you do it.'

Handing over the challenge was the last thing I wanted to do. I genuinely felt I was better equipped to bring home the meals. Tony suggested we toss for it and put a stone behind his back. I insisted Tara choose. She got the wrong hand. Hooray!

There were seven orange buoys floating; three marked the position of a star, a meal, while four were boobies. I had to dive for the tins underneath, bring each one in turn to the jetty, find the right key, hope for a star and dive for the next. One buoy, lodged eight feet up the cascade of the waterfall, was winking at me. I knew I had to go for it first and just hoped they had not been mean enough to make it a booby. I struck out across the pool, deliberately quashing thoughts of what might be lurking in the water and clambered up the rope ladder while the waterfall roared down on my head. I felt for the tin and pulled; it held fast. There was nothing for it but to use both hands, relinquishing my hold on the ladder. The tin came away and I crashed back into the water below. I was oblivious at the time, but had banged the corner of the tin hard into my cheekbone. By the time I got back to the jetty, the bump was already obvious to everyone else. Happily, the tin contained a star! I had been rewarded for tackling the most difficult first, but I was already very tired. The next three, two of which were much deeper than I thought I could possibly reach, were all boobies. My lungs were bursting. When I got back to the jetty and discovered yet another, a fourth, my expletive had to be deleted!

I gasped as I set off for the next. I had been diving down, and down, the tins were deep and heavy, I had had enough. But there were two more and each, by process of elimination, had to contain a star. I retrieved one and time was running out as I swam for the final tin. I dived and grabbed it but could not get back to the jetty in time. I needed another thirty seconds. I had got two meals.

We trekked back to the camp and I was longing for dry clothes, a mug of coffee and a collapse. In our absence 'they' had totally ransacked everything. The fire was out, bunks dismantled, the camp wrecked. My clothes were soaking, I was tired and my cheek was badly swollen, already turning black and blue. After a momentary sense-of-humour failure, I rallied and saw the funny side. It was a splendid joke! I knew I could get the bunks back together. It only needed common sense and elementary skill with a rope. Tony and Tara did not find the situation amusing. He was distraught to find his precious fire had been extinguished and we had a major set-to over the nonexistent embers, the first time we had crossed swords. Tony said he could do it himself if left alone. I shrugged and walked away. He accused me of putting damp leaves on the fire. He was probably right but I certainly wasn't going to admit it then! Wherever the fault lay, we failed to get the embers going despite idiotic attempts with the magnifying glass on the compass and my spectacles. There was no sun, so even an expert would fail, never mind a pair of bumbling amateurs! Tony and I must have looked ridiculous as we huffed and puffed and fanned without a flicker in return. In the end we had to admit defeat and were kindly provided with a box of matches in the Bush Telegraph. At last we got the water boiling and were able to eat – guess what? Rice and beans!

The next day dawned. I faced either the dubious delights of a day and a night alone with Tara or Tony, or eviction from the jungle, the joy of a hug from my husband, a hot bath, some champagne and real food. I knew I had done well on the swimming trial and thought my reaction to the ransacking would stand me in good stead. But the public wanted me out. I kept my composure at first but all my emotions welled up and spilled right over when my mother came on the screen, standing outside her flat in Cheshire, welcoming me home and promising the cottage pie would be waiting. 'Go on,' said Ant, 'Neil's waiting for you.'

I had just assumed Neil was back at the hotel. I ran towards the bridge, and into his arms as the fireworks went off around us. It was by far the longest time we had ever been apart. I hadn't realised how much I had missed him. The initial disappointment of my eviction began to soften, the sun was shining, the outside world was beckoning. It was good to be out. At the hotel there were interviews and debriefings, including another session with Sandra Scott. Had I learned anything about myself? Had it changed the way I felt about myself? Of course it hadn't, but I was to learn that it *had* changed the way others viewed me.

The next morning Tony was crowned 'King of the Jungle'. Afterwards I took Neil into the camp. It was an odd sensation not to have been able to share such an important experience and I wanted him to see it for himself. Also I wanted to say 'goodbye', more slowly and deliberately than I had been able the day before, to the area that had been home for a fortnight and was about to be returned to virgin rainforest, all trace of our invasion obliterated forever.

That evening we held the traditional 'wrap party' at the hotel round the pool. The programme had been a phenomenal success and everybody was on a high. Out on Monday, wrap on Tuesday, home on Wednesday. We arrived at Heathrow at 6.30 a.m. on Thursday morning and were collected by *This Morning* who had asked me to appear on the show that day with Granny, whom they had whisked down from Cheshire. She had worked out that that way she would get to see me sooner! Ten days later LWT screened a live reunion show where everyone was brought together. I had no problems with anyone, and was delighted to meet friends and family of the others, including Nigel Benn's wife and about three-quarters of his pack of children. The only person who studiously ignored me was Tara. I was sorry she felt like that but it is her decision and she has avoided me ever since, refusing to speak to or be photographed with me. I have managed to suffer this deprivation without counselling.

Having initially said no, I was so lucky to be given a second chance and would not have missed it for all the rice and beans in the world. I had certainly made amends to the Children's Wish Foundation, after our abysmal performance on *Who Wants to be a Millionaire?*, by raising nearly £100,000 for them. Apart from that, why had I done it? A commentator in the *Daily Telegraph* was complimentary about me personally (forgive me for quoting him but can you blame me?) and certainly identified one of my motives:

> As for Mrs Hamilton, I have always had a strong admiration for her. There is an unshakeable integrity about the woman, which has survived all the torments she has had to suffer in real life. I suspect that part of her reason for appearing on the programme was to protest to a television audience her husband's innocence of having accepted money in brown envelopes from the grotesque buffoon Mohamed Fayed. Good for her. For what it's worth, I think he is innocent, too.

Chapter Thirty

Media Mayhem

The Jungle was but part of my burgeoning new life as a 'media butterfly' and entertainer. I was astonished to read in the *Sunday Times* that I was, apparently, on a short list of 'most famous people' with Madonna, Kylie, Jerry and Liz. The columnist was making a point about modern celebrity.

I am sometimes accused of being 'publicity-crazed' but I never sought celebrity. In very public and inauspicious circumstances, I was thrown out of the career that had kept me busy and fulfilled for 26 years. There was no grand plan to forge another in the public eye. Neil and I just wanted to pick ourselves up, earn a living and start again. With politics firmly behind me, I gradually became involved in a new, exciting world of fun, frolic and sometimes fantasy. If it's legal, honest and faintly decent, then we are up for it! We don't take life, or ourselves, too seriously and this has led us into some unlikely situations.

Television is full of young vibrant people and working in the business helps us retain our youthful outlook. Neil and I were welcomed once a week as the resident Agony Uncle and Aunt on the *Big Breakfast*, that animated cartoon of a programme where noisy, bright, organised chaos reigned supreme. They probably regarded us as incipient geriatrics but apart from the nightmare of having to get up at 4.30 a.m. every Friday, it was lively, funky and gave us the illusion we were still teenagers!

I was at a loss to understand why we should be at all popular with young people but our 'fan club' among the student generation was growing. We were making guest appearances at nightclubs and student balls all over the country. We are older than most of their parents but seem to be regarded as 'cool' and fun to have around. It is a two-way attraction: we love the company of youngsters and it is only the intolerable noise level that drives us away in the early hours.

I found myself a cover girl of the left-wing political weekly the *New Statesman*, along with Cherie Blair and Pauline Prescott. We were apparently cosying up to each other like the political equivalent of *Footballers' Wives*, which was the subject of the accompanying article – was there such a beast? Head shots of the three of us had been superimposed on other bodies, glamorously clothed, complete with killer fingernails. It was a great collage, which clearly hoodwinked many people – some of my close friends were duped into thinking I had posed! I thought it highly entertaining and inventive but evidently Cherie was not amused.

We also became involved in some amusing advertising campaigns. Hush Puppies, launching a new range, were anxious to kick off their old-fashioned image and reach out to a younger, more fashion-conscious clientele without alienating their core, traditional customers. We were chosen as 'older, well-known personalities who reflect the attitude of the brand which does not take itself too seriously'. The theme was 'Old Dog, New Tricks'. Together with the basset hound, we, of course, were the 'old dogs'! It was a clever concept and we had an entertaining day in the East End re-creating several iconic scenes from cult movies – *Trainspotting, Pulp Fiction, Lock, Stock and Two Smoking Barrels*. I was asked to reproduce the infamous Sharon Stone leg-crossing scene from *Basic Instinct*, cigarette nonchalantly in hand. I protested that my legs were not my best feature but they persisted, I was persuaded, and it is a fun photograph, which happily caused apoplexy for some carping newspaper columnists.

The 118 118 directory enquiry service used our faces on the bodies of the two droopy-moustachioed runners in full-page newspaper ads, while the London Tourist Board produced a splendid TV commercial to highlight what could be visited for free – 'London's great when you're a little short.' With minimal dialogue, Neil and I rose from sleeping on a mattress on bare floorboards in a bare room, with no curtains and a naked light bulb – a reference to Neil's bankruptcy and our enforced house sale. Perhaps the funniest of all was Warner Music's TV advert for their *Ultimate Cheese Party Album* – all the party songs we love but dare not admit to. Amid scenes of gyrating wedding guests, Neil and I hammed it up and grooved to 'The Birdie Song', 'La Bamba', 'Macarena', 'YMCA' and many more. The inevitable slogan? 'Makes your party go with a swing – no matter who you've invited!'

Harry Hill devised a slot for us on his show and each week saw us doing something more ludicrous. The shoot was hilarious, starting with 'Inter-Species Tennis' against a horse and a donkey – yes, real ones on a real court. Fortunately, we won – at least it was made to appear as though we had! Subsequent weeks saw us racing each other rolling down a hill in 'ham' costumes; me, with Neil on my shoulders, getting up speed on an orange Space Hopper and then jumping over a double-decker bus and bursting into spontaneous combustion on landing. Jumping over the bus was easy, but I needed a body double for the flames – they were real! The wacky comic genius of Harry, a former hospital doctor who devises and writes his own material, spawns endless anarchic hilarity.

An invitation to strut our stuff in the *Rocky Horror Show* was truly irresistible! We had gone hand in hand to see the original production in the King's Road and now, on its thirtieth anniversary tour, we were to be part of the gang. The main cast remained the same but the 'Narrator' alternated. Sharing the role, Neil and I were booked to do a week in Oxford, Southampton, Birmingham and Milton Keynes. The production is electric, the music addictive and the cult show plays to huge audiences worldwide. Sex, drugs and rock and roll – what more could a girl want! The costumes are wild and wonderful but the audience seek to outdo any fantasy on the stage and the majority come dressed to kill. It is faintly unnerving to find yourself on stage in front of 3,500 fans, screaming, shouting, made-up to the eyeballs, in fishnets, suspenders and skimpy briefs – and that's just the men, many of whom are respectable middle-aged bank managers, accountants, policemen . . .

The Narrator's costume begins sedately enough but, for the finale, we both leapt on stage in fishnets, basque and high, high stilettos, joining in the immortal 'Time Warp', egging on the frenzied audience. We were welcomed and embraced by Jonathan Wilkes as Frank N Furter and the rest of the talented young cast. Waiting in the wings, observing the bizarre happenings on stage, was an intoxicating mix of nerves and exhilaration – We loved it but I began to worry Neil was becoming too attached to his stilettos!

I needed my wits about me when invited to appear again on *Have I Got News For You*, the first of its 2002 autumn series. On this occasion I was on Ian Hislop's team. Angus Deayton's penchant for cocaine and prostitutes had hit the headlines earlier and unknown to me, Ian and Paul had already expressed concern to the production company that his position was becoming untenable. He was there to make guests feel uncomfortable about *their* peccadilloes and failings, not himself to be the subject of their jokes. I went on the show to enjoy myself and give as good as I got. I did not deliberately plan to have a go at Angus – I like him, he's clever, witty, attractive and I knew my place: to be the butt of their barbs. But Angus provoked me too far when he used the 'D' word about Neil, calling him 'disgraced'. I cannot stop people using that word but I will not let it pass in my hearing. When attacked, I defend. I extended my arm to the full, sharply pointed finger just inches from Angus's nose, and angrily denounced him. I was furious. 'My husband does not commit adultery. My husband does not snort cocaine and my husband does not sleep with tarts. If anyone is disgraced around here it's *you*, Angus.'

I can only imagine what was going through his mind as he had to sit and endure my tirade. I was unaware, perhaps he was too, that the Sunday papers were about to expose yet more seedy behaviour on his part. He calmly turned back to the camera saying, with great sang-froid, 'Thank you, Christine, for making that clear.' I watched the following evening, felt I had been fairly edited, and got on with life. Meanwhile, Ian and Paul had confronted the programme-makers immediately afterwards, telling them this confirmed their worst fears. In the first of the series, I had undermined Angus's position as interrogator. They were not prepared to work with him any more. The weekend papers piled more fuel on his funeral pyre. Angus went, to be replaced by a succession of stand-ins, some more successful than others.

When I read of his departure, I wrote to Angus expressing my regret, which was genuine, reminding him my attack had been purely self-defence, wishing him well and a swift return to our screens. I never had a reply. Perhaps he did not receive the letter. I hope he does not bear a grudge because that would be against the spirit of the show, where everyone enjoys the reciprocal vitriol for its own sake and no-one seeks or gives any quarter.

More surreal adventures were to come when I took to the stage a few weeks later, as Fairy Battleaxe in *Jack and the Beanstalk* at the Yvonne Arnaud Theatre in Guildford, with Neil as the hapless, bankrupt King of Merrydale who had lost his all to Giant Blunderbore. The parts were perfect, I was well prepared for pantomime by twenty years of marriage to Neil and, in good panto tradition, I believe that Good does triumph over Evil, even if life takes some wonky turns on the way!

As Fairy Battleaxe I was able to fulfil every little girl's dream. I was born to be a fairy, adored every minute and had to be reminded to take off my crown and glittery false eyelashes before dashing into Guildford between shows for last-minute Christmas shopping! Fourteen years at the Westminster Palace of Varieties proved to be the ideal training for Neil's role as the impoverished King of Merrydale. The King was a bumbling hapless old fool, which taxed his acting abilities to the full! We had huge fun at all 45 performances while the old farce at Westminster plodded along its weary way. Politics tends to make people miserable and we were now in the grand old business of cheering them up.

For many children, panto is their first experience of live theatre with all the excitement of the lights, music, colour, magic and energy. Only the stony-hearted could fail to be enthused and enchanted by the wide-eyed, awestruck faces and roars of laughter from the hundreds of tiny theatregoers. It is a real responsibility on the cast, not just to amuse but also to plant the seeds of appreciation for a lifetime of live theatre. The cast was experienced and accomplished; Royce Mills was the beaming, booming, risqué Dame Trot, Michael Cochrane, equally experienced and accomplished, was the malevolent Fleshcreep, the Giant's fearsome minion on earth and Andy Collins was the wonderfully cheeky Silly Billy. Rula Lenska was subsequently cast as Jack – with her slender figure and amazing legs she was born to be a principal boy. Gerry Tebbutt, Head of Musical Drama at the Guildford School of Acting, directed and his third-year students provided the dauntingly versatile and talented ensemble.

There was just one snag. We were 'celebrity drop-ins' and had already prompted adverse comment and letters in the *Stage* – we were taking bread from the mouths of Equity members. Rula was not in favour of 'drop-ins', although she had signed on knowing we were already part of the cast, but we knew she was not alone in her misgivings. There would be plenty of people waiting, longing, for us to make a hash of it. We resolved to prove them wrong. The evening before rehearsals began I was sitting next to Danny La Rue at a showbiz charity dinner and expressed my nervousness. He reassured me, 'Darling – don't be ridiculous – you dropped out of the womb as an actress!'

Encouraged by this vote of confidence we presented ourselves at a deeply unglamorous, battered old hall in the back end of Guildford, which has since been pulled down. Rehearsals were tough but Gerry was patient and inspiring, urging us onwards to greater and better things each day. It was a nightmare trying to drill the lines into my head after decades of relative mental inactivity in politics. I was both amazed and horrified at how difficult it proved to be. Neil's task was even worse as he had a succession of 'nonsense' scenes and words, which had to be got right because each was the cue for someone else. He also had to practise the art of receiving plates of 'cream' in his face during the dairy scene – not as easy as it sounds!

At the dress rehearsal I popped on to the stage, wand aloft, in a puff of blue smoke, fairy frock and crown glittering in the stage lights. I screwed up the first line! Goodness knows what Rula was thinking standing in the wings, but Gerry was relaxed. 'Bad dress rehearsal, great first night. Don't even think about it, you'll get there.'

Snobs dismiss pantomime as easy, low-grade slapstick but everything, particularly the chaos, is carefully choreographed; timing is all. Entrances, exits and myriad cues follow each other with alarming speed. Concentration was vital to avoid colliding with the back end of Daisy, truly a multicultural, equal opportunities cow. Her front end (Jorden) came from Barnsley and her rear (Mario) from Mexico. When Jorden cut his head open and had to go to casualty, Mario moved to the front and a new rear end (Pauline) from Scotland moved in. Pauline was my understudy and was delighted to move up in the world by taking over Daisy's back end instead! Tap-dancing Daisy, with huge fluttering eyelashes, shaking legs and gloriously uncontrollable udder, was superlative. Absurdly endearing, Daisy received rave reviews from the critics – 'A cow beyond praise.' Charles Spencer, theatre critic of the *Daily Telegraph*, whose scathing comments can close a West End show, arrived one evening with his son. My wand quivered and Daisy really put the udder into shudder! Charles gave us all a glowing review:

> Christine proves a natural as the twinkling fairy, exuding a roguish bonhomie . . . Will someone please give this splendid gutsy couple their own sitcom series . . . the script would write itself . . . all they'd have to do is act naturally.

The *Sunday Telegraph* was equally enthusiastic:

> They take to their parts as to the manner born . . . they blend in so well you almost forget who they really are.

It was one of the happiest chapters of our lives, a truly joyful experience. Our friends of all ages came in their droves and we spent much of our wages on champagne and cola backstage afterwards! We drove down for one matinee with Granny and my nephew Henry (then eleven) who was to be responsible for getting them both back to London by train, while we stayed for the evening performance. As I was putting them into a taxi outside the theatre the driver said to Granny, 'Well, how was she?' My mother looked at me. 'Not bad for an amateur. But Neil was better – he *really* had to act, *she* was just herself.' Thanks, Mum, for that vote of confidence! Later, a friend who had seen the show said to her, 'Oh, wasn't it splendid and didn't Christine get such wonderful applause.' Granny did not disappoint: 'Yes, far more than she deserved!'

As well as his sparkling notices, there was an unexpected Christmas present for Neil. In a popularity poll he was voted fourth most interesting politician in Britain – and he'd been out of Parliament for five years!

Around that time I received an invitation from the University of York Wine Society to become their honorary patron. I hesitated, not certain whether I wanted to make the commitment, but was convinced when I read their motto, 'Oxford Spits, York Swallows'. My qualification, according to the chairman, was that I am 'a jovial individual with a lively reputation'.

They were not the only ones to think that. The BBC invited us to a party to celebrate the fortieth anniversary of *That Was the Week That Was* (TW3), the hugely successful 1960s satirical programme. We had no idea why we had been invited and assumed it was an enormous party. At Television Centre we were astonished to see only about 300 invitees. The TW3 survivors were there – David Frost, Lance Percival, Millicent Martin – and we were surrounded by a sea of famous faces ranging from Ronnie Barker, George Melly, Alan Whicker and Adam Faith, through Richard Stilgoe and Bernard Levin, to Shirley Anne Field and June Whitfield – and some newer ones like Mark Perry, already making his mark with *Dead Ringers*. Mingling were BBC hosts from Director-General Greg Dyke downwards. As a fellow alumnus of York University, I had always taken an interest in Greg's doings but had never met him, so I threaded my way across the room.

'Hello – and by the way, why have we been invited?'

'Because, Christine, you have just a whiff of scandal about you and you're great fun!'

Perhaps that was why we were invited to open the Erotica exhibition at Olympia in November 2003. I was not sure about that one and my immediate response was 'No way'. Neil, always less worried about 'what people might think', told me not to be ridiculous. After all, Ann Summers now inhabits the high street. Despite that, sex has never been taken entirely seriously in Britain – the land of Donald McGill seaside postcards and the divine Barbara Windsor – we tend to prefer hot-water bottles. The organisers were anxious to attract more middle-class, middle-of-the-road, heterosexuals to Erotica and saw us as the ideal combination of respectability, recognisability and sauciness.

Before the decision could be made, I needed advice and so I telephoned Sheila.

'Of course you must do it!' she enthused. 'But, *don't* let Neil out of your sight, *don't* pick anything up and above all, *don't* plug anything in!' Emboldened by her gusto I agreed, a trifle reluctantly, and off we swept to Olympia. It says something about the state of modern Britain that, whereas in previous years the Antiques Fair was held in the Grand Hall and Erotica relegated to one of the smaller halls, by 2003 the roles had been reversed! As we approached and saw the crowds flocking, it was not immediately apparent who was going to which exhibition apart, of course, from some obvious exceptions – people dressed in fancy gear who were clearly heading off in search of a Chippendale . . .

On arrival at Olympia, my fears were somewhat allayed when greeted in the inner sanctum by the Hon. Henry Cobbold, heir to Lord Cobbold, of Knebworth, whose ancestral home is a popular venue for rock and pop festivals, including the huge Robbie Williams concert earlier that year. The Erotica exhibition was his brainchild. Observing that other countries took festivals of erotica in their stride, Henry wondered why Britain did not. Needless to say the press were out in force. Just keep the blinkers on and remember Sheila's instructions. Fortified by a couple of glasses of fizz, I strode round the exhibition, happily enjoying the company of my burly minders, trying to resist the temptation to glance to right and left at the scantily clad girls and boys on the stands, offering all manner of bizarre merchandise. I was determined not to be caught unawares in a compromising position and resisted the dogged attempts of the photographers to get me to try pole dancing – not, by the way, to be confused with lap dancing. Apparently pole dancing, as well as being an erotic display in nightclubs, is also a cult exercise craze pursued by many, including Kate Moss and Dannii Minogue.

Apart from some practised exhibitionists (no politicians that I could recognise), the most noticeable feature was the normality of the visitors and the prevalence of apparently ordinary couples out for an afternoon's shopping, as though pushing a trolley around Sainsbury's. The Erotica exhibition is harmless fun and the fact that this ninth annual exhibition was visited by tens of thousands shows that Britain is becoming less and less neurotic about sex and sensuality. I relaxed sufficiently to agree that we should open the one at the G-Mex Centre in Manchester the following year. By then, I knew exactly what to expect, lay back and thoroughly enjoyed the whole experience.

As I did when performing *The Vagina Monologues* at the Playhouse during the Edinburgh Festival in 2003. They are highly entertaining (even if you don't have one) and alternately move the audience from hysterical laughter to anguish and back again. My only problem was the requirement to wear black, which necessitated purchasing my first ever little black dress, which has been unworn ever since. Shouting unmentionable four-letter words in front of 3,000 people was yet another liberating experience – roll on the next!

Chapter Thirty-One

Positively the Last Word?

For better for worse, we are just a normal, ordinary couple to whom rather extraordinary things seem to have happened. There have been times when even I felt as though I had lost touch with reality and was in a surround cinema watching myself appearing on several screens at once.

The media have seemed fascinated, indeed amazed that Neil and I have stuck together through thick and thin. It is, of course, much better news when people split up. I find it a sad reflection on society that a marriage which lasts through difficult times should be regarded as an object of curiosity. In today's throwaway world many marriage vows seem to be little more than just another disposable item – handy for the moment but soon discarded when the going gets tough. I didn't promise to obey my husband – does anyone really still do that? Perhaps it was better in Chaucer's time when women promised 'to be buxom to him' – it meant the same, obedient – but then people believed that God really was their witness so were more likely to keep their vows than in our increasingly secular society.

Neil and I are fundamentally opposite in character. My basic daily philosophy is 'if it's got to be done do it now and then you can forget about it and move on to something more interesting.' Neil's is the reverse 'it may not have to be done at all so don't do it until the last possible moment.' You can imagine the friction that might bring to daily life – and it does! Despite that, according to a leading astrologer our star charts are the most perfectly matched he has ever encountered. Perhaps the heavens were on our side from the start, although I have to say that if I had known then what I know now I would never have married a lawyer. If you need that explaining, then you haven't spent enough time with lawyers!

I am often asked what is the secret of a happy marriage and my answer is always the same. The most important ingredient is luck – to meet the right person. Then you need a bit of lust to get you off the ground, followed by deepening love and laughter to carry you through the turmoil of life. A little lolly might not go amiss but I suspect just as many 'wealthy' as 'poor' marriages come unstuck. Neil and I are not the first to discover you can survive a big financial dip without it torpedoing your relationship. People sometimes wonder why we have no children and the reason is simple – neither of us positively wanted them. But there are many actively in our lives. As well as family and godchildren, we have a clutch of 'honorary' children and maintain firm links with the rising generations. I adore young company and watching 'our' youngsters grow, develop and blossom is a constant joy.

Life, as John Lennon presciently observed, is what happens to you while you are busy making other plans. Certainly many events have taken us unawares but I am not complaining. We revel in our new and busy life in the media and elsewhere while retaining close friends in the political world. The centre of gravity of our activities has moved south and we finally left the Old Rectory in September 2003. In the process of moving, we 'enjoyed' some unusual food combinations as we chomped our way through the contents of freezers and store cupboards, while multiple journeys to the local charity shop cut swathes through the accumulations in my wardrobe. Some 'unconsidered trifles' provided rich pickings – a House of Commons watch (value maybe £10) fetched £60. My very last offering was my 'going away' hat which was a mistake 22 years earlier and certainly hasn't been worn since. Occasionally Neil fled the house for fear he would be swept up in my manic clearings!

Apparently the two most stressful things in life are moving house and divorce. Packing up your life in twenty-five containers and five pantechnicons is certainly hard work and we have left many dear friends and happy memories in the north-west. Indeed, one kind smallholder still regularly sends me half a dozen quail's eggs by post – like me, they are very robust and withstand the rough and tumble! It was a sad moment when we drove away, but few people ever get the opportunity to live in such a fabulous house and the grim times we endured there are totally eclipsed by wonderfully happy memories of love, friendship and the gales of laughter which always reverberated around the rooms, no matter how fierce the storms outside.

But life moves on – or, in our case, backwards. While working out the final months of Neil's bankruptcy and searching for a house nearer to London, we squashed into my little Battersea flat, exactly where we were over twenty-five years earlier before setting out on the uncharted seas of politics. Things are very different now. I feel totally liberated and delighted to be out of the whole beastly business. I rejoice in being a free spirit, unaccountable to anyone for my actions although I do have some difficulty explaining certain antics to Granny, who was a bit shocked when she read parts of this book. Yes, we lost our regular income, our predicted future security, and now happily freelance on a wing and a prayer, but we are not alone in that and have grown accustomed to the pace.

Looking for a house can be hard work, especially if your field of search has a wide radius, our only proviso being that the location had to be not more than one and a half hours from London, preferably in the direction of the prevailing wind, south westerly, but not excluding north west and south. House hunting is really just a form of dating. You register with the agency, they note your vital statistics – budget, location, number of bedrooms – then match you up with likely candidates, send the details and you decide which you fancy enough to seek a date. Particulars would come thudding through the letter box every day, most quite wrong for us, some tantalisingly gorgeous but way out of our reach, and few worth more than a cursory glance – like men, it being easy to tell instantly that they were unsuitable in some way. But houses are like spouses; if you look for perfection you will never get married. Our fancy was taken by a handsome Georgian house in Wiltshire which had been carefully renovated but left by the developer for the purchaser to complete, literally from scratch – it needed total plumbing, wiring, bathrooms, kitchen, heating, lighting – everything. A daunting task but, in the right hands, the end result would be very splendid. Bids were invited so we took the plunge and made an offer. But it was not to be, as someone bid significantly more and scooped the prize. My disappointment, although great, was only momentary as Neil immediately bundled me into the car and drove me down to see another property in Wiltshire, the particulars of which we had had for some weeks and for which he had been nursing a secret desire. It was not at all the kind of house I had envisaged we would move into but we were bowled over and it was love at first sight, warts and all.

And so, in December 2004, we moved into Bradfield Manor, a beautiful, medieval stone house, parts of which have seen six hundred years of history. Bradfield is quirky, rambling and romantic – a bit like Neil. Our possessions came happily tumbling out of their containers after 15 months of restriction and darkness and we were reunited with old friends including, of course, our cardboard Maggie Thatcher who is now back on duty to ward off burglars. We have been incredibly lucky to be able to rebuild a new life for ourselves, repair the hole in our finances, and once again live in a glorious house. But it has not happened without a lot of hard work and a determination not to be beaten.

Freed from the constraints of Slug and Fishface on 21 May 2004, Neil is now developing a business career away from politics and much of it also away from the spotlight, leaving me, the 'media butterfly', flitting from flower to flower. Among other things, Neil now recruits girls in Soho – yes, really! He is Chairman of an employment consultancy which sources and places senior secretaries and PAs and their office is just yards from Carnaby Street.

Our accuser, Nadine Milroy-Sloan, is currently serving three years at Her Majesty's pleasure for attempting to pervert the course of justice. I suspect the judge gave her a long sentence to warn others not to make false sexual allegations for profit. What she tried to do to us was bad enough – we could have found ourselves in jail for seven years – but her real crime was against genuine rape victims. Every time a girl cries wolf it makes it that bit harder for an actual victim to be believed.

No one had tackled him head-on before, but in Februay 2005, after a protracted struggle, Max Clifford was obliged to climb down and fully to retract, in open court, his defamatory remarks about us, in support of Milroy Sloan's lies. He also paid our entire legal costs and damages. Together with his own costs he must have spent many hundreds of thousands of pounds defending the indefensible. Ignoring the truth, he just took the risk that we were not in a position to defend ourselves. Thanks to our noble lawyers, who acted on a no win, no fee agreement, he was wrong.

And Mr Fayed? Whatever problems he has caused us are nothing compared with the hole he dug for himself. Following his own revelations during the trial that he withdrew annually enormous sums of money in cash from the Midland Bank in Park Lane and was in the habit of doling it out widely, the Inland Revenue decided to investigate possible tax irregularities.

It transpired that, unknown to the public, Fayed had an arrangement with the Revenue whereby he paid a fixed annual sum of income tax. This might have been in order except that the sum in question was a mere £240,000 – from a self-proclaimed billionaire. Fayed retained a foreign domicile (despite being a UK resident for over thirty years) and, as his major assets (Harrods, etc) are ultimately owned by other Fayed companies based in foreign tax havens, he could siphon any UK profits abroad free of UK income tax. Such tax avoidance schemes are perfectly lawful but, and this is the crucial point, if any exported profits re-enter the UK they fall into the tax net. The Revenue wanted to know, how was he funding his voracious appetite for cash from the Midland Bank if, as Fayed had claimed to them, he received only a small income in the UK? Dissatisfied with his answers, the Revenue cancelled the £240,000-a-year deal with retrospective effect and presented him with a tax bill for £32 million. As a result, he left the country for tax exile in Switzerland, able to return to the UK for only 90 days a year.

The Inland Revenue were, of course, also obliged to investigate our own tax affairs as a result of the verdict in the Fayed libel case. After a two-year investigation, trawling exhaustively through all our bank and credit card details since the mid-1980s checking both our income and our spending patterns (which would have varied had large sums of cash been injected), not only did they conclude that Fayed had not paid Neil cash for questions – or anything else – but they actually found we had overpaid some tax and qualified for a refund! The Revenue's highly trained forensic accountants, used to unmasking the most complicated tax frauds and enjoying unfettered access to our affairs, found no evidence whatsoever of illicit payments from Fayed, so we can only wonder what Sir Gormless Dopey (Downey) and later the jury found so compelling.

Most of my health problems have been resolved but I still carry the scars of past stress and a few uncertainties remain. People often kindly sympathise with the problems we have faced. Yes, things have been tough at times and we have had to battle through in the glare of publicity. But, if you asked everyone in almost any gathering to relate their experiences over the last ten years our 'little local difficulties' would pale into insignificance. Life certainly hasn't been dull and many people have contributed to the rich and colourful tapestry I have already enjoyed. I sometimes feel thanks are due to those who, by their actions both deliberate and unintended, have given me adversity and so enriched my life. Every bad moment passes and new excitements and experiences come along to assuage any pain. I always used to know the answer to the classic question, 'What will you be doing in five years time?' But now? We are happy to swim with the tide of our fortune and I no longer harbour any great ambitions. Growing old is mandatory but growing up is optional. So here I am, rapidly approaching pensionable age, having just enjoyed my first Saga cruise (as on board entertainment) and daily looking forward to fresh horizons and challenges. After she had endured so many grim times on our account, we were delighted to welcome Granny, still in full sail and independent in her 91st year, to preside over our first Christmas at Bradfield, with James, Fiona and all the children in attendance. Our only sadness was the absence of Grandpa, so I was denied the opportunity to give an honest answer, at last, to his perennial question, 'No problems, Blossom?' But life twirls on. Annually I am asked for my New Year resolution and it is always the same: 'Never to have a dull moment in the year ahead'. I intend that to continue.

Index